1, + Lunareay –
last 3 lectures

This book analyses County Mayo in Ireland from the Elizabethan pacification of the county to the first stage of the Land War in the nineteenth century. During those three centuries the county was transformed from being a remote, isolated, impoverished and hostile region of the country to being at the center of Irish politics and integrated into an agrarian capitalist economy.

The book is divided into two sections. The first contains an analysis of the county prior to the Great Famine, and provides the foundation for a core/periphery analysis of Mayo's economic development and its impact upon popular politics in the county. The second, employing a core/periphery analysis of the post-Famine economic and political transformation of the county, demonstrates that the structural changes that gave rise to the Land War occurred more rapidly in central Mayo than along its western coastline or eastern boundaries. This uneven development helps account for both the initial strength and rapid disintegration of the land movement in the county.

Past and Present Publications

Land and popular politics in Ireland

Past and Present Publications

General Editor: PAUL SLACK, *Exeter College, Oxford*

Past and Present Publications comprise books similar in character to the articles in the journal *Past and Present*. Whether the volumes in the series are collections of essays – some previously published, others new studies – or monographs, they encompass a wide variety of scholarly and original works primarily concerned with social, economic and cultural changes, and their causes and consequences. They will appeal to both specialists and non-specialists and will endeavour to communicate the results of historical and allied research in a readable and lively form.

For a list of titles in Past and Present Publications, see end of book.

Land and popular politics in Ireland

County Mayo from the Plantation to the Land War

DONALD E. JORDAN, JR

*Professor and Chair,
Program in the Humanities, Menlo College*

CAMBRIDGE
UNIVERSITY PRESS

Published by the Press Syndicate of the University of Cambridge
The Pitt Building, Trumpington Street, Cambridge CB2 1RP
40 West 20th Street, New York, NY 10011–4211, USA
10 Stamford Road, Oakleigh, Melbourne 3166, Australia

First published 1994

Printed in Great Britain at the University Press, Cambridge

A catalogue record for this book is available from the British Library

Library of Congress cataloguing in publication data
Jordan, Donald E.
Land and popular politics in Ireland: County Mayo from the
Plantation to the Land War / Donald E. Jordan Jr.
    p.   cm. – (Past and present publications)
Includes bibliographical references and index.
ISBN 0 521 32404 1
1. Mayo (Ireland: County) – Politics and government. 2. Mayo
(Ireland: County) – Economic conditions. 3. Land tenure – Ireland –
Mayo (County) – History. 4. Mayo (Ireland: County) – History.
I. Title.
DA990.M3J67 1994
941.7'3 – dc20   93–27945   CIP

ISBN 0 521 32404 1 hardback

WD

Contents

APPENDICES   314

Illustrations

TABLES

Acknowledgments

This book began as a Ph.D. thesis many years ago. Research for the thesis was generously funded by the Trustees of the Mabelle McLeod Lewis Memorial Fund and the Committee on Fellowships and Graduate Scholarships of the University of California, Davis. Additional research for this book was funded by the American Council of Learned Societies. To all three I wish to express my gratitude. Over the years of work on this study I have become indebted to many people for advice, direction, support, and encouragement. In particular, I wish to thank: Paul Bew, Louis Cullen, James Donnelly, Leonard Hochberg, Tony Judt, Joseph Lee, Joel Mokyr, the late T. W. Moody, Cormac O'Gráda, T. P. O'Neill, William Vaughan, and my thesis advisors, F. Roy Willis, Ted Margadant and William Hagen of the University of California, Davis.

Special thanks go to the late T. H. Aston for initially accepting the manuscript for inclusion in the Past and Present Publications series and to Charles Philpin, Associate Editor of *Past and Present*, for his encouragement and patience during the years it has taken me to complete the manuscript. David Miller of Carnegie Mellon University kindly read the entire manuscript and offered many very helpful comments. In addition, he took my data and generated Maps 4.1, 4.2 and 4.4 and Figure 2.1. I will always be in his debt. Elizabeth Grubgeld of Oklahoma State University did a close textual reading of the manuscript. Her criticisms and suggestions enabled me to clarify and improve the prose, logic, unity and argument of the manuscript. More importantly, her friendship and persistent encouragement over many years sustained me during lean periods when I despaired that this book would ever be completed. My gratitude to her is deeply felt. During the final stages of completing the manuscript I profited greatly from conversations with Anne Kane of UCLA, whose forthcoming Ph.D. thesis breaks new ground in our understanding of the Irish Land War. My heartfelt thanks go to her. Al Jacobs of Menlo College generously volunteered to read the page proofs with me. His careful reading found things that I did not, while his humor and good spirits transformed a tedious task into a pleasant one, for which I am very grateful.

Marean and Alex Jordan have put up with me during the many years of researching and writing of this book, while reminding me that there is much more to life than the travails of nineteenth-century Irish tenant farmers. This book is better because of their support and love, as am I.

Abbreviations

Bessborough Commission	*Her Majesty's Commission of Inquiry into the Working of the Landlord and Tenant (Ireland) Act, 1870*, 1881
CBS	Crime Branch Special Papers, State Paper Office
CSORP	Chief Secretary's Office, Registered Papers, State Paper Office
CT	*The Connaught Telegraph*
CTDA	Central Tenant's Defence Association
Devon Commission	*Her Majesty's Commission of Inquiry into the State of the Law and Practice in Respect to the Occupation of Land in Ireland*, 1845
FJ	*The Freeman's Journal*
OP	Outrage Papers, State Paper Office
PROI	Public Record Office, Ireland
PRONI	Public Record Office of Northern Ireland
Richmond Commission	*Royal Commission on the Depressed Condition of the Agricultural Interest*, 1881
RP	Rebellion Papers
SOC	State of the Country Papers
SPO	State Paper Office, Dublin Castle

Introduction

During the last quarter of the nineteenth century Ireland was convulsed by three periods of agrarian agitation, which together form one of the most important protest movements in recent European history. The first phase began in 1879, when economic crisis brought on by a confluence of bad weather, meager harvests and low prices undermined the post-Famine prosperity of larger farmers while devastating the fragile economies of the smaller farmers. The Land War quickly spread from the West of Ireland, where it began, into the East and South, until by the winter of 1880–1 the Irish National Land League could boast of hundreds of branches comprising over 200,000 members.[1] At its head was Charles Stewart Parnell, who managed to harness the agitation into the service of a revitalized Irish parliamentary party, in the process propelling himself into the leadership of the party at Westminster. An active party in parliament, supported by a massive agitation in Ireland, forced the Liberal government of William Ewart Gladstone to act on the Irish land question. Although the resulting Land Bill of 1881 fell far short of abolishing landlordism in Ireland, the ultimate goal of the land movement, it corrected some of the most glaring abuses of landlord power, established land courts to arbitrate rent disputes, and laid the foundation for the transfer of land ownership from landlords to working farmers.

The Land War marked a decisive stage in the emergence of agrarian capitalism in Ireland. By 1879 production for a cash economy was firmly established in the country, shaping political and social relationships. However, the continuing presence of landlordism prevented land from becoming a commodity that could be bought and sold, and meant that

---

[1] M. Davitt to J. Devoy, 16 Dec. 1880, in W. O'Brien and D. Ryan (eds.), *Devoy's Post Bag, 1871–1928*, 2 vols. (Dublin, 1948), II, p. 24.

rent levels would be arbitrarily set rather than fixed in accordance with price movements. While cattle prices rose rapidly during the first few decades following the Great Famine most Mayo farmers were able to pay their rents, which in many instances were not rising as rapidly as the prices they could fetch for their farm products. However, the fall in prices that came during the economic crisis of 1877–80 reduced the farmers' income and in many instances transformed rents from being a tolerable to an intolerable burden, bringing into question the rights of landlords to arbitrarily set rent levels in an era of free trade. Parnell summed up the feelings of many tenant farmers when he told an American reporter that the land agitation did "not attach so much importance . . . to mere reduction of rent," but sought to create a "natural state of affairs" in which land would become a commodity traded on the open market. Rents, where they remained, would be based on the "maxim that rent is merely a fair share of the profits of the land, and that when there are no profits there is no rent."[2] To many farmers, especially those with large holdings, the Land War was a struggle against an anachronistic land system that prevented their full participation in the free market economy. Led by former Fenians, ambitious parliamentarians and local politicians, the tenant farmers fought their landlords for control of the land in an open agitation, supplemented on occasion by bursts of nocturnal violence. While failing in the short run to establish themselves as landowners, the farmers succeeded in banishing from Ireland age-old habits of deference towards landlords, initiating an agrarian revolution that was completed in 1921, when the compulsory sale by landlords of tenanted land was enforced by the new Irish Free State government.

Until the 1970s, historians of the Land War concentrated their attention on its relationship to the larger national struggle for Irish self-government. This is not surprising, given the intimate connections between the land and national struggles, but it often meant that analyses of the land movement were tangential to analyses of the nationalist movement and its leaders. However, during the past two decades this partiality towards national political history has been offset by the publication of a series of monographs on the agricultural and social transformation that occurred in post-Famine Ireland, and the resultant changes in landlord–tenant relations. The earliest of these studies, most

---

[2] Interview with Albert Chester Ives, *New York Herald*, 2 Jan. 1880, reprinted in *Special Commission Act, 1888: Report of the Proceedings Before the Commissioners Appointed By the Act, Reprinted from The Times*, 4 vols. (London, 1890), I, pp. 187–8.

notably those by S. H. Cousens, James Donnelly, Jr., Joseph Lee, Cormac O'Gráda, Barbara Solow, and William Vaughan, paved the way for two conflicting interpretations of the social origins of the Land War and of the exercise of political power within the land movement. Samuel Clark, in his *Social Origins of the Irish Land War*,[3] argues that social and class antagonisms lessened in post-Famine Ireland, creating an environment in which a united peasantry could be mobilized against landlordism. In contrast, Paul Bew, in his *Land and the National Question in Ireland 1858–82*,[4] maintains that discord, not unity, characterized the land movement that was, at best, founded upon a fragile "class alliance" between large and small farmers rather than upon the rural solidarity found by Clark.

To a large extent these two interpretations, along with those presented in many of the studies that preceded them, are based upon analyses of social and economic change on the provincial or national levels. This approach, employing aggregated data, can illuminate major economic trends, but necessarily distorts economic and social organization at the local level, where the battle between landlords and their tenants was actually waged. Consequently, the questions regarding the political significance of rural class alignments raised by Bew's and Clark's studies can best be answered through an exposition of the complexities of local Irish society. Since the publication of these books, Irish social history has flourished to an unprecedented degree, resulting in numerous studies of local, county and regional history, including of late some that disregard the traditional administrative boundaries of provinces, counties, baronies or poor law unions in favor of complex spatial hierarchies based on the locations of urban centers, watersheds, railroads and a host of other variables.[5]

In many ways County Mayo is an ideal subject for a detailed study of the causes and the course of the Irish Land War. The agitation began

---

[3] Samuel Clark, *Social Origins of the Irish Land War* (Princeton, 1979).

[4] Paul Bew, *Land and the National Question in Ireland 1858–82* (Dublin, 1978).

[5] For examples of these latter studies, see the recent studies of Leonard Hochberg and David Miller. For example: "Regional Boundaries and Urban Hierarchy in Prefamine Ireland: A Preliminary Assessment," a paper presented to the Annual Meeting of the Social Science History Association, Washington, DC, October 1989; "Ireland on the Eve of the Famine: A Geographic Perspective," a paper presented at the National Center for Geographic Information and Analysis, Santa Barbara, California, March 1991; "Internal Colonialism in Geographic Perspective: The Case of Pre-Famine Ireland," forthcoming in L. Hochberg and G. Earle, *The Geography of Social Change* (Stanford).

there in April 1879, and Mayo remained an important center of the movement until 1881. As a result, the causes and organization of the rebellion must be sought first in Mayo. In consequence of its premier position, Mayo provides particularly rich documentation of the land agitation. Reporters, politicians and government investigators swarmed to the county, especially during the early stages of the agitation and again at the time of the celebrated "Boycott affair." In addition, the county's nationalist newspaper, *The Connaught Telegraph*, the voice of the land movement during its early stages, supplies a wealth of information on the political, social and economic situation in the county.

Mayo was an unlikely place for the Land War to begin. It was one of the most impoverished counties in Ireland and had a very limited history of agrarian protest prior to 1879. Over the previous 120 years agrarian protest movements in Ireland had been confined largely to the more prosperous counties of the eastern and central regions of the country, in which the social and economic convulsions associated with the developing market-oriented and cash-based economy had spawned frequent periods of agrarian violence. In County Mayo the conditions for a sustained and successful agitation were not in place prior to the Famine. In the seventeenth century Mayo experienced a significant transformation in landownership during which the Gaelic aristocracy was replaced on the land by Galway-based merchants, English "adventurers" and transplanted Irish, creating a host of grievances against the "usurpers" of the land and their descendants that fueled powerful oratory and fanned the flames of the agitation during the Land War. This transformation in landownership inaugurated the slow and uneven establishment of a market-based commercial economy in the county, which by the 1830s brought to Mayo the first signs of class divisions of the sort that had produced organized agrarian protest movements in central Ireland since the 1760s. These economic and political changes are the subject of Chapters 2 and 3.

During the three decades following the Great Famine of 1846–51, the pace of economic and political change in Mayo increased dramatically, bringing a livestock-based and capitalist economy along with a new farming and trading elite that by the 1870s was well positioned to structure political activity. These developments, detailed in Chapters 4 and 5, provide the immediate backdrop to and context for the Land War of 1879–81. Moreover, they provide an explanation for the clear geographic dimension of the agitation, which was not distributed equally throughout the county, but was concentrated in the rich plains and surrounding areas of south-central Mayo, where the livestock economy and its accompanying social and political changes were most evident.

In an attempt to understand this geographic dimension of the protest movement, I drew on the works of Michael Hechter, William Skinner and others to develop a core/periphery-based analysis of the social, economic and political development of County Mayo.[6] Without question, structuring an analysis of economic development around an artificial construct like a county is fraught with peril. As was the case with many Irish counties, Mayo was created by Elizabethan administrators towards the end of the sixteenth century. Their goal was not to create viable economic units but to replace the fluid tribal boundaries of the Celtic aristocracy with tidy English ones and in the process complete the pacification of Ireland. However, as it turned out, County Mayo is divided topographically into a central core and a surrounding periphery that affected significantly its economic development and contributed to making it an economic entity. The core begins with a narrow corridor encompassing the land around Killala and Ballina in north Mayo, widens out in mid-Mayo to include the land between Castlebar and Westport, and then continues south and east to the Galway and Roscommon borders. This central corridor contains much of the best pasture and tillage land in Mayo and was the area of the county where a livestock economy developed most fully following the Famine. It was the region of Mayo that experienced the heaviest Famine depopulation, largely as a result of the actions of evicting landlords who, anxious to redistribute the county's best farm land into more profitable large holdings, ejected many small holders during and immediately following the Famine. As a consequence, at the time of the Land War Mayo's large and middle-sized farmers were clustered in the center of the county, participating in the livestock economy that they had helped to establish. Most of the county's major towns were located in the core region, linked together by roads and, beginning in 1860, by railroads. The importance of these towns as centers of commerce, banking, credit, politics and

---

[6] Michael Hechter, *Internal Colonialism: The Celtic Fringe in British National Development, 1536–1966* (Berkeley and Los Angeles, 1975); Michael Hechter, "Internal Colonialism Revisited," in Edward Tiryakian and Ronald Rogowski (eds.), *New Nationalisms of the Developed West: Toward Explanation* (Boston, 1985), pp. 17–26; G. William Skinner, "Regional Urbanization in Nineteenth Century China" and "Cities and the Hierarchy of Local Systems," in G. William Skinner (ed.), *The City in Late Imperial China* (Stanford, 1977), pp. 211–49, 275–351. Also see: Hochberg and Miller, "Ireland on the Eve of the Famine: A Geographic Perspective," and "Internal Colonialism in Geographic Perspective: The Case of Pre-Famine Ireland."

administration, grew considerably following the Famine, as Mayo became more fully integrated into a market economy.

In contrast, the peripheral regions, consisting of mountainous, bog and poor quality land, sustained numerous small farmers living marginally in a family economy consisting of small-scale potato cultivation, rough grazing of a calf or two, the sale of a few cash crops, particularly eggs, and the wages from seasonal work in England or Scotland. Having witnessed relatively little Famine depopulation, the peripheral regions supported large populations that continued to subdivide the land into small holdings after such practices had been curtailed in the core areas. The periphery's towns, several of which were important market or ecclesiastical centers, provided many of the same services to the rural areas as did the towns of the core, but in a hierarchy of Mayo's towns, they would be of secondary importance by any measure.

It is important to stress that a core/periphery analysis does not expose the existence of two distinct farming cultures in Mayo, one "modern" or "modernizing" and one "pre-modern," locked in "tradition." Nor does it imply a strict territorial or economic division of the county. Mayo, like most western Irish counties, contains a patchwork of lowland pasture, cultivated land, bog, and mountain of varying degrees of agricultural potential. During the latter half of the nineteenth century, large and small holdings, and pasture and tillage land were scattered throughout the county. However, a core/periphery analysis does reveal differences in kinship structures, inheritance systems, and land use patterns between the two areas that suggest that the structural changes which Samuel Clark and others have identified as the social background for the Land War occurred more rapidly in central Mayo than they did along the western coastline or eastern boundaries of the county. The relationship that developed between the residents of the two zones was one characterized by a division of labor in which the periphery became an economic dependency of the core.

For a brief period during 1879 the interests of the various farming cultures in Mayo converged over the issue of rents. The nature of the post-Famine transformation of the county paved the way for this unity by establishing a farming class in which most members, regardless of farm size or tenure, were integrated into the commercial livestock economy and a shopkeeper class that was dependent upon the farmers' prosperity. Consequently, the fall in livestock prices after 1876, combined with a reduction in all other sources of farmers' income, drove the two groups together into an attack on rents paid to an increasingly alien and anachronistic landlord class. The leadership needed for an assault on rents came from a new political elite of farmers, shopkeepers, merchants, and professional men, all products of the post-Famine social, economic, and political transformation of Ireland. During the 1870s these emergent leaders, in a potent alliance with the county's Fenians, wrested a degree of political power in Mayo away from the gentry and the clergy. As examined in Chapters 6 and 7, in 1879 this locally based political alliance, strengthened by two years of economic crisis, supplied leadership in defiance of priests and landlords during the first heady months of the land agitation. Belatedly, the Catholic clergy joined the land agitation in an effort to retain their political influence in rural Ireland, but did so as auxiliaries to the movement's lay leadership. This redistribution of power in rural Ireland was the Land War's most significant contribution to Irish history, providing the base for political life in the Irish Free State after 1923.

The initial solidarity displayed by the land movement lends credence to Clark's thesis that structural changes within Ireland following the Famine succeeded in uniting farmers of differing classes with townsmen to form a "rural-urban coalition against a landed elite."[7] However, as analyzed in Chapters 8 and 9, the coalition was short-lived. The intrusion of capitalism into the Irish countryside provided the foundation for deep divisions between the large grazing farmers who farmed substantial tracts of land without owning them, and small tillage farmers who found their farms threatened with inclusion into grazing tracts, and who saw their aspirations for an equitable redistribution of the land blocked by the graziers.

To a large extent, the class conflict that surfaced in County Mayo during the fall of 1879 was part of a larger struggle within the Land League leadership between representatives of the large graziers, located primarily in eastern and southern Ireland, and advocates of the small western farmers. During the early 1880s, in an effort to make the land agitation truly national in scope, the League's central executive sought to draw the large eastern and southern graziers into the land movement. The "rent at the point of a bayonet" strategy adopted by the League during the summer of 1880 symbolized its embrace of the large farmers and apparent abandonment of the interests of the small western farmers. The new policy also marked a victory for those within the League leadership who sought to centralize control over the direction of the land movement.

[7] Clark, *Social Origins of the Irish Land War*, p. 263.

Clark has noted that one of the characteristics of the Land War that distinguishes it from pre-Famine forms of collective action is its national scope. The locally based, communally organized movements of the pre-Famine period were replaced by a national, associational collectivity that sought to change central government policies in the interests of the tenant farmers of Ireland.[8] This was indeed the case, but at least in the short run, the accomplishments of the Land League in wresting concessions from the government, such as the Land Bill of 1881, did not benefit all Irish tenant farmers equally. Moreover, the League's failure to defend the interests of the small farmers contributed markedly to their loss of faith in the small farm economy.

The experience of County Mayo makes it difficult to accept Clark's thesis that in the post-Famine period the "segment of the rural population that had been and remained comparatively insecure [the small farmers] became integrated at the national level into the same social group as a more secure segment [the larger farmers]. In this way the social basis was laid for an active collectivity that drew its support from both."[9] There is little doubt that the land agitation in Mayo was supported by all sections of the farming community and that the agitation was most vital during the early months while the broadly based anti-landlord coalition remained intact. It is also apparent that the major social and economic changes that occurred in post-Famine Mayo produced a politically active elite that was capable of mobilizing large and small farmers around the shared goals of rent reduction and land reform. However, the transitory nature of the farmers' alliance brings into question the components of its foundation. In Mayo, the land movement broke up internally long before government-sponsored land reform and repression formally curtailed the agitation, a victim of the fracturing of the popular front of tenant farmers and their townsmen allies.

In effect, there were two simultaneous agrarian revolutions in Ireland between 1879 and 1882: one by large graziers who wanted to be free of rents and landlords so they could fully profit from the market, and one by small farmers who wanted protection from eviction and free, equitable access to the land.[10] An open clash between these classes failed to materialize during the 1879–82 phase of the Land War, giving the

---

[8] *Ibid.*, pp. 350–65.

[9] *Ibid.*, pp. 364–5.

[10] A similar interpretation for the role of peasants during the French Revolution is made by Barrington Moore, Jr. in *Social Origins of Dictatorship and Democracy: Lord and Peasant in the Making of the Modern World* (Boston, 1966), pp. 69–74.

impression to most observers and many historians that rural Ireland had risen up in a united front against English landlordism. But tensions between them, compounded by disenchantment with the Land League, seriously weakened the land movement in County Mayo by the end of 1880. By then the small western farmers, whose plight had sparked the agitation, were forgotten by many members of the Land League's central executive and were virtually left out of the 1882 settlement between Parnell and the government, which officially closed the first phase of the Irish Land War. With their hopes to arrest the trend towards land consolidation dashed, vast numbers of Mayo's small farmers emigrated rather than remaining in Ireland to fight for land against the ascendant larger farmers, who were the true victors in the Land War.

Part 1

County Mayo prior to the Famine

1. *The natural and historical setting*

THE NATURAL SETTING

One of the four counties carved out of the kingdom of Connacht by Elizabethan administrators after 1570, Mayo is Ireland's third largest county, containing 2084 square miles arrayed in a complex pattern of land forms. Situated on the western edge of the European land mass, Mayo contains geological structures of great antiquity, especially the mountains along its Atlantic coast that date from the late pre-Cambrian era. The metamorphism of the physical landscape over the next 600 million years resulted in a dramatically uneven topography that has conditioned the patterns of human settlement and interaction in what has been for centuries Ireland's poorest county. The most significant topographic contrast is that between the relatively fertile central region of Mayo and the largely barren areas along the western coast and eastern boundaries of the county. From the time of the earliest inhabitants of the county, the central region of Mayo has been the nucleus of settlement and the avenue through which political, social, and economic changes penetrated Mayo. In contrast, residents of the peripheral regions, hindered by rough terrain, poor quality land, and few passable roads were cut off from contact with the more dynamic parts of the country.

The central corridor, stretching from Killala Bay in northern Mayo to the area east of Lough Mask in southern Mayo, contains some of the richest land in Connacht, although its use capability is limited when compared to the eastern and central regions of Ireland.[1] Mayo's most fertile soil is found east of Lough Mask in the northern portion of a limestone-based lowland that stretches south to County Clare. North of Lough Mask the lowlands are broken by a belt of drumlins, ice-moulded

---

[1] The Irish National Committee for Geography, *Atlas of Ireland* (Dublin, 1979), p. 28.

13

ridges appearing as low, rounded hills with generally fertile slopes, but with poorly drained hollows at their base. This drumlin-dotted lowland stretches north to Lough Conn, west to Clew Bay and east to a line running roughly from Claremorris to Swinford. It narrows through the Foxford gap north of Castlebar merging into the fertile valley of the Moy River, which stretches to Ballina. North-west of Ballina as far as Killala is another drumlin belt that stretches to the fertile strip on Mayo's north coast. This central core, which incorporates Mayo's two major seaports, Ballina and Westport, and the principal water and land routes to Galway and Dublin via Cong and Claremorris, is the county's central axis of communication, trade, and settlement. It is also the agricultural heartland of the county where the bulk of its tillage crops are grown and livestock raised.

The topography of eastern Mayo is a continuation of the lowlands of the center, but with eskers and kames, conical hills and ridges of lime-stone gravel replacing the rolling drumlins of central Mayo. As a result, the soil on the slopes is coarse while bog-filled hollows and lakes are frequent. This region, which includes eastern Mayo south of the Ox mountains, is of little agricultural value. In this it is similar to the land of western Mayo despite the topographical differences between the two regions. Western Mayo is dominated by the weathered roots of two ancient mountain ranges, divided at Clew Bay where the lowland corridor reaches the sea. The region south of Clew Bay consists of high mountains, laced with steep, fault-created valleys, while the outward slopes descend into large stretches of water-logged lowlands of blanket bog built up over mineral soil and ancient vegetation. North of Clew Bay a long line of mountains arcs across the desolate barony of Erris, dividing in two the largest formation of blanket bog in Ireland. Agriculture, and to a large degree human habitation, in western Mayo has been restricted to a narrow coastal strip that extends in an often-broken band from the Mullet peninsula in the north-west to Killary Bay in the south. This coastal strip, often no more than a mile in width, is bounded south of Clew Bay by steep mountains and barren foothills, while north of the bay it is confined by bogland reaching several miles to the mountain ranges of north-western Mayo.[2]

In part as a consequence of its remote location and inhospitable

---

[2] T. W. Freeman, *Pre-Famine Ireland: A Study in Historical Geography* (Manchester, 1957), pp. 242–68; T. W. Freeman, *Ireland: A General and Regional Geography*, 4th ed. (London, 1969), pp. 390–424; B. Buckley, "The Geology of Mayo," in B. O'Hara (ed.), *Mayo: Aspects of Its Heritage* (Galway, 1982), pp. 201–6.

terrain, Mayo has been rarely at the center stage of Irish history. Political, religious, and cultural changes have tended to come slowly to the west of Ireland and have rarely originated there. The rugged individuals who populated the region tended to resist fiercely external control, be it from Tara, Armagh, Dublin or London, although generally they were compelled to succumb in the end. Life in the west has been harder and starker than elsewhere in the country, but has proven to be a preservative for an indomitable spirit that has assured the survival, if not the prosperity of its people.

THE HISTORICAL SETTING

Excavations carried out over the past several decades suggest that northern Mayo may have been one of the first sites of human settlement in Ireland late in the mesolithic period.[3] Neolithic colonizers, arriving in Ireland during the fourth millennium BC, established northern Connacht as a major center of human habitation, as evidenced by its large number of megalithic tombs and monuments. Together with County Sligo to its north, Mayo displays one of the richest and densest clusters of neolithic sites anywhere in Europe. According to archaeologists Ruaidhri deValera and Sean O'Nuallain, Mayo contains the greatest number of court cairns recorded for any county in Ireland and the "most numerous homogeneous group of megalithic chambered long barrows in Britain and Ireland."[4]

Northern Connacht remained an important center of human activity during the Celtic iron age. According to the ancient tales, especially those comprising the Ulster Cycle, Connacht and Ulster provinces were rival centers of power within early Celtic Ireland, Connacht being associated with the legendary queen Mebd of Cruachan in County Roscommon. Several major tribes settled in Mayo, establishing combative dynasties that engaged in near continual struggles for power until the coming of the Normans in the twelfth century. By that time the dominant dynasty was that of the O'Connors, kings of Connacht and claimants to the high kingship of Ireland. The center of O'Connor power was outside Mayo, in Counties Roscommon, Sligo and north-eastern Galway, but the clan had fortifications at Westport and elsewhere in

[3] *Irish Times*, 17 August 1970.
[4] R. deValera and S. O'Nuallain, *Survey of Megalithic Tombs of Ireland, vol. II: County Mayo* (Dublin, 1964), pp. 115–17.

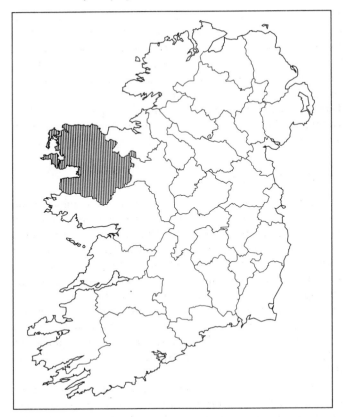

Map 1.1. Ireland showing location of County Mayo

Mayo and held sway over the major tribes through a complex series of family and military alliances.

The major tribes dominated a myriad of smaller kingdoms and vassal peoples. Society was aristocratic and hierarchical with bonds of personal loyalty and economic interdependence connecting the various classes. The lordship of the royal and warrior classes was maintained by the institution of clientship, whereby the several grades of commoners were supplied with a fief of cattle and guarantees of protection in return for a share in agricultural profits, homage and personal services.[5] The vast

---

[5] D. O'Corrain, *Ireland Before the Normans* (Dublin, 1972), pp. 42–4.

Map 1.2. The core and peripheral regions of County Mayo. Source: Adapted from The Irish National Committee for Geography, *Atlas of Ireland* (Dublin, 1978), p. 28.

majority of common farmers were pastoralists in a society where cattle rearing was both a source of food and an index of wealth and status. Farmsteads were dispersed, centering around a rath or ring fort containing houses, farm buildings and a farm yard or corral for sheltering the stock from bad weather and cattle raiders. Typically, the earthenwork rath was surrounded by a plot of tillage ground, probably quite small in the poor soil of Mayo, where cereals and some vegetables were grown. Beyond this was rough grazing ground, which in the west was generally held in common. From the large size of many raths it appears that there were a number of prosperous farms, although the number of well-to-do farmers and the degree of their prosperity is impossible to determine.[6] Periodic famines and continual warfare undoubtedly took their toll on a people whose lives were difficult in the best of times.

There is little evidence to suggest that the coming of Christianity to Mayo altered significantly the political structure or social and economic patterns of Celtic society. Tradition recorded or, as is likely, invented during the seventh century by Bishop Tirechan, a native of Mayo, has it that Saint Patrick personally brought Christianity to Mayo, and the county abounds with sites associated with his mission.[7] Regardless of how Christianity reached the county, Mayo's remoteness proved suitable for monasticism and eremiticism. In the absences of urban centers and the Romanized communities in which the Roman church had flourished on the continent and in England, Christianity in Ireland developed lacking a powerful diocesan system. In its stead, Irish Christianity developed around an archipelago of remote monasteries that functioned independently of central authority, but in close interaction with Celtic society.[8] A number of monasteries were founded in Mayo during the sixth and seventh centuries, including those at Cong, Balla, Meelick and Errew on Lough Conn.[9] Probably the most significant site was located in the heart of central Mayo at a place called Mayo of the Saxons or, more recently, Mayo Abbey. It was established in 665 by St. Colman, formerly Bishop of Scotland, who, following the defeat of his teachings regarding church organization and liturgy at the Synod of Whitby in 664, migrated with thirty English disciples to Mayo.[10] Mayo Abbey, like that at Cong, became a center of learning, drawing students from western Christendom. A measure of the county's importance as a Christian center came in 1152. At the Synod of Kells, convened to impose an ecclesiastical structure on Ireland and bring to an end the independence

---

6 *Ibid.*, pp. 49–58; F. H. A. Aalen, *Man and the Landscape in Ireland* (London, 1978), pp. 81–7.

7 L. Bieler, *History of Irish Catholicism, vol. I: St. Patrick and the Coming of Christianity* (Dublin and Melbourne, 1967), pp. 19–22; N. O'Muraile, "An Outline History of County Mayo," in O'Hara (ed.), *Mayo*, p. 12; H. T. Knox, *The History of the County of Mayo to the Close of the Sixteenth Century* (Dublin, 1908), pp. 26–8.

8 J. T. McNeill, *The Celtic Churches: A History, AD 200–1200* (Chicago, 1972); M. Dillon and N. Chadwick, *Celtic Realms* (London, 1967), pp. 151–96; K. Hughes, *The Church in Early Irish Society* (London, 1966).

9 O'Muraile, "An Outline History of County Mayo," p. 12.

10 Bede, *A History of the English Church and People*, rev. ed. (Harmondsworth, Middlesex, 1965), p. 208.

of the Irish church, Mayo Abbey and Killala were selected as centers of suffragan sees, while nearby Tuam, the center of the O'Connor kingship, became a metropolitan see.[11]

These episcopal arrangements were in place when, in 1169, Norman-Welsh adventurers intervened in an Irish quarrel at the invitation of one of the protagonists and with the blessing of Henry II, King of England. The Normans were quickly successful, prompting Henry to come to Ireland in 1171 to assure the continuing fealty of his barons and secure the homage of the defeated Irish chieftains. Henry, who came to Ireland the year after the murder of Thomas à Becket, was armed with a papal bull authorizing him to "proclaim the truths of the Christian religion to a rude and ignorant people, and to root out the growths of vice from the field of the Lord."[12] Henry assumed the Lordship of Ireland, authorized his Norman vassals to carve out territories for themselves, while accepting submissions from Irish chieftains hoping to obtain freehold titles to their lands backed by English authority.[13]

These momentous developments were slow to reach Connacht, in part because of its remoteness, but also because of the Treaty of Windsor of 1175. By the terms of the treaty, Henry recognized Ruaidhri O'Connor, King of Connacht, as High King of Ireland in those parts of the country unconquered by the Normans, including most of Connacht. It is doubtful that Henry took the treaty seriously, but the Anglo-Norman invasion of Connacht did not begin in earnest until 1227. In that year, Aedh O'Connor, King of Connacht, was forced to forfeit his claim to rule the province that was then granted as a fief, save for parts of present day County Roscommon, to Richard deBurgo. Ten years of warfare followed, during which the O'Connors fought to save their land, for a while aided by Henry III who was squabbling with Richard deBurgo's uncle, Hubert, the royal justiciar. However, once the deBurgos and Henry were reconciled, the conquest moved quickly and by 1237

---

[11] The diocese of Mayo was united to that at Tuam during the thirteenth century, then reappeared during the fifteenth and sixteenth centuries only to be absorbed again by Tuam during the seventeenth century. J. Watt, *The Church in Medieval Ireland* (Dublin, 1972), pp. 24–7; M. Dolley, *Anglo-Norman Ireland* (Dublin, 1972), pp. 39–42; O'Muraile, "An Outline History of County Mayo," p. 13.

[12] The Bull Laudabiliter was granted to Henry by Pope Adrian IV in 1156. E. Curtis and R. B. McDowell (eds.), *Irish Historical Documents, 1172–1922* (London and New York, 1968), pp. 17–18.

[13] Dolley, *Anglo-Norman Ireland*, p. 69.

deBurgo and his allies could parcel out the lands of Connacht with little threat from the native dynasties. DeBurgo reserved for himself most of the rich lowlands of central Mayo and Galway, letting out the remainder to his principal Anglo-Norman allies. The O'Connors and their native allies were pushed into north-eastern Connacht, present-day Counties Roscommon and Leitrim.[14]

The Anglo-Normans moved quickly to consolidate their conquest, building fortified castles in each fief and establishing Loughrea in County Galway as the center of the deBurgo lordship of Connacht. However, as was the case elsewhere in Ireland, the cultural conquest of the Gaels over the Normans proved at least as powerful as the military conquest of the Normans over the Gaels. Within a hundred years the Anglo-Norman families became indistinguishable from the Gaelic families in customs, dress and language. The two groups intermarried, fostered each other's children, shared the services of what the Statutes of Kilkenny called "tympanours, poets, story-tellers, babblers, rymours, harpers or any other Irish minstrels," and participated jointly in the internecine warfare that was a dominant feature of medieval Ireland.[15] In Mayo this process of Gaelicization was symbolized during the fourteenth century when the deBurgo family adopted the Gaelic patronymic MacUilliam, the MacWilliam. A number of other newly settled Anglo-Norman families followed suit.

Early in the fourteenth century the deBurgo lordship split, resulting in the growth of two rival dynasties. The Clanrickard Burkes, or MacUilliam Uachtarach (Upper MacWilliam) were centered in Galway while the Mayo Burkes, or MacUilliam Iochtarach (Lower MacWilliam), were centered in south-central Mayo. Much of the political history of Connacht until late into the sixteenth century is taken up by the rivalry between these two dynasties, each at the center of complex and ever changing factions and alliances of both Gaelic and Gaelicized families. Neither the temporary revival of the power of the Gaelic chieftains in Ireland during the latter half of the fourteenth century nor the authority of the crown was able to check the growing power of the Burkes and their clients in Connacht. Throughout the fifteenth century the two factions reigned supreme in their respective regions of Connacht.

---

[14] *Ibid.*, p. 136; Knox, *History of County Mayo*, pp. 54–6, 89, 101–5.

[15] The Statutes of Kilkenny, 1366, were drawn up in the forlorn hope of halting the Gaelicization of the Anglo-Normans. In the original, the quoted passage reads: "tympanours, fferdanes, skelaghes, ablers, rymours, clarsaghours." Curtis and McDowell (eds.), *Irish Historical Documents 1172–1922*, p. 53.

The Mayo Burkes operated independently of the crown, while the Clanrickard Burkes were nominally the king's official representatives in the province as sheriffs, but were rarely interfered with by the Dublin administration.[16]

This state of affairs was in sharp contrast to the orderly, centrally controlled realm that the Tudors sought to create after 1485. However, it was a considerable time before they could direct their attention toward the west of Ireland. Under the Lord Deputyship of Lord Leonard Gray (1536–40) Tudor authority was spread across the Shannon by the submissions of Gaelic and Anglo-Irish lords to Henry VIII. In Connacht Lord Gray's major success was in Galway where Ulick MacWilliam surrendered his lands to the crown, but was "regranted" them to be held from the king under English law. In addition, Burke was made the Earl of Clanricard. This policy of "surrender and regrant" had other successes in Galway, but appears to have had no impact in the territory of the Mayo Burkes where the Lower MacWilliam continued to exercise palatine jurisdiction.[17]

The Tudor pacification of Mayo began in 1570 under the direction of Lord Deputy Sir Henry Sidney and Sir Edward Fitton, who had been appointed to the new post of President of Connacht the previous year. In 1570 Fitton led a troop of Scottish mercenaries (Gallowglasses), cavalry, English foot soldiers and Gaelicized and Gaelic lords against a similar band put together by the Mayo Burkes. The outcome of the battle of Shrule was indecisive, although the MacWilliam submitted to royal authority soon thereafter. However, within a year Fitton was back to again confront a rebellion of the Mayo lords, this time more successfully with the submission of the MacWilliam and his allies lasting until 1579, when they joined the Desmond rebellion centered in Munster. Under Fitton's presidency (1569–75) the shiring of Connacht was undertaken. County Mayo was composed roughly of the territory of the Lower MacWilliam lordship and ten baronies were created in the county, each containing the land of one or more of the sublordships controlled by Gaelicized Anglo-Norman lords. In 1576 the MacWilliam "received his Country at my [Sidney's] Hands, by Way of Seneschalship, which he

---

[16] K. Nicholls, *Gaelic and Gaelicised Ireland in the Middle Ages* (Dublin, 1972), pp. 148–9.

[17] G. A. Hayes-McCoy, "The Royal Supremacy and Ecclesiastical Revolution, 1534–47," in T. W. Moody, F. X. Martin, F. J. Byrne (eds.), *A New History of Ireland, vol. III: Early Modern Ireland, 1534–1691* (Oxford, 1976), p. 48; Knox, *History of County Mayo*, pp. 168–9.

thankfully accepted," and an English sheriff was appointed to the newly formed county.[18]

More important than the shiring of Connacht from the point of view of Elizabethan administrators was the regularizing of revenue, so that the governance of the province could be made self-supporting, and the curtailing of the independent authority of the lords over their lands, tenants and clients. In an agreement negotiated with the Connacht lords in 1585, known as the Composition of Connacht, the government attempted to accomplish these goals. According to one administrator, the purpose of the settlement was:

> to take away the greatness of the Irish lords . . . that the inferior subject might be freed from their Irish customs, cuttings and unreasonable exactions, and by knowing what was their own . . . be drawn to depend ever after upon the state, and not on those Irish lords or gentlemen: which also might not only much avail her majesty in time of any stirs or revolts, by drawing the common people from following the great chief lords, but also bring a more certainer yearly rent or revenue into her majesty's coffers.[19]

Under the terms of the settlement, the subscribers agreed to pay a yearly rent to the crown of ten shillings on each quarter of tillage or pasture land, rather than the periodic and uncertain exactions that had been demanded previously. Irish titles and offices were abolished, including that of the MacWilliam, and the system of primogeniture was substituted for the Gaelic practice whereby the sept as a whole determined inheritance rights and land settlement.[20] Moreover, land holders were to fix certain and regular rents for their tenants along lines similar to those of their indenture of composition with the crown.[21]

---

[18] Letter from Sir Henry Sidney, 27 April 1576, printed in Knox, *History of County Mayo*, pp. 183–4.

[19] Henry Docwra, "A Narration of the Services Done by the Army Ymployed [sic] to Lough Foyle." Quoted in G. A. Hayes-McCoy, "The Completion of the Tudor Conquest and the Advance of the Counter-Reformation, 1571–1603," in Moody, et al. (eds.), *A New History of Ireland*, III, p. 109.

[20] Mary O'Dowd has shown that there were considerable variations of land tenure and inheritance customs among Gaelic families in Sligo by the sixteenth century, with many having adopted English practices long before the Composition. "Land Inheritance in Early Modern Sligo," *Irish Economic and Social History*, 10 (1983), pp. 5–18.

[21] A. M. Freeman (ed.), *The Compossicion Booke of Conought* (Dublin, 1936), pp. 104–19; Lord Deputy Sir John Perrot to Secretary of State Sir Francis Walsynghan, 10 July 1587, *Calendar of State Papers Relating to Ireland, 1509–1670*, 24 vols. (London, 1860–1912), *1586–1588*, pp. 381–3.

Fiscally the Composition was a success. The province began to pay for itself, at least when rebellion was sufficiently curtailed to allow for the collection of the rent. The level of taxation was not excessive, especially since many great lords were allowed certain of their lands free of composition rent.[22] In addition, many tenants were relieved to have their rents fixed and the power of their lords curtailed by English law. However, the limitations imposed on the prestige and power of the Gaelic and Gaelicized lords proved to be a major source of contention.

Responsibility for administering the Composition fell to Sir Richard Bingham, President of Connacht from 1585 to 1595, who was confronted with regular rebellions on the part of what he termed the "low country" or "loose" Burkes of Mayo and their allies. With lulls and periodic submissions to royal authority, the Mayo lords, in a dizzying and continually changing array of alliances and loyalties, remained in rebellion from 1585 to 1601. The two major issues in the rebellions were the abolition of Gaelic titles and offices and the limitations placed on the relationship between lords and their tenants and clients. According to a declaration issued in November 1586 by the rebels:

resistance to composition [handwritten margin note]

> we do protest and declare in our consciences, that the abolishing and taking away of the name of M'William from the competitors thereof, and the extinguishing of the other lordships and seigniories, from the gentlemen and chiefs of the septs and surnames of the country by the late composition, and the restraining of them from their cuttings and spendings and exactions [from their tenants] hath been the only beginning of the said rebellion, and the chief ground and principal cause which moved these gentlemen who were authors of it to enter into the same . . .

The rebels feared that the restraints placed on their "accustomed cuttings and extortions upon their tenants . . . would shortly make their churl their master, and that the gentlemen were like to become beggars for want of their cuttings and spendings and such other exactions as they compelled their tenants to yield unto them at their own devotion."[23]

Lords upset not because of loss of revenue but loss of autonomy [handwritten margin note]

In most instances, the lords were concerned more with the undermining of the foundations of their status and independence than with the possible reduction of their revenues. Under the terms of the Composition probably few Mayo lords suffered grievous financial loss. Their ability,

---

[22] B. Cunningham, "The Composition of Connacht in the Lordships of Clanricarde and Thomond, 1577–1641," *Irish Historical Studies*, 24 (1984), pp. 4–8.
[23] *Cal. of State Papers, Ireland, 1586–88*, pp. 199, 203.

after 1585, to fix rents on their tenants and hold some of their demesne land tax free probably compensated for the loss of their customary rights to cess for troops, charge entertainment and travel expenses, and extract labor services, goods and rents from their tenants and sub-lords.[24] However, in Ireland lordship involved more than land and revenue. An Irish lordship was over people, not over the territory they occupied, and status rested on the number of people one "lorded" over – i.e., the number of one's clients.[25] Since this system was maintained as much by images of status and authority as by actual rights and power, the elimination of Gaelic titles and offices weakened the cultural bonds between lord and client, presaging the end of the Gaelic order.

The lords fought tenaciously for the restoration of their titles, and with them their arbitrary rights over their clients. On occasion, these struggles broke the local boundaries in which they were normally confined and took the form of a national crusade against the English. According to Bingham, the Mayo lords threatened to seek a MacWilliam in Spain if the local claimant was denied the title and lamented that "so mighty a nation" should "so long [be] subject unto a woman." This attack on the queen was accompanied by a pledge that "the Pope and the King of Spain shall have the rule of us, and none other."[26] However, more often than not, the rebels were interested only in securing the restoration of Gaelic titles to men of their liking, while retaining the advantageous features of the Composition. Accordingly, they were unable to present a united front against English authority with the rebels divided frequently into the rival camps of the various claimants to titles and land.

The divisiveness of the rebels was illustrated in December 1595, when Hugh Roe O'Donnell of Donegal, leader along with Hugh O'Neill of the great rebellion of 1595–1603, came to Connacht to consolidate his influence in the province. At a gathering of the great lords of northern Connacht, assembled to choose a MacWilliam and inaugurate him

---

[24] The nature and degree of the lords' ability to exact revenue and other "cuttings and spendings" varied greatly. They are summarized in Nicholls, *Gaelic and Gaelicised Ireland*, pp. 31–7. See also, Cunningham, "The Composition of Connacht," pp. 7–8 and G. A. Hayes-McCoy, "Gaelic Society in Ireland in the Late Sixteenth Century," in G. A. Hayes-McCoy (ed.), *Historical Studies*, 4 (London, 1963), pp. 48–9.

[25] Nicholls, *Gaelic and Gaelicised Ireland*, pp. 22–3.

[26] "A Discourse of the Services Done by Sir Richard Byngham in the County of Mayo, Within the Province of Connaught, For the Quieting of the Said Country, the Suppression of the Burkes as Revolted There, and the Overthrow of the Scots Who Lately Invaded the Same Province in July, August, and September 1586," in *Cal. of State Papers, Ireland, 1586–88*, p. 172.

according to ancient rituals, O'Donnell, exercising near regal authority, picked from the eight claimants the man with the least right to the title. As a consequence, O'Donnell alienated the Mayo Burkes and their allies who soon made peace with the queen's forces, seriously weakening the rebellion in northern Connacht. In 1600, in an apparent attempt to strengthen his personal authority, the new MacWilliam offered his allegiance to the queen and promised to bring O'Donnell and his allies to England dead or alive. He assured the queen that "being lineally descended from England since the last conquest, [he] hath nothing to do with the Irishry, but in respect of some former wrongs done unto him, thinking by their assistance to be helped, and not for any love he protested he bare [sic] them." In return for his services, he requested an earldom, 150 foot soldiers and 50 cavalry in the queen's pay, and £1000 sterling.[27] His offer and requests, except for the £1000, were accepted and a plan was drawn up for him to carry out his aim.[28] However, for unknown reasons the plan was never carried out and in 1601 the MacWilliam, isolated from many of his countrymen, joined O'Donnell in a campaign for the relief of the Spanish troops at Kinsale. Following the defeat of the Irish, he fled to Spain with O'Donnell, marking the end of the MacWilliam title. The following year his archrival for the MacWilliamship, Captain Thomas Bourke, successfully petitioned the queen for a grant of the seignory for County Mayo, based in part on his loyal support of the English cause and "his good service at Kinsale."[29] Within a few years, he became Viscount Bourke of Mayo under the new order of English rule in Mayo. The MacWilliam title and the world it symbolized were gone for ever.

PLANTATION AND TRANSPLANTATION IN MAYO

Mayo did not figure largely in the Irish policies of James I, which were directed towards the plantation of Ulster and adherence to the crown by Old English recusants. Officially, the county was regarded as the location of "the most barbarous and dangerous people in all Ireland," who "to this day [are] so much given to idleness that their only

[27] A. Blackwell to Captain Thomas Lee, 26 July 1600, *Cal. of State Papers, Ireland, 1600*, pp. 258–60.

[28] Sir Robert Cecil to Captain Thomas Lee, December 1600(?), *Cal. of State Papers, Ireland, 1600–1601*, p. 104.

[29] Sir George Carew to Secretary Cecil, 9 March 1602, *Cal. of State Papers, Ireland, 1601–1603*, p. 321.

dependence is upon the depredation and spoils of pirates . . . "[30] Their
continued willingness to pay the exactions of the chieftains' families,
even though such payments had been outlawed by the Composition, was
particularly worrisome to the Dublin authorities, since this custom was
seen at the root of the sixteenth-century rebellions.[31] Plans to develop
fishing and ship-building industries on the Mayo coast were received
cordially by the government in the hope that an end to idleness would
bring an end to instability and rebelliousness in the county.[32] However,
plans for these industries to employ 20,000 people never materialized
and on the death of James I in 1625 the county was still considered poor
and barbarous.

During the reign of Charles I two plantation schemes were put forward
for Counties Roscommon, Sligo and Mayo, in part motivated by a desire
to civilize the natives. According to a memorandum drawn up in
support of the first plantation scheme in 1628, a plantation would lessen
the dependence of the populace on the old lords' families, "ascertain,
settle, and establish his Majesty's tenures for ever hereafter," bring
Protestantism, double the king's revenue, "mix the British with the
natives, and so avert rebellion" and set a good example to the natives
to "become laborious," and "set up Englishmen who can hold the
office of magistrate." However, the scheme was so devised as to be of
primary benefit to its local promoters, and thus did not secure royal
favor.[33]

A more ambitious scheme was put forward in 1635 by Lord Deputy
Viscount Wentworth (Earl of Strafford after 1640). Under its terms, a
royal claim to the land of counties Roscommon, Sligo, Galway and Mayo
was to be established, with one-quarter of the confiscated land to be set
aside for plantation. In July, Wentworth traveled to Connacht to preside
over inquisitions at which the king's title was to be established and his

---

[30] "Project for Fishing in Ireland," undated papers from the reign of James I, *Cal. of State
Papers, Ireland, 1615–1625*, p. 579.

[31] "Memorandum of the Benefits Which Will Arise to His Majesty by a Plantation to Be
Made in the Counties of Roscommon, Sligo and Mayo, 1628," *Cal of State Papers, Ireland, 1647–1660*, pp. 128–9.

[32] *Ibid.*, p. 56, "Petition for Captain Payliff for Fishing Rights from Achill to the Stags
of Broadhaven" (about 1625); Lord Deputy to the Privy Council, 14 March 1623, and
"Project for Fishing in Ireland," *Cal. of State Papers, Ireland, 1615–1625*, pp. 403–4,
579.

[33] "Memorandum on the Benefits Which Will Arise . . . by a Plantation . . . in the
Counties of Roscommon, Sligo and Mayo," *Cal. of State Papers, Ireland, 1647–1660*,
pp. 128–9; A. Clarke, "Pacification, Plantation, and the Catholic Question, 1602–23,"
in Moody et al. (eds.), *A New History of Ireland*, III, p. 242.

grace appealed to by the resident owners who wanted to keep their lands. On 31 July, he held an inquisition at Ballinrobe at which a jury of Mayo landowners was compelled to declare the king heir to all the land in the county.[34] Since the plan proposed to confiscate the land of the Old English as well as the Gaelic landowners, some of whom were well placed at court, its implementation was delayed by rigorous protests. Moreover, in a time when land was readily available in Virginia, there were few takers for land in the west of Ireland. In Mayo, some land was allocated to planters, but few acres were actually planted by the time the scheme collapsed with the trial and execution of Strafford in 1641.

A gradual drift away from Celtic practices towards those favored by the English characterized the period of relative peace between 1601 and 1641. The inquisition held by Wentworth in July 1635, at which Mayo landowners came forward to declare their title to the land, revealed that the great bulk of the land was held in small parcels by several thousand smallholders, the great majority of whom were descended from the Anglo-Norman families that had settled in the county following the conquest. During the late sixteenth and early seventeenth centuries they had been joined by a sizeable number of Galway merchants who used their wealth from trade to purchase land, often in rich central Mayo, and by a handful of Elizabethan administrators who purchased land in the county they had helped to subdue.[35] As a result of the changed political climate imposed by the Tudors, traditional notions of status, wealth and power gave way. No longer was status determined by the number of clients one could command, but by the size of one's estate and the wealth to be derived from it. Land ownership and inheritance rights came to rest increasingly with the individual not with the family, as had been the case before the Composition. The Strafford Inquisition revealed an accelerated pattern of consolidation and expansion of lands into personal estates on the English pattern during the early decades of the seventeenth century. Gradually, Mayo society was becoming one split into two groups – large landowners and tenants. The former were becoming increasingly Anglicized and Protestant, while the latter remained Roman

---

[34] Similar proceedings were carried out in the other counties of Connacht, with only County Galway refusing to grant the king title until the jury was arrested, imprisoned, fined and bullied into compliance. A. Clarke, "The Government of Wentworth, 1632–40," in Moody, et al. (eds.), *A New History of Ireland*, III, pp. 253–6, 263.

[35] W. O'Sullivan (ed.), *The Strafford Inquisition of County Mayo* (Dublin, 1958).

Catholics whose religious and economic position deteriorated during the century.[36]

The pace and character of the transformation of rural Connacht was altered dramatically during the middle of the century by the rebellion of 1641–52 and by the Cromwellian conquest and resettlement of the country. Mayo's role in the rebellion was marginal. The county fell to the rebels in December 1641, two months after the outbreak of the rebellion in Ulster. Shortly afterwards, one of the many massacres to occur in the early months of the rebellion took place at Shrule, when a group of Protestants fleeing Mayo was plundered and killed by the escort taking it to safety in a Galway fort.[37] Thereafter, the county remained in rebel territory, but for the most part not in active rebellion. The county capitulated in July 1652, when its governor, Sir Theobald Bourke, third Viscount Mayo, whose ambiguous feelings toward the rebellion probably helped keep the county relatively peaceful, surrendered.[38]

At the conclusion of hostilities the Cromwellian government found itself pressed to meet its obligations and promises in the form of Irish land to the "adventurers" who had loaned it money for subduing Ireland and to the soldiers whose pay for service in Ireland was in arrears.[39] In addition, the Commonwealth owed money to "such persons, their executors, administrators or assigns, bodies politic or corporate as have lent monies upon the public faith."[40] On 12 August 1652 parliament passed the Act of Settlement designed to punish the Irish for rebellion by the forfeiture of vast quantities of land, which could then be used to satisfy the Commonwealth's creditors. The bill outlined a series of "Qualifications" by which the guilt of the Irish nation was to be determined. Possibly 80,000 persons were condemned to death and the forfeiture of their estates by the Act, although in the end only several

[36] J. M. Graham, "Rural Society in Connacht, 1600–1640," in N. Stephens and R. E. Glasscock (eds.), *Irish Geographic Studies in Honour of E. Estyn Evans* (Belfast, 1970), pp. 192–208.

[37] R. Bagwell, *Ireland Under the Stuarts and During the Interregnum*, 3 vols. (London, 1909–16), II, pp. 6–7.

[38] *Ibid.*, II, p. 311, in February 1653 Viscount Mayo was tried and executed for complicity in the Shrule massacre of 1642; R. Dunlop (ed.), *Ireland Under the Commonwealth: Being A Selection of Documents Relating to the Government of Ireland from 1651 to 1659*, 2 vols. (Manchester, 1913), I, p. 198.

[39] K. S. Bottigheimer, *English Money and Irish Land: The "Adventurers" in the Cromwellian Settlement of Ireland* (Oxford, 1971), pp. 76–134.

[40] C. H. Firth and R. S. Riat (eds.), *Acts and Ordinances of the Interregnum, 1642–1660*, 3 vols. (London, 1911), II, p. 733.

hundred were actually executed.[41] Less guilty "papists" were to forfeit their estates and accept either banishment from the country or resettlement on land elsewhere in Ireland. Those to be resettled received a parcel of land proportional to their guilt – normally one-third or two-thirds the value of their original estate. After considerable controversy and confusion as to how these provisions were to be carried out, the Council of State resolved during June and July 1653 that the government's debts would be met with land in Ulster, Leinster and Munster provinces. The Irish residents of those provinces would be transplanted west of the Shannon to Connacht and County Clare in accord with the Act of Settlement. This order was accepted by the parliament on 26 September. Under the terms of the Act of Satisfaction, no Irish were to be settled in port towns in the west or within four miles of the sea or the Shannon river, the hope being to set the Irish apart from the new Protestant settlers while also denying them easy access to their Catholic brethren on the continent.[42] In June 1655 it was announced that proprietors in Connacht whose lands were to be seized for distribution to the newcomers were to receive reduced parcels elsewhere in the province.[43]

Reserving Connacht for the Catholic Irish proved difficult due to the insufficient quantity of land elsewhere in Ireland with which to satisfy the soldiers' demands. In addition, the Council of State for Ireland gave confusing directions for the assignment of land in Connacht and County Clare to the commisioners established at Loughrea, County Galway.[44] In 1654 Counties Leitrim and Sligo and the barony of Tirawley in County Mayo were set aside for the soldiers, substantially reducing the amount of land the Loughrea commissioners had for distribution to the transplanted Irish.[45] In February 1656, in an attempt to regularize the transplantation of Irish Catholics to Connacht, the Council of State decided that the remaining baronies of Mayo, with the exception of Gallen, were to be reserved for transplantees from Ulster. The people

---

[41] *Ibid.*, II, pp. 598–603; S. R. Gardiner, "The Transplantation to Connaught," *English Historical Review*, 14 (1899), pp. 702–4, 708.

[42] Firth and Riat (eds.), *Acts and Ordinances*, II, p. 722; Bottigheimer, *English Money and Irish Land*, pp. 132–4.

[43] Dunlop, *Ireland Under the Commonwealth*, II, pp. 522–3.

[44] *Ibid.*, II, pp. 387–9.

[45] R. C. Simington (ed.), *Books of Survey and Distribution, vol. II: County Mayo* (Dublin, 1956), pp. xlviii–l; R. C. Simington (ed.), *The Transplantation to Connacht, 1654–58* (Shannon, Ireland, 1970), pp. x–xi.

already transplanted to these baronies were to be moved elsewhere in the province.[46] In May the Council suggested, in apparent contradiction of the February decree, that portions of Mayo be made available for settlers originally assigned to County Leitrim, since the latter county was "a place of such natural strength" as to make unwise the settling there of Catholics. A further contradiction of the February decree, which indicates the confusion and indecision engendered by the plantation of County Mayo, was an official announcement that two-thirds of the county

> hath been already assigned for the satisfaction of [soldiers'] arrears
> . . . and is tenanted with English inhabitants for the most part; and
> forasmuch as it is thought advisable that the other remaining third part
> (being the maritime part and bordering most upon the sea) should be
> likewise planted with English . . . it is thought fit and ordered . . . that
> no Irish be permitted to set down within the said county.

This announcement, based more on wishful thinking than on the actual state of affairs in Mayo, was reversed within a month when permission was granted to the Loughrea commissioners to plant Irish on lands previously reserved for English, including the coastal zone that was now reduced to one mile.[47]

As was the case elsewhere in Connacht, the Cromwellian settlement of Mayo was chaotic. Often, it was carried out callously, indiscriminately and in apparent violation of the principles established by the 1652–3 acts and directives. Moreover, its administration was officially characterized as being prone to "frustration, fraud and injustice."[48] In the midst of this confusion, approximately 200 grants of land in Mayo were given to planters from elsewhere in Ireland. Approximately 119,494 "profitable" Irish acres, or roughly 52 percent of the profitable acres in Mayo, were granted by the commissioners.[49] Although Mayo had been set aside for

---

46 Inhabitants of Counties Down and Antrim were to be allocated land in the baronies of Clanmorris, Carra and Kilmaine. Inhabitants of the remaining Ulster counties were to be allocated land in the baronies of Murrisk, Burrishoole, Erris and Costello and four baronies in County Galway. Dunlop, *Ireland Under the Commonwealth*, II, pp. 566–7.

47 *Ibid.*, II, pp. 601, 608–11.

48 Quoted in Simington (ed.), *The Transplantation to Connacht*, p. vii.

49 All of the data for this discussion of the Cromwellian settlement of County Mayo are derived from *ibid.*, pp. 185–229 and Simington (ed.), *Books of Survey and Distribution, vol. II: County Mayo*. The acreage figures used are those taken by Simington from the "List of Transplanted Irish, 1655–1659" found in the Ormonde Manuscripts. Historical Manuscript Commission, *The Manuscripts of the Marquis of Ormonde*, 2 vols. (London, 1899), II, pp. 114–76. Every effort has been made to eliminate the duplicate acreages found in the Simington text in the form of joint holdings. When a grant

Table 1.1. *Cromwellian land grants in County Mayo, by barony*

Barony	Irish acres granted	% of arable acres in barony	% of arable acres in county
Burrishoole	9,229	56.4	4
Carra	5,473	28.6	2.4
Clanmorris	9,986	44.3	4.3
Costello	17,169	69.2	7.5
Gallen	13,789	46.8	6
Kilmaine	12,201	33	5.3
Murrisk	5,521	52.5	2.4
Tirawley	10,164	16.5	4.4
Grants in two or more baronies	35,962		15.7
County totals	119,494		52

Sources: Simington (ed.), *The Transplantation to Connacht, 1654–58*, pp. 185–229; Simington (ed.), *Books of Survey and Distribution*, II, pp. 15–204.

grantees from Ulster, only 5 percent of the transplanters came from the province. Rather, the largest numbers came from Munster, 71 or 38 percent, and Connacht, 69 or 37 percent, with an additional 25 or 13 percent coming from Leinster. No place of origin was listed for nine of the transplanters. By far the largest group, 48 or 26 percent, came from County Galway, with thirty of those coming from Galway city. Most of this latter group were merchants, many stemming from ancient Galway families, who were deprived of their livelihood by the Act of Satisfaction which banned the Irish from port towns.

Land was granted in all Mayo baronies except for the half barony of Erris, which was exempted presumably because its small band of profitable land was located along the coast, from which the Irish were barred. As can be seen from Table 1.1, most baronies had 40–70 percent of their profitable land decreed to transplanters. The major exception was Tirawley, which had been set aside for Cromwellian soldiers rather than transplanters. The eastern half of the county was more heavily granted than was the west, and the land decreed was distributed evenly between

included land in two or more counties, it was split equally among them when the proportions could not be determined from the text. As a result of the numerous ambiguities in the available data, all figures in the following discussion should be taken as rough estimates. The discussion is based on figures derived from 186 separate grants for which data were available in the Simington text. An Irish acre contains 7840 square yards, 62 percent larger than an English acre of 4840 square yards.

Table 1.2. *Sizes of Cromwellian Land Grants in County Mayo*

Size of grant (Irish acres)	% of grants
2001+	5.4
1001–2000	9.2
501–1000	19
401–500	5.4
301–400	11.4
201–300	14.1
101–200	18.5
1–100	16.8

Barony	Average size of grant (Irish acres)
Burrishoole	1154
Carra	365
Clanmorris	587
Costello	390
Gallen	431
Kilmaine	531
Murrisk	613
Tirawley	484
County average	642

Source: Simington, *The Transplantation to Connacht, 1654–58*, pp. 185–229.

those areas defined as being in the county's core and peripheral areas. As illustrated by Table 1.2, most of the grants were relatively small, roughly half being for 300 acres or less, with only a handful being in excess of 2001 acres.

On the face of it, it would appear that the Cromwellian resettlement produced a major transformation of land ownership in Mayo, with over half of the profitable acres being taken up by outsiders. However, a comparison of the names of the transplanters with the names of land-owners contained in the *Books of Survey and Distribution* reveals that possibly as few as 24 percent of the grantees or their families were in possession of their Mayo land by the 1690s.[50] Although it is impossible to trace with any accuracy the process of land inheritance and transfer between the 1650s and 1690s, the absence of transplanters or their descendants by the end of the seventeenth century is unmistakable. No

---

[50] For a discussion of the origin and purpose of these volumes, see: R. C. Simington (ed.), *Books of Survey and Distribution, vol. I: County of Roscommon* (Dublin, 1949), pp. xxi–xxxi.

doubt many grantees never took up their grants, possibly because they were able to hold on to their family land by one means or another, while others sold their newly acquired land at the earliest opportunity. Not surprisingly, transplanters from other counties in Connacht were more willing or able to stay in Mayo than were those from elsewhere in Ireland; 51 percent of the grantees from Connacht appear to have stayed, while only 33 percent from Munster, 11 percent from Leinster and 2 percent from Ulster were willing to settle permanently in the far west.

The Cromwellian transplantation scheme was a transitional stage in the transformation of land ownership in Mayo. It completed the destruction of the old order, which had been initiated by the Composition of 1585, but it did not set in place the new order of landowners who would, for the most part, control Mayo during the eighteenth and nineteenth centuries. That distinction belongs to the various instruments of title to Irish lands enacted during the reign of Charles II, to the sale between 1701 and 1703 of land forfeited by Jacobite rebels following the 1688–9 war and to the chaotic land market of the last half of the seventeenth century.

The restoration of Charles II in 1660 raised hopes among the expropriated landowners of Ireland that they would be restored to their land.[51] Charles appeared sympathetic to the Catholics and royalists of Ireland, but found that there was not sufficient land in the country to satisfy the claims of the displaced Irish and of the Protestants who held the land with the support of the English parliament and army. Two parliamentary measures, the Act of Settlement of 1662 and the Act of Explanation of 1665, were enacted with the purpose of resolving the land question in Ireland, but in the end they did little more than confirm the Cromwellian settlement and the numerous land purchases that had accompanied it. A select group of royalists and others who "merited [royal] grace and favour" or who had "eminently suffered for their adhering to the authority of his Majesty or his late father" were specified in the Act of Settlement to have their land restored. In Mayo, this included Viscount Dillon, the largest landholder in the county, the Earl of Clanricarde, John Browne of The Neale and a handful of smaller landowners. Several major landowners in Mayo, Col. Garret Moore and

[51] *Ibid.*, pp. xiv–xix for the land question in Ireland during the Restoration; J. G. Simms, "The Restoration, 1660–85," in Moody, et al. (eds.), *A New History of Ireland*, III, pp. 420–9; W. F. T. Butler, *Confiscation in Irish History* (Port Washington, New York, 1970 reprinted, Dublin, 1917), pp. 165–205.

Viscount Mayo, were added to this list in the Act of Explanation.[52] Nine other Mayo landowners are listed in the *Books of Survey and Distribution* as holding land as a result of decrees of innocence issued by the courts of claims established by the Act of Settlement.[53]

It appears that few other Mayo Catholics and royalists who had been removed from their land during the Commonwealth were restored. However, a great number of planters and purchasers received certifications confirming their claim to the land. The pretense for the two acts was the declaration that measures passed during the Cromwellian period were void at law. Consequently, Irish land distributed during the Commonwealth, with the exception of church land, land belonging to Trinity College, Dublin and the land of "innocents," was vested in the crown by the Act of Settlement. Under the terms of the acts, courts of claims were established to investigate the land claims of transplanters, soldiers and purchasers and to issue certificates to those whose claim was deemed valid. In Mayo, the titles to approximately two-thirds of all holdings listed in the *Books of Survey and Distribution* were credited to certificates issued under the provisions of one of the two acts and to patents issued after 1675 to Connacht and Clare transplanters who had yet to receive legal titles to their allotted land. Another 18 percent of the land was held by quit rents, payable to the government on land forfeited after 1641, and fixed in the Act of Settlement of 1662. Accordingly, the titles to approximately 84 percent of the profitable land in Mayo can be attributed to the Acts of Settlement and Explanation. It is far from clear in the *Books of Survey and Distribution* which recipients of these certificates and patents were transplanters, soldiers, purchasers or the descendants of pre-Cromwellian landowners. Of the 187 landowners listed for Mayo, roughly 40 percent, holding approximately 9 percent of the land, appear to be descended from transplanters or soldiers. Another 50 percent or so, holding approximately 57 percent of the land, seem to be descended from pre-1641 landowners, although in many instances they did not hold the same land as their ancestors.[54]

The final stages of the seventeenth-century land redistribution in Ireland had little lasting effect on Mayo. Only 7 of the 457 estates forfeited by Jacobite supporters were in Mayo. J. G. Simms concludes

---

[52] 14 and 15 Chas. 2, c. 2, secs., xxv, ccxxv; 17 and 18 Chas. 2, c. 2, secs., cxciv, cciv.

[53] Simington (ed.), *Books of Survey and Distribution: County of Mayo*, pp. 15–204.

[54] *Ibid.*, these estimates are based on comparing the "proprietors' names [anno 1641]" and the "to whom soe disposed" columns. They should be taken as very rough estimates.

that the seven Mayo Jacobites, including Walter Bourke and Henry O'Neill who were outlawed for treason, all fled to France, forfeiting 14,717 acres.[55] This land was purchased in 1702–3 through the Trustees' sales by four individuals, two of whom already owned extensive land in the county, and by the Hollow Sword Blades company, a London firm recruited by the government to purchase those properties that were not sold at auction.[56]

With the Trustees' sales of forfeited land the seventeenth-century transformation of land ownership in Mayo came to an end, although some disputed title cases remained in litigation until the middle of the eighteenth century. A little over half of the land remained in the hands of families that held land in the county in 1641, over half of whom were descended from Elizabethan administrators or Galway families who settled in the county during the fifty years prior to 1641. Few of the pre-Elizabethan Gaelic or Gaelicized Old English families remained owners of land in Mayo by 1703, although several of them, such as the Bourkes and the Dillons, remained sizeable land holders. The majority of the landowners were Protestants, although Catholics retained a larger portion of the land in Connacht than elsewhere in Ireland. Nollaig O'Muraile estimates that 39 percent of the land was in Catholic hands in 1703, down from 88 percent in 1641.[57] As illustrated in Table 1.3, two major landowners, Viscounts Dillon and Mayo, held between them over one-third of the "profitable" land in the county, while another four, Col. Garrett Moore, Sir Arthur Gore, the Protestant Archbishop of Tuam and the Protestant Bishop of Killala, held estates in excess of 5000 profitable acres. Of these six landowners who held between them almost half of the county, only Gore, who held vast tracts in the barony of Tirawley, was new to the county. The others had managed to survive the turbulent land exchange of the last half of the seventeenth century with their estates intact, and in some instances enhanced substantially. At the other end of the spectrum, 65 percent of the landowners in Mayo held less than 10 percent of the land in estates of less than 500 acres.

Although a sizeable proportion of land in the county remained in the hands of long-established Mayo families, the loyalties of those families

---

[55] J. G. Simms, *The Williamite Confiscation in Ireland, 1690–1703* (Westport, Connecticut, 1976 reprinted, London, 1956), pp. 41, 65.

[56] *Ibid.*, pp. 151–2.

[57] *Ibid.*, p. 196, Simms places in the 25–49 percent category the proportion of Catholic landowners in Mayo in 1703; O'Muraile, "An Outline History of County Mayo," pp. 21–2.

Table 1.3. *Size of estates in County Mayo, 1703*

Size of holding (Irish acres)	Number of holdings	Proportion of profitable land in County Mayo
20,000+	2	34
5000–10,000	4	13
3000–4999	7	12
1000–2999	30	24
500–999	23	8
100–499	71	8
1–99	50	1

Notes and sources: Simington (ed.), *Books of survey and Distribution*, II, pp. 15–204. Because of ambiguities in the data, these figures can only be taken as estimates.

had shifted dramatically during the seventeenth century. Traditional loyalties to kin and bonds between lords and clients, which Mayo notables had fought tenaciously to preserve at the end of the sixteenth century, were gone forever by the end of the seventeenth century. The new loyalty was to the land, to the estates they had managed to retain and acquire during the tumultuous last half of the century. These attitudes towards the land and its tenants were seen in Ireland as being Protestant and English, but were nonetheless adopted by landowners who were neither. By the beginning of the eighteenth century it was clear that the retention of land and the maintenance of position and authority required acceptance of the established church and acknowledgment that power emanated from London. During the first third of the eighteenth century many of those old Mayo families that had not yet done so converted to the established church.[58] Mayo landowners rapidly joined the ranks of the emerging Anglo-Irish ascendancy class, which during the eighteenth century was to define itself as the Irish nation, but in doing so estranged itself from the actual tillers of the soil who formed the vast majority of the county's population.

[58] Simms, *The Williamite Confiscation in Ireland*, p. 160.

2. Economy and society, 1691–1846

No Help I'll Call

No help I'll call till I'm put in the narrow coffin.
By the Book, it would bring it no nearer if I did!
Our prime strong-handed prop, of the seed of Eoghan
– his sinews are pierced and his vigour is withered up.

Wave-shaken is my brain, my chief hope gone.
There's a hole in my gut, there are foul spikes through my bowels.

The Sionainn, the Life, the musical Laoi, are muffled
and the Biorra Dubh river, the Bruice, the Brid, the Boinn.
Reddened are Loch Dearg's narrows and the Wave of Toim
since the Knave has skinned the crowned King in the game.

Incessant my cry; I spill continual tears;
heavy my ruin; I am one in disarray.
No music is nigh as I wail about the roads
except for the noise of the Pig no arrows wound.

That lord of the Rinn and Cill, and the Eoghanacht country
– want and injustice have wasted away his strength.
A hawk now holds those places, and takes their rent,
who favours none, though near to him in blood.

Our proud royal line is wrecked; on that account
the water ploughs in grief down from my temples,
sources sending their streams out angrily
to the river that flows from Truipeall to pleasant Eochaill.

I will stop now – my death is hurrying near
now the dragons of the Leamhan, Louch Lein and the Laoe are
    destroyed.
In the grave with this cherished chief I'll join those kings
my people served before the death of Christ.

Aogan O'Rathaille[1]

The effect of the seventeenth-century transformation of land ownership on the peasants of Mayo is difficult to gauge. Following the lead of Gaelic poets such as Aogan O'Rathaille, one of whose poems heads this chapter, historians and Gaelic revivalists of the late nineteenth and early twentieth centuries lamented the loss of the Gaelic and Old English lords. They argued that the destruction of the Gaelic system had left the Irish peasants impoverished, alienated and leaderless. According to Daniel Corkery, the most skilful and influential proponent of this view of the eighteenth century, "hidden Ireland" was one in which "poverty was its only wear – poverty in the town, the cabin, the person, the gear, the landscape. Civic life was not only broken, but wiped away . . . Life did no more than just crawl along, without enough to eat, unclothed, fever-stricken, slow: how could it have a thought for anything beyond mere existence from day to day!"[2] Led by Louis Cullen, contemporary historians have argued that eighteenth-century Ireland was not as bleak as Corkery assumed and that the literary evidence, on which Corkery relied, is far from conclusive in support of his thesis.[3] Cullen charged Corkery with taking at "their face value rhetorical references to their circumstances by the poets, which are general, conventional and imitative, and conveying what may be described as the aristocratic sense of loss or grievance at the revolution in land ownership." Cullen argued that "while the poetry suggests alienation, and may even have helped to keep a feeling of alienation alive, it does not constitute evidence of the existence of a community, oppressed economically or socially."[4]

---

[1] Aogan O'Rathaille (Egan O'Rahilly), trans. by Thomas Kinsella in S. O'Tuama and T. Kinsella (eds.), *An Duanaire, An Irish Anthology: 1600–1900 Poems of the Dispossessed* (Philadelphia, 1981), pp. 165–7.

[2] D. Corkery, *The Hidden Ireland* (Dublin, 1924; ref. from paperback ed., Dublin, 1967), p. 36.

[3] L. M. Cullen, "The Hidden Ireland: Re-Assessment of a Concept," *Studia Hibernica*, 9 (1969), pp. 7–47.

[4] *Ibid.*, pp. 18, 28.

THE GROWTH OF AN INTERREGIONAL MARKET ECONOMY

Although evidence is meager on the condition of the vast majority of Mayo residents during the first half of the eighteenth century, it is doubtful that the changes in land ownership had an immediate or wrenching effect on them. Rather, their lives continued to be governed by social and economic forces set in motion during Elizabethan times. No doubt, this continuity was furthered by the presence of a large number of pre-1641 landowners who had managed to retain land in the county. Yet, for the most part, they were not the descendants of Gaelic families who might have harbored some vestige of the old patron–client relationship with their tenants. They were heirs of Galway merchants and Elizabethan administrators who took up land with the hope of profiting from it. They viewed their tenants as vehicles to that end, replacing bonds of personal loyalty between owner and tiller with contractual relationships that, as the eighteenth century progressed, became increasingly responsive to market forces. Gone were the relatively prosperous small proprietors who were in the process of formation prior to 1640.[5] They had either become or been replaced by tenant farmers who had little claim to the land other than as lease-holders and rent-payers. Increasingly, they were vulnerable to rent raises and eviction, although the degree to which these occurred is impossible to determine.

As early as 1710 a wave of cattle houghing and other forms of assault on livestock began in Iar Connacht, the region of County Galway that adjoins the south-western corner of County Mayo. The Archbishop of Dublin attributed these assaults to rent raises, evictions and the conversion of tillage land to grazing, an analysis supported by recent research.[6] In the first reference to the maiming of livestock having spread to County Mayo, the Archbishop of Tuam, John Vesey, reported to the

---

[5] Graham, "Rural Society in Connacht, 1600–1640," p. 205.

[6] J. G. Simms, "The Establishment of the Protestant Ascendancy, 1691–1714," in T. W. Moody and W. E. Vaughan (eds.), *A New History of Ireland, vol. IV: Eighteenth Century Ireland, 1691–1800* (Oxford, 1986), pp. 9–10; S. J. Connolly, "The Houghers: Agrarian Protest in Early Eighteenth Century Connacht," in C. H. E. Philpin (ed.), *Nationalism and Popular Protest in Ireland* (Cambridge, 1987), pp. 139–62; S. J. Connolly, "Law, Order and Popular Protest in Early Eighteenth Century Ireland: The Case of the Houghers," in P. J. Corish (ed.), *Historical Studies XV: Radicals, Rebels and Establishments* (Belfast, 1985), pp. 51–68; W. E. H. Lecky, *A History of Ireland in the Eighteenth Century*, 8 vols. (London, 1906), I, pp. 361–5.

government on 22 January 1712 that 300 head of cattle had been killed in the county during the previous week.[7] One Mayo landlord whose cattle and sheep had been houghed in March 1712, Sir Arthur Shaen, had settled Protestant tenants on the Mullet estate that his father had acquired during the seventeenth century. These tenants believed that they were the targets of the attacks on livestock and petitioned the President of Connacht, Sir Henry Bingham, thanking him for arresting troublesome "papists" whose land they had been given. The petitioners reported that the "natives" had "effectively ruined" them "by the most secret artifices of stealing our cattle, to the number of seventy-five, within the space of nine months, besides our sheep without number, not to mention the plundering of our gardens [and] stealing our corn."[8] Although it appears likely that the wave of agrarian outrage that struck Connacht between 1710 and 1712 was the consequence of the growing insecurity and resentment felt by the Catholic tenantry, the 2 percent growth in the number of households in County Mayo paying hearth tax between 1702 and 1712 would not support the notion of wide-spread evictions or land conversion during the first decade of the eighteenth century.[9] Nonetheless, this agrarian protest, as limited in scope as it probably was, might well be seen as evidence of an awareness on the part of tenant farmers of their increased vulnerability, especially at the conclusion of three years of poor harvests in Ireland.[10]

The degree to which Mayo and other western counties became part of an interregional market economy during the eighteenth century and the speed of their integration with the national economy has been disputed by historians. In 1960 Patrick Lynch and John Vaizey put forward an interesting although largely discredited thesis that pre-Famine Ireland could be characterized as having two economies: a "maritime economy" that included the east coast and the cities of Limerick and Galway that was monetized and linked to England; and a "subsistence economy" in the rest of the country. The subsistence sector, which they argued was sharply and territorially set off from the maritime economy, contained a "society

---

[7] Public Record Office, London, S. P. Vesey to Dawson, 22 Jan. 1712, 63/367, fo. 243. Ref. from Connolly, "The Houghers," p. 143.

[8] P. Knight, *Erris in the Irish Highlands and the Atlantic Railway* (Dublin, 1836), p. 64. Knight dates this petition as having been sent during the reign of Queen Anne (1702–14).

[9] See Table 2.1, p. 46 below.

[10] L. M. Cullen, *An Economic History of Ireland Since 1660* (London, 1972; ref. from 1976 pbk. ed.), p. 43.

without a market."[11] Although the Lynch and Vaizey thesis was a useful and stimulating break from the nationalist view of eighteenth-century Ireland as being in a continual state of destitution, its division of the country into two geographically distinct zones did not take into account the degree to which a monetary and market economy had reached even the most remote regions of rural Ireland by the middle of the eighteenth century, if not earlier. As Joel Mokyr puts it: "there were indeed two Irelands, but they were not geographically separate as Lynch and Vaisey [sic] suggested. Instead, they were living alongside each other, intertwined and mutually dependent though utterly different in their degrees of commercialization, economic attitudes, agricultural techniques and so on."[12] As noted above, topographically and economically County Mayo can be divided into a central corridor banded east and west by peripheral regions.[13] Although Mayo contains relatively distinct territorial divisions that influenced the development of its economic and social structure, the county's core and periphery were mutually dependent and both were characterized by a mixture of commercial and subsistence economies.

There is little data on the structure of the Mayo economy during the first half of the eighteenth century, or on the degree to which it was involved in interregional trade. However, there is no reason to suspect that the more fertile and accessible regions of central Mayo were less commercialized than similar regions in neighboring County Sligo, for which there is some evidence. Between 1752 and 1773 an enterprising County Sligo landlord, Charles O'Hara, compiled a report on the economic development of his county.[14] He reported that at the beginning of the eighteenth century there was "no foreign" and little interregional

---

[11] P. Lynch and J. Vaizey, *Guinness's Brewery in the Irish Economy, 1756–1876* (Cambridge, 1960), pp. 9–36. For criticisms of the "dual economy" thesis, see: R. D. Crotty, *Irish Agricultural Production: Its Volume and Structure* (Cork, 1966), pp. 306–7; L. M. Cullen, "Problems in the Interpretation and Revision of Eighteenth Century Irish Economic History," *Transactions of the Royal Historical Society*, 5th series, 17 (1967), pp. 1–22; J. H. Johnson, "The Two 'Irelands' at the Beginning of the Nineteenth Century," in Stephens and Glasscock (eds.), *Irish Geographical Studies in Honour of E. Estyn Evans*, pp. 224–43; J. Lee, "The Dual Economy in Ireland, 1800–1850," in T. D. Williams (ed.), *Historical Studies VIII* (Dublin, 1971), pp. 191–201; R. J. Raymond, "A Reinterpretation of Irish Economic History (1730–1850)," *The Journal of European Economic History*, 2 (1982), pp. 655–8; J. Mokyr, *Why Ireland Starved* (London, 1983), pp. 20–2.

[12] Mokyr, *Why Ireland Starved*, p. 20.

[13] See Map 1.1, p. 16 above.

[14] Public Record Office of Northern Ireland (PRONI), Charles O'Hara of Nymphsfield, "A Survey of the Economic Development of County Sligo in the Eighteenth Century" (typed manuscript), T.2812/19/1.

demand for the agricultural products of County Sligo and little cash in the county's economy. However, this situation began to change as early as 1710 when the needs of the North American colonies and of the British and French navies brought an increased demand for Irish beef.[15] With this increased trade in Irish beef, much of it centered in south-central Ireland, "the graziers of Munster turned their grounds to feeding, and came towards the Connaught fairs for their store cattle." According to O'Hara, by the 1720s the demand for store cattle in County Sligo was resulting in a rise in rents and "many villagers" being turned off their land and replaced with cattle.[16] However, Cullen cautions that the rent increases of the 1720s had more to do with the falling in of leases set at "unrealistically low" levels during the 1690s than with rising demand for store cattle or population pressure.[17]

It is impossible to determine the extent to which tenants were put off their land. O'Hara cites the decline in the hearth money returns for 1727 as evidence for a reduction in the number of County Sligo tenant farmers, although he later claimed that some of these tenants returned to their farms when beef prices dropped in 1728.[18] Hearth tax records indicate that between 1726 and 1732 the number of houses paying tax in County Sligo declined by 10 percent, while in County Mayo the decline was 5 percent.[19] However, in both instances, the decline in tax-paying households was probably the result of a series of bad harvests and famine conditions that struck Ireland in 1727–9. O'Hara reported that the linen industry, which arrived in the west of Ireland during the early decades of the eighteenth century, "was the preservation of many families" during the hard times of the 1720s.[20] Without doubt, O'Hara exaggerates the extent of the linen industry in the county. Nonetheless, from the 1720s efforts by the Linen Board to encourage the growing and spinning of flax in counties Mayo and Sligo met with increasing success as the needs of Ulster weavers for yarn grew steadily.[21] However, prior to mid-century

---

[15] Cullen, *An Economic History of Ireland Since 1660*, pp. 54–6.

[16] O'Hara, "Survey," pp. 6–7.

[17] Cullen, "Problems in the Interpretation and Revision of Eighteenth-Century Irish History," p. 17; Cullen, *An Economic History of Ireland Since 1660*, pp. 44–5.

[18] O'Hara, "Survey," p. 7.

[19] D. Dickson, C. O'Gráda, S. Daultrey, "Hearth Tax, Household Size and Irish Population Change, 1672–1821," *Proceedings of the Royal Irish Academy*, lxxxii, c, no. 6 (1982), p. 177 and Table 2.1.

[20] O'Hara, "Survey," p. 7.

[21] E. L. Almquist, "Mayo and Beyond: Land, Domestic Industry, and Rural Transformation in the Irish West" (Boston University, Ph.D. thesis, 1977), pp. 22–34.

the trade in linen yarn, like the trade in store cattle represented little more than a tentative, fragile economic link with the commercial markets of the east and south-east and through them with Europe and North America. Poor communication and transportation links with the east coast ports limited the county's access to the export trade while rough seas and poor quality ships made hazardous the transportation of stock from Mayo's ports.[22] As a consequence only a minority of farmers participated in this trade and few profited to any great extent. Nonetheless, this interregional trade introduced both the towns and rural areas of County Mayo to a unified cash-based economy that to an ever-increasing extent was based on an Irish export trade in cattle and linen.

The picture we get of County Mayo during the first half of the eighteenth century is one of a population highly vulnerable to poor harvests, fluctuating agricultural prices and famine. Successive bad harvests brought famine to Ireland in 1728–9 and 1740–1 and near-famine conditions in 1744 and 1756–7.[23] By all accounts, the famine of 1740–1 was the most devastating of the century, when a series of bad harvests was followed by a frost that lasted seven weeks in late 1739 and early 1740. The frost destroyed the potato crop, leaving large sections of the Irish population with a lack of food. By the spring of 1741 the weakened population was racked by epidemics of typhus and dysentery, which probably resulted in more deaths than did starvation.[24]

In the far west of Ireland the crisis of 1744–5, brought on by an excessively wet August in 1744 followed by a winter snow and torrential spring rains in 1745, may have been even more severe than that of 1740–1. O'Hara reported:

> on the 24 of August a violent storm with rain so totally destroyed it [the corn crop] that not one acre in ten was worth reaping . . . In January this was succeeded by a violent fall of snow which covered the whole face of the country until the latter end of March, so that all kind of fodder being consumed the people fed their cattle with corn. The food was too hot for them in their weak condition, the cattle died, and the people starved for want of the corn. There is no misery which

---

[22] Freeman, *Pre-Famine Ireland*, p. 117; J. O'Donovan, *The Economic History of Livestock in Ireland* (Cork, 1940), p. 213.

[23] Cullen, *An Economic History of Ireland Since 1660*, p. 68; L. M. Cullen, "Economic Development, 1691–1750," in Moody and Vaughan (eds.), *A New History of Ireland, IV*, pp. 145–7.

[24] M. Drake, "The Irish Demographic Crisis of 1740–41," in T. W. Moody (ed.), *Historical Studies VI* (London, 1968), pp. 101–24.

famine can induce that did not afflict our country the following year [1745].[25]

Charles O'Conor of Belanagare in County Roscommon, which borders Mayo on the east, wrote in his diary on 5 June 1745 that "famine more devilish now than in the summer of 1741, and all Ireland threatened with the same judgement." On 28 July he recorded: "famine in steady progress, without a grain of harvest, barley or potato, and without a bite of bread now except for what came from beyond the seas. That is the most astonishing experience in the world."[26] The impression of these diaries that the crisis of 1744–5 was more severe in the west than had been the famine of 1740–1 is supported by an analysis of the number of houses paying hearth tax.

POPULATION SIZE AND CHANGE DURING THE EIGHTEENTH CENTURY

The house counts supplied by hearth tax collectors provide the only data available from which to estimate population size and change during the eighteenth century. Begun in 1662 and available in an irregular but continuous series from 1706 to 1791, these counts have long been recognized by demographers and historians as a valuable source for estimating the population of Ireland.[27] The counts were made by "collectors" who forwarded to Dublin abstracts giving the number of hearth and house totals for each parish as well as of the houses exempt from tax because their inhabitants were widows or had been deemed by the local magistrate to be below the poverty line. To the degree that decreases in the number of taxed houses reflect the mortality, migration and poverty associated with famine or severe hardship, fluctuations in the house counts provide a rough barometer of economic activity.[28]

Recently, Stuart Daultrey, David Dickson and Cormac O'Gráda have subjected this series to its most serious scrutiny and have developed new

25 O'Hara, "Survey," p. 8.
26 Síle Ní Chinnéide, "Dhá leabhar nótaí le Séarlas O'Conchubbhair," *Galvia*, I (1954), pp. 38–9, quoted and translated in Cullen, "Economic Development, 1691–1750," pp. 146–7.
27 K. H. Connell, *The Population of Ireland* (Oxford, 1950), pp. 3–15; G. O'Brien, *The Economic History of Ireland in the Eighteenth Century* (Dublin and London, 1918), pp. 9–12.
28 Returns of exempt houses have not survived prior to the 1770s. S. Daultrey, D. Dickson, C. O'Gráda, "Eighteenth-Century Irish Population: New Perspectives from Old Sources," *Journal of Economic History*, 41 (1981), pp. 610–11, 616–18.

estimates of households and population as well as the first analysis of eighteenth-century regional and county population change.[29] They found strong regional contrasts in the rate of population change, but in general concluded that

> one can sense two phases in the history of the Irish population growth before the 1820s. In the first eighty years of the hearth tax, from the 1660s to the 1740s, the record seems one of growth frustrated, the potential checked by the Williamite wars, the harvest crisis of the late 'twenties and early 'forties, and the relatively high level of migration to the port cities. In the following eighty years the potential for growth was realized.[30]

As illustrated in Table 2.1 and Figure 2.1 the population of County Mayo followed this pattern. During the first quarter of the eighteenth century the population of the county rose approximately 37 percent, or at an annual rate of 1.9 percent. This rate set County Mayo as one of the fastest growing counties in the country, a distinction it also had during the last fifteen years of the seventeenth century.[31] However, during the second quarter the population of County Mayo, along with that of the country as a whole, fluctuated in accord with the economic climate. Between 1726 and 1732 the population declined by 6.5 percent, no doubt in large part as a consequence of the famine of 1728–9. However, the famine of 1740–1 seems to have only slowed the rate of population growth in the county. Between 1732 and 1744 the population rose despite the famine, although at the reduced annual rate of 0.56 percent, only to drop 5.3 percent between 1744 and 1749 in response to the economic crisis of the middle of the decade. By 1753, the last year, prior to 1791, when reliable population estimates can be derived, the population of the county had risen by 8.7 percent or 42 percent greater than it had been in 1706.

THE COMMERCIALIZATION OF MAYO AGRICULTURE, 1750–1830

The unbroken rise in the population that began during the 1750s corresponded with a slow, often interrupted, expansion of the county's economy that lasted until the second decade of the nineteenth century.

---

[29] *Ibid.* and Dickson et al., "Hearth Tax, Household Size and Irish Population Change."
[30] Dickson et al., "Hearth Tax, Household Size and Irish Population Change," p. 174.
[31] *Ibid.*, pp. 161, 163; Daultrey et al., "Eighteenth-Century Irish Population," p. 622.

Table 2.1. *Household and population estimates, County Mayo, 1706–1841*

Date	Households	Households adjusted 14%	Households adjusted 34%	Household size	Population lower estimate	Population upper estimate
1706	9211	10,501	12,343	4.8	50,403	59,245
1712	9,397	10,713	12,592	4.8	51,420	60,442
1718	9,967	11,362	13,356	4.8	54,539	64,108
1725	12,615	14,381	16,904	4.8	69,029	81,140
1726	12,742	14,526	17,074	4.8	69,724	81,957
1732	12,163	13,866	16,298	4.7	65,159	76,603
1744	12,709	14,488	17,030	4.8	69,544	81,744
1749	12,038	13,723	16,130	4.8	65,872	77,428
1752	12,815	14,609	17,172	4.8	70,124	82,426
1753	13,085	14,917	17,534	4.8	71,602	84,163
1791	20,210	21,827	21,827	5.3	120,043	120,043
1821	53,051				293,112	310,259
1831	62,367				366,328	372,556
1841	70,522				388,887	399,581

Notes and Sources: Household totals for 1706–91 are taxed houses compiled from published reports by Dickson, O'Gráda and Daultrey; 1821 and 1831 totals are taken from the censuses of those years. Dickson, O'Gráda and Daultrey argue that the totals for the years 1753–91 are too unreliable to be used, and are not included above. For the years 1706–53 they estimate that the published household totals under-record the number of households by between 14 and 34 percent. For 1791 they estimate that the official totals under-report the number of households by 8 percent. Columns 3 and 4 above adjust the household totals according to these estimates. Estimates of the number of persons per household are also derived from Dickson, O'Gráda and Daultrey and are used to compute the lower and upper estimates of the county's population for the years 1706–91. The lower figure for 1821, 1831 and 1841 are the official totals published in the censuses. The upper estimate for these three years is computed using Lee's appraisal that the 1821 census under-reports the population by 5.85 percent, the 1831 census by 1.7 percent and the 1841 census by 2.75 percent. Dickson, O'Gráda and Daultrey, "Hearth Tax, Household Size and Irish Population Change, 1672–1821," pp. 125–81; Daultrey, Dickson and O'Gráda, "Eighteenth Century Irish Population: New Perspectives from Old Sources," pp. 601–28; J. Lee, "On the Accuracy of the Pre-Famine Irish Censuses," in J. M. Goldstrom and L. A. Clarkson (eds.), *Irish Population, Economy and Society: Essays in Honour of the Late K. H. O'Connell* (Oxford, 1981), pp. 37–56; *House of Commons Journals, Ireland* XV (1792–92), appendix cxcvii–ccii; *Abstract of Answers and Returns, Pursuant to Act 55 Geo. 3, For Taking an Account of the Population of Ireland in 1821: Part IV. Province of Connaught,* PP 1824 (577), xxii, p. 788; *Abstract of the Population Returns, 1831: Part VI. Province of Connaught,* PP 1833 (634), xxxix, p. 382; *Report of the Commissioners Appointed to Take the Census of Ireland for the Year 1841,* PP 1843 [504[, xxiv, pp. 400–1.

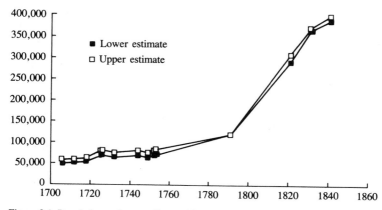

Figure 2.1. Population estimates, County Mayo, 1706–1841

As was the case elsewhere in Ireland, the growth of County Mayo's economy was linked to the rising agricultural prices that resulted from the growing demand for Irish products in Britain and its colonies. Although the county had almost no direct international trade until the early decades of the nineteenth century, by the middle of the eighteenth century it had entered into a trade network that was fueled to a large extent by external demand. During the last half of the eighteenth century the landlords, farmers and cottiers of County Mayo endured unpredictable weather, frequent credit crises and the vicissitudes of the Irish, British and colonial markets to develop gradually a market-oriented, cash-based economy that was remarkably vibrant by the end of the century. As early as the 1760s, Charles O'Hara, writing from adjacent County Sligo, was convinced that the economic fortunes of even the lowliest cottier or subtenant were tied to an external market. In his entry for 1760, O'Hara proclaimed that "the lower people now rely more on their industry [primarily linen and calf-rearing], which opened an access to other markets, in case of scarcity at home."[32]

Unfortunately, there is no remotely comparable survey of the economy of County Mayo during the eighteenth century, which when combined with the dearth of economic information, makes it difficult to chart the growth of the county's economy. The extensive economic data contained in the appendices to the *Journals of the House of Commons of*

[32] O'Hara, "Survey," p. 24.

Table 2.2. *Grain exports from the Port of Newport, 1749–1790*

Date	Oats quarters	Barley quarters	Wheat quarters	Oat flour barrels
1749	96			
1750				
1751				
1752				
1753	6			52
1754				
1755				30
1756 to 1773	No exports recorded			
1774	525	666		99
1775				
1776				
1777				
1778				
1779				
1780				
1781				
1782				
1783	334	66		100
1784				
1785		1333	160	
1786	7	2160	200	
1787	721	1110		
1788	1184			80
1789	818	279		
1790	749	312	879	520

Source: House of Commons Journals, Ireland, XII (1786–8), Appendix, cccliii; XIV (1790–1), Appendix ccxcii.

Ireland include few references to County Mayo. However, it is possible to compile from this source two indices that provide some idea of the level of Mayo's economic activity during the second half of the eighteenth century, at least as regards the grain trade. The appendices record grain exports from Irish ports from 1700 to 1790. Newport, County Mayo's major port during the eighteenth century, had no recorded exports prior to 1749. Thereafter, as illustrated in Table 2.2, grain exports from Newport were spotty until 1785 when they became regular, no doubt in response to the rise in prices that became sustained after 1785. Table 2.3 records national average prices for oats (Mayo's major cash crop), barley and wheat between 1738 and 1840. It illustrates

Table 2.3. *Irish grain prices, 1738–1840 (prices per cwt.)*

	Oats		Barley		Wheat	
	s.	d.	s.	d.	s.	d.
1738–48	3	4	3	0	6	7
1749–58	4	10	4	4	8	3
1759–68	5	7	3	6	8	6
1769–78	5	1	3	9	9	5
1781–85	4	10	5	0	9	9
1789	7	8	8	2	10	0
1800–5	8	4	9	8	15	10
1806–10	9	6	10	4	17	8
1812–15	10	2	11	4	17	6
1816–20	9	10	10	3	15	11
1821–25	6	11	7	6	11	6
1826–30	8	10	9	5	13	1
1831–35	6	4	7	2	10	6
1836–40	7	9	8	6	13	9

Sources: Crotty, *Irish Agricultural Production*, Table 4, p, 21, Table 67C, p. 283; as adapted by O'Neill, *Family Farm in Pre-Famine Ireland*, Table 2.1, p. 73.

clearly the dramatic rise in grain prices between 1785 and 1815, when the end of the Napoleonic wars brought an end to the thirty-year economic boom. There is no comparable index for prices in County Mayo. However, we do know that in 1811, during the peak of the Napoleonic boom period, oats were selling in Westport for 5s. 10d. per hundredweight, barley for 10s. 2d. and wheat for 10s. 10d.[33] Although barley prices were equivalent to the national average, oat and wheat prices were substantially lower, as would be expected given the distance from the major grain markets and ports of eastern Ireland.

A stronger indication of the growth of commercial agriculture in Mayo can be seen in the county's trade with Dublin. Table 2.4 and Figure 2.2 illustrate the grain, malt and flour recorded as being sent from Mayo to Dublin in consequence of a 1758 act of parliament designed to better supply Dublin with food.[34] Under the terms of the act and its subsequent

[33] E. Wakefield, *An Account of Ireland: Statistical and Political*, 2 vols. (London, 1812), II, p. 213.

[34] 31 Geo. II, c. 3 (3 Mar. 1758). On the bounty see A. Young, *A Tour of Ireland: With General Observations on the Present State of that Kingdom, Made in the Years 1776, 1777, 1778, and Brought Down to the End of 1779* (London, 1780). References from A. W. Hutton's edition, 2 vols. (London, 1892), II, pp. 155–91; Connell, *Population of Ireland*, pp. 270–1; J. H. Andrews, "Land and People, c. 1780," in Moody and

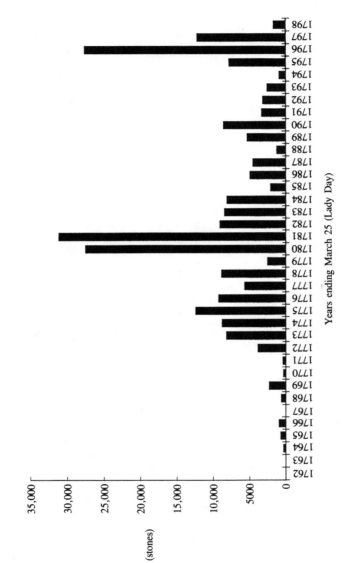

Figure 2.2. Grain and malt, County Mayo to Dublin, 1764–1798

Table 2.4. *Grain, malt and flour transported from County Mayo to Dublin, 1762–1798*

Year	Bere & barley (stones)	Wheat (stones)	Oats (stones)	Malt (stones)	Meal (stones)	Total (stones)	Flour (cwt)	Sum paid £	s.	d.
1762	0	0	0	0	0	0	0			
1763	0	0	0	0	0	0	0			
1764	0	0	385	0	0	385	0	3	16	2
1765	0	0	754	0	0	754	0	7	1	7
1766	0	0	1018	0	0	1018	0	11	1	9
1767	0	0	0	0	0	0	0			
1768	0	0	674	0	0	674	0	6	5	1
1769	0	248	56	2026	0	2330	0	61	3	9
1770	0	0	388	0	0	388	0	4	7	3
1771	0	0	481	0	0	481	0	5	7	9
1772	0	537	944	2413	0	3894	0	85	13	8
1773	0	0	381	7849	0	8230	0	214	17	5
1774	0	2369	653	4953	842	8817	0	203	17	10
1775	0	582	1854	9945	60	12,441	0	311	19	6
1776	0	502	1754	5512	1532	9300	0	201	0	1
1777	0	0	180	5516	0	5696	0	157	0	0
1778	0	0	716	8187	0	8903	0	226	13	0
1779	0	0	224	2336	0	2560	0	64	1	11
1780	0	0	144	27,108	336	27,588	0	776	1	0
1781	0	440	0	30,788	0	31,228	0	896	18	9
1782	0	5538	1094	2522	0	9154	0	130	15	7
1783	0	4218	1542	2690	74	8524	100	138	13	11
1784	0	166	1264	6766	0	8196		177	5	3
1785	0	0	158	1989	0	2147	0	43	17	9
1786	0	0	190	4826	0	5019	0	106	10	11
1787	0	803	2009	1473	312	4597	0	68	17	11
1788	0	770	535	0	0	1305	108	32	4	10
1789	205	0	0	5182	0	5387	622	221	8	4
1790	240	641	0	7751	0	8632	156	206	7	7
1791	169	0	71	3119	0	3359	0	77	7	3
1792	0	0	1057	2167	0	3224	320	121	7	7
1793	0	536	340	1752	0	2628	912	217	14	7
1794	0	0	646	0	317	963	170	44	1	1
1795	80	0	882	6913	0	7875	0	162	10	2
1796	1819	0	1471	20,607	3812	27,709	462	664	0	3
1979	0	0	3502	1728	7011	12,241	1748	530	6	2
1798	0	0	0	561	1181	1749	630	149	13	11

Sources: House of Commons Journals, Ireland XII (1786–88), appendices clxiii, ccclxxxi, dxcix; *House of Commons Journals, Ireland*, XIII (1789–90), appendices xlvii, cclxv; *House of Commons Journals Ireland*, XIV (1790–91), appendix liii; *House of Commons Journals, Ireland*, XV (1792–94), appendices clviii, cclxxxiii, cccclx; *House of Commons Journals, Ireland*, XVI (1795–96), appendices xxxi, cclxv; *House of Commons Journals, Ireland* XVII (1796–98), appendices xcvi, ccclxx; *House of Commons Journals, Ireland*, XVIII (1799), appendix lii.

revisions a bounty was paid to persons bringing corn and flour to Dublin, initially by land carriage, but later by canal or coastal transportation. As Arthur Young pointed out in his criticism of the bounty system, the great bulk of the money paid out went to the traditional grain-growing counties of the east and midlands.[35] However, even Young's tables, compiled from the Irish House of Commons' *Journals*, indicate that the impoverished counties of the west of Ireland supplied an increasing amount of corn and flour to Dublin during the thirty-six years of the bounty program. As illustrated in Table 2.4 and Figure 2.2, the farmers of County Mayo participated in the bounty program beginning in 1764, two years after its inception. Although the county never contributed as much as 1 percent of the grain sent to Dublin in any given year (0.97 percent in 1781 was the high point) and only 0.0031 percent of the total over the course of the program, its involvement in this interregional grain market demonstrates the slow expansion of the commercialized sector of the Mayo economy to include tillage products.

By the early decades of the nineteenth century export-based commercialized agriculture had reached the more remote areas of the county's periphery. The Mullet peninsula that juts out from the northwestern coast of the half-barony of Erris is a case in point. It is separated from central Mayo by a 30 mile stretch of blanket bog which, until the 1830s, was traversed by only the meanest of roads. Traveling in the county in 1801 to conduct a county survey for the Dublin Society, James MacParlan, described the roads across the half-barony of Erris as "completely bad and devious." The road north from Newport through the barony of Tirawley he called "a burlesque upon roads . . . a satire upon the county."[36] In an 1831 report prepared for the Lord Lieutenant, Sampson Carter described the district as "wild" consisting of "vast tracts of boggy swamps, chiefly waste, interspersed with a few lakes and unculturable mountains." He recommended road construction in the district as a means of subverting crime, bringing employment, facilitating trade and civilizing Erris through easier contact with the inland regions of the county.[37]

Vaughan (eds.), *A New History of Ireland*, IV, pp. 247–8. Full accounts of the bounties paid appear in the appendices to the *Journals of the Irish House of Commons*; see note on sources for Table 2.4.

[35] Young, *A Tour of Ireland*, II, pp. 167–9.

[36] J. MacParlan, *Statistical Survey of the County of Mayo* (Dublin, 1802), pp. 93–4.

[37] State Paper Office, Dublin Castle (SPO), Outrage Papers (OP), 1831, Sampson Carter to Colonel Gossett, 9, Feb. 1831, B/1.

However, although commerce and communication between Erris and central Mayo were restricted severely by poor roads and difficult terrain, the half-barony's protected harbors in Broadhaven and Blacksod bays and a fertile strip of land along the Mullet peninsula enabled the western-most farmers and landlords of Mayo to attempt to profit from rising prices and agricultural commercialization. During the early decades of the nineteenth century the two principal landowners of the Mullet peninsula, William Henry Carter, with an annual rental income in 1831 of £3000, and Major Denis Bingham, whose Erris properties brought in £2000 annually, established towns and arranged for the Fishery Board to construct piers in order to facilitate a coastal trade. Binghamstown was the smaller and less successful of the two in large part due to the unwillingness of Major Bingham to expend any money to promote trade. Sampson Carter described it in 1831 as having five to six slated houses, sixty "indifferent cottages" and no "positive trade and no encouragement apparently for any species of industry." Ten years later Caesar Otway called Binghamstown a "monument to failure . . . sinking fast into decay in consequence of its too great proximity to its younger sister, Belmullet."[38] Both Carter and Otway were more enthusiastic about Belmullet, established in 1825 at the point where the Mullet peninsula is attached to the mainland by a narrow isthmus. Carter described it as having thirty-two "good slated houses" and thirty-four "comfortable thatched cottages."[39] Otway praised the town's owner William Henry Carter for giving birth to prosperity in the region. He reported that prior to the establishment of Belmullet "there was not a tradesman residing [on the Mullet peninsula]; they were obliged to be brought at great inconvenience from the interior of the country."[40] By 1831 there were "three persons engaged moderately in the corn trade" in Belmullet, carrying on trade with Scotland, England and other parts of Ireland. In January of that year, a year of near famine due to the failure of the potato crop, a Glasgow-bound ship left Belmullet carrying 120 tons of oats while another waited at the quay and others were expected.[41] In 1812 E. Wakefield reported that "in many parts of Mayo . . . the establishment of corn buyers who ship oats for Scotland, has proved the means of exciting the farmers to sow many hundreds of acres that would have been

[38] Ibid.; C. Otway, *Sketches in Erris and Tyrawly* (Dublin, 1841), pp. 51–2.
[39] Carter to Gossett, 9 Feb. 1831.
[40] Otway, *Sketches in Erris and Tyrawly*, pp. 48–9.
[41] Carter to Gossett, 9 Feb. 1831; SPO. OP, 1831, William [surname illegible] to William Henry Carter, 7 Jan. 1831, B/1; Freeman, *Pre-Famine Ireland*, p. 266.

covered only with sour grass . . . "[42] It appears that by the 1830s the Scottish market had spread its influence to Mayo's remotest regions.

Although commercial agriculture geared to an external market penetrated both the core and the periphery of County Mayo by the early decades of the nineteenth century, it is difficult to gauge its impact on the various classes of farmers within the county. Without question, export-geared agriculture was dominated by major landowners, such as the Marquis of Sligo, and a select group of farmers who were well-informed and had the knowledge and wealth required to obtain a decent yield from the poor soil that plagued much of the county.[43] The great majority of Mayo's farmers worked small plots, often held in common, and baffled landlords, agents and travelers with what appeared to be inefficient and primitive methods of tillage. MacParlan reported in 1801 that he found agriculture in the county to be "still in a very backward state, and in no very great progress of improvement . . . The ploughs and harrows are of the old bad kind, very badly constructed and the work miserably executed."[44] Yet, while the farming methods and implements may not have been up to the standards of agricultural reformers, MacParlan, like Young before him, found that many Mayo farmers cultivated several market crops and often reared livestock that made their way to the major fair at Ballinasloe, County Galway.

Many of Mayo's small farmers held their land jointly or in "rundale."[45] Under the rundale system, which may have its roots in Celtic, Iron Age Ireland, land was leased to one or several tenants who oversaw its distribution among as many as twenty or thirty co-partners. Most often the land, frequently an entire townland, was divided into two or three categories distinguished by quality. Each co-partner was given a portion of each type of land based upon the portion of the rent he or she paid. In some regions of the county tenants had little idea of how many acres of land they held, calculating their holdings as so many "pounds worth."[46]

---

[42] Wakefield, *An Account of Ireland*, I, p. 380.

[43] For Lord Sligo's farming and reclaiming efforts during the 1770s, see: Young, *A Tour of Ireland*, I, 250–60.

[44] MacParlan, *Statistical Survey of the County of Mayo*, p. 13.

[45] The only thorough analysis of the rundale system in Ireland is: D. McCourt, "The Rundale System in Ireland: A Study of Its Geographical Distribution and Social Relations" (The Queen's University, Belfast, Ph.D. thesis, 1950). Also see: A. R. H. Baker and R. A. Butlin, *Studies of Field Systems in the British Isles* (Cambridge, 1973), pp. 580–618. For Mayo, see: Almquist, "Mayo and Beyond," pp. 81–104.

[46] National Library, Ireland (NLI), Report of Samuel Nicholson, Civil Engineer and Land Valuator, upon the estates of Sir Robert Lynch Bloose, Baronet, lying in the Baronies

In other areas the land was allocated on a complex system of "cow's grass" (*fear bo, collop* or *sum*) or the number of cattle each co-partner was allowed to graze on the land.[47]

Systems for periodically redistributing the land varied throughout Mayo. In some areas, such as the half-barony of Erris, divisions usually took place every two or three years, with each tenant receiving a *collop*, or the grazing for one cow, for each 30s. of rent paid.[48] The Very Rev. John Patrick Lyons, Dean of Killala and Parish Priest of Kilmore Erris, described the system to the Devon Commission. Every two years

> a man got a ridge of good, a ridge of middling and a ridge of bad land, in different parts of the field in proportion to his rent . . . Generally four men in the village take the land, and become what they call head of quarters; and then they take in with them a certain number of other tenants to become co-partners; but the four men are the parties who are generally responsible to the landlord. They are the persons who determine the number of *sums* and the quantity of tillage land to which each of the tenants is entitled in proportion to the rent to which he is liable.[49]

In addition to overseeing the distribution of the lots, the head of quarters or headsmen were the acknowledged arbitrators and organizers of the agricultural life of the community. According to one early-nineteenth-century traveler in Erris, the headsman

> is deputed to cast the lots every third year, and to arrange within the community what work is to be done during the year in fencing and probably reclaiming a new field, or for "setting the bin" as it is called, i.e., the number of heads of cattle of each kind . . . that is to be put on the farm for the ensuing year . . . he is advisor of the villagers, their spokesman on certain occasions, and a general man of influence on many matters connected with the village.[50]

The headman's role was crucial for the efficient functioning of the rundale system, although it appears that he acted within the bounds set

of Carra and Clanmorris, and County Mayo, 1844, MS 2725, pp. 30–1. Reference from Almquist, "Mayo and Beyond," p. 97.

47 McCourt, "The Rundale System in Ireland," p. 42.

48 Testimony of Rev. Peter Geraghy, *Evidence Taken Before Her Majesty's Commissioners of Inquiry into the State of the Law and Practice in Respect to the Occupation of Land in Ireland, Pt. I*, PP 1845 [616], xx, p. 410 (hereafter Devon Commission); McCourt, "The Rundale System in Ireland," pp. 76–7.

49 *Devon Commission, Minutes of Evidence, Pt. II*, PP 1845 [606], xix, p. 154.

50 Knight, *Erris in the Irish Highlands*, p. 47. A similar account can be found in Otway, *Sketches in Erris and Tyrawly*, p. 357.

by village custom, what Wakefield called a "rude system of village law."[51]

Ideally, the rundale system was similar to the "infield–outfield" system of England and Scotland, where the nucleated village, or *clachan* as it was called in parts of Ireland, was situated amidst the richest land, which in turn was surrounded by mountain or grazing land of inferior quality. .However, in Ireland, with its complex maze of arable, rough pasture and bog lands, the distribution of land among co-tenants was fraught with conflict. Most often the holdings tended to be scattered in small strips and patches with some effort having been made to guarantee that the various tenants should have a share of each grade of land. Not surprisingly, the equity of the distribution system was often called into question by disgruntled co-partners who took to the courts to seek redress.[52] Wakefield reported "continual wrangling and pertinacious litigation, for trifles, scarcely worth a straw," while the outspoken proprietor of the Castlebar newspaper, the *Telegraph*, told the Devon Commission that holding the land in common and the regular changing of lots led to perpetual squabbling and fighting.[53]

Despite the regular disputes and litigation that the system of co-tenancies begot, it persisted in Mayo long after it had been eradicated in most other Irish counties. The reasons are not difficult to identify. The rundale system provided a means through which grazing land could be shared and seaweed fertilizer and peat could be distributed equitably. In addition, it fostered a general spirit of co-operation that minimized the risks associated with cultivating fragile crops on poor soil. In McCourt's words: "with little technique in ameliorating soil conditions, the slightest natural advantage assumed an importance disproportionate to a modern economy. Dispersion of strips and patches through a townland was a natural result, and simple solution to the problem of ensuring equal quality as well as quantity."[54] Moreover, in a period of rapidly increasing population, the rundale system provided easy access to the land for the growing numbers of farm families. Under pressure from children, the scattered holdings were subdivided regularly into thirds or quarters of *collops*, known in Mayo as *gurlas*, or eighths of a "cow's

---

[51] Wakefield, *An Account of Ireland*, I, p. 271.

[52] Almquist, "Mayo and Beyond," pp. 99–102.

[53] Wakefield, *An Account of Ireland*, I, p. 271; Testimony of the Hon. Frederick Cavendish, *Devon Commission, Minutes of Evidence, Pt. II*, p. 423.

[54] McCourt, "The Rundale System in Ireland," pp. 38–9.

grass," called *toe* or *cleet*.[55] The result was a proliferation of small-holdings that left the arable land over-cropped and the rough pasture over-grazed. According to statistics compiled by the Devon Commission, which was charged with inquiring into the occupation of land in Ireland, 58 percent of the land in County Mayo was held in common or joint tenancy in 1845.[56]

On these small plots Mayo's farmers raised barley, oats, flax and potatoes in varying combinations, fertilizing primarily with seaweed.[57] In general, oats were raised for the export market, barley for the illegal distillers, flax for local linen manufacture and potatoes for consumption. As the population rose during the decades leading up to the Famine of 1846–50, the proportion of the land devoted to potatoes grew steadily, with the potato portion of a given farm rising in an inverse ratio to the size of the holding. Increasingly, smallholders whose farms were getting smaller as their families got bigger became single crop farmers, with little land available for cash crops. For the most part, by the 1830s only middle-sized farmers and the gentry, especially those with land in the fertile regions of the center or coastal corridor, were able to participate in the export market to any appreciable degree.

One advantage of the rundale system was that it provided most tenants with access to grazing land and the services of a herd. MacParlan reported in 1801 that in Murrisk barony "most villagers have one or two cows, and one horse, besides a few sheep, in proportion to their tenures."[58] This was likely the case in most parts of the county. In the more fertile regions farmers bought yearlings either from local breeders or at the major livestock fair at Ballinasloe, County Galway. In the rougher, less fertile regions, considered unsafe for yearlings, farmers purchased two-year-olds. These bullocks were kept for a year or two before being sold at Ballinasloe or one of the ninety-seven small cattle fairs that occurred each year in Mayo. Between the fall harvest and spring planting, the cattle, along with any sheep or pigs the villagers possessed, were allowed to graze freely over the stubble of the previous harvest, before being taken to upland rough pasture for the summer months. The poorer small farmers "most frequently" divided the "house

---

[55] *Ibid.*, p. 42.

[56] Almquist, "Mayo and Beyond," pp. 210–11, 357; *Devon Commission, Appendix, Pt. IV*, PP 1845 [672], xxii, Appendix 94, pp. 280–3.

[57] For the course of crops and agricultural methods, see: Almquist, "Mayo and Beyond," pp. 173–8 and MacParlan, *Statistical Survey of the County of Mayo*, pp. 13–37.

[58] MacParlan, *Statistical Survey of the County of Mayo*, p. 41.

Table 2.5. *County Mayo cattle prices, 1775 and 1801, price per head*

Year	Yearlings	Bullocks	Dry cows	Milch cows
1776	10s. 6d.–£3 10s.	£4–£6		
1801	£1 10s.–£7	£9 9s.–£18	£4–£10 10s.	£6–£15

Sources: 1776 prices are those that Mayo farmers received at the Ballinasloe fair, the major livestock fair in western Ireland: Young, *A Tour of Ireland*, I, pp. 247, 249, 258. 1801 prices are those of local County Mayo fairs: MacParlan, *Statistical Survey of the County of Mayo*, p. 52.

and the potatoes with the calves and cows from December till April," after which they were taken to graze on the mountain sides. According to MacParlan, the cattle that were reared in this fashion brought the lowest prices in the market, while the highest prices were reserved for those reared in the fertile central corridor by the large graziers and gentry, who supplemented grazing with hay, straw and "artificial grasses," such as clover.[59] The range of prices obtained for cattle in 1776 and 1801, illustrated in Table 2.5, demonstrates that superior cattle brought substantially higher prices and that cattle prices soared during those twenty-five years.

The degree to which the farmers of Mayo benefited from the rising prices of grain and livestock is difficult to gauge. In his study of County Cavan during the same period, Kevin O'Neill argues that prior to the substantial grain price rise after 1785, farmers were caught in a "self-limiting device" through which increases in income were matched by increases in rent. Only after 1785 did farm incomes rise at a faster rate than rents, thus providing the tenants with an increase in their net income and some capital with which to enter more fully into the expanding market economy.[60] Unfortunately, the limited rental data available for County Mayo makes it difficult to substantiate a similar argument. Touring Mayo in 1776, Young reported that rents in the county had trebled over the previous forty years, although they had fallen slightly between 1771 and 1776. He found that rents had stabilized by 1776 and were showing a "tendency to rise."[61]

According to Almquist's analysis of the few available rent ledgers for

---

[59] *Ibid.*, pp. 52–6; Young, *A Tour of Ireland*, I, pp. 247, 249, 258.

[60] K. O'Neill, *Family and Farm in Pre-Famine Ireland: The Parish of Killashandra* (Madison, 1984), pp. 72–3.

[61] Young, *A Tour of Ireland*, I, p. 259.

the county, the rise in rents that Young reported for the years up to 1776 became dramatic between 1787 and 1810, up as much as 75 percent on sections of the O'Donnell estate in the barony of Burrishoole. Almquist discovered that between 1810 and 1830, as the economy cooled following the war-time boom, rents rose only slightly.[62] Respondents to the Poor Law Commission in 1836 estimated that rents in the county were on the average of £1 to £1 10s. per acre of arable land.[63] This would represent an approximate doubling of rents since Young's findings of 1776, although this must remain a very rough estimate.

Although it is clear that rents did increase between 1750 and 1830, there is no way to determine with any accuracy the amount of marketable grain or livestock that any farming class had available or to gauge the ease or difficulty that Mayo farmers had in meeting the rent demands. Presumably, those tenant farmers with reasonable sized holdings of fertile soil, and who could resist the demands of heirs to split the holding, were able to increase their production to meet the needs of the market and raise their income despite rent increases. At the other end of the scale, the small farmers holding infertile land in joint-tenancy were ill-equipped to profit fully from the new market opportunities and by the 1830s were finding the rent difficult to meet. This was especially the case following the collapse of the domestic linen industry, which many small farmers had relied on to earn cash with which to pay the rent.

THE LINEN INDUSTRY AND THE GROWTH OF THE CENTRAL CORRIDOR

Without doubt, the most dynamic sector of the Mayo economy during the second half of the eighteenth century was the linen industry. The roots of Mayo linen production date to the early eighteenth century when the inability of Ulster's weavers to procure sufficient quantities of yarn from local sources fostered the spread of flax cultivation and spinning into northern Connacht. Almquist, in his thorough study of the linen industry in County Mayo, found the earliest evidence of linen spinning dates from

---

[62] Almquist, "Mayo and Beyond," pp. 127–32.

[63] *Poor Inquiry (Ireland): Appendix (F) Containing Baronial Examinations Relative to Con-Acre, Quarter or Score Ground, Small Tenantry, Consolidation of Farms and Dislodged Tenantry, Emigration, Landlord and Tenant, Nature and State of Agriculture, Taxation, Roads, Observations on the Nature and State of Agriculture: and Supplement*, PP 1836 [38], xxxiii, pp. 445–55.

the 1720s. He speculates that linen manufacture took off in the county after 1730 and became a "boom industry" after 1750.[64] Initially, Mayo's contribution to linen manufacturing was the growing and spinning of flax, with the spinning carried out largely by farm women in cottages scattered around the linen markets of the central corridor – Ballina, Castlebar, Foxford, Hollymount, Minola, Westport and Newport.[65] During the early decades of the linen industry in Mayo the bulk of the yarn spun in the county was transported north by jobbers to supply the weavers of Ulster. A group of Quaker weavers from Ulster who settled in Newport in 1720 in response to the establishment of a weaving colony by Captain Pratt, found a "want of livelihood" and eventually left the county.[66] However, by 1760 Ulster weavers found the county a profitable place to settle as improving landlords encouraged and financed a weaving industry. By 1770 about £10,000 worth of linen cloth was sold in Mayo, increasing to £17,500 by 1783.[67] In 1790 a local newspaper reported that the linen trade had become "the principal source of wealth and independence of the county."[68]

Mayo's principal towns grew and prospered in response to the linen trade. This was especially true of the major linen market towns – Castlebar, Ballina, Westport and Newport – all of which bustled with linen-related industries. For example, Castlebar, the chief linen town in the county, had received a patent in 1609 from James I to hold a market, one of six Mayo towns to obtain such patents during the early seventeenth century.[69] The patent had been obtained by the town's owner, John Bingham, brother of the merciless Elizabethan governor of Connacht, Richard Bingham. Three years later the king granted the town a charter of incorporation, establishing it as the center of royal authority in Mayo.[70] In 1763, Sir Charles Bingham, Member of Parliament for County Mayo, ensured that his town would establish itself as the leading linen center in the county by creating a "premier market" in response to

---

64 Almquist, "Mayo and Beyond," pp. 28–36.

65 *Ibid.*, pp. 33–5, 65, 68–70.

66 K. L. Carroll, "Quaker Weavers at Newport, Ireland, 1720–1740," *Journal of the Friends' Historical Society*, 54 (1976), pp. 15–27.

67 Almquist, "Mayo and Beyond," pp. 51–7.

68 Quoted in Cullen, *An Economic History of Ireland Since 1660*, p. 63.

69 The other five were Cong (1604), Ballinrobe (1605), Shrule (1606), Killala (1613) and Ballindine (1627). *Report of the Commissioners Appointed to Inquire Into the State of the Fairs and Markets in Ireland*, PP 1852–3 [1674], xli, p. 44.

70 S. Lewis, *A Topographical Dictionary of Ireland*, 2nd ed., 2 vols. (London, 1840), I, p. 288; C. Woodham-Smith, *The Reason Why* (London, 1953), pp. 16–17.

an incentive funded by the Irish Linen Board. The result was an immense jump in the amount of linen sold at the Castlebar market, from less than 10,000 yards in 1762 to 33,000 in 1764 and 49,000 in 1765.[71] Traveling in Mayo in 1776, Arthur Young found Castlebar to be "greatly rising from manufactures." A linen hall built in the town in 1790 was soon overflowing with linen to be sold and looms and spinning wheels to be distributed.[72]

Similar activities were going on elsewhere in the county. In Westport, Young discovered that Lord Altamont had made "great exertions" to establish linen weaving in the town:

> In order to establish it, he built good houses in the town of Westport, and let them upon very reasonable terms to weavers, gave them looms, and lent them money to buy yarn, and in order to secure them from manufacturing goods, which they should not be able readily to sell, he constantly bought all they could not sell, which for some years was all they made; but by degrees, as the manufacture arose, buyers came in, so that he has for some time not bought any great quantity . . . This year he has also given such encouragement as to induce a person to build and establish a bleach linen-green and mill. The progress of this manufacture has been prodigious, for at first Lord Altamont was the only buyer, whereas for the two years past there has not been less than £10,000 a year laid out at this market in linen; yet with all this increase, they do not yet weave a tenth part of the yarn that is spun in the neighborhood.[73]

At the end of the century possibly as many as 200 weavers from Ulster arrived in Westport, supplementing the activities of the local weavers. Ballina, in north-central Mayo, which had had a linen market since at least the 1730s, was also a bustling manufacturing center by the end of the century.[74] In 1798, a colony of northern weavers brought to the village of Mullifaragh near Ballina by the Earl of Arran, numbered 1000.[75] A traveler to the town in about 1800 found that the "primitive looking domiciles" he passed were a "hive of manufacturing energy and industry":

---

[71] Almquist, "Mayo and Beyond," p. 51.

[72] *Ibid.*, p. 67; Young, *Tour of Ireland*, I, p. 250.

[73] Young, *Tour of Ireland*, I, pp. 255–6.

[74] *Ibid.*, I, p. 247.

[75] J. Stock, *A Narrative of What Passed at Killala in the County of Mayo and the Parts Adjacent During the French Invasion in the Summer of 1798, by an Eye-Witness*, G. Freyer (ed.) (Ballina, Ireland, 1982), p. 66 (hereafter: *Bishop Stock's Narrative*).

The number of pots outside the doors gave me to understand that the localities were abodes of linnen [sic] and woolen weavers. The "click, click" of the shuttle, the smack of the reel and the chuzz of the spinning wheel soon convinced us that the occupiers of mud hovels could enjoy the comforts of a palace provided that manufacturing industry held its kingly sway.[76]

The linen trade and the wealth it brought to Mayo gave rise to other industries. The same traveler to Ballina, George O'Malley, gazed in wonder at

a street which shot straight as an arrow . . . each side . . . lined with a row of tables and stalls from end to end. There was a large quantity of animal food for sale and from the thronged state of the market I concluded that Ballina was a place of unusual prosperity. . . . We returned to the Cross and saw a long line of tables running westward with piles of felt hats for sale. Opposite in another long line, the brogue markets had their standings arranged. Hatters and brogue makers were exchanging their value for money fast.[77]

In Westport, the first decades of the nineteenth century witnessed the establishment of a distillery which by the 1830s was producing 60,000 gallons of whiskey a year, two breweries, at least five flour, corn and oat mills, all water powered, and several cotton and linen manufacturing factories, including one that contained twenty-four power looms.[78]

The economy of Mayo was clearly booming. One Justice of the Peace from Islandeady, located between Westport and Castlebar, reported to a parliamentary committee in 1835 that during the years of the Napoleonic Wars "the condition of the poor . . . was prosperous in the extreme."[79] To the limited degree that this was the case, the primary beneficiaries were the inhabitants of the towns and farms of the lowland corridor whose leading position in the Mayo economy was solidified by the economic growth the county experienced between 1750 and 1830. Based on the limited data available, Almquist found that the major areas of flax growth and spinning in the county were in the baronies of Tirawley, Carra, Kilmaine and Clanmorris, all of which were principally located in

---

[76] Quoted in Cullen, *An Economic History of Ireland Since 1660*, p. 63.

[77] *Ibid.*, p. 81.

[78] Lewis, *Topographical Dictionary of Ireland*, II, pp. 699–700.

[79] *Poor Inquiry (Ireland): Appendix (E) Containing Baronial Examinations Relative to Food, Cottages and Cabins, Clothing and Furniture, Pawnbroking and Savings Bank, Drinking and Supplement Containing Answers to Questions 13 to 22 Circulated by the Commissioners*, PP 1836 [37], xxxii, p. 19.

the central core of Mayo.[80] These were the regions with the easiest access to the market towns, both those in Mayo and those in the neighboring counties of Sligo and Galway. The markets of Sligo funnelled yarn and cloth from the spinners and weavers of northern Mayo to Ulster, England and Scotland, while the great cloth and cattle fairs at Ballinasloe linked Mayo manufacturers and farmers to the markets of Leinster and Munster provinces.[81] The farm families of central Mayo were quick to take advantage of the opportunities for a cash income which the labor-intensive domestic linen manufacture offered. Spinning, a task confined largely to women and girls, became during the latter half of the eighteenth century an important source of the cash needed to pay rent. Contemporaries recorded that women spinners in County Mayo could earn from 4d. to 13d. per day. Almquist estimates that this income could provide one-third to one-half of the farm rent.[82]

In contrast, farmers living in the peripheral regions of the county, especially those in the western parishes, remained in relative isolation until the 1830s when the first roads penetrated into the bog-strewn western lands. Prior to that, travelers who attempted journeys into these inaccessible regions reported great obstacles and long delays to their progress.[83] The farmers of the periphery remained poor potato and grain cultivators largely cut off from the inroads of commercialized farming or industry.

During the 1820s technological changes in spinning and the gradual substitution of cotton for linen in the English market undermined the domestic linen economy of Mayo. Mayo's women hand loom spinners could not compete in quality or quantity with the machine spun yarn of Ulster, while the spinning mills established in Westport and elsewhere in Mayo were hurt by their distance from the major cloth markets in eastern Ireland. As late as 1823 optimism about the future of Mayo's linen trade remained high. Denis Browne, MP, told a parliamentary committee looking for ways to increase employment in Ireland that the market for Irish linen was "unlimited." An English linen merchant with

---

[80] Almquist, "Mayo and Beyond," pp. 64–7.

[81] *Ibid.*, pp. 52–3; Cullen, *An Economic History of Ireland Since 1660*, p. 59; Cullen, "Economic Development, 1750–1800," pp. 180–1.

[82] Almquist, "Mayo and Beyond," pp. 71–3; Cullen, *An Economic History of Ireland Since 1660*, pp. 62–3.

[83] J. G. Simms, "Connacht in the Eighteenth Century," *Irish Historical Studies*, 11 (1958), pp. 120–1; Lewis, *Topographical Dictionary of Ireland*, II, p. 357; also see: Aalen, *Man and Landscape in Ireland*, p. 183.

considerable business in Ireland, including County Mayo, told the same committee that the market for Irish cloth, especially for imitations of German linen, was growing and would continue to do so.[84] However, within a decade the optimism was gone and Mayo's remaining spinners were selling their yarn at greatly reduced prices.[85] A traveler to Castlebar in 1835 found "great numbers of women" on market day "holding a hank or two of yarn of their own spinning," offering "their trifling commodities for sale." He found that they "could not earn by spinning more than a penny or two-pence a day, and hundreds of them attended the market whose earnings for the whole week did not exceed sixpence or ninepence."[86] A Church of Ireland clergyman reported from Ballinrobe in 1836 that "the colony of poor weavers brought from the North some years ago have no remunerating price for their linen at 6d. or 6½d. per yard, the material being too costly in proportion to the price of the cloth; some of them are to be more compassioned than the labourers . . . "[87]

The collapse of the linen industry rippled throughout the Mayo economy, dashing hopes that the economic growth of the previous century would continue. Writing his topographical dictionary in 1837, Samuel Lewis described the abandoned newly built warehouses, quays and harbors as symbols of the decline of the principal towns of Mayo in the wake of the loss of the linen trade.[88] W. M. Thackeray, in his *Irish Sketchbook*, commented on the unused warehouses in the "pseudo-commercial port" of Westport and derided the Irish for over-building in anticipation of what he felt had been an insignificant level of commerce:

There was a long, handsome pier (which no doubt, remains at this present minute) . . . As for the warehouses, they are enormous; and might accommodate, I should think, not only the trade of Westport, but of Manchester too. There are huge streets of these houses, ten stories high, with cranes, owners' names, etc. marked Wine Stores, Flour Stores, Bonded Tobacco Warehouse and so forth. . . . These dismal mausoleums, as fast as pyramids, are the places where the dead trade of Westport lies buried – a trade that, in its lifetime, probably was

---

84 *Report from the Select Committee on the Employment of the Poor in Ireland*, PP 1823 (561), vi, pp. 50, 58.
85 Almquist, "Mayo and Beyond," pp. 149–69.
86 Quoted in *ibid.*, p. 153.
87 *Poor Inquiry (Ireland): Appendix (E)*, Supplement, p. 24.
88 Lewis, *Topographical Dictionary of Ireland*, I, p. 289, II, p. 699. Also see: Freeman, *Pre-Famine Ireland*, p. 245, *The Parliamentary Gazetteer of Ireland*, 2 vols. (Dublin, London and Edinburgh, 1846), II, p. 247.

about as big as a mouse. Nor is this the first nor the hundredth place to be seen in this country, which sanguine builders have erected to accommodate an imaginary commerce. Mill-owners over-mill themselves, merchants over-warehouse themselves, squires over-castle themselves . . . [89]

The continued export of grain and livestock from Mayo sustained the economy of the central corridor following the collapse of the linen industry. The grain trade was aided during the 1830s by an improved network of roads constructed by the Board of Works and by the introduction of steamships plying the waters between Liverpool, Glasgow and the ports of western Ireland.[90] In 1835, Ballina, soon to be the most important commercial center in Mayo, had exports valued at £70,568, consisting of 8839 tons of corn, 453 tons of provisions, 40 tons of kelp, 6¼ tons of hides and 6 tons of feathers. In 1836, Westport, still the largest port in Mayo, exported corn, meal and flour valued at £87,000.[91] The livestock trade profited from the completion in 1836 of the Grand Canal from Dublin to Ballinasloe, County Galway, providing water transportation to the Dublin docks for those Mayo farmers who sold their stock at the "Great October Fair" in Ballinasloe.[92] However, this economic activity was confined to a minority of Mayo farmers – those with the land, resources and acumen to profit despite a contracting economy. They were sustained in this effort by the network of market towns, roads and trading links that had been built up during the trade boom of 1750–1820. During those seventy years Mayo had been brought into the realm of nation-wide commerce, with its central, lowland corridor as the major axis of trade and communication between the county and the rest of the British Isles.

MAYO ON THE EVE OF THE GREAT FAMINE

For the bulk of the county's farming population the last two decades prior to the Famine of 1846–50 were a time of economic decline. Respondents

[89] W. M. Thackeray, *The Irish Sketchbook* (London and Glasgow, n.d.), p. 263.

[90] Cullen, *An Economic History of Ireland Since 1660*, pp. 113, 122–3; Freeman, *Pre-Famine Ireland*, pp. 109–16.

[91] Freeman, *Pre-Famine Ireland*, pp. 263–4; *The Parliamentary Gazetteer of Ireland*, I, p. 124.

[92] Cullen, *An Economic History of Ireland Since 1660*, p. 122; Freeman, *Pre-Famine Ireland*, pp. 118–19; O'Donovan, *An Economic History of Livestock in Ireland*, pp. 165, 260.

from Mayo to a questionnaire sent out by the Poor Law Commission in 1836 were nearly uniform in answering in the negative to the first part of the following question: "Is the general condition of the poorer classes in your parish improved, deteriorated, or stationary, since the Peace, in the year 1815, and in what respects? Is the population of the parish increasing or diminishing?"[93] In order to analyze these responses Joel Mokyr and Cormac O'Gráda constructed what they termed the "Subjective Impoverishment Index." They assigned the following values to the responses: −2 to "much deteriorated," −1 to "deteriorated," 0 to "unchanged," 1 to "improved" and 2 to "much improved." They found that for Ireland as a whole the mean value of the responses was −0.43 while that for County Mayo was −1.02, indicating the most precipitous decline of living standards of any county in Ireland.[94] Applying Mokyr's and O'Gráda's index on a baronial basis within Mayo produces the breakdown illustrated in Table 2.6.

Without question this index is based on a small and subjective survey. For example, parish priests were more likely to emphasize the deterioration of their parishioners' standard of living than were justices of the peace. Nonetheless, the fact that 81 percent of the respondents to the questionnaire (30 of 37), along with the vast majority of those who testified in person before the commissioners, believed that the situation in the county was bad and getting worse leaves little room for controversy. The county was going through an economic transformation in which deindustrialization and rapid population growth were undermining the limited prosperity that had developed during the preceding seventy years, and putting excessive pressure on the land to feed and support the populace. Not surprisingly, as Table 2.6 indicates, the decay was most pronounced in the peripheral regions of the county. The western and eastern boundaries of the county had played only a marginal role in the economic growth of the late eighteenth and early nineteenth centuries. As that growth was curtailed and then to a large degree halted, those regions most distant from the market towns and the remaining trade centers were the first to suffer. Given the poor quality of the land, the residents of the periphery had the fewest resources to fall back upon.

---

[93] *Poor Inquiry (Ireland), Appendix (E) Supplement*, pp. 18–29.

[94] Joel Mokyr and Cormac O'Gráda, "Poor and Getting Poorer? Living Standards in Ireland Before the Famine," *Economic History Review*, 2nd ser., 41 (1988), pp. 211–15. A similar index, without the county breakdown appears in Mokyr, *Why Ireland Starved*, p. 12.

Table 2.6. *"Subjective Economic Change Index" : County Mayo, 1815–1835*

Barony	Number of respondents	Value	Core/ periphery
Burrishoole	2	−2.00	Primarily in periphery
Carra	4	−0.25	Core
Clanmorris	3	−1.00	Primarily in periphery
Costello	2	−1.00	Periphery
Erris	2	−1.00	Periphery
Gallen	2	−1.50	Periphery
Kilmain	9	−0.22	Core
Murrisk	6	−1.83	Periphery
Tirawley	7	−1.57	Periphery
County Mayo	37	−1.05	

Notes and sources: For core/periphery refer to Map 1.2, the core and peripheral regions of County Mayo, p. 17 above. *Poor Inquiry (Ireland): Appendix (E), Supplement*, pp. 18–29. J. Mokyr and C. O'Gráda, "Poor and Getting Poorer? Living Standards in Ireland Before the Famine," *Economic History Review*, 2nd ser., 41 (1988), pp. 212–15. The slight discrepancy between Mokyr's and O'Gráda's value of −1.02 and my −1.05 is the result of the number of respondents we excluded for not having experience in the county dating back to 1815. Mokyr and O'Gráda used 43 respondents for Mayo while I used 37.

Respondents to the questionnaire joined with those who testified in person before the Commission in attributing major responsibility for the pauperization of the small tenantry to the rising population and resultant subdivisions of holdings. Sir Samuel O'Malley, a landlord with extensive property in Mayo, summed up the view of many landlords when he told the Commissioners that "all the landlords of this barony [Murrisk] are aware that small tenants cannot accumulate capital; but the reason of this inability is not to be sought in the highness of rents, but in the progressive and habitual subdivision of farms, and in the custom of looking to the land alone as a way of getting food." After complaining of landlords who "screw out of the small tenantry what they can" and of high rents for bad land, Revs. Patrick Dwyer and P. McManus, priests in the barony, acknowledged the prevalence of subdivision, although they placed part of the blame on landlords who wished to increase the number of 40 shilling freehold voters, prior to their disenfranchisement in 1829.[95]

[95] *Poor Inquiry (Ireland): Appendix (F)*, pp. 40–1, 85.

The "manufacture" of 40s. freeholders through landlord-encouraged subdivision had been common in Mayo prior to 1829.[96] However, its contribution to the subdivision of holdings was insignificant when compared to the impact of the rapid growth of the population. As discussed above, the population of County Mayo began an unbroken period of growth in the middle of the eighteenth century. The growth rate accelerated regularly until the third decade of the nineteenth century. At the time of the 1831 census the population of the county stood at approximately 370,000, having risen 20–25 percent over the preceding ten years. The economic troubles associated with the collapse of the linen trade appear to have affected population growth during the 1830s with the population rising only 6 to 7 percent, to stand at between 390,000 and 400,000 at the time of the 1841 census.[97] Although the rate slackened during the 1830s, the continued growth of the population was noted by many of the respondents to the Poor Commission questionnaire.[98] Father McManus noted that not only had "minute subdivision" resulted in small holdings, it had "led to much waste in the numerous fences." He maintained that 5 percent of the land was "utterly lost" to fences, although he noted that the loss was "no loss to the landlord, as the waste was always surveyed on the tenant." Fr. McManus concluded that "the people are aware of it [the waste], but they cannot help it, they are so numerous."[99]

With few agricultural statistics or estate records extant, it is impossible to determine the pace or extent of subdivision in the county prior to the Great Famine. Without question, it was extensive, both on land held in severalty and that held in rundale, a system of tenancy containing no checks to extensive subdivision.[100] Landlord efforts to halt the practice were feeble and ineffectual in most instances. In 1836, Sir Samuel O'Malley told the Poor Inquiry Commissioners: "Clauses against subletting have been almost universally inserted in recent leases . . . but without any effect, as the landlords have been quite unable to enforce them

---

[96] See testimony of Dominick Browne, MP for Mayo: *Minutes of Evidence Taken Before the Select Committee of the House of Lords Appointed to Inquire into the State of Ireland, More Particularly With Reference to the Circumstances Which May Have Led to Disturbances in That Part of the United Kingdom*, PP 1825 (521), IX, pp. 585–7.

[97] See Table 2.1, p. 46 above.

[98] *Poor Inquiry (Ireland), Appendix (E), Supplement*, pp. 18–29 and *Appendix (F), Supplement*, pp. 18–29.

[99] *Ibid., Appendix (F)*, p. 84.

[100] Almquist, "Mayo and Beyond," p. 123.

in any instances . . ."[101] Similarly, some ambitious improving landlords attempted to end joint-tenancy and consolidate the smallholdings into what they felt would be more productive and lucrative large farms.[102] However, these efforts could not stem the tide of subdivision within the county. By 1841 Mayo was the most extensively subdivided county in Ireland with 72.6 percent of all holdings being between 1 and 5 acres.[103] In addition, Mayo had the lowest per acre and per capita land valuation, and, according to the 1841 Census, the greatest rural population density of any county in Ireland.[104]

As a consequence of rapid population growth, the proliferation of smallholdings, deindustrialization and the reduction of the limited inter-regional trade that had developed during the previous eighty years, County Mayo became increasingly impoverished during the two decades prior to the Great Famine. As was the case elsewhere in Ireland, the county's small farmers turned more and more exclusively to the potato for sustenance, as it was a crop capable of producing an adequate supply of food on a small parcel of land. Mokyr has demonstrated that the most impoverished regions of Ireland, those in which the small farmers and cottiers had little cash for food, were those where potato cultivation was the most intense. By his calculations, County Mayo had the lowest per capita income in Ireland in 1836, leaving its growing population increasingly dependent on the least expensive food available: the potato. In 1845 nearly 30 percent of the acreage under cultivation in the county

[101] *Poor Inquiry (Ireland), Appendix (F)*, p. 85. One landlord to insert no-subletting clauses into leases was Lord Lucan, holder of a vast estate in central and western Mayo: *Devon Commission, Minutes of Evidence, Pt. II*, p. 436.

[102] *Poor Inquiry (Ireland), Appendix (F)*, pp. 83–5, 145–8, Supplement, pp. 18–29; Almquist, "Mayo and Beyond," pp. 104–16; *Devon Commission, Minutes of Evidence, Pt. II*, pp. 382, 396–7, 416.

[103] A table listing the proportion of smallholdings per county appears in Almquist, "Mayo and Beyond," p. 356. The only counties approaching Mayo in the proportion of small-holdings are Roscommon (63.9 percent); Galway (63.1 percent); Sligo (60.8 per cent). *Report . . . Census of Ireland for the year 1841*, pp. 454–5.

[104] Almquist argues that the method for calculating population density employed by the census commissioners, dividing rural population into square miles of "arable" land, is inaccurate because their measurement for arable land was not consistent for all counties. He argues that a more accurate figure can be arrived at by dividing the 1841 rural population into the 1851 census data for square miles of grass, crop and fallow. By this second calculation, Mayo has a population density of 364 per square mile compared to the official 1841 census figure of 475. Mayo drops from being the most densely populated county to being the 8th most densely populated. Almquist explains the discrepancy as being the result of the commissioners' difficulty in classifying the marginal land along the western seaboard. "Mayo and Beyond," pp. 206–10, 350–4. *Census of Ireland, 1841*, p. xiii.

was devoted to potatoes; the highest proportion and the highest per capita acreage of potatoes of any county in Ireland.[105]

Two consequences of this dependence were a further decommercialization of the county and the increased vulnerability of the population to the failure of its fragile staple crop. For the most part, the potato was not a commercial crop. It was heavy to transport, subject to rotting or sprouting if stored and was in general uneconomical as a cash crop. The Poor Inquiry Commissioners were told that it was uneconomical to transport potatoes the 15 miles from Ballina to Westport, even though the prices might be doubled. Sir Samuel O'Malley followed this, saying that: "Potatoes cannot be conveyed any distance by a person whose object is profit . . . "[106] Moreover, few small farmers had a surplus to sell, even locally. The more fortunate farmers, those with larger holdings, continued to grow cash crops, especially wheat, barley or oats.[107] But as the population grew and the size of holdings shrank, the number and proportion of farmers with no cash crop grew significantly. In effect, the slow and incomplete process of commercialization of the county was reversed during the two decades prior to the Great Famine by the collapse of the linen trade and the movement towards single-crop, subsistence agriculture.[108] For many, the only commodity for which there was a market was labor. But with little work available in the county, many were forced to travel to England and Scotland at harvest time in the hope of sending back enough money to pay the rent.[109]

The vulnerability of the poor of Mayo to the failure of the potato crop was demonstrated regularly during the half-century before the Great Famine of 1846–50. A lengthy list of crop failures published with the 1851 census revealed four major and eleven partial potato crop failures

---

[105] J. Mokyr, "Irish History With the Potato," *Irish Economic and Social History*, VIII (1981), p. 29; Mokyr, *Why Ireland Starved*, pp. 10–12, 262. For an account of pre-Famine potato husbandry in County Mayo, see: Almquist, "Mayo and Beyond," pp. 172–9.

[106] *Poor Inquiry (Ireland), Appendix (E)*, p. 6.

[107] *Ibid., Appendix (F)*, pp. 215–16.

[108] E. Hoffman and J. Mokyr, "Peasants, Potatoes and Poverty: Transactions Costs in Pre-Famine Ireland," in Gary Saxonhouse and Gavin Wright (eds.), *Research in Economic History, Suppl. 3: Technique, Spirit and Form in the Making of Modern Economics: Essays in Honor of William N. Parker* (Greenwich, Conn., 1984), pp. 115–39.

[109] According to the 1841 census, County Mayo had the greatest number of seasonal migrants of any county in Ireland, although the census takers were not certain how many of these people stayed permanently in England and Scotland. *Census of Ireland, 1841*, pp. xxvi–xxvii. For pre-Famine seasonal migration to Britain, see: Almquist, "Mayo and Beyond," pp. 225–8; for the post-Famine period see Chapter 4 below.

in Ireland between 1815 and 1845.[110] It is unclear how many of these failures affected County Mayo, although it is likely most did. William Wilde, the author of the census list noted that the potato failures of 1821 and 1831, both the result of cold, wet weather, hit the coast of County Mayo with particular ferocity.[111] Spotty contemporary accounts give the impression that the potato failed somewhere in the county nearly every year. For example, the Poor Inquiry Commissioners were told that in the area around Westport "in ordinary seasons there is one-fifth of the population who have not a sufficiency of even this food [poor quality 'lumper' potatoes]; and years of scarcity are so frequent, that they must enter largely into any calculation of the general condition of the people of this parish."[112] Serious distress as a result of the near total failure of the potato crop afflicted the county in 1816, 1822, 1831 and 1835. In all these instances alternative food was available, but the growing number of subsistence farmers had not the funds to purchase it. Denis Browne, MP, told the Select Committee on the Employment of the Poor in Ireland that during the 1822 distress the grain stores in Mayo were full, but that the poor had no money to buy. "In short, there was plenty for every one; there was no deficiency of anything, but the means of buying."[113]

In a memorial to the Marquis of Anglesey, Lord Lieutenant of Ireland, requesting public works to provide income, the "clergy, gentlemen, merchants and other residents" of the half-barony of Erris explained the condition of much of the populace:

Why no Revolts as in France 30 & 40yrs before (Bread riots)

> That owing to the great failure of the potato crop in every part of this extensive and populous barony the main support of three-fourths of the inhabitants is cut off – and unless some prompt and effectual remedy be immediately applied, the horrors of 1822, which can never be forgotten by your memorialists, and the very idea of which alone has already had the effect of creating terror and confusion throughout the barony, must be renewed with aggravated suffering.

> That a population of 20,000 souls at least being deprived of their *staple in linen*, have no description of trade or manufacture by which to palliate approaching famine, which has commenced they doubt not

---

[110] *The Census of Ireland for the Year 1851, Part V: Tables of Deaths, vol. I*, PP 1856 [2078-I], xxix, pp. 41–235; O'Connell, *The Population of Ireland*, pp. 144–5.

[111] *Census of Ireland, 1851, pt. v*, pp. 239–40.

[112] *First Report From His Majesty's Commissioners for Inquiring Into the Condition of the Poorer Classes in Ireland, Appendix (A) and Supplement*, PP 1835 (369), xxxii, pt. 1, p. 373.

[113] *Report from the Select Committee on the Employment of the Poor in Ireland*, p. 50.

in an auspicious moment for your memorialists shall devise some means of relief, they must eventually fall victims to want, anarchy and confusion, and every evil work.[114]

Subscriptions from local merchants, clergy and some landlords, funds collected in England by the Parish Priest, J. P. Lyons, and a national relief fund assisted the poor in purchasing the potatoes that were shipped in.[115] In 1835 distress returned, although Father Lyons reported in May that it was more limited than in 1831. Again committees were formed, funds distributed and potatoes brought in from Scotland and eastern Ireland to enable the county to withstand another failure of its staple crop.[116] In all three major crop failures as well as the numerous limited ones, the issue was not the availability of food, but the availability of money to purchase the food. As the Coast Guard commander at Belmullet reported to his superiors in 1831: "there are potatoes in the country . . . yet . . . those having them will not sell them at a price the poor can buy them at – nor can the holders be obliged to sell at such a rate."[117] Food other than potatoes was generally prohibitively expensive and was increasingly incongruous with the potato culture that Hoffman and Mokyr argue the poor of Ireland were "locked" into.[118]

In many ways the experience of County Mayo during the century before the Great Famine was not unlike that of other parts of the country. The county was brought gradually into a cash-based economy that included manufacturing and trade within Ireland and with England and Scotland. As a result, Mayo prospered to an unprecedented degree between the 1780s and 1815. However, it is important not to exaggerate the growth, commercialization or wealth of the Mayo economy. When compared to the more fertile and accessible counties of the east and midlands, Mayo's economic development was mediocre at best. Moreover, it was limited to a large extent to those farmers and traders living in or near the market towns and ports of central Mayo: what I have called the county's "core." It was in the core where spinning and weaving, rearing livestock and growing grain, all for distant markets, enabled many farmers to meet their rents and even prosper. Farmers living in the county's "periphery" along the western coast and eastern boundary were much less likely to participate in and profit from the commercial

---

114 SPO, OP, 1831, Memorial . . . 12 Jan. 1831, B/1.
115 *Ibid*, J. P. Lyons to . . . Lord Plunket . . . , 10 Jan. 1831.
116 SPO, OP, 1835, Distress in Mayo, 350D; *Poor Inquiry (Ireland), Appendix (E)*, p. 6.
117 SPO, OP, 1831, Lt. Nugent to Inspector General of the Cost Guard, 11 Jan. 1831, B/1.
118 Hoffman and Mokyr, "Peasants, Potatoes, and Poverty," pp. 137–8.

economy. Many had a small cash crop or a few livestock, but hampered by poor land and roads, they remained near destitute, although to a large extent able to pay their rents. The post-Napoleonic War drop in grain prices and collapse of the county's domestic linen industry demonstrated the fragility of Mayo's economy and the vulnerability of its population. Economic growth had been rapid and geared almost exclusively to an external market. This made Mayo's spinners, weavers, traders and commercial farmers dependent upon market forces over which they had no control. Their vulnerability was made all the greater by their distance from the markets and the marginality of the county's involvement in the national and international markets. When those markets weakened after 1815, the west of Ireland was the earliest sufferer, a suffering made more extreme by the lack of a local market to fall back on. The economic growth of the previous generation had been too rapid and too short-lived for the development of a local market of any depth, yet it left a legacy and an infrastructure of commercial activity that was the foundation for more substantial growth following the Great Famine.

3. Pre-Famine popular politics and rural protest

I do not consider myself an unnecessary alarmist, but when I see the whole of the lower orders bound to each other by an oath which they observe inviolably, when I see these persons every night patrolling the country breaking open houses, seizing arms, levying contributions, and committing horrible outrages with perfect impunity, when I find the terror of the name of ribbon man to be greater than that of the law, and that no magistrate has yet found one individual bold enough or honest enough to give information to conviction of these miscreants, and yet that they sit quietly down without making any exertions, seeing all this I cannot but consider the law and the power of the country to be in the hands of a rebellious rabble, who if left much longer unchecked will attempt to declare themselves openly the lords and masters of the land.

(J. E. Strickland to Denis Browne, 16 January 1820)[1]

As was the case with the economy, popular politics and rural protest in County Mayo remained on the periphery of national life during the half-century before the Famine. Only with the unexpected landing of the French at Killala in August 1798 did County Mayo have a brief moment in the spotlight of radical politics. Even this event, as Roy Foster states in his recent history of modern Ireland, was little more than a "footnote to Irish history."[2] Prior to 1798 the county had been virtually untouched by organized agrarian protest movements such as those of the Whiteboys and Rightboys, which disturbed large sections of the south and midlands during the 1760–80s.[3] Rural protest entered Mayo quickly and violently

---

[1] SPO, State of Country Papers (hereafter SOC), 1820, 2175/1.

[2] Roy Foster, *Modern Ireland, 1600–1972* (London, 1988), p. 280.

[3] For these movements see J. S. Donnelly, Jr., "The Whiteboy Movement, 1761–5," *Irish Historical Studies*, 21 (1978–9), pp. 20–59; J. S. Donnelly, Jr., "The Rightboy

during the 1790s, first in 1793 when the half-barony of Erris exploded briefly in opposition to the Militia Bill of that year, and then following the French landing in 1798.[4] In both instances the protests were quickly and bloodily repressed, leaving little or no leadership to build on the experiences of 1793 and 1798 or to galvanize the populace to further action. Of the rebel leaders who were fortunate enough to escape the gallows, many fled to the wilds of Connemara and Erris or to France. Those in Connemara and Erris remained a threat in the eyes of the authorities, but for the most part abandoned political activity for banditry and smuggling.[5]

The Mayo rebellions of the 1790s were staged in the context of the Irish nationalist struggle against England organized by the United Irishmen. Mayo rebels, like those in other parts of Ireland, borrowed from their French allies vaguely understood Enlightenment notions of liberty and the rhetoric that accompanied them, but adapted those ideas to meet local circumstances. On his arrival in Killala, the French General Humbert distributed copies of a stirring proclamation headed "Liberty, Equality, Fraternity, Union!" In it he called on "Brave Irishmen" to shed their blood "in the sacred cause of liberty." In the colorful words of Rev. James Little, who had the misfortune of being Church of England Rector at Lackan, near Killala, in 1798: "the Phantom exhibited to them was a deceptious picture of the temple of Liberty with its stately portals highly coloured & striking in front, while the conflagrations Massacres & bodies of mangled victims were hardly discernible in the background of

---

Movement, 1785–8," *Studia Hibernica*, 17–18 (1977–8), pp. 120–202; J. S. Donnelly, Jr., "Irish Agrarian Rebellion: The Whiteboys of 1769–76," *Proceedings of the Royal Irish Academy*, lxxxiii, c (1983), pp. 293–331; M. R. Beames, *Peasants and Power: The Whiteboy Movements and their Control in Pre-Famine Ireland* (Brighton and New York, 1983); J. Lee, "The Ribbonmen," in T. D. Williams (ed.), *Secret Societies in Ireland* (Dublin and New York, 1973), pp. 26–35; M. Bric, "Priests, Parsons and Politics: The Rightboy Protest in County Cork, 1785–1788," T. Garvin, "Defenders, Ribbonmen and Others: Underground Political Networks in Pre-Famine Ireland," M. R. Beames, "The Ribbon Societies: Lower-Class Nationalism in Pre-Famine Ireland," all in C. Philpin (ed.), *Nationalism and Popular Protest in Ireland* (Cambridge, 1987), pp. 163–90, 219–63.

4 T. Bartlett, "An End to Moral Economy: The Irish Militia Disturbances of 1793," in Philpin (ed.), *Nationalism and Popular Protest in Ireland*, pp. 208–10.

5 SPO, SOC, 1802, Lord Sligo to Alexander Marsden, 13 June and 23 June 1802, 1021/20. Denis Browne, MP for Mayo, told a House of Commons committee in 1823 that ultimately a deal was struck with the surviving rebels to allow them to go to America. *Report from the Select Committee on the Employment of the Poor in Ireland*, p. 52. R. Hayes, *The Last Invasion of Ireland* (Dublin, 1937; reprinted 1979), p. 259.

French landing of 1798

the picture."[6] However, while the rhetoric of 1798 was that of national liberty and "indefeasible" fights, what compelled Mayo farmers to abandon the harvest and join the French were local pressures, ages-old grievances, sectarian fears, as well as the chance to settle old scores and plunder. In this, Mayo rebels differed little from those elsewhere in Ireland where local issues and antagonisms dominated the rebellion, to the consternation of the leadership of the United Irishmen. What distinguished Mayo was its lack of radical tradition. There had been no Ribbonmen or Defenders to define issues and establish forms of protest prior to the 1790s.

Eye-witnesses and historians have commented on the comic appearance of the Mayo rebels, strutting about in fragments of French uniforms, indiscriminately discharging the weapons the French so liberally distributed, drinking heavily and plundering with abandon. As Marianne Elliott has recently put it: "A strange air of festivity reigned in Killala."[7] These were not experienced, organized or sophisticated rebels. They were country people, isolated from political developments in Dublin, Ulster, France or America. They embraced the French as deliverers who could restore the land to its rightful owners, or at least reduce the rent, and rid the countryside of Protestants. The world was to be "turned upside down," history reversed and justice restored to the native, Catholic Irish. These notions had an emotive power that, when unleashed by the stirring appearance of the French soldiers, inaugurated a radical tradition in the county, and began a slow process of articulating issues that would become more concrete during the early decades of the nineteenth century.

Rev. Little may have been more correct than he knew when he attributed the rebellious spirit of a hitherto passive people to "a certain alleviation of . . . poverty which took place for some time previous to the Invasion." After discussing the growing market for grain, livestock and linen from Mayo, Rev. Little concluded that "from all these circumstances, operating suddenly, the profits of land were perhaps doubled, before there was time from the expiration of leases, to make a proportion

6 W. H. Maxwell, *History of the Irish Rebellion in 1798* (London, 1903), p. 225; J. Little, "Little's Diary of the French Landing in 1798," *Analecta Hibernica*, 11 (1941), N. Costello (ed.), p. 66. Photostat of original proclamation appears in Hayes, *The Last Invasion of Ireland*, facing p. 22.
7 Marianne Elliott, *Partners in Revolution: The United Irishmen and France* (New Haven and London, 1982), p. 224. Most accounts of the conduct of Mayo rebels take their lead from *Bishop Stock's Narrative*.

encrease of rent: so that the generality of the peasantry found themselves raised from great poverty to a state of more comfortable accommodation, which was to them a sort of affluence . . . "[8] Rev. Little understood that an increasing number of the people of Mayo had something concrete to gain from rebellion – for the first time. This is not to say that poverty was not both common and extreme. Many of the rebels and most of the country people around Killala were very poor. One French captain who accompanied General Humbert to Killala later wrote of how stunned he and his fellow soldiers were at the extreme poverty of the "semi-savages" they saw everywhere. "Never can a country have presented such a wretched prospect."[9] Yet, this may well have been a revolt driven as much by hope for a better future as by the desperation of a destitute people.

The market economy, introduced into the country during the previous half-century, had increased the value of the land, changed ages-old farming practices, and raised both the hopes and anxieties of Mayo farmers. These conditions gave birth to the spirit of rural protest that was to develop and mature in Mayo after 1790. Between the Act of Union of 1800 and the Great Famine of 1846–50, peace in the county was disrupted not infrequently by rural protest. Often these protests were echoes of movements occurring on a large scale elsewhere in Ireland, although the county was the starting point for the first nineteenth-century wave of rural protest, that of the Threshers. By the standards set in the south and midlands, Mayo's protests were relatively mild and short-lived, the county remaining on the periphery of Ireland's radical rural politics. Yet, beginning with the French landing in 1798, Mayo established a tradition of oath-bound secret societies ready to respond to local grievances and terrorize those who violated their codes.

[handwritten marginal note: Begining of Secret Societies]

THE FRENCH LANDING AND REBELLION IN MAYO, 1798

In September 1797 the provincial committee of the Society of United Irishmen, meeting in Dungannon, pronounced the province of Connacht to be reasonably well organized, with a number of new recruits brought

---

[8] Little, "Little's Diary of the French Landing," pp. 70–2.
[9] J. L. Jobit, "Journal de l'expedition d'Irlande suivi de notes sur le General Humbert qui l'a commande," *Analecta Hibernica*, 11 (1941), N. Costello (ed.), p. 15.

into the organization during the previous year.[10] Undoubtedly, this was an optimistic assessment, despite the efforts in Mayo of James Joseph McDonnell, a Westport barrister and friend of Theobald Wolfe Tone, who was well connected to the leadership of the United Irishmen. Reports coming to Dublin from local magistrates testify to the swearing in of new United Irishmen in counties Mayo, Sligo and Galway during 1797, but it is unlikely that this had resulted in the establishment of viable county committees.[11] Rev. Little noted that "a few profligate persons of the lower order [were] charged with administering the United Irishmen's oath to a few others of their own description," but "it seemed as if they regarded it . . . little . . . "[12] Given the gentry and middle-class composition of the urban-based United Irishmen, its lack of success in County Mayo is hardly surprising. The county had almost no middle class and its gentry, led by Denis Browne, had remained aloof from both the Catholic and national struggles of the 1790s, to the great frustration of Tone.[13] According to Tone, any successes the United Irishmen had in Connacht were attributable to the Defenders, who made their appeal directly to the small farmers and laborers.[14]

The Defender movement began as the Catholic response to the violent attacks of the Protestant Peep-o'-Day Boys and the Orange Order during the sectarian battles fought in County Armagh during the 1780s and 1790s. Although Defenderism had its roots in Ulster's sectarian bloodshed, its appeal went far beyond simple hatred of Protestants. As Thomas Bartlett has argued, Defenderism was "a complex web of archaic and modern forces . . . remarkably adept at fusing local grievances with an anti-protestant, anti-English, anti-state ideology . . . "[15] Defender

10 R. Musgrave, *Memoirs of the Different Rebellions in Ireland* (Dublin, 1801), p. 560; C. L. Falkiner, *Studies in Irish History and Biography* (London, 1902), p. 262.

11 SPO, Rebellion Papers (hereafter RP), information, Feb. 1797, 620/28/279; magistrates of County Sligo, 620/30/99; information, 18 Mar. 1797, 620/36/25; information, 620/30/129; L. Comyn to –, 21 May 1797, 620/30/129. Reference from R. B. McDowell, *Ireland in the Age of Imperialism and Revolution, 1760–1801* (Oxford, 1979), p. 476, n. 35. Also see, Lecky, *A History of Ireland in the Eighteenth Century*, IV, p. 139. On McDonnell, see: Hayes, *The Last Invasion of Ireland*, pp. 275–8.

12 Little, "Little's Diary of the French Landing," p. 69.

13 R. B. O'Brien (ed.), *The Autobiography of Theobald Wolfe Tone, 1763–1798*, 2 vols. (Dublin, 1910), pp. 136–41, 147, 156; McDowell, *Ireland in the Age of Imperialism and Revolution*, p. 408.

14 Falkiner, *Studies in Irish History*, p. 266.

15 T. Bartlett, "Select Documents XXXVIII: Defenders and Defenderism in 1795," *Irish Historical Studies*, 24 (1985), pp. 374–5. Also see: D. W. Miller, "The Armagh Troubles, 1784–95," in S. Clark and J. S. Donnelly, Jr. (eds.), *Irish Peasants: Violence and Political Unrest, 1780–1914* (Madison, 1983), pp. 155–91.

ideology involved deeply-rooted bitterness within the Catholi~
munity over the land confiscations of the seventeenth century ¿
Penal Laws of the eighteenth. It appealed to the vague but fervently held
belief of many Irish farmers in their historic right to the land. It opposed
the payment of tithes to an alien church and taxes to an alien government, demanded the reduction of rents and, in general, responded to the
hopes and fears of the Catholic poor. It held out the hope that a social
revolution assisted by the French as the Gaelic world's long-awaited
foreign deliverers, would overturn Protestant domination and bring
social, economic and political justice.[16] The fact that the French Revolution, which sparked such hopes, had been secular and that the French
hoped to enlist Protestant support in their campaign against England did
little to diffuse the millennial hopes of Ireland's Catholic poor. Again to
quote from Rev. Little:

> the fatal French revolution, operating on minds confused with claims
> of indefinite privileges, had made them giddy extravagant &
> insatiable: this dreadful event . . . has left the Roman Catholic mind
> here in uncertain suspense, a prey to devouring wishes; not actuated by
> what is, but what was, conscious of indulging in intemperate ambition
> & apprehensive that the wisest & broadest measures of general safety
> & utility subsequently taken are only a counter-plot to operate their
> eternal depression.[17]

During the mid-1790s the Defenders and United Irishmen formed an
alliance designed to merge the popular appeal of Defenderism with the
political aspirations of the United men. Although they did not understand
it at the time, by merging with Defenderism the United Irishmen assured
that the revolution they had planned to be secular and national would be
sectarian and local. It was an effective alliance that propelled the radical
movement into hitherto untouched regions of the country, including into
County Mayo.

The extent to which Defenderism established itself in Mayo is
difficult to gauge. The county was not as infected as were the neighboring counties of Sligo, Roscommon and Galway, in which Defender
riots and assemblies had been reported to Dublin authorities by

---

[16] Bartlett, "Selected Documents," pp. 377–8, 385–6; M. Elliott, "The Origins and Transformation of Early Irish Republicanism," *Internat. Rev. Social Hist.*, 23 (1978), pp. 405–28; Foster, *Modern Ireland*, pp. 271–3; J. S. Donnelly, Jr., "Propagating the Cause of the United Irishmen," *Studies: An Irish Quarterly*, 65 (1980), pp. 5–23.

[17] Little, "Little's Diary of the French Landing," pp. 153–4.

1795.[18] Nonetheless, there is evidence that Defenderism had appeared in Mayo as early as 1793, where it was described as a "plebeian association" hostile to tithes and to the dues paid to the Catholic clergy.[19] Although the evidence is scanty, it is quite likely that this early appearance of Defenderism in Mayo was the result of the increasing contacts between the county's spinners, weavers and traders with their counterparts in the linen-manufacturing counties of the north. This network among Ireland's growing rural workforce was a major conduit of political ideas to the most remote parts of the country.[20]

After 1795 the politicization of Mayo's lower orders was greatly accelerated by the appearance of several thousand Catholic refugees from the province of Ulster. They were fleeing from the Peep-o'-Day Boys and the Orangemen who plundered their homes and, in many cases, forcibly expelled them from the north. This sectarian violence, rooted in competition between Catholics and Protestants for land and employment in the linen manufacturing regions, spiraled out of control following the "Battle of the Diamond" on September 21, 1795.[21] Many of the fleeing Catholics, a large number of them weavers, migrated to Connacht. In November some sixty northern migrants, mostly weavers, waited on James Cuffe, Esq., MP in Ballina, to seek tenancies in his town of Ballinrobe.[22] Eight months later, in a letter to Dublin Castle, Denis Browne reported that 490 families from the north, containing nearly 2000 people had "taken shelter in and about Westport." He indicated that he and his brother, Lord Altamont, would aid them to the degree they could, although they were first having "their characters and intentions . . . scrutinized" by the military.[23] In late July,

18 Public Record Office, London, Home Office Papers (hereafter PRO, HO), Extracts from Letters, etc., in the Office of the Chief Secretary Relative to the Defenders, July 1795, 100/58/198–201. Reference from Bartlett, "Selected Documents," pp. 384–5, n. 10. Also see, T. Garvin, "Defenders, Ribbonmen and Others: Underground Political Networks in Pre-Famine Ireland," p. 226.

19 PRO, HO, 100/44. Reference from McDowell, *Ireland in the Age of Imperialism and Revolution*, p. 463, n. 4.

20 Elliott, "The Origins and Transformation of Early Irish Republicanism," p. 406.

21 P. Tohall, "The Diamond Fight of 1795 and the Resultant Expulsions," *Seanchas Ardmhacha*, 3 (1958), pp. 17–50; Lecky, *A History of Ireland in the Eighteenth Century*, III, pp. 421–49.

22 Tohall, "The Diamond Fight of 1795 and Resultant Expulsions," pp. 35–6; Lecky, *History of Ireland in the Eighteenth Century*, III, pp. 442–3.

23 SPO, RP, D. Browne to T. Pelham, 29 June 1796, 620/23/206. Reference from P. Hogan, "The Migration of Ulster Catholics to Connaught, 1795–96," *Seanchas Ardmhacha*, 9 (1979), p. 289, n. 2.

Lord Altamont put the number of migrants from Ulster to Mayo at 4000.[24]

These migrants brought to Mayo harrowing tales of the outrages they had suffered at the hands of Protestants, instilling in the local Catholic population a fear of an impending nationwide massacre of Catholics. In addition, they brought a mistrust of the government and the landed gentry for having so miserably failed to protect them. In July 1796 a concerned Lord Altamont informed Dublin Castle that he had been told by a reliable source that the idea that "the persecutions in the North have been fomented by government . . . has gained belief, and has disaffected a great body of the Catholics of every rank."[25] It seems certain that these northerners, who impressed James Cuffe as being "much more intelligent than the natives," brought more to Mayo than harrowing tales and political savvy, they also seem to have brought their experience of organizing for political ends.[26]

According to Falkiner, "clubs and meetings soon became numerous" in Mayo following the arrival of the northerners with local magistrates detecting "active plotting of rebellion" in the neighborhood of Ballina by early 1798.[27] Sir Richard Musgrave, writing in 1801, had been informed by a magistrate from Ballina, Rev. Neligan, that:

> the petty shop-keepers, mechanicks and servants, of the popish persuasion, used to hold frequent meetings at the low tippling houses in Ballina, and its vicinity, which induced well-grounded suspicions that they entertained designs of a treasonable tendency; particularly as such associations were constantly attended by some of the northerners, who were active and zealous in making proselytes to their pernicious doctrines. They also kept up a constant intercourse with their friends in the north, by means of emissaries, who passed and re-passed in the guise of hawkers and peddlers.[28]

Rev. Neligan further reported that after "a few lashes of a cat-o'-nine tails" an unfortunate peddlar disclosed the existence of a wide conspiracy and supplied the names of many conspirators. According to Musgrave,

---

[24] Lecky, *History of Ireland in the Eighteenth Century*, III, p. 442. This estimate on Lord Altamont's part is probably excessive. Lists of migrants and their destinations appear in Hogan, "The Migration of Ulster Catholics to Connaught" and Tohall, "The Diamond Fight of 1795 and Resultant Expulsions." Also see: Elliott, "The Origins and Transformation of Early Irish Republicanism," p. 424, n. 59.

[25] Lecky, *A History of Ireland in the Eighteenth Century*, III, p. 441.

[26] *Ibid.*, p. 443.

[27] Falkiner, *Studies in Irish History*, pp. 263, 265.

[28] Musgrave, *Memoirs of the Different Rebellions in Ireland*, p. 567.

Neligan was "astonished at the number and respectability of the persons concerned in it," including half of the local yeomen infantry.[29] Similar reports of attempts by northerners to swear in United Irishmen/Defender recruits in the area around Newport and Westport provide further evidence of the presence of active treasonable associations in Mayo by the time the French arrived in 1798.[30]

Although United Irishmen/Defender organizations existed in Mayo by August 1798, it does not appear that they took an active role in the rebellion that accompanied the French invasion. Without question, men whose political consciousness was nurtured within the organization and who had taken the United Irish oath were active rebels. However, they acted more as individuals than as members of the United Irishmen or Defenders. There is no evidence that large numbers of United Irishmen/ Defenders flocked to Killala to join the French or that their leaders assumed positions of importance in the rebellion. Moreover, accounts of rebel leaders supplied by Bishop Stock and Musgrave do not link them to the United Irishmen/Defender movement, nor to the communities of exiled northern weavers.[31] According to Marianne Elliott, "rumours of extermination and Orange atrocities, feeding upon the existing Catholic fears of the community of presbyterian weavers at Ballina, succeeded where the more formal attempts of the United men [to organize Connacht] had failed, and people flocked into Killala from surrounding areas to join the French."[32]

Without question, the fear of and animosity towards Protestants on the part of Mayo Catholics fueled the rebellion that accompanied the French landing. However, Mayo was spared the sectarian excesses of County Wexford, where large numbers of Protestants were massacred. Indeed, Bishop Stock reported with pleasure that "not a drop of blood was shed by the Connaught rebels, except in the field of war."[33] However, the homes of Protestant gentry were sacked and looted in the neighborhoods of Killala and Castlebar as was the Protestant church at Castlebar and the homes and meeting house of Presbyterian weavers at Mullifaragh, near Ballina. At one point as many as 120 Protestants were imprisoned at Ballina by Catholics led by Fr. Owen Crowley, who reportedly

---

[29] *Ibid.*, p. 268.
[30] Lecky, *A History of Ireland in the Eighteenth Century*, IV, pp. 90–1.
[31] *Bishop Stock's Narrative*, pp. 9, 36, 47, 51, 59; Musgrave, *Memoirs of the Different Rebellions in Ireland*, pp. 582–98.
[32] Elliott, *Partners in Revolution*, p. 224.
[33] *Bishop Stock's Narrative*, p. 19.

denounced the prisoners as "a parcel of hereticks" [sic], with "no more religion than pigs." He warned them that they would "be put to death with greatest torture."[34]

For many Catholics the rising of 1798 marked an apocalyptical struggle between good and evil, Catholic and Protestant. One traveler in Mayo during the French occupation noted in his journal that many people believed that prophecies of the disappearance of Protestantism and the restoration of the land to Catholics were coming true and that it was the work of God.[35] However, the victory of Catholicism was apparently not going to be an easy one. Mayo was rife with rumors of an impending massacre of Catholics by Orangemen carrying inextinguishable black candles. Musgrave, who maintained that the entire rebellion was a popish plot, gives the following colorful description of the rumors:

> A few days before the French landed, a report was industriously circulated, that the Protestants had entered into a conspiracy to massacre the Roman catholicks [sic], and that they would not spare man, woman, or child. It was said that, for this purpose, a large quantity of combustible stuff had been introduced by the orangemen, who made a kind of black candles of it; that they were of such a quality, that they could not be extinguished when once lighted; and that in whatever house they should be burnt, they would produce the destruction of every person in it.[36]

Little noted in his diary that "these Orangemen in buckram with their black candles of inextinguishable flame, filled the imagination of my neighbours with the image of a universal conflagration, and made the people eager to fly to arms."[37] Exactly who these "Orangemen" were was never clear, since as both Rev. Little and Bishop Stock note, few if anyone calling themselves by that name resided in Mayo. However, in the popular mind Orangemen became associated with Protestants in

---

[34] Musgrave, *Memoirs of the Different Rebellions in Ireland*, pp. 571–3, 585–7, 598, 607, and appendix pp. 163–4; *Bishop Stock's Narrative*, pp. 34–5, 70–3; "Little's Diary of the French Landing," pp. 113, 133, 142.

[35] Musgrave, *Memoirs of the Different Rebellions in Ireland*, p. 599. For a discussion of millenarianism in pre-Famine Irish rebellions, see: P. O'Farrell, "Millenialism, Messianism, and Utopianism in Irish History," *Anglo-Irish Studies*, 2 (1976), pp. 45–68; J. S. Donnelly, Jr., "Pastorini and Captain Rock: Millenarianism and Sectarianism in the Rockite Movement of 1821–4," in Clark and Donnelly (eds.), *Irish Peasants*, pp. 102–39; Donnelly, "Propagating the Cause of the United Irishmen," pp. 15–20.

[36] Musgrave, *Memoirs of the Different Rebellions in Ireland*, p. 566.

[37] "Little's Diary of the French Landing," p. 87.

general and especially with the unfortunate colony of Presbyterian weavers at Mullifaragh.[38]

Both Rev. Little and Musgrave place a major share of the responsibility for this sectarianism on Carmelite friars resident in Ballina. Musgrave was convinced that the order had been "perverted to the purpose of associating men for the express purpose of committing treason, murder, sacrilege, and robbery, with every other inferior crime, which depravity might suggest or opportunity afford." Similarly, Rev. Little believed that the Carmelites constituted "not a religious, but a factious or anti-Orange association."[39] According to Musgrave, the Carmelite friars, assisted by local priests, enlisted many Mayo Catholics into a confraternity of believers who were assured that membership would insure eternal happiness and protection from danger, both temporal and spiritual. Upon the payment of one shilling, the initiated were given an asbestos plaque inscribed with the letters IHS (Jesus, Savior of Mankind), to be worn around the neck. The "supernatural" power of this talisman to resist fire was attributed to the priest's blessing of the "scapular," as it was popularly called. Musgrave reports that "bags of them . . . [were] sent to fairs and markets, and sold to the credulous multitude."

> This soon became the signal by which those of the true faith were to know each other, and the rallying point for those devotees who carried on the crusade against the heretics; and a shop was opened soon after the landing of the French, where all the sons of Erin, with their pikes in their hands, were supplied with scapulars at regulated prices . . . These were intended, not only to unite them more strongly against the common enemy, but to arm them with fresh courage and protect them from danger in the hour of trial.[40]

Little maintains that the Carmelite confraternity provided Catholic rebels with an opportunity to pursue "the objects of their unlawful ambition under the mask of Religion" and to compel the clergy, "however reluctantly," to go along rather than lose face and credibility with the people.[41]

---

[38] *Ibid.*, p. 142; *Bishop Stock's Narrative*, p. 66.

[39] Musgrave, *Memoirs of the Different Rebellions in Ireland*, p. 564; "Little's Diary of the French Landing," p. 67.

[40] Musgrave, *Memoirs of the Different Rebellions in Ireland*, p. 565. A similar amulet, prepared out of cloth and sold by priests, was worn in Connemara during the 1820s to ward off evil and disease. See: H. Blake and Family (attributed), *Letters from the Irish Highlands* (London, 1825), pp. 115–17.

[41] Little, "Little's Diary of the French Landing," pp. 66–7.

It is unlikely that the small and diminishing Carmelite community in County Mayo played the sinister role ascribed to it by Musgrave and Little, although the confraternity could well have focused the hatred of Protestants and the millenarian hopes of the Catholic community.[42]

Without question, a handful of priests played an active role in the rebellion, but few influenced the course of events to a significant degree.[43] In fact, the rebellion that accompanied the French landing, while bringing forward some military leaders of distinction, produced few leaders interested in defining local issues and building a solid, popular base for radical agrarian action in County Mayo. Lists compiled from the accounts of Stock and Musgrave and the work of Richard Hayes contain the names of fifty-four men prominent in the rebellion, twelve of whom were priests. Of the twenty-eight lay leaders listed for whom some biographical information was included, twenty-six were men of substantial property, gentlemen of old Mayo families, merchants, tradesmen, professionals, or members of their families. Only two were identified as small farmers, although presumably there were some farmers among the remaining fourteen for whom no biographical information was available.[44] These were the men who led battalions of villagers to join the French at Killala or Castlebar, were created

[42] According to P. R. McCaffrey, the historian of the Carmelite order in Ireland, a Carmelite convent was founded in Ballinsmale (Ballynamall), County Mayo in 1356. There is no townland by this name listed in the townland survey that accompanied the census of 1901 or in any of the nineteenth-century census reports. There is a Ballinsmaula townland in the parish of Kilcolman in the Barony of Clanmorris, a considerable distance from Ballina. In 1750 there were only sixty-eight Carmelites in all of Ireland. By 1840 there were twenty-six, with only two in Ballinsmale. In an official report prepared in 1840 for the Father General, Fr. John Colgan states: "The convent at Ballinsmale is a private house, in a ruinous state, and the church seems to be a stable. The prior, who is advanced in years, seems to be able to do nothing towards improving this state of things." P. R. McCaffrey, *The White Friars: An Outline Carmelite History* (Dublin, 1926), pp. 369, 436; J. L. McCracken, "The Ecclesiastical Structure, 1714–60," in Moody and Vaughan (eds.), *A New History of Ireland*, IV, p. 92.

[43] Richard Hayes lists the most prominent priests involved in the rising in Mayo and elsewhere. "Priests in the Independence Movement of '98," *Irish Ecclesiastical Record*, 5th ser, 66 (1945), pp. 261–70. See also, Musgrave, *Memoirs of the Different Rebellions in Ireland*, pp. 582–90 and B. Hoban, "Dominick Bellew, 1745–1812: Parish Priest of Dundalk and Bishop of Killala," *Seanchas Ardmhacha*, 6 (1972), pp. 363–6.

[44] *Bishop Stock's Narrative*, pp. 9, 36, 47, 51, 59; Musgrave, *Memoirs of the Different Rebellions in Ireland*, pp. 582–90, 600–1; Hayes, "Priests in the Independence Movement," pp. 261–70.

officers by the French and fought with them, or who participated in committees of public safety that helped preserve some degree of order.

Although these lists are far from exhaustive or definitive, they do point clearly to the lack of small farmers in positions of leadership. This is hardly surprising given their impoverishment and the lack of a radical tradition. Their role was a reactive one consistent with their ill-defined but ardently held motives for joining the rebellion. Rev. Little speculates, probably accurately, that the seventeenth-century loss of land to Protestants and the penal laws of the eighteenth century remained sources of bitterness and hatred towards Protestants and fostered the belief that the removal of Protestants from the county would bring prosperity to the Catholic majority and a restoration of traditional Gaelic society with the security of tenure it was thought to contain.[45] The rebellion, then, was to be a social revolution that would restore the natural order of things, reverse the history of the previous two centuries and guarantee to the Irish their historic claim to the land and the wealth it produced.

The reactive character of the rebellion was due to the unexpectedness of the French landing, which meant that the rebellion it sparked was unplanned and not a response to a building up of tensions in the county. Consequently, it was not able to survive the defeat of the French and the brutality of the loyalist troops who entered Mayo a month after the French landed.[46] Moreover, the French and their United Irishmen allies had little interest in or affinity with the as yet inchoate grievances and goals of Mayo farmers and would have found the imposition of local issues or local leaders to be counter to their purposes. The settling of old scores and the venting of religious hostilities, fueled by a strong but ill-defined sense of historic injustices were not goals or forms of revolution that appealed to the French or United Irishmen. Consequently, while the Mayo tenantry rose to the occasion provided by the French and joined with enthusiasm they never seized the initiative or made the revolt their own. With the defeat of the French and the wanton massacre of the rebels, the rebellion died away. It furthered little the process of defining issues and creating a sophisticated organization capable of a sustained,

---

[45] "Little's Diary of the French Landing," pp. 146–59.
[46] Bishop Stock reported that about 400 rebels were killed in Killala alone during the suppression of the rebellion. *Bishop Stock's Narrative*, pp. 91–9; also see Lecky, *History of Ireland in the Eighteenth Century*, V, pp. 64–8.

purposeful period of revolt. However, it helped establish a tradition of revolt in the county, which bore fruit in the first decades of the nineteenth century.

THRESHERS AND RIBBONMEN

During the forty years prior to the Great Famine of 1846–50 Mayo, like many Irish counties, was regularly disturbed by popular protest. In sharp contrast with the protests of the 1790s, those of the first half of the nineteenth century were in response to specific grievances and were led by local men, often organized in oath-bound secret societies. Opposition to tithes, priests' fees, grand jury and vestry cesses, rent levels, the price of grain and the shipping of grain out of the county replaced vague longings for a return to a previous, more just order, as the goals of Mayo's rebels. Their activities alarmed local authorities, but were relatively insignificant when compared with seriously disturbed counties such as Roscommon, Tipperary, Limerick, Clare or Westmeath. The county was not proclaimed under the various insurrection acts of the period and requests to Dublin for additional troops to quell disturbances were generally turned down for lack of sufficient cause. Nonetheless, during the first half of the nineteenth century the county entered the mainstream of popular politics in Ireland, developing patterns of protest and leadership comparable to those in the traditionally active parts of the country.

While the agitation that became endemic to Mayo shared forms of protest and grievance with that in other counties, it did not reflect the complex social divisions that were manifested in other, more economically developed, sections of Ireland. In the wealthier, more market-oriented, cattle raising counties of the midlands, where agrarian conflict during the pre-Famine years was most extensive, it often took the form of struggles between laborers and farmers over access to the land, especially to the small potato plots that the landless rented on an annual basis from tenant farmers rather than directly from the landlords. Joseph Lee, who first developed this thesis on the class-based nature of pre-Famine rural protest, argued that the lack of significant agrarian outrage in the west could be attributed to a smaller proportion of laborers and a less developed distinction between farmers and laborers.[47] Subsequent

---

[47] Lee, "The Ribbonmen," p. 28. James Donnelly summarizes the debate over the class base of agrarian protest in "The Social Composition of Agrarian Rebellions in Early

analysis of the 1841 census by David Fitzpatrick has revealed that the proportion of laborers to farmers in the west was above the national average, with Mayo's being 349 laborers per 100 farmers. Nonetheless, as Fitzpatrick acknowledges, laborers in the west were likely to occupy land, so the distinction between laborer and farmer was blurred.[48] In a county where 34 percent of those holding land in single family tenancies held 5 acres or less and another 32 percent held between 5 and 10 acres, and with the majority of small farm families holding lands jointly, most families survived on a combination of the produce of their land and labor for others. As one farmer and land surveyor told the Devon Commission in 1845, in Counties Mayo and Sligo "we have no people . . . who are only small farmers; they are all of a class of labourers, if they can get labour . . . "[49]

There is little surviving evidence from which to develop a clear sense of the social composition of agrarian radicals in pre-Famine Mayo. The general impression given is that they were primarily small farmers and laborers, that amorphous group probably best referred to as the rural poor. In this they differed little from members of secret societies elsewhere in pre-Famine Ireland. As was the pattern nationwide, bonds of neighborhood and kinship were as important, if not more so, as class in uniting the rebels, who moved easily back and forth between rebellion and banditry.[50] Rebel combinations in Mayo were highly localized, frequently consisting of bands of kin who had little formal connection with similar bands elsewhere in the county. Not surprisingly, these secret combinations often formed first in the wilds of Erris, Tirawley or Connemara, areas long associated with bandits and smugglers, some of whom were 1798 rebels who had escaped prosecution or execution. Membership in the secret societies appears to have been fluid and informal with bonds of solidarity and common purpose forged more by an awareness of kin and community than by the formal oaths that were part of the *modus operandi* of secret societies. Despite this loose structure and the lack of the class divisions that fostered violence

Nineteenth-Century Ireland: the Case of the Carders and Caravets, 1813–16," in P. J. Cornish (ed.), *Radicals, Rebels, and Establishments* (Belfast, 1985), pp. 151–4.

[48] David Fitzpatrick, "The Disappearance of the Irish Agricultural Labourer, 1841–1912," *Irish Economic and Social History*, 7 (1980), pp. 77, 88. Also see: D. Jordan, "Land and Politics in the West of Ireland: County Mayo, 1846–82" (University of California, Davis, Ph.D. thesis, 1982), pp. 377–9.

[49] *Devon Commission, Minutes of Evidence*, pt. 1, p. 389; *Appendix, Pt. IV*, pp. 280–3.

[50] Clark, *Social Origins of the Irish Land War*, pp. 65–104; Beames, *Peasants and Power*, pp. 53–62.

Cardiny

elsewhere in Ireland, Mayo's pre-Famine agrarian rebels carried out an agitation that was much more complex and coherent in its aims, methods and organization than anything the county had seen previously.

The Threshers, Ribbonmen and Steel Boys who disrupted Mayo prior to the Famine adopted methods of operation that had long been the stock in trade of Irish agrarian rebels.[51] They disguised themselves by blackening their faces. They dressed in white smocks, sometimes with a belt of straw. They raided the countryside for arms, prepared threatening notices and administered oaths, both to formalize the bonds of loyalty between members of secret societies and to compel non-members to carry out orders or adhere to the principles of the rebels. For example, in October 1806, during the campaign against clerical fees, James McPhadeen was visited one night at midnight by a mob of Threshers who swore him against his will to carry a threatening message to the local priest advising him to lower his fees. As part of the same campaign, people were sworn not to make payments to priests or go to confession. Similarly, at various times the residents of whole villages or districts were sworn not to pay rent, tithes or other payments until told to do so by the rebels.[52]

Those who broke their oaths, violated the code of the rebels, or were otherwise deemed obnoxious were subjected to attacks on their person, property or stock. The forms of assault were the common ones in pre-Famine Ireland: houghing of cattle, burning of grain stacks, breaking open of pounds, carding of individuals, terrorizing others late at night, and in rare instances, murder. For example, near Ballaghaderreen in July 1807, according to a report submitted to authorities in Dublin, Luke Manion was "found guilty by the new would be legislators on two counts, first for being a herd and secondly for selling potatoes at a rate that exceeded their regulations, and on sentencing passed, the poor man was immediately carded."[53] In contrast to the case in the more

---

[51] Beames, *Peasants and Power*, pp. 62–88.

[52] W. Ridgeway, *A Report of the Proceedings Under a Special Commission, of Oyer and Terminer, and Goal Delivery for the Counties of Sligo, Mayo, Leitrim, Longford and Cavan, in the Month of December 1806* (Dublin, 1807), pp. 136–47; Testimony of The Most Reverend Oliver Kelly, Titular Archbishop of Tuam, *Second Report from the Select Committee on the State of Ireland, 1825*, PP 1825)129 continued), viii, p. 259; SPO, SOC, 1822, Capt. W. Smith to Col. O'Hara, 14 Feb. 1822, 2291/3; SPO, OP, 1831, 9 Jan. 1831, W/3; SPO, OP, 1831, J. Dawson to E. G. Stanley, 15 Jan. 1831, B/1; *Telegraph or Connaught Ranger*, 9 Jan. 1831.

[53] SPO, SOC, 1807, W. Seymour to Dublin Castle, 15 July 1807, 1120/47; numerous other examples can be found in SPO, OSC and SPO, OP.

prosperous regions of Ireland, no clear pattern emerges as to the social composition of the victims of agrarian violence in pre-Famine Mayo. Certainly, herds, process servers, tithe proctors, and food hoarders bore a considerable amount of the violence, but the rural poor were not exempt when they broke with the solidarity demanded by the secret societies.[54]

The tone, form and issues of the renewed agitation were set by the Threshers who disrupted the county, with varying degrees of intensity, between 1805 and 1819, when Thresher activity was incorporated into the nation-wide Ribbonmen movement that struck Mayo periodically until the Famine. As was to be the case throughout the pre-Famine agitation in Mayo, access to land and disputes between farmers over tenancies were not significant issues. These were issues that were to surface in a substantial way only after the Famine, when a transformed economy brought tension between large and small farmers, and when County Mayo inaugurated for the first time a protracted period of rural agitation with nation-wide significance.[55] Prior to the Famine, the issues that sparked agrarian protest and violence were, in the words of Denis Browne, MP for the county, "all kinds of payments, whether of tithes, industry, labour or farming . . . "[56] These "payments" were concerns that united rather than divided the farming community, focusing their animosity toward clergy, magistrates, merchants, landlords and those who worked for or collaborated with them.

Although agrarian disturbances disrupted Mayo throughout the pre-Famine decades, the most intense periods were 1806–7, 1819–20, 1822–3 and 1830–2. The first of these periods of unrest occurred amidst the economic boom associated with the Napoleonic Wars, while the latter three were linked directly to the deterioration of the Mayo economy and to serious potato failures. During the first period rural agitation focused to a significant degree on the fees and tithes paid to the clergy, both Catholic and Protestant. The post-Napoleonic slide of the economy, marked in 1816 by the county's first major failure of the potato crop, saw a shift of emphasis on the part of rural agitators. As crop failure became

---

[54] For the victims of violence elsewhere in Ireland see: Clark, *Social Origins of the Irish Land War*, pp. 66–73; Beames, "Rural Conflict in Pre-Famine Ireland: Peasant Assassinations in Tipperary, 1837–1847"; P. E. W. Roberts, "Caravats and Shanvests: Whiteboyism and Faction Fighting in East Munster, 1802–11," in Clark and Donnelly (eds.), *Irish Peasants*, pp. 84–5.

[55] See Chapter 4 below.

[56] Ridgeway, *A Report of the Proceedings Under A Special Commission*, p. 134.

endemic during the 1820s, while the population continued to grow, an increasingly destitute people turned away from anti-clerical agitation to focus their attention on rents, the price of provisions and the export of grain out of the county. These concerns, which pitted the rural poor against landlords, large farmers and merchants, introduced a divisiveness into popular politics that had not been the case with the anti-clerical agitation of the first decades of the century.

Opposition to clerical fees and tithes had been rallying points for agrarian rebels in Ireland since the middle of the eighteenth century. Both surfaced in Mayo in 1806 in an apparent reaction to a substantial increase in fees and tithes coming at a time of rising prices throughout Ireland. During this period of general inflation the Threshers appear to have taken upon themselves the task of establishing and enforcing a code of behavior based on their notion of what was just. Interestingly, given the overwhelming proportion of Catholics among the rural poor, the fees charged by priests were seen to be no less oppressive or unjust than the tithes and fees charged by the Anglican clergy.[57] In 1806, at the beginning of the campaign against clerical fees, Thresher notices to priests made it clear that they were demanding reductions in priests' fees and tithes "in proportion."[58] At this stage of the agitation, the issue was economic, not sectarian. Both priests and rectors were singled out by the Threshers because their financial requests were judged to be excessive by a code designed to regulate most, if not all, prices, fees and taxes.

The fees charged by priests for the essential rites and services of Catholicism were leveled frequently, and in the opinion of many, excessively. With no other sources of income, priests charged for baptisms, marriages, last rites, private masses and expected (or demanded) a high level of hospitality when hearing confession or administering communion in private homes.[59] A member of the Blake family of Connemara, writing in 1823, described clerical demands for hospitality as follows:

> The rites of the Roman catholic church, in Ireland at least, are all performed at home; except indeed the marriage ceremony, which

---

[57] Testimony of The Most Reverend Oliver Kelly, *Second Report from the Select Committee on the State of Ireland, 1825*, p. 259.

[58] Ridgeway, *A Report of the Proceedings Under A Special Commission*, pp. 228, 231–2.

[59] For an account of the sources of priests' income see, S. J. Connolly, *Priests and People in Pre-Famine Ireland, 1780–1845* (Dublin, 1982), pp. 47–53, 243–4, and J. A. Murphy, "The Support of the Catholic Clergy in Ireland," in J. L. McCracken (ed.), *Historical Studies*, 5 (London, 1965), pp. 103–21.

occasionally takes place in the priest's house. Twice a year he comes round the parish, for the purpose of confession; and in the different villages, takes up his station in some snug cabin, where he expects to be treated with white bread, tea, sugar, and whiskey. Those who, in more prosperous times, probably esteemed the entertainment of this reverend guest as an honour, now frequently complain of it as a burden. A poor woman who, on the last of these occasions, walked four miles in search of a teapot, gave as her reason, that neither bread, butter, nor milk, would be considered acceptable without the addition of tea and spirits. Nay, it is a fact, that a priest, on the Sunday previous to commencing his rounds, gave public notice after mass, that as tea, sugar, and flour were to be had in the neighborhood, there would be no excuse for those who were not prepared.[60]

Blake went on to report that "the magnitude of the dues of the church, and the severity with which they are exacted, is a topic on which they [rural Catholics] do not scruple to express their sentiments."[61] According to the Catholic Archbishop of Tuam, many Catholics felt that "the demand of the priest upon them were so many, that they could not answer them" for in addition to fees for services, the clergy expected dues as high as 2s. per family payable at Easter and Christmas, as well as contributions for construction and maintenance of chapels and schools.[62]

In a celebrated instance in Minola, County Mayo in October 1806 the parish priest was advised to "have his coffin convenient" if he did not reduce his fees to what had been the "usual custom" prior to a recent 230 percent increase in fees for baptisms and a 130 percent increase for private masses. On the same Sunday in the parish of Kilcolmen, 10 miles from Minola, the priest was similarly told that the "rules" laid down by the Threshers were that fees should be reduced to "half a guinea [10s. 6d.] for marriage, 19s. ½d. for christening and 1s. 1d. for mass . . . " Furthermore, Fr. Nolan of Minola was told to take what he was offered for holding stations in private homes and not to ask or expect anything more.[63]

60 Blake, *Letters from the Irish Highlands*, pp. 100–1.

61 *Ibid.*, p. 103.

62 Testimony of The Most Reverend Oliver Kelly, Titular Archbishop of Tuam, *Second Report From the Select Committee on the State of Ireland, 1825*, p. 259; Testimony of Denis Browne, MP, *First Report From the Select Committee on the State of Ireland, 1825*, PP, 1825 (129), viii, p. 30.

63 Ridgeway, *A Report of the Proceedings Under a Special Commission*, pp. 137, 145, 227–8, 232.

For the most part, Anglican clergy, who used proctors to collect the tithe, were spared direct threats such as this. Rather, the Threshers directed their actions against the proctors and pound keepers who distrained stock when tithes were not paid. Pounds were broken into and stock released or damaged, grain taken as payment of the tithe was burned or scattered and those involved in the collection of the tithes were harassed and intimidated as the Threshers attempted to enforce their code and force a reduction in the tithes. In Mayo, where the potato crop was exempt from the tithe, the burden of supporting the Anglican church fell on the grain and flax crops, the major sources of cash with which the county's small farmers paid the rent.[64] Their burden was increased by a method of collection that was corrupt, subject to bribery, and the source of great profits for the tithe proctors. In February 1806, at the beginning of the anti-tithe agitation, Lord Rosslyn described the method of collection in Mayo as follows:

> In general, the clergyman lets his tythes to a tythe proctor or farmer for a gross sum. This person sometimes makes an agreement with the tenants separately for as much as he can get and always for a considerable profit; and this is by far the most favourable mode for the tenants and the least common.
>
> For the most part, the tythe proctor puts up the tythes of the different villages or subdivisions of the parish to auction; which takes place commonly at night, and the bribes are encouraged by great quantities of whiskey.
>
> In order to indemnify himself the buyer must either exact a very high price from the cultivator or take them in kind.
>
> The practice is obviously calculated to take from the people as much as profitable, and they do, in fact, pay more in proportion than farmers do in England, or in Ireland under any other mode of management.

Lord Rosslyn went on to say that the dissatisfaction of the people was with the exorbitant profits made by the proctors and the "rigorous and vexatious measures" that were "not infrequently resorted to enforce the payments . . . "[65] By 1820, Denis Browne reported that the clergy were

---

[64] SPO, SOC, 1806, Lord Rosslyn to Lt. Gen. Lloyd, 6 Feb. 1806, 1091/47; testimony of The Most Reverend Oliver Kelly, *Second Report from the Select Committee on the State of Ireland, 1825*, p. 259. For a history of the tithe in Ireland and its method of collection, see: A. MacIntyre, *The Liberator: Daniel O'Connell and the Irish Party, 1830–1847* (London, 1965), pp. 167–75; D. Bowen, *The Protestant Crusade in Ireland, 1800–70* (Dublin, 1978), pp. 156–8.

[65] SPO, SOC, 1806, Lord Rosslyn to Lt. Gen. Lloyd, 6 Feb. 1806, 1091/47.

"glad to get any person who will take the risk of collecting his tythes and that person takes care to pay himself well from the produce of the country."[66]

However, during the 1820s, as the economy of Mayo declined sharply, the rate or method of tithe collection, or the payment of fees to their priests, ceased to be central concerns for many Mayo farm families. The issue of fees paid to the Catholic clergy surfaced periodically until 1842–3, but as Sean Connolly notes, it became less violent and less pressing as the status of the increasingly disciplined Catholic clergy rose, and as its members became more responsive to the worsening plight of their flocks.[67] By 1830 the anti-tithe campaign faded as an issue for agrarian rebels, to be taken up during the 1830s by the constitutional agitation of priests, townsmen, large farmers and some landlords. Increasingly, the central concern of Mayo's rural poor was their inability to make any of the payments demanded of them, including those for rent, seed or food. During the early stages of rural agitation in Mayo the Threshers had attempted to fix the price of potatoes as part of their code, but for the most part had directed their violence against farmers rather than merchants.[68] However, in the wake of the poor potato harvests of 1816 and 1822 and plummeting grain prices, the concern of Mayo's secret societies focused on the price and availability of food, with their ire directed at town-based merchants. A threatening notice posted in Ballina in October 1830 referred to merchants who shipped grain out of the county as "bigoted, black, bloodthirsty foes" of the "poor, distressed inhabitants of Mayo" and called on the people to deal only with "liberal and freehearted" merchants.[69]

Agitation to prevent the shipping of grain out of the county began in Ballina which, as noted in the previous chapter, had become one of Mayo's more important trading and manufacturing centers with its merchants and weavers profiting from the county's expanding economy. On 25 February 1817 the prospect of food being sent out of the county brought "a mob consisting of five hundred persons" to the house of Colonel King, RM. According to Col. King, they were "carrying with them several carts laden with meal intended to be sent by land carriage to the town of Sligo, which they admitted they had seized upon, and

---

66 SPO, SOC, 1820, Denis Browne, 23 Jan. 1820, 2175/9.
67 Sean Connolly, *Priests and People in Pre-Famine Ireland*, pp. 248–55.
68 SPO, SOC, 1807, W. Seymour, 15 July 1807, 1120/47; SOC, 1812, Statement on Outrage that Occurred 7 May 1812, 1408/22.
69 SPO, OP, 1830, C/74.

declaring in the most violent and outrageous manner their determination of not allowing provisions of any sort to be conveyed out of the county." This incident, which ended with the killing of two rioters by the military and with an attack on the home of a grain merchant, followed a period of growing tension over the export of provisions. A week earlier the grain merchants of Ballina had petitioned the Lord Lieutenant for a military escort for the £30,000–£40,000 worth of grain they had ready for export, but feared to do so because of threats from the "working and lower classes."[70]

A more violent and drawn out engagement over the question of shipping grain occurred at Belmullet during the winter of 1830–1, again in the context of extreme distress resulting from a very poor potato harvest, the loss of income from linen and the general deterioration of the Mayo economy. According to Rev. J. P. Lyons, RC Rector of Kilmore-Erris, during the summer of 1830 "ill disposed persons under the name of 'Steel Boys' created great disturbance in Erris by levelling kilns, destroying the corn of obnoxious individuals, demolishing pounds and terrifying the peaceable and well-meaning inhabitants by threats and menaces." These Steel Boys began their agitation among the mountain people of Erris with their initial object being to prevent food being sent out of the country; however, these "nocturnal legislators soon enlarged their views and proceeded to enormities . . . "[71] Nightly, large numbers of people were summoned by the sound of horns and were sworn to prevent the export of oats and, in the words of the Protestant vicar, "the empounding of cattle for rent, the serving of process for recovery of tithe, rent and other debts [and] the distillation of illicit spirits."[72] By winter the Steel Boys had expanded out of the mountains. Rev. Lyons reported that the evening of the November fair "the whole street of [Belmullet] was a scene of riot and uproar . . . Strangers from Westport and elsewhere were beaten and insulted by persons from the mountains because they could not reply to the pass-word of the Ribbon system, and even the Police were frequently threatened and told not to shew their heads."[73]

---

[70] SPO, SOC, 1817, Rt. Hon. Col. King, 22, 27 Feb., 6 Mar. 1817 and William Jackson, 28 Feb. 1817, 1833/18–21.

[71] SPO, OP, 1831, State of Belmullet, J. P. Lyons to The Rt. Hon. Lord Plunket, Lord High Chancellor of Ireland, 10 Jan. 1831, B/1; *The Telegraph or Connaught Ranger*, 1 Dec. 1830.

[72] SPO, OP, 1831, J. Dawson to E. G. Stanley, 15 Jan. 1831; Lieut. Nugent to Inspector General of the Coast Guard, 11 Jan. 1831, B/1.

[73] *The Telegraph or Connaught Ranger*, 1 Dec. 1830.

Agitation on the central issue of the shipping of grain came to a head on 10 January 1831 when 800 protesters marched into Belmullet demanding that the oats stored in town not be loaded on to a ship waiting in the harbor to take it to Liverpool. In addition, the protesters demanded that the price of provisions, especially of potatoes, be fixed at a level that the poor and starving could afford. Ultimately, the disturbances subsided early in February with the arrival of a force of marines and with the receipt and distribution at cost of two shiploads of potatoes ordered by the merchants of Belmullet.[74]

The agitation of 1830–2 was not confined to the half-barony of Erris on Mayo's far west coast, nor was it limited to the issue of grain exports. In petitions to the Lord Lieutenant calling for more police and troops, county magistrates meeting in Crossmolina and Killala in January 1831 reported "nightly assemblages of men collected by the call of bugles . . . for the purpose of breaking and levelling pounds, of swearing new members to their lawless association and of contriving further outrage." The magistrates further reported that the goal of these nocturnal actions and of daylight meetings was the reduction of rents, taxes and tithes.[75] Also in January, the residents of Kilmeena, near Newport, were sworn not to pay rent, tithes or taxes before their grievances could be heard at a mass meeting in Westport. This action prompted their parish priest to print a broadside in which he condemned his parishioners for having brought "indelible disgrace on yourselves and your parish." He attached a long letter from Daniel O'Connell, written a few days earlier, in which O'Connell reminded the people of Ireland that he had "often cautioned them against the folly, the drivelling, disgusting folly, of secret societies [and] the horrible impiety of illegal oaths."[76] Near Foxford in central Mayo an armed band of men, whose leader wore a white sash and a white cloth on his head, destroyed pounds before being dispersed by the military. *The Telegraph or Connaught Ranger* reported that the "peasantry" had become "so daring . . . that large bodies of them have even ventured in day light to stop the carts conveying oats to Ballina, and have levied contributions of three shillings on each."[77]

---

[74] SPO, OP, 1831, W. Jones to W. H. Carter, 11 Jan. 1831; D. Bingham to E. G. Stanley, 11 Jan. 1831; Lieut. Nugent to J. Dunkain, 28 Jan. 1831; S. Carter to Col. Gossett, 9 Feb. 1831, B/1.

[75] SPO, OP, 1831, J/3, K/3.

[76] SPO, OP, 1831, W/3 and O/6; *The Telegraph or Connaught Ranger*, 19 Jan. 1831.

[77] *The Telegraph or Connaught Ranger*, 15 Dec. 1830; 23 Feb. 1831; SPO, OP, 1831, B/24.

The distress that sparked these actions was grave and widespread. A committee appointed in February 1831 by the Marquis of Sligo to look into the causes of the distress reported a "general failure of crops" due to an excessively wet summer in 1830, "want of employment everywhere," and the collapse of the linen industry.[78] By July over 200,000 people in the county were receiving relief from the Mayo Central Committee, which by the end of August when the distress began to abate, had distributed over £40,000 worth of aid.[79]

Mayo went through regular periods of distress between 1832 and the Great Famine that began in 1846. However, the county did not experience another period of widespread and sustained rural protest until the late 1870s. During the 1830s and 1840s popular political activity in Mayo was largely constitutional in nature and had a triple purpose of abolishing tithes, calling for a repeal of the union with Britain, and breaking the monopoly that the Browne family had on Mayo's parliamentary seats. These campaigns were part of nation-wide ones, inspired and sponsored by Daniel O'Connell and carried out by largely middle-class and Catholic nationalists. In Mayo, the tone and class foundation of these campaigns were revealed in *The Telegraph or Connaught Ranger*'s account of O'Connell's first visit to the county in January 1837. The procession past Sheridan's Hotel, where O'Connell was staying, was of tradesmen, marching in order by trade and headed by Mr. Morris, "one of the most respectable and wealthy townsmen, who had been entrusted by his brother tradesmen with their address." At the dinner in O'Connell's honor the newspaper reported:

> There never, on any occasion was before assembled in Mayo, so much of the respectability, wealth, talent, and public spirit of its inhabitants – the elite of the ancient houses – the most wealthy of its resident gentry – the venerated and patriotic Catholic clergy – the intelligent and active commercial men of the county, and those honest and patriotic men who first united to overthrow the faction by which we were so long opposed.[80]

In this environment the rural poor, who so recently had risen in protest against the merchants and townsmen who were O'Connell loyalists, stayed in the background. They attended the massive anti-tithe and Repeal meetings and periodically committed outrages in support of popular parliamentary candidates but left the initiative and direction to

[78] *The Telegraph or Connaught Ranger*, 16 Mar. 1831.
[79] *Ibid.*, 13 July 1831; 31 Aug. 1831.
[80] *Ibid.*, 25 Jan 1837.

priests, strong farmers and townsmen.[81] By March 1841 *The Telegraph or Connaught Ranger* could report that the county was tranquil and that secret societies in Mayo were as "rare as birds of Paradise." [82]

Without question the class divisions that fueled agrarian protest and violence elsewhere in pre-Famine Ireland were beginning to develop in Mayo during the century prior to the Famine. However, they were not yet developed sufficiently to provoke sustained agitation. The neighboring county of Roscommon was disturbed by secret societies regularly during the final decade prior to the Famine, especially over the issue of the availability and cost of conacre plots.[83] However, in Mayo, where the conacre system was insignificant and where joint tenancies provided access to land for most of the poor, and where the distinction between farmers and laborers was less well defined, agrarian protest largely vanished after 1832.[84] Pre-Famine Mayo did not experience to a significant degree competition for land between aggressive strong farmers and the rural poor, as few farmers were yet in a position to profit from securing additional land at the expense of their vulnerable neighbors. Given the limited amount of good land in the county, an agrarian economy that remained centered on grain cultivation did not promote the creation of large numbers of strong farmers. It is significant that pre-Famine agitation was scattered randomly around the country, with only the port cities receiving any special attention during the 1820s and early 1830s. As illustrated on Map 3.1, of the fifty-two incidents of agrarian violence or secret society activity, twenty-eight occurred in the periphery, twenty-four in the core, although given that only 45 percent of the county's population lived in the periphery, its per capita level of agrarianism was significantly higher than that of the core.[85] It was not until the post-Famine transformation of the county into a market-oriented

---

81   Examples of these outrages can be found in: SPO, OP, 1832, 1833, 1834.

82   *The Telegraph or Connaught Ranger*, 10 Mar. 1841.

83   Lee, "The Ribbonmen," pp. 28–35; Beames, *Peasants and Power*, pp. 42–53, 120–4, 230.

84   The lowering of rents, including conacre rates, was occasionally included as a demand of Mayo's agrarian rebels, but never emerged as a primary issue to the degree that it did in many parts of Ireland, including County Roscommon. Denis Browne, MP, attributed this to the fact that in Mayo more land was let directly by landlords and not by "middlemen and land jobbers." SPO, SOC, 1820, 23 Jan. 1820, 2175/9.

85   Incidents of agrarian violence or secret society activity were compiled from government reports and newspaper accounts. For a comparison with the 1879–81 period of agitation, see Map 5.2, p. 191 below. The per capita levels of rural protest are one incident per 5832 people in the periphery and one per 8457 in the core. *Abstract of Population Returns, 1831*, p. 39.

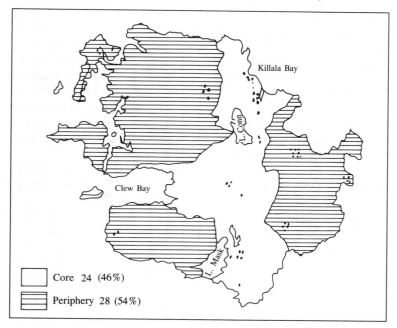

Map 3.1. Distribution of rural protests within the core and periphery, 1806–1837

livestock economy that the social and economic foundation was in place to position agrarian agitation to a large degree in the county's central corridor, where conflicts over land pitted small farmers against livestock graziers and their commercial allies, and both against landlords whose rents were increasingly viewed as being oppressive and anachronistic.

From its first appearance following the French landing of 1798, agrarian agitation in County Mayo was conditioned by fluctuations in an economy that from the middle of the eighteenth century was slowly, hesitantly, but steadily, being transformed into a market-based and capitalist one in which forces external to Mayo often determined whether the county's economy would grow or contract. During the nineteenth century, these economic fluctuations periodically sparked agrarian conflict, established the issues that fueled it, and influenced the forms of protest and the degree of class conflict or collaboration exhibited by the agitation. In contrast to the situation in the more prosperous regions of Ireland, the conditions that led to class-based conflicts among tenant farmers were not yet in place in pre-Famine Mayo. The poor quality of the land and distance from the markets delayed until after the Famine the full establishment of a livestock-based economy with its attendant competition for land between graziers and tillage farmers. Moreover, the persistence of rundale leasing and extensive subdivision guaranteed access to potato ground to most Mayo small farm families, which dampened the market for conacre rentals that was so divisive elsewhere in Ireland. It was only in times of great despair and near famine, beginning in the 1820s, that rural protest in pre-Famine Mayo began to exhibit anything approaching class conflict. In those instances the rural poor directed their protest against merchants who set prices and attempted to ship grain and potatoes out of the county, rather than against other farmers.

The agrarian protest that began and matured in pre-Famine Mayo established patterns that continued into the more complex social and economic environment of the 1870s and 1880s. Most significantly, in generally prosperous times the county's farmers displayed a considerable degree of solidarity, despite a growing disparity between the wealth and security of the substantial graziers and the small farmers, who continued to comprise 90–95 per cent of the county's farming community.

Part 2

The post-Famine transformation of County Mayo

4. *Economy and society, 1846–1877*

For the Commander of the "Eliza"

Routine patrol off West Mayo; sighting
A rowboat heading unusually far
Beyond the creek, I tacked and hailed the crew
In Gaelic. Their stroke had clearly weakened
As they pulled to, from guilt or bashfulness
I was conjecturing when, O my sweet Christ,
We saw piled in the bottom of their craft
Six grown men with gaping mouths and eyes
Bursting the sockets like spring onions in drills.
Six wrecks of bone and pallid, tautened skin.
"Bia, bia,
Bia". In whines and snarls their desperation
Rose and fell like a flock of starving gulls.
We'd known about the shortage but on board
They always kept us right with flour and beef
So understand my feelings, and the men's,
Who had no mandate to relieve distress
Since relief was then available in Westport –
Though clearly these poor brutes would never make it.
I had to refuse food: they cursed and howled
Like dogs that had been kicked hard in the privates.
When they drove at me with their starboard oar
(Risking capsize themselves) I saw they were
Violent and without hope. I hoisted
And cleared off. Less incidents the better.

Next day, like six bad smells, those living skulls
Drifted through the dark of bunks and hatches

> And once in port I exorcised my ship
> Reporting all to the Inspector General.
> Sir James, I understand, urged free relief
> For famine victims in the Westport Sector
> And earned tart reprimand from good Whitehall.
> Let natives prosper by their own exertions;
> Who could not swim might go ahead and sink.
> "The Coast Guard with their zeal and activity
> Are too lavish" were the words, I think.
>
> Seamus Heaney, *Death of a Naturalist*[1]

The Famine of 1846–50 marks a major turning point in the economic and social development of modern Ireland. Famine depopulation and post-Famine land clearances and emigration accelerated a trend, established before the Famine, of consolidation of holdings into larger, more profitable ones. The reduction in the number of subsistence producers which the Famine brought about allowed for a larger market surplus for those who retained land, and cleared the way for the fuller commercialization of Irish agriculture. A rise in livestock prices, stimulated by a growing British beef market, further encouraged the consolidation of holdings and a switch from tillage to livestock farming. These demographic and economic changes brought new wealth and prominence to those with sizeable holdings of good pasture land. Within the agrarian community the class balance between the various classes of farmers shifted markedly to the advantage of the larger farmers, whose agricultural, inheritance and marriage practices became the norm for Irish society.[2]

These structural changes occurred more slowly in Mayo than they did in the more prosperous counties of Ireland. There were proportionally fewer large farm families in Mayo to lead the way by taking full advantage of the dynamic of the post-Famine economy. The county, and especially its periphery, remained peopled with small farmers who married early and worked tillage farms that were regularly subdivided to meet the land hunger of the next generation. Nonetheless, the process of the consolidation of holdings and the shift from labor-intensive tillage farming to labor-extensive grazing did occur, bringing with it conflicts over land and tensions within the farming community. While the lines of

---

[1] In Seamus Heaney, *Poems 1965–1975* (New York, 1980), pp. 24–5.
[2] J. Lee, *The Modernisation of Irish Society* (Dublin, 1973), pp. 1–20.

division between large farmers, concentrated in central Mayo, and the small farmers increasingly relegated to the peripheral regions cannot be precisely drawn, following the Famine Mayo developed more fully than previously into a county that contained two economies and two social systems – one concentrated in but not confined to the core and one concentrated in but not confined to the periphery.

FAMINE AND EVICTIONS IN MAYO 1846–1852

The Great Famine of 1846–50 hit the western seaboard of Ireland with particular severity, since a large percentage of the population in this area was almost totally dependent upon the potato for sustenance. As was the case elsewhere in Ireland, the first clear signs of the appearance of potato rot caused by the fungal disease *Phytophthora Infestans* came with the fall harvest of 1845. In October *The Telegraph or Connaught Ranger* reported that the appearance of rot had caused a "panic" that had driven up grain and flour prices at "an alarming pitch." In an editorial comment, the newspaper's editor, Frederick Cavendish, called on landlords to protect their tenants from the prospect of famine and on the government to prevent grain or potatoes from leaving Irish ports.[3] The first actual deaths by starvation in the county came the following August. Even before the Famine, pressure on the land and on the fragile potato crop from the rapidly increasing population had resulted in a gradual rise in the number of deaths recorded in Mayo.[4] In 1843 there were 4.3 percent more recorded deaths than there had been in 1842, and in 1844 there were 8.3 percent more than in 1843. However, the first dramatic rise in mortality occurred as a result of the partial failure of the potato in 1845, when 3090 people died in Mayo, an increase of 34.4 percent over the previous year.[5] By the end of 1846 reports were coming in from all parts of the county of famine-related deaths and by March 1847 "famine fever" (either typhus or relapsing fever), the real killer during the Famine, was well established in Mayo.[6]

---

[3] *The Telegraph or Connaught Ranger*, 1 Oct., 15 Oct., 19 Nov. 1845.

[4] For a discussion of the methodological problems associated with recorded mortality figures prior to and during the Famine, see: S. H. Cousens, "Regional Death Rates in Ireland During the Great Famine, From 1846–1851." *Population Studies*, 14 (1960), pp. 55–74 and Mokyr, *Why Ireland Starved*, pp. 263–8.

[5] Almquist, "Mayo and Beyond," pp. 237–8.

[6] C. Woodham-Smith, *The Great Hunger* (London, 1962), pp. 110, 168, 188–90, 199; T. P. O'Neill, "The Organization of Relief, 1845–52," in R. D. Edwards and T. D. Williams (eds.), *The Great Famine* (New York, 1957), p. 233; S. H. Cousens, "The

Relief efforts, either by the government or by private charity, could not cope with such massive starvation and disease, even in the rare instances when relief was administered liberally and efficiently. The various governmental attempts at relief for Ireland – food depots, public works projects, soup kitchens and poor law relief – were all attempted in Mayo with limited success.[7] For example, during 1847 over 70 percent of the population of all of Mayo's poor law unions received some rations, but the organization of the kitchens was slow, leaving many people in extreme distress, especially those too sick or weak to trek to the kitchens and wait in long lines.[8] The poor law guardians to whom the relief of distress was turned over in 1847 were, in Mayo as elsewhere, hopelessly ill-equipped for the task. In many unions rates were almost impossible to collect from reluctant or absentee landlords so union indebtedness was widespread.[9] Prior to the Famine, the Westport Board of Guardians required a warship, two revenue cruisers, "two companies of the 69th Regiment, a troop of 20th Hussars, fifty police, two police inspectors and two stipendiary magistrates" to aid their rate collectors. During the Famine, the Castlebar guardians had to offer a cut of 2s. 6d. per pound collected in order to find anyone to accept the post of rate collector.[10] Despite these efforts, the Westport union was £800 and the Castlebar union was £3000 in debt at the beginning of the Famine. As a consequence of its indebtedness, the Castlebar union was not admitting people in late 1846 even though other unions in the county were operating beyond their capacity. Not surprisingly, many of the county's unions were never able to meet the need or the government's expectations of them and eventually collapsed under the strain.[11]

Private charity was equally unsuccessful. The Society of Friends,

---

Regional Variation in Mortality During the Great Irish Famine," *Proceedings of the Royal Irish Academy*, 63, C, no. 3 (1963), p. 131.

[7] The most thorough account of these efforts is J. S. Donnelly, Jr., "Famine and Government Response, 1845–6," "The Administration of Relief, 1846–7," "The Soup Kitchens," "The Administration of Relief, 1847–51," in W. E. Vaughan (ed.), *A New History of Ireland V: Ireland Under the Union, I, 1801–70* (Oxford, 1989), pp. 272–85, 294–331.

[8] Woodham-Smith, *The Great Hunger*, p. 287; O'Neill, "Organization of Relief," p. 242; Donnelly, "The Soup Kitchens," pp. 310–13.

[9] *Copies or Extracts of Correspondence Relating to the State of Union Workhouses in Ireland*, PP 1847 [766], lv, pp. 7, 27, 33–4, 49–50, 57–60; Cousens, "Regional Variation in Mortality," pp. 137–8.

[10] Woodham-Smith, *The Great Hunger*, p. 175; O'Neill, "Organization of Relief," p. 248.

[11] *The Telegraph or Connaught Ranger*, 28 Oct. 1846; Woodham-Smith, *The Great Hunger*, pp. 175–7, 311–12.

whose efforts during the Famine are still remembered in Ireland with gratitude, found it difficult to set up an effective organization in Mayo, while many landlords, the other source of private relief, ignored or were unable to assist their starving tenantry.[12] Those landlords who made a serious effort to help their tenants shared the distress of Colonel Vaughan Jackson, a Mayo landlord who wrote, "no men were more ill-fated or greater victims than we resident proprietors, we are consumed by the hives of human beings that exist on the properties of the absentees. On my right and my left are proprietors such as I allude to. I am over-whelmed and ruined by them. The proprietors *will do nothing.* All the burden of relief and employment falls on me . . . "[13] Reportedly, Jackson had liquidated many of his assets in order to devote himself to the aid of his tenants. The largest landlord in Mayo, the Marquis of Sligo, personally maintained the Westport workhouse when no other money was available and joined with Sir Robert Bloose and George Henry Moore to charter the *Martha Washington* to bring 1000 tons of flour from New Orleans to Westport. Moore, in addition, donated £1000 of his race horse winnings for famine relief and left bowls of food on the steps of Moore Hall for his tenants to take away.[14] However, all efforts at relief were hopelessly insufficient given the magnitude of the crisis. In January 1849 *The Telegraph or Connaught Ranger* summed up the state of the county as follows: "From the four quarters of the county we hear of nothing but ruined landlords, levelled cabins, emaciated human beings, crawling about, and deaths without end: the inanimate bodies, nine out of ten, consigned to their kindred earth without coffins."[15]

Estimates vary on the number of people who succumbed to starvation and Famine-related diseases in Mayo between 1846 and 1850. Cousens estimates the excess mortality, i.e. the number of deaths that occurred in the county less the number who would have died during a comparable normal period, at 50,124.[16] In an econometric analysis of available data, Joel Mokyr has argued convincingly that Cousens' estimates, based on

[12] Woodham-Smith, *The Great Hunger*, pp. 157, 316; S. H. Cousens, "The Regional Pattern of Emigration During the Great Irish Famine, 1846–51," *Transactions of the Institute of British Geographers*, 28 (1960), p. 127.

[13] Quoted in Woodham-Smith, *The Great Famine*, p. 319.

[14] *Ibid.*, pp. 299, 364; M. G. Moore, *An Irish Gentleman: George Henry Moore, His Travels, His Racing, His Politics* (London, n.d.), pp. 106, 123-5.

[15] *The Telegraph or Connaught Ranger*, 3 Jan. 1849.

[16] Cousens, "Regional Death Rates in Ireland," pp. 67, 71. The recorded number of deaths in Mayo for these years was 41,893. *The Census of Ireland for the Year 1851, Part VI: General Report*, PP 1856 [2134], xxxi, p. li.

Famine-related deaths recorded in the 1851 census, are low. Mokyr calculates excess death rates as a residual of the "counterfactual" population of each county in 1851 (if birth and death rates had remained constant between 1846 and 1851) less the recorded 1851 population, after subtracting Famine emigrants. He derives an upper and lower estimate of the Famine death rates per county, with the primary difference being whether averted births are counted as Famine casualties.[17] For County Mayo, Mokyr arrives at an upper-bound estimate of excess Famine mortality of 120,000 and a lower-bound estimate of 100,000, representing the highest rate of any county in Ireland.[18] He attributes the high rate in Mayo and other western counties to dependency on potatoes for food, low incomes per capita, the lack of an urban population, high rates of illiteracy and a substantial proportion of farms under twenty acres.[19] Cousens maintains, and there seems no reason to dispute this, that the highest Famine mortality occurred in County Mayo during 1847, when relief efforts were at their most inadequate, and then dropped slowly between 1848 and 1850.[20]

Emigration was the second source of Famine-related depopulation. Although no adequate county-based statistics on emigration are available before 1851, it appears certain that emigration from County Mayo was high during the Famine years. Kerby Miller noted that the counties of north Connacht, including Mayo, were among the few in Ireland to experience both high rates of excess mortality and high rates of emigration during the Famine.[21] In his pioneering work on regional

---

[17] Joel Mokyr, "The Deadly Fungus: An Econometric Investigation into the Short-Term Demographic Impact of the Irish Famine, 1846–1851," *Research in Population Economics*, 2 (1980), pp. 245–7; Mokyr, *Why Ireland Starved*, pp. 264–7; the debate and findings are summed up in J. S. Donnelly, Jr., "Excess Mortality and Emigration," in Vaughan (ed.), *A New History of Ireland*, V, pp. 350–2.

[18] These numbers are derived from assuming an 1846 population of 410,000 and annual excess mortality estimates of 7.2 percent and 5.84 percent between 1846 and 1851. I am indebted to Joel Mokyr for providing me with his estimates of Mayo's 1846 population and excess mortality, which are not included in his published works. He stresses that they are "estimates based on assumptions" and suggests that he may have underestimated Famine migration, which would lower "a bit" his estimates of excess mortality.

[19] Mokyr, *Why Ireland Starved*, pp. 267–75.

[20] Cousens' figures are as follows: during 1847 4–5 percent of the population died as a result of the famine; during 1848 and 1849 3–4 percent died; during 1850 1–2 percent died. "Regional Variation in Mortality," pp. 129–48.

[21] Kerby Miller, *Emigrants and Exiles: Ireland and the Irish Exodus to North America* (New York, 1985), p. 293; also see Donnelly, "Excess Mortality and Emigration," p. 355.

patterns of Famine emigration Cousens argues that since there was little internal migration during the Famine, a simple way of calculating roughly the number of emigrants from a given county was to subtract the Famine-period decline in population from the estimates of excess mortality.[22] This method, employing Cousens' estimate of 50,124 excess mortality in Mayo during the Famine, results in a population loss due to emigration of approximately 64,264.[23] This estimate is similar to that of Mokyr who computes Famine emigration as the residual of the "counterfactual" population of Mayo in 1851 less excess mortality and the recorded population in 1851. Mokyr's estimates of Famine emigration range from 50,000 to 70,000 depending on whether his lower or upper estimate of excess mortality is employed.[24] A working estimate of 60,000 for Famine emigration would mean that approximately 44 percent of the county's Famine population loss was attributable to emigration.

The Famine resulted in the first substantial wave of emigration from the poor counties of the west of Ireland. According to Miller, during the thirty years prior to the Famine, the bulk of emigrants to North America came from "Ulster, Leinster, and certain highly commercialized districts of Munster and east Connaught" with Protestants outnumbering Catholics until the 1840s. Nonetheless, from the 1820s an increasing number of emigrants came from the poorer, Irish-speaking regions of the west, including the most remote regions of County Mayo.[25] During the Famine, north Connacht, including Mayo, saw many residents depart for North America. In Mayo it appears that many people who had savings and saleable possessions left at the early signs of blight and then remitted money to family members who joined the exodus during the latter years of the Famine. Others fled with their rent money before they could be evicted and their possessions distrained for back rent.[26]

Yet, for tens of thousands of Mayo's poor, the passage fare of 50 to 75 shillings was impossible to raise, leaving them at the mercy of their

---

[22] Cousens, "The Regional Pattern of Emigration," pp. 119-20.

[23] *Ibid.*, p. 121. This would include emigrants to Britain as well as those to North America.

[24] These estimates are derived by assuming an 1846 population of 410,000 and that the pre-Famine annual growth rate of 1.6 percent would have continued without the Famine. This would mean a "counterfactual" 1851 population in Mayo of 444,000. Again, I am indebted to Professor Mokyr for providing me with these estimates, which are not included in his published works.

[25] Miller, *Emigrants and Exiles*, pp. 193–201.

[26] *Ibid.*, p. 293; Cousens, "The Regional Pattern of Emigration," pp. 123, 127.

landlords and the various relief systems.[27] Few landlords were willing or able to assist their tenants to emigrate, no doubt because so many were bordering on financial ruin themselves. Some did use their positions as magistrates to aid people to emigrate by giving sentences of transportation to the colonies to felons who committed crimes solely for the purpose of enabling them to flee Ireland. For example, Westport barrister Michael Shaughnessy told the Select Committee on Poor Laws that he agreed to transport a number of felons after being satisfied "that they had no alternative but starvation or the commission of crime."[28]

One alternative available to landlords unwilling or unable to aid their tenants was to evict them. During the course of the Famine, as rents went unpaid and poor law rates rose, a number of Mayo landlords removed unwanted tenants, often, in the words of one landlord, without giving "one damn where the people went to."[29] Many landlords faced with demands from family, creditors and poor rates to maintain pauper tenants felt they had no choice but to evict. By 1848 poor rates in the Ballina, Ballinrobe, Castlebar and Westport Poor Law Unions were between 3s. and 3s. 6d. per £1 valuation annually, while the rate in the Swinford Union was an exceptionally high 6s. 3d.[30] According to the law, landlords were responsible for the levy for all tenants whose holdings were valued at £4 or less. In Mayo, where 75 percent of all occupiers held land valued at £4 or less, the poor law rates were exceptionally burdensome, with many landlords having to pay the entire rate.[31] One consequence of this situation was an unwillingness or inability on the part of many landlords to pay the rates, leaving the union workhouses desperate for funds. Even the largest and most prosperous landholders in the county, the Marquis of Sligo and the Earl of Lucan, were unwilling or unable to pay their rates. In 1848 Lord Sligo owed £1648 in back rates to the Westport Union, although as noted above he did maintain the workhouse at his own expense. Lord Lucan owed £309 to the Westport Union

27 O. MacDonagh, "Irish Emigration to the United States of America and the British Colonies During the Famine," in Edwards and Williams (eds.), *The Great Famine*, pp. 361–2.

28 *Ibid.*, pp. 324–5; Woodham-Smith, *The Great Hunger*, pp. 376–7.

29 *Papers Relating to Proceedings for the Relief of the Distress and State of Unions and Workhouses, Sixth Series, 1848*, PP 1847–8 [955], lvi, p. 240.

30 *A Return in Continuation of Parliamentary Papers No. 311, . . . of the Valuation of Each Electoral Division in Ireland . . .*, PP 1849 (198), xlix, p. 244.

31 *A Return from the Poor Law Commissioners, Showing . . . Each Union in Ireland [and] . . . Each Electoral Division . . .*, PP 1846 (262), xxxvi, pp. 34–5.

and £692 to the Castlebar Union, with which he was involved in an acrimonious battle over the accuracy and justness of its demands upon him.[32]

Evicting pauper tenants was one means of easing one's liability for poor rates, much to the distress of poor law officials for whom the evicted tenants were an additional burden. For example, poor law commissioners were angered when John Walsh of Castlehill, Crossmolina, who was £63 18s. in arrears on his poor rates, evicted his tenants on the Mullet peninsula, thus compelling the Ballina union to assume their maintenance.[33] Undeterred by the anger of the commissioners, Walsh leaped into eviction with vigor. A few days before Christmas 1847 he employed a company of soldiers to protect his agent, son and shepherd as they went through his Mullet properties unroofing houses. Several days later, when he learned that many of his evicted tenants were sleeping in lean-tos or makeshift tents in the rubble of their former homes, he ordered his shepherd to destroy these shelters and force the tenants on the road. Some of those evicted told poor law inspectors of sleeping out in the open or under hay ricks, and of the death of family members from exposure since they could not gain admission to the overcrowded workhouse at Ballina.[34] Another Mullet landlord, Mr. Lyons, reportedly thought himself "deeply aggrieved by his tenantry" for their failure to pay their rent. He too evicted wholesale from his properties near Binghamstown.[35]

Many landlords shared the dilemma of the Marquis of Sligo, who postponed evicting tenants on his vast estate until late in 1848. He wrote to Lord Monteagle in October 1848 that he had not received any rents for three years and had to borrow £1500 in order to pay poor rates. He claimed to have "struggled hard not to eject" but was now "under the necessity of ejecting or being ejected . . ."[36] Lord Sligo later maintained that he evicted selectively in an effort to safeguard not only his interests but those of as many of his "honest" tenants as possible. His thinking is revealed in a letter he wrote to his cousin George Henry Moore in 1852. Moore, MP for Mayo, had been unwilling to evict any of his tenants during the Famine and continued to allow the subdivision of holdings on

[32] *Papers Relating to the Proceedings For Relief . . . Sixth Series, 1848*, pp. 543–7.
[33] *Ibid.*, p. 223.
[34] *Ibid.*, pp. 213, 218–19; Woodham-Smith, *The Great Hunger*, pp. 319–20.
[35] *Papers Relating to the Proceedings for Relief . . . Sixth Series, 1848*, pp. 219, 223.
[36] Lord Sligo to Monteagle, 8 Oct. 1848, Monteagle Papers. Quoted in Woodham-Smith, *The Great Hunger*, p. 364.

his estate. Sligo censured Moore for his "neglect to attend to the rent paying of [his] tenants." He went on:

> Here is a contrast between my estate and Sir Samuel's [O'Malley] and yours will be as Sir Samuel's case if you do not mind and however it may suit you to say that you did not sanction it – you must on reflection feel that the cause you follow is tending to exterminate your tenantry. Sir Samuel O'Malley's property in Chancery owed five or six years rent. It is in Kilmeera and the houses are being levelled till at least half are evicted or legally removed. In Clare Island it is contemplated to evict every soul.
>
> In Ld. Sligo's estate large evictions were carried out – but care was taken to select those who showed a desire to be honest – they were in all cases put back and though the really idle and dishonest are put off, the honest are freed from all and given a new fairly valued rent.
>
> In consequence ¾ of Sir Samuel's tenants will be put out and perhaps ¼ of Lord Sligo's. In each case the landlord is responsible . . . You will be a second Sir Samuel . . . you are morally bona fide the exterminator . . .
>
> In my heart's belief you and Sir Samuel do more ruin and injure and persecute and exterminate your tenants than any man in Mayo.
>
> You will disagree in toto – time will show who saves most of his tenants and most of his rents . . . [37]

According to press reports, Lord Sligo evicted large numbers of people in 1850–1, filing papers in Quarter Sessions showing rents in arrears from two to six years for those evicted.[38] Without access to the rent ledgers it is not possible to know whether these evictions and house levelings were carried out according to the principles set down in the letter to Moore.

The Earl of Lucan, Lord Lieutenant of County Mayo and the holder of 60,570 acres in the county, cleared away a large portion of his pauper tenants beginning in June 1848. Frequently Lucan, who reportedly said that he "would not breed paupers to pay priests," cleared entire townlands of tenants.[39] The incomplete Lucan rent ledgers for 1848–73 list 429 families "by arrears removed" or "by hanging gale removed"

---

[37] Quoted in J. Hone, *The Moores of Moore Hall* (London, 1939), pp. 158–60.

[38] *The Telegraph or Connaught Ranger*, 9 Jan. 1850, 22 Jan., 2 July, 19 Nov. 1851.

[39] *Ibid.*, 7, 21 June 1848; F. Dun, *Landlords and Tenants in Ireland* (London, 1881), p. 233.

between 1848 and 1851, with the greatest number of evictions occurring in November 1849.[40]

Often Lucan would convert the land from which tenants had been evicted from tillage to pasture for cattle and sheep and then either keep it in his own possession or lease it to large ranchers. Typical was the townland of Liscromwell, located in the lowlands a few miles from Castlebar in the parish of Aglish. Ten families were evicted from thirteen plots in May 1849 for a total arrears of £168 7s. 8½d. Six years later, at the time of the government valuation of land in Ireland, the townland of Liscromwell was held by the Earl of Lucan in fee with a shepherd's house as the only building.[41] In another instance, Lucan evicted 2000 people and leveled 300 houses between 1846 and 1849 in Ballinrobe parish, one of the richest grazing regions in Mayo. In 1856 he gave a twenty-five-year lease on this Cloona Castle estate to a Scottish farmer, James Simpson, for an annual rent of £2200.[42] In 1881 Simpson told the Richmond Commission investigating the depressed condition of Irish agriculture that before the Famine there were no large grazing farms such as his in the region, but that vast areas had been cleared during and immediately following the Famine. He said that the cleared tenants and their descendants "are now the pool for agricultural labourers" who "still pine for the land."[43]

Although accurate records on evictions were not kept until 1849, it is possible to derive a fair estimate from the records kept of ejectment decrees granted by the courts during the years 1846–8. As can be seen from Table 4.1, the number of evictions rose steadily from 1846 to 1848 and then rose sharply during 1849–50, remaining high until 1853, before beginning a sharp decline. Figure 4.1 demonstrates that this pattern was quite different from that for Connacht province or for Ireland as a whole. The rate of evictions in Mayo, when calculated per 1000 holdings, was

---

[40] "Hanging gale" refers to the practice of giving tenants a six-month grace period on payment of rents. This was a widespread practice on Irish estates. Public Record Office, Ireland (PROI), Business Records, Mayo 13, Lucan Rent Ledgers, 1848–73. In 1978 the original was in possession of Michael J. Egan, Castlebar, who kindly permitted me to use it prior to its filming by the PROI.

[41] *Ibid.*; *General Valuation of Rateable Property in Ireland, County Mayo, Valuation of the Several Tenements in the Union of Castlebar* (Dublin, 1857), p. 4. Hereafter referred to as *General Valuation*.

[42] Lucan Rent Ledgers; Dun, *Landlords and Tenants in Ireland*, p. 238; *Royal Commission on the Depressed Condition of the Agricultural Interest: Minutes of Evidence*, Vol. *I*, PP 1881 [C 2778-U], xv, p. 89. Hereafter cited as *Richmond Commission, Minutes of Evidence*.

[43] *Richmond Commission, Minutes of Evidence, I*, pp. 401–3.

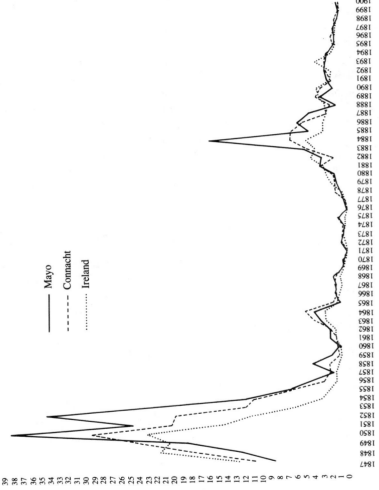

Figure 4.1. Evictions per 1000 holdings, 1847–1900

Table 4.1. *County Mayo evictions, 1846–1900*

Year	Families evicted	Families reinstated[a]	Evictions less reinstatements	Year	Families evicted	Families reinstated[a]	Evictions less reinstatements
1846	263	(39)	224	1874	157	(142)	15
1847	528	(79)	449	1875	66	(30)	36
1848	630	(95)	535	1876	12	(6)	6
1849	1115	420	695	1877	32	(16)	16
1850	1755	367	1388	1878	47	(20)	27
1851	1408	551	857	1879	77	(34)	43
1852	1329	208	1121	1880	106	56	50
1853	1017	232	839	1881	244	130	114
1854	474	71	403	1882	291	182	109
1855	516	273	243	1883	399	219	180
1856	164	14	150	1884	756	197	559
1857	67	2	65	1885	245	88	157
1858	178	26	152	1886	463	264	199
1859	73	0	73	1887	412	268	144
1860	44	2	42	1888	1210	1166	44
1861	100	19	81	1889	693	588	105
1862	106	24	82	1890	745	690	55
1863	117	0	117	1891	605	527	78
1864	180	36	144	1892	939	853	86
1865	37	0	37	1893	1286	1205	81
1866	83	26	57	1894	1028	952	76
1867	70	17	53	1895	713	668	45
1868	62	0	62	1896	1117	1071	46
1869	27	7	20	1897	591	539	52
1870	31	(18)	13	1898	556	525	31
1871	21	(17)	4	1899	855	827	28
1872	49	(22)	27	1900	419	385	34

Notes:

[a] At the discretion of their landlord, evicted tenants could be reinstated either as tenants or as caretakers who managed their former holdings for their landlord. Under the terms of Section 7 of the Land Act of 1887, tenants in arrears on their rent received a simple notice from their landlord, which reclassified the tenant as a caretaker until such time as he or she could pay up their rents, or be turned out of their holdings. This accounts for the sharp upswing in the number of formal evictions and reinstatements after 1887. See L. P. Curtis, Jr., *Coercion and Conciliation in Ireland, 1880–1882* (Princeton, NJ, 1963), p. 337.

( ) estimates. For explanation see Appendix 1.

Source: Returns compiled by Royal Irish Constabulary. See Appendix 1.

somewhat lower than the national and Connacht averages until 1850, but was substantially higher between 1851 and 1854.

One explanation for Mayo's somewhat lower level of Famine evictions was that many of the county's smallholders gave up their land as a prerequisite for obtaining relief. They did so under the provisions of the "Gregory" or "quarter acre" clause of the Irish Poor Relief Extension Act of 1847.[44] Named after William Gregory, MP for Dublin, who suggested it, the clause stipulated that any tenant holding land in excess of one-quarter acre was ineligible for relief. The vice-guardians of the Castlebar Union reported in 1848 that "many landlords are accepting surrenders from their small tenantry" so that they would be eligible for relief.[45] In some instances landlords followed the practice of Lord Oranmore or Sir Samuel O'Malley, who were willing to take formal surrenders of holdings from their tenants and then reinstate them as caretakers so they would be eligible for relief without losing their holdings.[46] In other cases landlords abused the provisions that allowed the tenant to retain his or her cottage by demanding the surrender of the house as well as the land and then having it demolished. In many instances tenants simply abandoned their holdings and ran for the emigrant ship without informing their landlords, so that the passage money would not be distrained for rent. As a result of these surrenders and abandonments, Mayo landlords were spared the need to go to court to obtain a decree for ejectment during the Famine. Only after the Famine had passed, and the surviving tenantry were beginning to recover, did Mayo landlords need to embark upon wholesale clearances through court proceedings.

These post-Famine clearances of pauper tenants from the land were, to a large degree, in response to rising livestock prices. Prices for livestock, especially for "store" cattle that were sold to other farmers for fattening, had risen at a faster rate than had prices for tillage crops from at least the 1830s, but this trend accelerated after the Famine. From a low point in 1850, the prices of cattle at the Ballinasloe October fair, the "greatest" fair in the west of Ireland, doubled by 1855 then continued to rise steadily at an average rate of £2 per year until 1880.[47] According to estimates appearing in *Thom's Irish Almanac*, beef prices at Ballina, Co. Mayo

---

[44]   10 and 11 Vict., c. 31, s. 10.

[45]   *Papers Relating to Proceedings For the Relief of Distress and State of the Unions and Workhouses in Ireland, Fifth Series, 1848*, PP 1847–8 [919], lv, p. 435.

[46]   *Papers Relating to Proceedings for the Relief of Distress . . . Seventh Series, 1848*, PP 1847–8 [999], liv, pp. 186–7.

[47]   R. M. Barrington, *Notes on the Prices of Irish Agricultural Produce: A Paper Read Before the Statistical and Social Inquiry Society of Ireland, Wednesday 1st March 1893* (Dublin, 1893), p. 4. For a discussion of the price rise, see: B. Solow, *The Land Question and the Irish Economy, 1870–1903* (Cambridge, Mass., 1971), pp. 94–7.

doubled between 1851 and 1876, rising from 35s. 5d. to 70s. per cwt. of 112 pounds. Mutton prices rose from 42s. 7½d. to 70s. per cwt. over the same period.[48] Grain prices fluctuated wildly after the Famine, wheat prices being 21 percent lower nationally in 1876 than in 1840. Oats, the principal grain crop grown in Mayo, rose 19 percent in price over the same years and 74 percent between the low point of 1851 and 1876.[49] In Ballina, according to the *Thom's* estimates, the price of oats rose 73 percent between 1851 and 1876, a substantial rise, but not one that could keep pace with the rise in livestock prices.[50]

The significance of this shift in prices away from tillage and towards livestock was not lost on "improving" landlords. Many hoped that after clearing their lands of insolvent small farmers they could guarantee their incomes by letting land to large graziers, hopefully from England or Scotland, who would be capable of making improvements on the land and working it profitably. Apparently English and Scottish farmers were anxious to settle in the west of Ireland. One estate agent estimated that in 1858 about 800 English and Scottish farmers held farms in Counties Galway and Mayo, with especially heavy concentrations in the regions of Newport, Westport and Hollymount in Mayo, and Tuam and Ballinasloe in Galway.[51]

In addition to clearances made by established landlords, who sought to increase the income from their estates, were those carried out by the purchasers of insolvent estates. In Mayo, as elsewhere in Ireland, large numbers of landed proprietors were tottering on the brink of insolvency prior to the Famine. Their inability to collect rents during the Famine destroyed many of them. Possibly one quarter of all Irish landlords were bankrupt or nearly so by 1848, with the number in the west probably substantially higher.[52] Under the terms of the Encumbered Estates Act of 1849 a special court was established to facilitate the purchase of bankrupt or financially weak Irish estates. The sponsors of the bill hoped

[48] *Thom's Irish Almanac and Official Directory for the Year 1880* (Dublin, 1880), p. 679.

[49] T. Barrington, "A Review of Irish Agricultural Prices," *Journal of the Statistical and Social Inquiry Society of Ireland*, 15 (1927), pp. 251–2.

[50] *Thom's 1880*, p. 679.

[51] T. Miller, *The Agricultural and Social State of Ireland in 1858*, pp. 7, 12. Reference from P. Lane, "The General Impact of the Encumbered Estates Act of 1849 on Counties Galway and Mayo," *Journal of the Galway Archaeological and Historical Society*, 33 (1972–3), pp. 66–7.

[52] J. S. Donnelly, Jr., *Landlord and Tenant in Nineteenth Century Ireland* (Dublin, 1973), p. 43.

that these estates would be bought by English and Scottish gentlemen who would possess the capital and the ability to bring about a vast improvement in the state of Irish agriculture. These hopes were never fulfilled as many of the purchasers were Irish who, anxious to realize a quick profit, cleared their newly acquired land and established grazing farms, thus driving up the rate of post-Famine evictions.[53]

DEMOGRAPHIC CHANGE IN POST-FAMINE MAYO

As was the case throughout Ireland, the Famine inaugurated a period of population decline in County Mayo that saw the population drop 27 percent between 1851 and 1901. This population loss was not distributed evenly throughout the county. The massive population loss during the Famine was heavier in central Mayo, the area designated above as the core, and lower in the periphery, especially the eastern periphery, where one parish, Kilmovee, actually experienced a 6 percent increase in population between 1841 and 1851. In a pattern that was to continue until the 1880s, the poorest regions of the county suffered less depopulation than did the more prosperous lowlands, as can be seen from a comparison of Maps 4.1 and 4.2. Between 1851 and 1881 many parishes that experienced the least population loss between 1841 and 1851 actually gained in population, despite a 10 percent drop for the county as a whole. All of the five parishes that lost 15 percent or less of their population between 1841 and 1851 gained population during the subsequent thirty years. Of the ten parishes that lost 15–25 percent of their population between 1841 and 1851, eight experienced a population gain by 1881. At the other extreme, all the parishes that experienced a depopulation in excess of 40 percent between 1841 and 1851 continued afterwards to decline in population, often at very high rates.

The salient components of Famine depopulation – death and emigration – were present throughout the county. It is impossible to isolate statistically one or the other of these factors on a regional basis, but it seems safe to assume that Famine mortality was the least likely of the two to contribute significantly to the regional variation in depopulation. At the time of the Famine all regions of Mayo contained a considerable number of people who were heavily dependent on the potato and who suffered severely when it failed. On the other hand,

[53] *Ibid.*, pp. 49–51; Lane, "The General Impact of the Encumbered Estates Act," pp. 44–51.

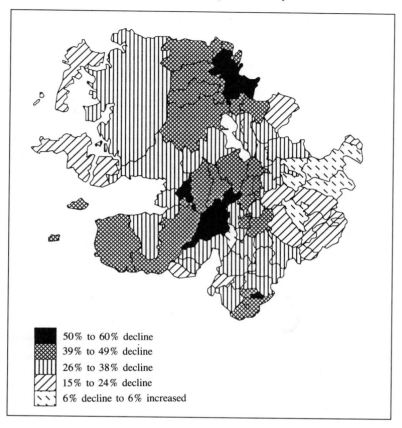

■ 50% to 60% decline
▨ 39% to 49% decline
‖ 26% to 38% decline
⁄ 15% to 24% decline
＼ 6% decline to 6% increased

Map 4.1. Rural population change, 1841–1851, by parish, County Mayo. Source: *The Census of Ireland 1851, Part 1*, pp. 455–513. Note: Populations of the towns of Ballina, Killala, Westport, Hollymount, Cong, Castlebar and Ballinrobe excluded.

emigration, at least that forced by eviction, may have accounted for the heavy depopulation from the fertile lowlands. This was the area where there was the greatest incentive for landlords to clear the land of tenants and amalgamate holdings into large grazing farms. Although none of the poor law unions for which statistics on farm sizes were compiled in 1847 consisted entirely of good quality lowland, Ballinrobe had a larger share than any other union in Mayo. During the Famine the union was ravaged by death and evictions, especially in 1848, compelling *The Telegraph or Connaught Ranger* to compare its fate to that of Skibereen in County

Table 4.2. *Population of County Mayo, 1851–1901*

Year	Males	Females	Total	Percentage change
1851	133,264	141,235	274,499	
1861	125,636	129,160	254,796	−7.18
1871	120,877	125,153	246,030	−3.44
1881	119,421	125,791	245,212	−0.33
1891	107,498	111,536	219,034	−10.68
1901	97,564	101,602	199,166	−9.07

Source: W. E. Vaughan and A. J. Fitzpatrick (eds.), *Irish Historical Statistics: Population, 1821–1971* (Dublin, 1978), p. 14.

Cork.[54] The effect of Famine evictions in the union is evident when comparing farm size in 1847 and in 1851. Between those years the number of farms of 15 acres or less fell from 75 to 61 percent, while the median size of farms rose from 17 to 26 acres.[55] This was the pattern in all poor law unions whose territory included portions of the central lowlands. It appears that many of the families displaced by the evictions that made the amalgamation of holdings possible took to the emigration ships or migrated elsewhere in Ireland or to Britain.

Famine depopulation was lowest in the eastern periphery, especially in the Swinford union, which comprised much of the eastern portion of the county. Cousens has argued that regions such as that comprising the Swinford union were spared excessive Famine depopulation and experienced population growth after 1851 due in large part to the availability of wasteland that could be reclaimed and converted into smallholdings for people who would otherwise be compelled to emigrate.[56] According to the commissioners of the 1851 census, Mayo had the largest area of unclaimed wasteland of any county in Ireland. The commissioners estimated that between 1841 and 1851, 10.9 percent of that wasteland had been reclaimed, lowering the proportion of such land

[54] *The Telegraph or Connaught Ranger*, 7 June 1848, 3 Jan. 1849.
[55] In order to create four new unions for County Mayo, the poor law unions were reorganized in 1850. The eastern portion of the Ballinrobe union was separated off to form the Claremorris union. For purposes of comparison, the figures for 1851 include both the Ballinrobe and Claremorris unions. The 1851 figure for the Ballinrobe union as it was constituted in 1851 shows a drop in the proportion of holdings 15 acres or less to 64 percent and a rise in the median size of holdings to 30 acres. See Table 4.6, pp. 137–8 below.
[56] S. H. Cousens, "Emigration and Demographic Change in Ireland, 1851–1861," *Econ. Hist. Rev.*, 2nd series, 14 (1961), pp. 278–88.

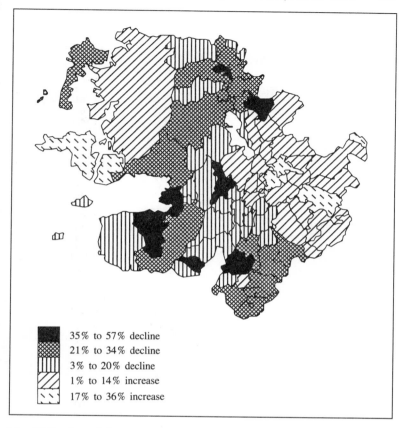

35% to 57% decline
21% to 34% decline
3% to 20% decline
1% to 14% increase
17% to 36% increase

Map 4.2. Rural population change, 1851–1881, by parish, County Mayo. Source: *The Census of Ireland 1881, Part 1, vol. 3*, pp. 285–353. Note: Populations of the towns of Ballina, Killala, Westport, Hollymount, Cong, Castlebar and Ballinrobe excluded.

in the county from 58.8 percent to 47.68 percent.[57] In 1845 R. Griffith, the General Valuation Commissioner for Ireland, estimated for the Devon Commission that 58.7 percent of the land of Mayo was unclaimed. Comparing Griffith's estimate with that contained in the 1841 census would indicate that little reclamation had gone on between 1841 and 1845, when the population of the county was rising.[58] Rather,

[57] *Census of Ireland, 1851: General Report*, pp. x–xii.
[58] *Devon Commission Report*, PP 1845 [605], xix, p. 51.

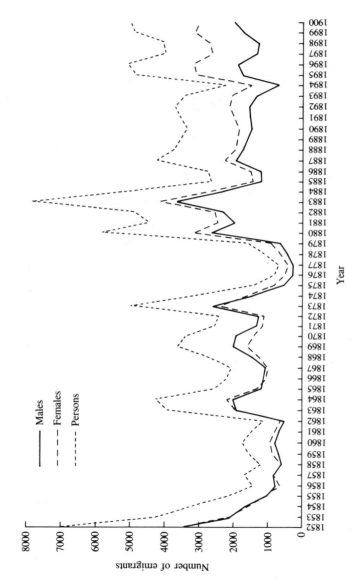

Figure 4.2. Emigration, County Mayo, 1852–1900

the bulk of the decennial reclamation appears to have occurred during the Famine, when it would seem improbable that a starving population would have much time or energy for clearing and draining new lands. This was the assumption of K. H. Connell in his study of the reclamation of waste land in Ireland:

> When starvation was almost universal, it can hardly be supposed that the peasants had either the resources or the incentive to drain mountain and bog as never before. And, moreover, when death and emigration caused neighbors to vacate their holdings it is unlikely that the need to clear fresh land seemed as urgent as in former years.[59]

Yet, in eastern Mayo land was reclaimed during the Famine and it seems reasonable to suggest that the people doing the reclamation had been evicted from land in the more fertile lowlands. In eastern Mayo they found land of marginal quality that held little incentive for landlord-initiated consolidation. The result was low Famine depopulation and rapid repopulation during the following decades.[60]

The regional variations in levels of population growth and decline in post-Famine Mayo were further reinforced by differing levels of natural increase (i.e., excess births over deaths) within the county. Between 1861 and 1871 the rate of natural increase in Mayo, when calculated by poor law union, varied from 12–15 percent in the central and northwestern sections of the county to 16–19 percent in the east and in the parishes of Achill and Burrishoole in the west. Between 1871 and 1881 all of eastern and western Mayo had rates of 12–15 percent, while the rate in the central strip fell to between 8 and 11 percent.[61] By 1901 the division was even sharper. Between 1891 and 1901 the poor law unions that included portions of central Mayo had levels of natural increase ranging from 5.1 percent in the Ballinrobe union to 7.5 percent in the Ballina union, while the Belmullet and Westport unions had rates of 11.3 percent and 9.5 percent respectively. In the unions of east Mayo, Swinford had a rate of 9.3 percent and Claremorris a rate of 9 percent.[62]

The decline in the number of births that characterized post-Famine

[59] K. H. Connell, "The Colonization of Waste Land in Ireland, 1780–1845," *Econ. Hist. Rev.*, 2nd series, 2 (1950), p. 48.

[60] Cousens, "Emigration and Demographic Change," p. 280.

[61] S. H. Cousens, "The Regional Variations in Population Changes in Ireland, 1861–1881," *Econ. Hist. Rev.*, 2nd series, 17 (1964), pp. 306, 314.

[62] *The Census of Ireland for the Year 1901, Part I: Area, Houses and Population: Also the Ages, Civil or Conjugal Condition, Occupations, Birthplaces, Religion and Education of the People, Vol. IV, Province of Connaught, No. 3, County of Mayo*, PP 1902 [Cd. 1059-II], cxviii, p. 104.

Ireland is generally attributed to a rise in the age of marriage, an increase in the number of people not marrying, and the high rate of emigration of potential parents.[63] Prior to the Famine, marriage patterns tended to be conditioned by the ease with which land on many estates could be subdivided among all heirs and by the potato, which enabled a large family to be fed on a small parcel of land. In impoverished counties such as Mayo, where land was easily subdivided and where the practice of impartible inheritance of land had not yet found acceptance, there were few restraints to early marriages since the new couple would have little difficulty obtaining a potato patch. Stemming from the work of K. H. Connell, it has long been accepted by Irish historians that the practice of early and frequent marriages was the norm throughout pre-Famine Ireland.[64] However, recent research has demonstrated that O'Connell's analysis of pre-Famine marriages failed to account for the complexity of a rapidly changing set of practices. It now seems certain that many farmers, especially the more substantial ones who tended to be clustered in the wealthier eastern and central regions of Ireland, were engaged in complex and carefully calculated marriage and inheritance practices prior to the Famine that established stringent terms over the possibility and the timing of marriage. S. J. Connolly suggests that future research on pre-Famine marriage in Ireland might

> reveal the existence of two groups within the farming community: a minority of larger occupiers, among whom marriage was postponed almost or entirely as long as it was to be in post-Famine Ireland, and a larger group of small farmers, deeply concerned with the implications of marriage for the orderly transfer of property from one generation to the next, but nevertheless willing to subdivide the family holding in order to allow their sons to marry while still in their twenties.[65]

Such a division of marriage practices was noted in pre-Famine Mayo in 1825. In testimony before a parliamentary committee the Catholic

---

63 For discussions of Irish demographic history during the nineteenth century, see: B. M. Walsh, "A Perspective on Irish Population Patterns," *Eire–Ireland*, 4 (1969), pp. 3–21; K. H. Connell, "Land and Population in Ireland, 1780–1845," *Econ. Hist. Rev.*, 2nd series, 2 (1950), pp. 278–89; K. H. Connell, "Peasant Marriage in Ireland: Its Structure and Development Since the Famine," *Econ. Hist. Rev.*, 2nd series, 14 (1962), pp. 502–33; Lee, *Modernisation of Irish Society*, pp. 1–9. For a brief discussion of regional differences in depopulation in Mayo, see: Almquist, "Mayo and Beyond," pp. 239-42.

64 K. H. Connell, *The Population of Ireland, 1750–1845*.

65 S. J. Connolly, "Marriage in Pre-Famine Ireland," in A. Cosgrove (ed.), *Marriage in Ireland* (Dublin, 1985), p. 83.

Archbishop of Tuam, Oliver Kelly, reported that among the more prosperous farmer/weavers in the vicinity of Westport and Newport there was "an indisposition . . . to contract improvident marriages." He continued:

> I did observe that in those prosperous districts the marriages were not so frequent as I found them in the more impoverished districts . . . I have perfectly on my recollection that the circumstance [in the prosperous districts] struck me at the time, and that I did inquire amongst the people how it happened; and the reply I received was that they had no idea of entering into the matrimonial state until they could acquire a competency for their own support, and the support of a family. In other parts of the country, where I observed very considerable poverty, I found a greater indifference about their future comforts than among persons in a more prosperous situation in life.[66]

For the majority of Mayo's small farmers the lack of hope for an improved future combined with few restraints on the subdivision of holdings and the survival of the rundale system, meant there was little incentive to limit marriage or to impose lofty financial expectations on it. A Catholic curate, speaking in 1836 before a royal commission, summed up the beliefs of many of the county's smallholders when he reported that they were "induced to marry by feeling that their condition cannot be made much worse, or, rather, they know they can lose nothing, and they promise themselves some pleasure in the society of a wife."[67]

The near elimination of rundale and the gradual increase in the median size of holdings following the Famine brought a slow transformation of marriage practices in rural Mayo, although as David Fitzpatrick has recently noted, farmers in the West tended to marry younger and in larger numbers than their counterparts in the east until the last third of the nineteenth century.[68] One consequence of the Famine, in Mayo as elsewhere, was that there was a larger proportion of farmers who were more likely to engage inrestrictive marriage practices. As Lee has noted, "a disproportionate number of Famine survivors belonged to classes with above average age at marriage . . . Even had age at marriage remained unchanged within social groups, the reduction in the proportion of earlier marrying strata would have raised average age at marriage."[69]

---

[66] *Second Report from the Committee on the State of Ireland, 1825*, p. 247.
[67] *Poor Inquiry (Ireland), Appendix (F)*, p. 43.
[68] David Fitzpatrick, "Marriage in Post-Famine Ireland," in Cosgrave (ed.), *Marriage in Ireland*, pp. 117–20.
[69] Lee, *Modernisation of Irish Society*, p. 4.

In this new environment it became increasingly the norm for the timing of marriage and the choice of a partner to be controlled by parents who were concerned above all with the commercial advantages of the marriage. Encouraged by the unwillingness of many post-Famine landlords to countenance the further subdivision of their land and by their own heightened expectations, the prime concern of many parents was to preserve the farm intact by leaving it in its entirety to one heir and to provide a dowry to allow at least one daughter to marry well. To the male heir, not necessarily the eldest son, fell the privilege of marrying. The landless sons were left either to emigrate or to remain celibate since, without land, marriage was improbable. Even the inheriting son was often prevented from marrying until he came into the land on or near the death of his parents. The pattern was similar for daughters, with the one chosen or willing to marry into a neighboring farm family being provided with a suitable dowry while her sisters were left to emigrate or remain unmarried. Marriage negotiations were protracted, parents of potential brides being concerned primarily with assurances of when and under what circumstances their prospective son-in-law would come into the land. Parents of potential grooms were equally concerned with the amount of cash, stock and/or land that their prospective daughter-in-law's dowry contained. Frequently, the couple had little or no say in these matters.[70]

One consequence of these restrictive marriage practices was an increase in celibacy, although its spread was slower in the west than in the east.[71] Two frequently employed indices of late and infrequent marriage are the proportion of young men and women who are married and the proportion of fertile adults who never marry.[72] As can be seen from Figure 4.3, the proportion of married young men and women fell in Mayo from 1871, while the percentage of fertile adults who never married rose steadily. The figures indicate that the restrictive marriage practices associated with the post-Famine period began to have a significant impact in Mayo after 1871. Brendan Walsh has calculated that the marriage rate per 1000 single women fell more rapidly in Mayo after 1871 than in any county in Ireland. At the same time, according to Walsh's figures, the fertility rate (children under 1 year of age per 1000

---

[70] Fitzpatrick, "Marriage in Post-Famine Ireland," pp. 116–29.

[71] *Ibid.*, pp. 117–18.

[72] Cousens, "The Regional Variations in Population," pp. 315–18; B. Walsh, "Marriage Rates and Population Pressure: Ireland, 1871 and 1911," *Econ. Hist. Rev.*, 2nd series, 23 (1970), pp. 148, 151.

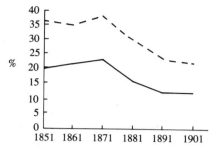

A. Proportion of those between 15 and 34 years
of age who were married

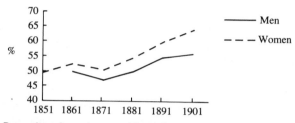

B. Proportion of men between 15 and 64 and women
between 15 and 44 who never married

Figure 4.3. Proportions of single and married in some age categories, County Mayo, 1851–1901. Source: *Census of Ireland, 1851, Part VI*, p. 577; *Census of Ireland, 1861, Part V*, p. 419; *Census of Ireland, 1871, Part II, Vol. IV, No. 3*, pp. 361–3; *Census of Ireland, 1881, Part I, Vol. IV, No. 3*, pp. 361–2; *Census of Ireland, 1891, Part I, Vol. IV, No. 3*, pp. 361–2; *Census of Ireland, 1901, Part I, Vol. IV, No. 3*, pp. 108–9

women aged 15–45) in the west remained high despite a national downward trend. Walsh charts a demographic transition between 1871 and 1911 in which the west of Ireland was transformed from a region with high marriage and fertility rates to one with a low marriage level but continued high fertility and argues that a primary cause of this transformation was the desire on the part of Mayo's farmers to secure higher living standards by reducing the population pressure on the land. With fertility within marriage remaining high, Walsh argues that restraining from marriage was an accepted means of controlling the population.[73]

Surprisingly, the indices of age and frequency of marriage do not show

[73] Walsh, "Marriage Rates and Population Pressure," pp. 148–62.

a wide diversity between the core and the peripheral areas of County Mayo. As indicated in Figure 4.4, in 1871, when the census first contains breakdowns of age and conjugal status by poor law union, the Ballinrobe and Swinford unions were roughly equivalent in both the proportion of young men and women who were married and the proportion of fertile adults who were not married. Until 1891 both unions followed similar paths in the decline in the number of young adults who were married and the rise in the number of celibates. Yet, by 1901 the two unions were experiencing quite different marriage patterns as the Swinford union reversed course and drifted back to early and frequent marriages.

From these indices it would appear that there was very little difference between the marriage patterns in the center and the periphery during the last third of the nineteenth century. However, when the marriage rate (marriages per 1000 population) of the two unions is compared, a wide divergence appears. In 1864, at the time of the first registration of marriages, births and deaths, the Swinford union had a marriage rate of 6.3 while the Ballinrobe union had one of 2.95. These were respectively the highest and lowest rates in the county, with the county average being 4.6. However, by the beginning of the twentieth century the marriage rate in the two unions had converged. In 1901 the rates were 4.5 for the Swinford union, 3.5 for the Ballinrobe union and 3.9 for the county of Mayo.[74]

The explanation for the seeming disparity between the two indices is most probably found in differences in the rate of emigration between the core and the periphery within County Mayo. While the emigration statistics do not reveal the districts within the county from which emigrants departed, it seems probable that by the 1870s, if not earlier, Mayo's high number of emigrants came to a large degree from the poorest regions of the county, in contrast to the situation during the Famine. Walsh theorizes that by the 1870s population growth had resulted in a scarcity of land in those regions that experienced growth during the thirty years following the Famine.[75] As a consequence of this new land shortage, subdivision of holdings slowed down, less new land

---

[74] *First Annual Report of the Registrar General of Marriages, Births, and Deaths in Ireland, 1864*, PP 1868–9 [4137], xvi, pp. 46, 50; *Thirty-Eighth Detailed Annual Report of the Registrar General (Ireland), Containing a General Abstract of the Number of Marriages, Births and Deaths Registered in Ireland During the Year 1901*, PP 1902 [Cd. 1225], xviii, pp. 40, 46.

[75] Walsh, "Marriage Rates and Population Pressure," pp. 158–9.

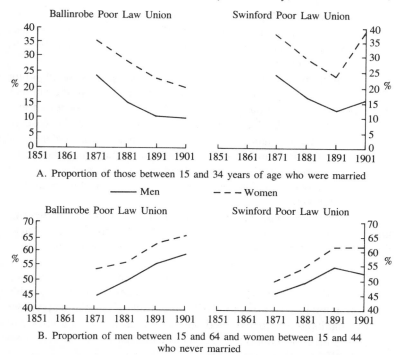

Figure 4.4. Proportions of single and married in some age categories in the Ballinrobe and Swinford Poor Law Unions. Source: Same as for Figure 4.3

was available, and many people who would have stayed in Mayo had land been available, opted to go to America.

In the Swinford union the number of men aged between 15 and 34, which had risen steadily from 1851 to 1881, fell from 6909 in 1881 to 6562 in 1901. Over the same period the number of women in this age bracket fell more sharply from 8893 to 7823 due to the substantially higher rate of emigration among women.[76] The growing divergence in the emigration rate of men and women after 1888 no doubt contributed to the sharp upswing in the percentage of women aged between 15 and 34 in 1901 who were married, as fewer young women were available to

[76] *The Census of Ireland for the Year 1881, Part I: Area, Houses, and Population, Vol. III, Province of Connaught, No. 3, County of Mayo,* PP 1882 [C 3268-III], lxxix, p. 362; *Census of Ireland, 1901, Part I, Vol. IV, No. 3,* p. 109.

marry. Similarly, the slight rise in the proportion of married men can also be attributed to emigration, since with the departure of the landless young men the proportion of men with access to land and thus to marriage would increase.

In the Ballinrobe union the gradual decline in the proportion of young men and women who were married and the gradual rise in the number of celibates continued unabated from 1871 to 1901. This occurred less from a scarcity of land due to overpopulation, as was the case in the Swinford union, than from the slow but steady consolidation of holdings in the Ballinrobe union. These consolidations limited the amount of land available for new families as market-oriented and aggressive farmers took up the farms of their less fortunate or less resolute neighbors.

Although by the end of the century marriage patterns in the two unions, representing Mayo's core and periphery, had coalesced to a large degree and conformed to the national pattern of late and infrequent marriages with many left celibate, the reasons for this change were significantly different in the two regions. Among small farmers, concentrated in but not exclusive to the periphery, the demographic transformation began during the 1870s as a result of population pressure on the smallholdings that limited land available to new families and compelled many to emigrate. It is significant that small farmers were driven to abandon their marriage traditions in order to preserve a share of the small farm economy for the fortunate few who could secure land. In contrast, the more prosperous farmers clustered on the good land of central Mayo adopted prudent marriage practices that were calculated to increase the size of their holdings and to better capitalize on the dynamic post-Famine livestock economy.

THE POST-FAMINE LIVESTOCK ECONOMY

The Famine inaugurated a process whereby old patterns of land use and settlement were replaced by new ones revolving around the grazing of cattle and sheep on compact holdings held by individual farmers. This process had its origins in pre-Famine Mayo, but the pace of change accelerated following the Famine. Between 1847, the first year for which reliable statistics are available, and 1851, the number of cattle in Mayo rose from 79,148 to 116,930. There were 173,596 cattle in 1876 and 191,497 in 1900, representing an increase of 142 percent over the fifty-three years. The number of sheep rose 225 percent over the same years.

In order to graze this livestock, the amount of land in Mayo devoted to grass, meadow and clover increased from 485,651 statute acres in 1851, or 38.8 percent of the total acreage in the county, to 595,843 acres, or 44.9 percent of the total in 1900. During the same period, the proportion of acres that was devoted to crops declined from 10.6 percent to 7.2 percent, while the proportion of wasteland declined from 50.6 percent of the county's acreage to 47.9 percent.[77]

This massive growth in the number of livestock was not limited to the richer grazing land of central Mayo, but affected all regions in the county, as both small and larger-sized farmers attempted to take advantage of the buoyant prices. However, the process of conversion from tillage to grazing was most rapid in the lowlands where quality grass farms were easily established. As can be seen from Maps 4.3 and 4.4, the central corridor contained the best quality land with the highest government valuation.[78] In 1881 the valuation of land in the parishes comprising the central corridor was often in excess of 10s. per acre, while the parishes in the western periphery were consistently under 3s. and those in the eastern periphery were rarely above 5s. per acre. Tables 4.3 and 4.4 illustrate that between 1851 and 1876 the increase in the number of acres under grass, meadow and clover in those poor law unions that contained large portions of the more fertile center (Ballina, Killala, Ballinrobe) was achieved by converting crop and waste land to grazing tracts.

The most marked example was the Ballinrobe union, containing the best grassland in Mayo, where the proportion of land under crops fell

---

[77] See Tables 4.3, 4.4, 4.5.

[78] The government valuation of Ireland (Griffith's Valuation) was compiled between 1852 and 1865 by Sir Richard Griffith and a well-trained team of valuers. It was carried out in response to an act of parliament providing for a valuation of all tenancies in Ireland, which could be used for assessing county rates, poor rates and income taxes. The rental value of each holding was arrived at after a careful examination of the soil, fertility, climate and proximity to markets. Based upon these variables, a market price of an estimated yield of crops and stock was arrived at and a rental value was fixed. The valuation was never updated and estimates are that by the late 1870s it was 20–33 percent below the market value of the land. Nonetheless, the valuation was considered by Irish tenant farmers as a fair rental and any rents above the valuation were considered excessive. For a discussion of the valuation and the controversies surrounding it see: Solow, *The Land Question and the Irish Economy*, pp. 58–68 and W. E. Vaughan, "A Study of Landlord and Tenant Relations in Ireland Between the Famine and the Land War, 1850–78," (Trinity College, Dublin University, Ph.D. thesis, 1974), pp. 371–5. I wish to thank Dr. Vaughan for kindly granting me permission to read his thesis in the Trinity College Library.

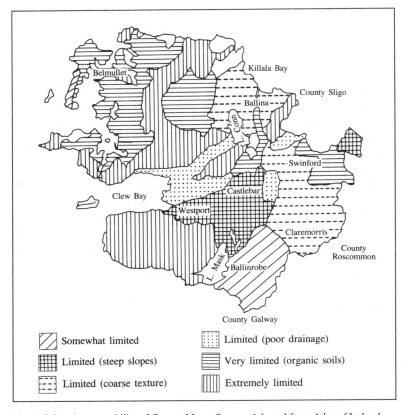

Map 4.3. Land use capability of County Mayo. Source: Adapted from *Atlas of Ireland*, p. 28

16.9 percent and the proportion of waste land fell 24.1 percent. Since the Ballinrobe union suffered a high rate of depopulation during the Famine, no doubt much of the land listed as waste in 1851 had been cropped prior to the Famine, making the conversion to grass at the expense of cropland even more extreme than the 1851 figures indicate. As Table 4.6 illustrates, the median farm size in the Ballinrobe union increased from 17 to 26.6 acres between 1847 and 1876. In sharp contrast is the Swinford union on Mayo eastern periphery where subdivision rather than consolidation of holdings remained the norm until the twentieth century. Both before and after the Famine the Swinford union had the lowest

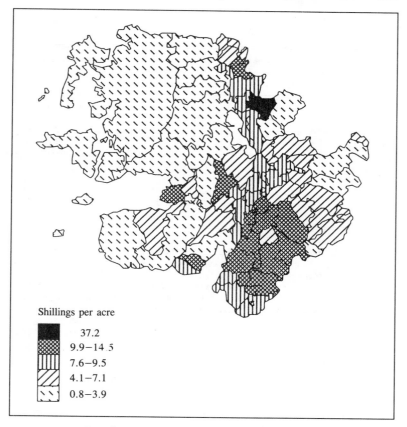

Map 4.4. Valuation of land, 1881, by parish, County Mayo (shillings per acre). Source: *The Census of Ireland, 1881, part 1: area, houses and population, vol. III, province of Connaught, no. 3, County Mayo*, pp. 285–353

median farm size and the highest proportion of farms at 15 acres or less in Mayo. Although the median size of holdings increased county-wide after 1847, the most sizeable increases occurred in those poor law unions that contained the county's best land. The process of conversion of the land in the center was especially rapid during and immediately following the Famine when evictions moved people from good land in the center to poor land on the periphery.[79] In addition, efforts by landlords to eliminate

[79] *Richmond Commission, Minutes of Evidence, I*, p. 103.

Table 4.3. *Proportion of land under crops, grass and waste in County Mayo in 1851, 1876 and 1900, by Poor Law Union*[a] *(percent)*

	Area under crops			Area under grass			Area under waste		
	1851	1876	1900	1851	1876	1900	1851	1876	1900
Mayo	10.6	11.1	7.2	38.8	42.3	44.9	50.6	46.6	47.9
Poor Law Unions									
Ballina	14.7	13.2	8.2	33.3	38.3	42.4	52.3	48.5	49.6
Ballinrobe	15.9	13.2	8.9	47.5	58.3	60.9	37.0	27.1	30.2
Belmullet	4.2	5.0	3.7	29.4	13.9	18.5	63.6	81.2	77.7
Castlebar	12.2	12.8	8.0	45.0	53.0	57.6	42.9	34.2	34.6
Claremorris	21.0	20.9	14.0	54.0	61.5	65.8	25.1	17.6	20.2
Killala	7.3	6.6	4.4	25.2	33.9	37.4	67.5	60.0	58.1
Swinford	19.7	20.7	12.8	36.8	50.7	64.3	43.5	28.6	23.0
Newport/Westport	5.3	5.5	3.9	30.8	40.0	34.7	63.9	54.8	61.4

Notes and sources:
[a] *The Census of Ireland for the Year 1851, Pt. II, Returns of Agricultural Produce in 1851*, PP 1852–3 [1589], xciii, pp. xxi–xxii, xxx, 36, 44, 92, 134, 162, 329, 473, 560, 613, 673; *Agricultural Statistics of Ireland for the Year 1876*, PP 1877 [C. 1749], lxxxv, pp. 34–7, 44; *Agricultural Statistics of Ireland, with Detailed Reports for the Year 1900*, PP 1901 [Cd. 557], lxxxviii, pp. 27–9, 58–9, 74–5. Grass includes land listed in the *Agricultural Statistics* as meadow, clover and grass. Waste includes all non-urban land not listed as either crops or grass. This includes land listed as fallow, woods and plantations, bogs and marsh, barren mountain and water. The Newport and Westport unions were combined after 1876.

Table 4.4. *Percentage of change in land use in County Mayo, 1851–1876 and 1876–1900, by Poor Law Union*

	Change in area under crops		Change in area under grass		Change in area under waste	
	1851–76	1876–1900	1851–76	1876–1900	1851–76	1876–1900
Mayo	4.6	−34.3	14.9	6.8	−8.5	3.6
Poor Law Unions						
Ballina	−10.2	−38.2	16.1	10.3	−7.3	2.3
Ballinrobe	−16.9	−32.5	22.8	4.7	−24.1	8.0
Belmullet	20.7	−26.2	−52.8	33.3	28.4	9.3
Castlebar	−2.0	−37.3	9.4	8.7	−26.1	2.6
Claremorris	−1.0	−33.1	14.1	7.1	−30.0	14.9
Killala	−10.4	−32.7	34.7	10.5	−11.8	−2.4
Swinford	4.9	−38.3	37.9	25.8	−34.2	−20.6
Newport/Westport	7.4	−28.5	32.9	−12.6	−11.5	12.1

Notes and sources: Same as Table 4.3.

Table 4.5. *Percentage increase in number of cattle and sheep in County Mayo, 1851–1876 and 1876–1900, by Poor Law Union*

	Cattle		Sheep	
	1851–76	1876–1900	1851–76	1876–1900
Mayo	48.5	10.3	126.3	30.6
Poor Law Unions				
Ballina	43.9	8.3	98.6	48.5
Ballinrobe	40.8	42.5	106.5	29.7
Belmullet	36.8	9.3	79.1	59.2
Castlebar	60.2	6.3	163.5	33.1
Claremorris	58.6	7.2	110.6	10.5
Killala	32.0	0.0	20.0	52.1
Swinford	45.7	7.3	189.4	4.2
Newport/Westport	53.6	8.7	94.0	91.2

Notes and sources: Same as Table 4.3.

the last vestiges of the rundale system furthered the process of consolidation of holdings.[80]

By 1879 approximately 14 percent of all farmers in Mayo held land in excess of 50 acres. Roughly 40 percent of these farmers held land of little value in the mountains and bogs of Western Mayo, while another 25 percent held marginal land along the eastern border of the county. This left roughly 1750 farmers, or 5 percent of all occupiers of agricultural land in Mayo, who farmed sizeable holdings in the central corridor and who could lay claim to being called medium or large-sized farmers in terms of both the amount of land they held and its quality.[81] They were the only tenant farmers in Mayo who could truly afford to work their land to its full potential by improving the land and stocking it with quality animals. James Simpson, the largest tenant farmer in the county, told the Richmond Commission that good quality stock could only be produced on improved land. He had a 3000 acre farm on the plains of Mayo in the Ballinrobe union that in 1862 he stocked with 1300 ewes, 1400 lambs, 150 bullocks and heifers, and 200 store cattle.[82] He estimated that it took £5 to £6 per acre to lay down grass seed, drain and fence good quality land such as his in order to prepare it for producing good stock that could

[80] Jordan, "Land and Politics in the West of Ireland: County Mayo, 1846–82," pp. 101–4.
[81] *The Agricultural Statistics of Ireland for the Year 1879*, PP 1880 [C 2534], lxxvi, p. 9.
[82] H. Coulter, *The West of Ireland: Its Existing Condition and Prospects* (Dublin, 1862), p. 174. Store cattle were young cattle that would be sold to others for fattening.

Table 4.6. *Proportion of holdings of various sizes in County Mayo, by Poor Law Unions*

	1 acre or less %	1–5 acres %	5–15 acres %	15–30 acres %	30–50 acres %	50–100 acres %	100–200 acres %	200–500 acres %	500+ acres %	Total number of holdings	Median holding in acres
Mayo											
1847	4.4	19.5	44.5	18.6	13.0					53,003	
1851	2.9	14.2	44.0	23.4	15.4					34,810	
1876	5.7	12.7	42.6	25.1	6.7	3.6	1.8	1.2	0.5	37,026	24.3
1900	5.8	9.6	41.8	26.3	8.0	4.7	2.1	1.3	0.5	36,341	30.2
Poor Law Unions											
Ballina											
1847	3.0	28.5	44.0	16.1	5.3	1.5	1.0	0.3	0.2		16.6
1851	1.5	12.2	47.2	24.6	5.6	3.8	3.4	1.4	0.3	4025	29.2
1876	11.9	7.2	41.5	23.6	7.0	4.5	2.8	1.2	0.3	4297	27.1
1900	8.8	7.4	39.6	25.5	8.1	5.5	3.0	1.8	0.3	4170	31.1
Ballinrobe											
1847	5.6	32.6	36.9	12.0	7.0	3.2	1.9	0.6	0.2		17.0
1851	4.7	20.9	38.3	18.3	6.9	5.3	3.5	1.9	0.2	4416	29.9
1876	11.0	15.0	36.0	23.5	6.0	4.3	2.3	1.5	0.3	4775	26.6
1900	11.9	12.3	37.6	22.7	7.0	4.4	2.3	1.6	0.3	4827	27.5
Belmullet											
1851	2.0	18.6	28.0	18.1	10.0	9.3	5.9	6.0	2.1	2125	68.8
1876	1.4	31.5	42.0	12.8	3.0	2.3	2.1	3.1	1.8	2503	43.0
1900	2.2	10.0	48.5	17.2	6.2	7.7	3.4	2.8	2.0	2254	52.4
Castlebar											
1847	3.1	15.9	46.2	20.2	10.3	3.0	1.0	0.2	0.1		19.4
1851	2.1	15.3	44.0	22.3	7.4	4.8	2.2	1.3	0.2	4532	26.0
1876	6.4	9.8	45.5	24.0	7.3	3.8	1.8	1.2	0.1	5007	24.2
1900	4.8	8.5	44.1	27.1	7.5	4.9	2.0	1.0	0.1	4954	24.9

Claremorris											
1851	2.2	9.7	46.2	29.2	7.0	2.7	1.4	0.8	0.1	4437	22.5
1876	4.1	8.9	41.7	30.5	8.2	4.4	1.5	0.8	0.0	4661	23.3
1900	3.2	7.0	41.9	31.0	9.8	4.6	1.7	0.8	0.0	4510	24.5
Killala											
1851	0.7	17.9	35.3	24.1	7.9	4.8	4.1	3.9	1.2	1550	48.4
1876	8.8	6.8	29.7	28.1	11.4	6.8	3.6	3.1	1.8	1735	53.5
1900	8.1	7.9	28.2	27.8	11.4	8.6	3.2	3.1	1.6	1579	52.6
Newport											
1851	6.2	12.9	29.7	21.0	13.4	11.5	1.8	1.2	2.2	1972	50.9
1876	3.6	36.3	32.5	14.0	6.2	3.7	1.2	0.8	1.7	2657	33.9
Swinford											
1847	7.7	18.8	55.9	13.8	2.6	0.7	0.3	0.1	0.0		11.5
1851	2.5	12.2	55.7	23.5	3.7	1.6	0.5	0.2	0.0	7136	15.4
1876	5.1	6.5	51.0	29.9	5.1	1.5	0.4	0.2	0.0	8259	16.9
1900	2.7	6.5	51.0	31.4	5.9	1.5	0.5	0.2	0.0	7888	17.5
Westport											
1847	7.0	44.7	29.8	7.8	4.8	2.6	2.3	0.4	0.5		19.4
1851	3.4	13.3	41.1	23.5	7.8	5.9	3.1	1.3	0.5	4116	31.6
1876	5.9	11.7	40.1	22.8	8.9	4.7	2.9	1.6	1.5	3416	41.1
1900	2.1	16.1	33.4	21.7	10.2	5.9	3.1	1.6	1.5	6159	42.4

Notes and sources: Returns of Agricultural Produce in Ireland in the Year 1848, PP 1849 [1116], xlix, p. lx; The Census of Ireland, 1851: Pt. II, pp. iv, 36, 44, 92, 134, 162, 329, 473, 560, 613; Agricultural Statistics, 1876, pp. 34–7, 44; Agricultural Statistics, 1900, pp. 10, 20; Devon Commission, Pt. IV, Appendices, pp. 280–3. The available statistics on size of holdings for 1847 and 1851 group all holdings of 30 acres or more into one category. The total number of holdings for County Mayo do not equal the sum of holdings in the poor law unions as the boundaries do not correspond exactly. The poor law unions in County Mayo were reorganized in 1850. The original five unions were broken up and four new ones (Belmullet, Claremorris, Kilalla, Newport) were formed. Later the Newport and Westport unions were combined. In order to calculate the median size of holdings, I set the median of the final category (+500 acres) at 1000 acres. The figures for 1847 are estimates derived from reports submitted to the Devon Commission by clerks of poor law unions.

fetch a high price in the market. Additional money would be needed, he reported, to either purchase or plant turnips to feed the stock during the winter.[83] Simpson further improved his herds by careful breeding with selected stock that he imported into Mayo.[84] While not all large farmers worked their land as intelligently as did Simpson, many overstocking in hopes of a quick profit, it was these large farmers in the county's center who gained most from the period of rising agricultural prices and from the general prosperity of the years 1850 to 1876.

The case was much different for the small farming majority in Mayo. In Simpson's words, "the capital of a great many of those small farmers consists of their families."[85] Their land tended to be of marginal value, located in areas where there was little incentive for landlords to clear the land of smallholders. Much of this land was of such poor quality that it had never been used for tillage, except for potatoes and possibly a small poorly tended oat crop. Cattle and sheep had been its chief product for years and, following the Famine, the small farmers increased the number of their stock in the time-honored way of converting wasteland into rough grazing land. As can be seen from Table 4.4 those unions that contained lands on the periphery (Swinford, Newport/Westport, Belmullet) actually showed an increase in the amount of acreage under tillage at the same time as the number of acres under pasture was increasing. Both were carved out of the waste lands, the amount of which declined heavily in all cases.

In his study of the social origins of the Land War, Samuel Clark contends that because farmers in these regions could expand their pastures by encroaching on waste land, the post-Famine "development of a livestock economy represented in *relative* [his emphasis] terms an even greater boom . . . than to those in most other parts of the country." He explains that the ability of small farmers to breed a few calves or graze a few sheep on marginal lands allowed them to "enjoy benefits of the livestock trade" to a limited extent and to "make better use of their meager resources than they could in an economy based on commercial crops."[86] This was the case in County Mayo where livestock husbandry on marginal land had been a primary feature of the small farm economy for at least a century before the Famine. The rising price for cattle

---

[83] *Richmond Commission, Minutes of Evidence, I*, pp. 397–404.
[84] Dun, *Landlords and Tenants in Ireland*, pp. 239–40.
[85] *Richmond Commission, Minutes of Evidence, I*, p. 404.
[86] Clark, *Social Origins of the Irish Land War*, pp. 109–10.

and sheep after the Famine was no doubt welcomed by small farmers who increased the number of their stock, but it did not stimulate any major structural change in the agrarian economy of the small farm regions of Mayo. Cattle and sheep grazed on marginal or mountainous land, much of it, especially along the western seaboard, still held in common.

The quality of stock raised by smallholders on this marginal land was poor, since they had few resources with which to improve the grass, supplement the grazing diet with turnips or mangels or monitor the breeding stock. James Simpson complained before the Richmond Commission in 1881 that store cattle of inferior quality and bringing low prices flooded local markets and depressed the cattle market in general to the detriment of graziers like himself.[87] Finlay Dun, traveling in Mayo in 1881 confirmed that graziers in the Ballinrobe area had a low opinion of the stock bred in Mayo's peripheral regions, preferring to buy calves for fattening in Counties Kilkenny, Westmeath, Limerick and Roscommon.[88] A decade later inspectors sent by the newly formed Congested Districts Board commented regularly on the poor quality of the cattle they found. Reporting from Swinford, one inspector wrote: "The livestock are of a very inferior description. The people are extremely careless in the breeding of their stock, seldom exercising any foresight in the selection of breeding animals . . . The bull let for the smallest fee is usually the one most in request . . . "[89] Not surprisingly, stock of this description, when sold at a year or two of age, brought a low price. One inspector reported that the "worst description of cattle" did not realize half the normal price.[90]

One consequence of the poor prices that their store cattle could command was that few small farmers could pay their rent and meet expenses in the post-Famine cash economy without some means of supplementing their income. It was often attested that small farmers in Mayo would have had difficulty making ends meet even if they held their land rent free. In 1881 Rev. Patrick Lyons, CC, Castlebar, told the Bessborough Commission investigating the working of the 1870 land act that the tenant farmers of Achill in western Mayo were unable to live on their land for more than four or five months a year, much less meet their

---

[87] *Richmond Commission, Minutes of Evidence, I*, pp. 397, 401.
[88] Dun, *Landlords and Tenants in Ireland*, p. 242.
[89] Trinity College Library, Dublin, Base-Line Reports to the Congested Districts Board, 1892–98, p. 398.
[90] *Ibid.*, p. 405.

rents, without additional sources of income.[91] Two opportunities were available to Mayo farmers for procuring additional cash earnings: seasonal work in England or Scotland and the sale of farm produce such as eggs for the English market.

The most important source of cash beyond that obtained from the sale of stock was seasonal work in Britain. As early as 1853 *The Telegraph or Connaught Ranger* bemoaned the "exodus from Mayo":

On our way to and from Claremorris on Wednesday last, we saw no less than 74 adult persons on the road from Balla to that town, on their route to England. Some of these were from Castlebar, who stated to us they would not be working here for 9d. or 10d. per day, without meat or drink, while they could get from 2s. 6d. to 3s. per day in England . . . In some instances we saw fathers and mothers carrying their weak children on their backs. In Claremorris we were informed no day passes that at least from 90 to 100 persons, bound for England, do not enter that town by the same road . . . From Erris and Tyrawley the exodus is daily equally large by the Ballaghaderreen route.[92]

In 1880, at the time of the first post-Famine enumeration of seasonal migrants, Mayo sent 10,198 migrants to Britain. Cormac O'Gráda suggests that this figure, based upon enumerations made by the Royal Irish Constabulary, probably represented only 60 percent of the actual number.[93] Accordingly, the number of seasonal migrants from Mayo in 1880 may have been as high as 17,000. Whichever figure is employed, Mayo sent nearly half of Ireland's seasonal migrants to Britain, far outdistancing all other counties in the country.

The usual pattern was for migrants to leave in late spring or early summer, often on Midsummer's Day, 24 June, the morning after the "festivities of St. John's Eve."[94] The great majority of Mayo harvesters set out by rail to Dublin or Drogheda and then to Lancashire for hay cutting, with smaller numbers going to Lincolnshire and Cambridgeshire

---

[91] *Report of Her Majesty's Commissioners of Inquiry Into the Working of the Landlord and Tenant (Ireland) Act, 1870, and the Acts Amending the Same, Vol. II: Digest of Evidence, Minutes of Evidence, Pt. 1*, PP 1881 [C 2779-I], xviii, p. 551 (hereafter, Bessborough Commission).

[92] *The Telegraph or Connaught Ranger*, 4 May 1853.

[93] *Agricultural Statistics, Ireland, 1880, Report and Tables Relating to Migratory Agricultural Labourers*, PP 1881 [C 2809], xciii, p. 7; C. O'Gráda, "Seasonal Migration and Post-Famine Adjustment in the West of Ireland," *Studia Hibernica*, 13 (1973), pp. 56–7.

[94] CDB, Base Line Reports, pp. 295, 307, 416; K. Danaher, *The Year in Ireland* (Cork, 1972), p. 151.

for grain harvesting or to Cheshire, Warwickshire or Staffordshire for potato harvesting.[95] A small number of harvesters from the west coast of Mayo left directly by boat for potato harvesting in Scotland. By the 1880s seasonal migration was almost exclusively a male operation. Women and young children were left at home to manage the farm for five to seven months. In Achill, however, women migrated along with the men. Rev. Anthony Waters of Castlebar told the Bessborough Commission that in Achill he "saw whole families going off in the spring, and locking the doors and sending their cattle off to the mountains and going over wholesale . . . and then coming back about the 1st of August."[96] Ten years later the Congested Districts Board inspector in Achill reported that "all the females and a few men go to Scotland, working in Lanark, Ayr and Mid Lothian. The great majority of the male labourers proceed to Lancashire, Cheshire and Yorkshire. The average earnings for men are from £9 to £10 cash and £1 10s. value of clothes purchased. The average earnings for women are from £5 to £7 cash and £1 10s. value of clothes purchased."[97]

O'Gráda calculates that the amount earned by harvesters dwindled steadily from £10 to £15 during the 1860s to from £8 to £10 during the 1890s with the average Mayo harvester being able to send back or return with about £8 for their five to seven months of labor in Britain.[98] The CDB inspectors estimated that during the 1890s a "family in ordinary circumstances" would earn 20-25 percent of their cash income from seasonal work in Britain. In Achill, where both men and women migrated and where the land was exceptionally unremunerative, seasonal migration brought 73 percent of annual income.[99]

While all regions of Mayo sent some seasonal migrants to Britain, the greatest flow came from the eastern periphery. As can be seen from Table 4.7, the Swinford union, where whole villages were often emptied of their adult males during the summer months, had the highest rate of seasonal migrants in Mayo. In addition, the Swinford and Claremorris unions had the highest rates in Ireland. Not surprisingly, those unions that show the highest rate of seasonal migrants were also those where subdivision of holdings and early marriages persisted and where post-Famine repopulation was most complete.

---

[95] CDB Baseline Reports, pp. 295–416; Almquist, "Mayo and Beyond", pp. 249–50.
[96] *Bessborough Commission, Vol. II Minutes of Evidence, Pt. I*, p. 543.
[97] CDB, Baseline Reports, p. 339.
[98] O'Gráda, "Seasonal Migration and Post-Famine Adjustment," p. 69.
[99] CDB, Baseline Reports, pp. 295–416.

Table 4.7. *Seasonal migration in County Mayo per 1000 population, by Poor Law Union, 1880*

	Rate RIC	Rate adjusted
County Mayo	41.7	69.5
Poor Law Union		
Swinford	91.6	152.5
Claremorris	57.0	95.0
Castlebar	46.0	60.0
Newport	34.5	56.5
Ballina	17.7	29.5
Belmullet	16.8	27.5
Westport	14.1	23.5
Ballinrobe	13.3	22.2
Killala	12.0	20.0

Sources: O'Gráda, "Seasonal Migration and Post-Famine Adjustment", p. 61; *Agricultural Statistics, 1880 . . . Relating to Migratory . . . Labourers*, pp. 7–9.

The sale of farm produce was also an important source of income for many small farm families. Turf for fires, sea kelp for fertilizer, potatoes and oats were all sold, but the most important source of income for many families came from the sale of eggs for the English market. Management of family egg production and sale was almost exclusively in the hands of women and children, who were responsible for farm maintenance while the men were away. Those living in remote districts tended to sell their eggs to small shopkeepers or to peddlers who then forwarded the eggs to dealers in the towns who sent them by rail or ship to Britain. In some of the most remote regions of Mayo, eggs were bartered for tea, sugar and tobacco, which were carted into the back country by "creeleen women," so named by the "creels" or baskets that they had strapped onto their backs.[100] It was often several days before the eggs reached the "eggler" or exporter who, if the price was low, might hold back the eggs for several weeks until the price rose. As a consequence, Mayo eggs were often three to four weeks old before they reached the wholesaler in Britain. Not only were the eggs often stale, they were neither washed nor packaged with the care of their Danish competitors and consequently could not command the best prices on the English or Scottish market.[101]

[100] *Ibid.*, pp, 328, 344; Almquist, "Mayo and Beyond," pp. 255–6.
[101] CDB, Baseline Reports, p. 351.

Nonetheless, egg sales provided farm families with a "labor-intensive domestic economic pursuit which required little initial capital . . . and . . . was directly tied to the marketplace."[102] Almquist calculated that in 1880 the sale of eggs may have yielded £42,500 to the Mayo economy.[103] In 1892, CDB inspectors reported estimates of £70,000 in egg sales annually from the Swinford, Ballaghaderreen and Ballyhaunis regions of eastern Mayo, £10,000 from Castlebar and £6000 from Crossmolina, with equally large sales from Ballina and Westport.[104] Clearly, the sale of eggs was an important element in the small farm economy of County Mayo.

Almquist suggests that it might be possible to view egg production as a substitute for the pre-Famine domestic linen manufacture. It employed the same members of the family, produced a similar income and, like domestic spinning, provided the cash necessary for the maintenance of the small farm economy.[105] Along with seasonal migration, the sale of eggs and other farm produce allowed Mayo's small farm families to continue the subdivision of holdings, perpetuate early and frequent marriages and helped make possible the survival of the potato economy and the repopulation of the land following the Famine.[106] In short, these cash producing activities were part of an economic strategy that allowed for the continuation of a pre-Famine economy in a rapidly changing post-Famine economic world that was cash-based. The poor remained poor, but adjusted their family economies to meet the demands of the new economic environment. They supplied inexpensive yearling calves to the large graziers and sold cheaply their labor and farm produce on the English market. Yet they remained primarily potato cultivators, preserving a small farm culture in which hardship was pervasive, but which provided rights to the land for all family members.

The vulnerability of this small farming majority was demonstrated between 1859 and 1864 during the only serious agricultural depression and near-famine to occur in Ireland between the Great Famine and the Land War. The west of Ireland was hardest hit by a bizarre cycle of drought and heavy rains that combined to bring about a return of the potato blight, the ruin of much of the wheat and oat crops, and fodder

---

[102] Almquist, "Mayo and Beyond," 255.
[103] *Ibid.*, p. 258.
[104] CDB. Baseline Reports, pp. 314, 318–19, 332, 344, 352, 426.
[105] Almquist, "Mayo and Beyond," pp. 254, 258–9.
[106] O'Gráda, "Seasonal Migration and Post-Famine Adjustment," pp. 247–62.

and fuel famines that weakened stock and left households without turf.[107] In Mayo the most severe distress was in the western periphery and especially in the half-barony of Erris, where in 1862 Henry Coulter found "the greatest wretchedness and poverty I have yet witnessed."[108] In October 1861 *The Telegraph or Connaught Ranger* summed up the situation as follows:

> Never, within the memory of the oldest amongst us, except the tragic and eventful years of '46 and '47, were there more dismal prospects than these which usher in the Winter of 1861. About the first day of July last, never was there a better prospect of a rich and plentiful harvest, and never did a hardy and industrious people make greater efforts in the preceding spring to secure so great a blessing. But in the beginning of the month of July those prospects began to assume a different character. The rains of Heaven fell day after day and night after night – floods succeeded floods, and five times and more were the lowlands of our river sides and their teeming crops of meadow, and oats, and potatoes buried, for acres around, under the watery element.
>
> Alas! alas! the stern and melancholy result is but too visible to all. There is a fuel-famine already; the potatoes are gone; the corn crop is below average; and to bring a climax upon this sad state of things, a disease among the pigs – that great staple of the poor man's comfort – leaves many a poor family without the means of paying rents, or meeting the many other necessary demands upon them.[109]

The loss of the potato was the greatest threat to the smallholders of Mayo since the tuber remained the staple of most diets. Coulter reported that in parts of Mayo half the potato crop was lost, while a statement issued in April 1860 by the landlords and clergy of Erris reported that half of the population of the half-barony was starving.[110] In July 1863 the entire small farming population of the parish of Kilgeever went to the workhouse at Westport to ask to be admitted. Only 95 of the 600 people were taken in by the already crowded facility.[111] To survive, small farm families were compelled to sell at low prices what they could salvage from their oat crop or borrow from "Gombeen" men in order to purchase

---

[107] J. S. Donnelly, Jr., "The Agricultural Depression of 1859–64," *Irish Economic and Social History*, 3 (1976), pp. 33–46.

[108] *The Telegraph of Connaught Ranger*, 1 Jan. 1862.

[109] *Ibid.*, 9 Oct. 1861.

[110] Coulter, *The West of Ireland*, pp. 180, 207–8; *The Telegraph or Connaught Ranger*, 18 Apr. 1860.

[111] *The Telegraph or Connaught Ranger*, 1 July 1863.

indian meal (maize) to feed their families and obtain cash with which to pay their rent.[112]

Disease and shortage of fodder decimated many herds in Mayo causing, in Coulter's words, an "enormous loss of cattle sustained by small farmers."[113] The *Irish Farmer's Gazette* reported in 1860 that thousands of sheep in Mayo died of starvation while the *Mayo Constitution* noted that the "finest lands of the province are waste, and no tenants can be had to take [them]."[114] Between 1859 and 1864 the number of cattle in Mayo dropped from 166,178 to 117,338, while the number of sheep declined from 260,780 to 238,814.[115]

A full-scale famine in Mayo was averted by the efforts of numerous relief committees and by the availability of indian meal. According to Donnelly, "the really crucial change in the position of the West since the Great Famine . . . lay in the availability of cheap alternative supplies of food and in the recent elaboration of sophisticated networks of wholesaling, retailing and credit which ensured broad distribution whenever the potato crop failed."[116] Despite improved trading, credit and relief systems that curtailed dramatically actual starvation, sharp increases in evictions and emigration between 1862 and 1864 indicate that many Mayo small farmers lost their holdings and were forced to leave.[117] In a scathing editorial *The Telegraph or Connaught Ranger* commented:

During [the last quarter of 1862] bailiffs, drivers, process-servers . . . did great execution among the . . . occupants of this county. The landlords and the Gombeen lords had a regular race for the product of the harvest. While the unfortunate [tenants] were gathering in and converting the harvest into money, his Honor's bailiffs and the Gombeen process-servers were as busily employed in distributing their favours. The one side succeeded in the service of ten thousand odd civil bills – the other distributed as many ejectments. Twenty thousand civil bills and ejectments in the quarter ending 31st December 1862, proclaim the state of Mayo in terms too plain and explicit to require note or comment.

---

[112] *Ibid.*, 28 Jan. 1863; Coulter, *The West of Ireland*, pp. 160, 180. For a discussion of "Gombeen" men see pp. 167–9 below.

[113] Coulter, *The West of Ireland*, pp. 247–8.

[114] Quoted in Donnelly, "The Irish Agricultural Depression of 1859–64," pp. 38, 40.

[115] *The Agricultural Statistics of Ireland for the Year 1859*, PP 1861 [C 2763], lxii, p. 147; *The Agricultural Statistics of Ireland for the Year 1864*, PP 1867 [C 3766], lxxi, p. 147.

[116] Donnelly, "The Irish Agricultural Depression of 1859–64," pp. 48–9.

[117] See Figures 4.1 and 4.2 above.

Now, taking it for granted that the Gombeen harpy and the landlord seized on the same individual in each case – the former claiming the money, the latter the land or the rent, or, rather, both – and allowing five to a family in the case of the insolvents, the result will show an amount of destitution added to the previous pauperism of the county heartrending to contemplate.[118]

The deprivation, eviction and emigration that threatened the small farmers was, for the most part, not shared by the larger ones who could ride out the depression on the profits from previous years.[119] The widespread adoption of livestock raising following the Famine had not created an integrated society in County Mayo by 1862, nor had it by 1879. Rather, it altered the structure of, but did not diminish, a long-standing division in the county between a progressive economic elite concentrated in the core, and the rural poor, spread throughout the county, but particularly prevalent in the periphery. In pre-Famine Mayo the economic elite consisted to a large extent of the merchants and traders who participated in linen manufacture and trade or those who supplied goods and services to the lively linen centers. Prosperous farmers existed, but their economic significance was relatively minor. This changed dramatically after the Famine. The collapse of the linen trade and the subsequent rise in livestock prices established the large grazing farmers as the primary members of the new economic elite. They formed an agrarian capitalist class who shaped a society in which production for a cash economy defined social and political relationships.

LANDLORDS AND RENTS

Curiously, in this new post-Famine economic environment many landlords in County Mayo, as was the case elsewhere in the country, made little effort to increase their rental income in order to profit fully from rising stock prices. Landlords were hardly objects of pity. Their rents were paid regularly and their tenants were relatively docile until the economic crisis of 1877–80, yet it is generally agreed by Irish economic historians that, on the whole, rents did not increase in proportion to the rise in agricultural prices.[120] Vaughan computed that the worth of

118 *The Telegraph or Connaught Ranger*, 28 Jan. 1863.
119 Coulter, *The West of Ireland*, p. 170.
120 This case is most thoroughly presented in Solow, *The Land Question and the Irish Economy*, especially pp. 57–77, 89–120, and Vaughan, " A Study of Landlord and Tenant Relations in Ireland between the Famine and the Land War, 1850–78." Vaughan

agricultural produce in Ireland rose from £28.7 million in the early 1850s to £40.5 million by the mid-1870s. During the same years he estimated that rents rose from £10 million to £12 million. He argues that Irish landlords would have needed post-Famine rent rises of "at least" 40 percent in order to give them "a proportionate share in the increased wealth of agriculture."[121] Solow came to similar conclusions. Examining adjusted figures of land value assessed for income tax purposes, she found that rents rose a "modest" 12 percent from a little over £11 million in 1865 to between £12,776,000 and £13,305,000 in 1880. This rise occurred, she argues, during a time of "steeply rising prices" and "great prosperity" representing "very nearly a success story" for Irish farmers.[122] Both Vaughan and Solow stress that the farmers were the chief beneficiaries of the post-Famine price rises.

Their research has discredited the traditional nationalist image of the rapacious, rack-renting post-Famine landlord. While such characters existed, providing fuel to the fires of the land agitation, few today would claim that the majority of Irish landlords raised their rents to extraordinary high levels following the Famine. Yet O'Gráda, and following him Paul Bew, have suggested that while rents did not rise significantly on most Irish estates, the decline in the number of tenant farmers, combined with rising agricultural prices, increased the landlords' share of the value of Irish agriculture after the Famine.[123] In addition, Irish landlords invested as little as 3 to 4 percent of their rental income in improvements to their estates between 1850 and 1875, thus increasing their immediate profits.[124] In general, it appears that Irish landlords profited handsomely from their estates with little capital outlay and only

has summarized his findings in "Landlord and Tenant Relations in Ireland Between the Famine and the Land War, 1850–1878," in L. M. Cullen and T. C. Smout (eds.), *Comparative Aspects of Scottish and Irish Economic and Social History* (Edinburgh, n.d.), pp. 216–26. Also see W. Vaughan, "An Assessment of the Economic Performance of Irish Landlords," in F. S. L. Lyons and R. A. J. Hawkins (eds.), *Ireland Under the Union, Varieties of Tension: Essays in Honour of T. W. Moody* (Oxford, 1980), pp. 173–99.

[121] Vaughan, "An Assessment of the Economic Performance of Irish Landlords," pp. 181, 187.

[122] Solow, *The Land Question and the Irish Economy*, pp. 61–2, 69–70, 120.

[123] C. O'Gráda, "Agricultural Head Rents, Pre-Famine and Post-Famine," *Economic and Social Review*, 5 (1974), pp. 390–1; Bew, *Land and the National Question in Ireland, 1858–82*, pp. 27–8.

[124] C. O'Gráda, "The Investment Behavior of Irish Landlords, 1850–75: Some Preliminary Findings," *Agricultural History Review*, 23 (1975), pp. 151, 154. For a discussion of landlord-funded improvements that is more favorable to landlords, see: Solow, *The Land Question and the Irish Economy*, pp. 77–85.

moderate rent increases. According to Vaughan, most landlords chose a middle ground between wholesale clearances and high rent rises on the one extreme and no evictions or rent increases on the other.[125]

Very little nineteenth-century rental data from estates in County Mayo survived the IRA bombing campaign of the 1920s, the dissolution of Irish estates and dispersal of landlord families, and the callous disrespect for materials from the "colonial" period that long hampered archive preservation in Ireland. In addition, the descendants of several Mayo landlords have chosen to deny scholars access to their valuable records. Despite these difficulties, I was able to ferret out from public and private archives rental data from several Mayo estates. In addition, a great deal of information on rents is contained in the Minutes of Evidence of the commission chaired by the Earl of Bessborough that was charged with investigating the workings of the Landlord Tenant Act (Ireland), 1870. Rather than group this rental data together in general indices to produce rent averages in Mayo, in the following discussion of rents I have isolated rents on the various estates in order to illustrate the great discrepancies that existed from estate to estate and from farm to farm on a single estate. This method assures that rent levels on the highly rented estates, which provided powerful weapons to the orators of the Land League, are not obscured by rent levels on the many low or moderately rented estates in the county. Ultimately, the tenant farmers revolted against rents, evictions and landlords not because rents were too high or evictions too frequent, based upon an arbitrary standard prepared by economic historians, but because in their estimation rents and evictions had to be further reduced or eliminated. Solow mildly scoffs at the farmers who complained to the Bessborough Commission about a single rent rise in 50 or 100 years, but these rises were nonetheless grievances stored up until they became ammunition during the Land War.[126]

The majority of Mayo landlords appear to have been content with regularly remitted low or moderate rents. Few attempted to raise their rents commensurate with the rise in agricultural prices while many made no effort to increase rents at all during the twenty-five years between the Famine and the Land War. One landlord who regularly raised the rents on his estate was the Marquis of Sligo, owner of the largest property in

---

[125] Vaughan, "An Assessment of the Economic Performance of Irish Landlords," p. 176.
[126] Solow, *The Land Question and the Irish Economy*, p. 75.

County Mayo and the third largest landowner in Ireland.[127] Lord Sligo explained his actions in a letter to the Bessborough Commission:

> There was a great Famine in Ireland thirty years ago, and when, after it, I wiped off great arrears of rent . . . I let the land at nominal rents. All was in confusion. I had no idea of making them permanent. I told the tenants that the rents were only temporary and low to help them to recover themselves, and to repair the houses, etc., and put pig sties outside instead of inside the houses. I determined from the first to raise the rent by degrees, and not all at once, to a fair and moderate rate. The rent at the first arrangement was far less than the old rate . . . I believe the rents now to be fair and moderate.[128]

He informed the commissioners that following the 1875 rise in rent, one based on a re-evaluation of the farms on his estate, small tenants were paying, on the average, 14 percent over the government valuation of their farms.

Lord Sligo may have thought that his rents were fair and reasonable, but those of his tenants who appeared before the Bessborough Commission disagreed. For example, Patrick M'Ginn, a tenant of Lord Sligo in the townland of Arderry, told the commissioners that between 1853 and 1869 his rent had been raised three times from £28 to £98. Rather than accept Lord Sligo's argument that the rent rises were justified by the low rates charged following the Famine, M'Ginn claimed that "according as we improved the land he raised the rent."[129] Other tenants on the Sligo estate echoed M'Ginn's complaint about steep and regular rent increases with the bulk of them having received their most recent rise in 1875, as a result of the re-evaluation of the estate. Edward and Thady Heraghty presented to the commission the following letter that they received in March 1875 from Lord Sligo's agent Sydney Smyth:

> The Marquis of Sligo having directed me to revalue the farm you hold in Claddy, and for which you pay a rent of £40, we have done so, and consider that your rent should be increased to £55, over and above the rates and taxes, including the landlord's portion of county cess and poor rate. The increased rent to commence from the 1st November

---

[127] The Sligo family retains possession of an extensive collection of estate records but, in keeping with a long-standing policy, denied me permission to examine them. A report on the papers prepared by Sir John Ainsworth appears in the *National Library Report on Private Collections*, no. 24.

[128] *Bessborough Commission, Vol. III, Minutes of Evidence, Pt. II*, PP 1881 [C 2779-II], xix, p. 1370.

[129] *Ibid.*, Vol. I, p. 530.

last. In this new letting the Marquis will reserve to himself all game, turf, turbary and timber, and royalties, as is usual on the estate, and I request your consent to this within one week.[130]

The eleven tenants of Lord Sligo who supplied the Bessborough Commission with full particulars on the 1875 rent rise had their rents increased an average of 29–44 percent above the government valuation.[131] James Daly, editor of *The Connaught Telegraph*, and the best informed nationalist in Mayo, provided the commission with rental information for seven townlands owned by Lord Sligo. On these townlands the rent ranged from 17–35 percent above the government valuation.[132]

The Earl of Lucan also had a reputation for being zealous in assuring that he would get what he felt to be the full value from his 60,570 acre Mayo estate. Unlike the Marquis of Sligo, who increased his rents regularly, Lord Lucan appears to have raised his rents spasmodically during the twenty years following the Famine. The incomplete Lucan rent rolls covering the period 1848–73 present no consistent pattern of rent increases or of rent levels within the estate. A sampling of fifty-eight farms on which rents and valuations could be compared revealed that in 1870 rents were on the average 14.5 percent above the valuation. Alexander Larminie, Lord Lucan's agent, told the Bessborough Commission that in 1881 rents were 20–25 percent above the valuation.[133] As can be seen from Table 4.8, rent levels were not evenly distributed on the Lucan estate, with tenants on the smallest holdings paying the highest rents when compared to the valuation of their holdings.[134] It appears that most small farmers on the Lucan estate had their rents raised an average of 10 percent during the two years following the completion of the government valuation of Mayo in 1857. No consistent pattern emerges from the rent ledgers that would allow for conclusions as to why some rents were raised while others were left untouched, but small farmers who took land during the 1850s and 1860s were required to pay a higher rent relative to the valuation than tenants

---

130 *Ibid.*, p. 531.
131 *Ibid.*, pp. 531–5.
132 *Ibid.*, p. 568. For an evaluation of Daly's testimony see: Lee, *Modernisation of Irish Society*, p. 69.
133 Lucan Rent Ledgers; *Bessborough Commission, Vol. II, Minutes of Evidence, Pt. I*, p. 527.
134 Vaughan found that in Ireland as a whole, tenants on the smallest holdings paid the highest rent. See: "A Study of Landlord and Tenant Relations in Ireland," p. 57.

Table 4.8. *Average percentage by which rents exceeded the government valuation on the Lucan Estate, County Mayo (percent)*

Size of holding (Irish Acres)	1850	1860	1870
Under 30	38.1	39.5	54.5
30–100	1.4	3.6	3.1
101–500	2.5	8.2	11.9
501–1000		7.1	10.1

Notes and sources: An Irish acre is equivalent to 1.62 statute or English acres. Sample of 58 farms, Lucan Rent Ledgers, 1848–73; *General Valuation, Unions of Castlebar, Westport and Ballinrobe.*

in possession of their land at the time of the Famine. Few of the small farmers who had their rents raised in the late 1850s experienced additional increases prior to the beginning of the land agitation in 1879. Tenant farmers with larger plots were likely to experience two rent increases, each averaging 13.5 percent during the period covered by the extant rent ledgers, one in 1858 or 1859 and a second in 1867 or 1868. These rent increases, while substantial, do not seem to have exceeded the farmers' ability to pay, as the rent rolls show few tenants in arrears during the twenty years following the Famine. However, it must be remembered that Lord Lucan cleared large areas of his land of pauper tenants during and immediately after the Famine, thus reducing the number of small farmers who would be most likely to go into arrears during the 1860s and 1870s.

A sharp contrast to the practices of Lords Sligo and Lucan is provided by Baron Clanmorris, whose rent on his 12,337 acre Mayo estate remained at or below the government valuation for the majority of his small tenants. For example, in 1877 the rents on his Foxford estate were 31 percent below the government valuation. A year later the holdings in the Bellas townland were reorganized and the rents were raised to the valuation, but the rent on the other four townlands of the Foxford estate remained unaltered through 1888, when the extant rent ledgers end. The great bulk of Lord Clanmorris' tenants were smallholders, 39 percent of whom were paying £2 or less in rent and 63 percent of whom were paying £4 or less in 1878. The rents for these smallholders averaged 23–37 percent below the government valuation of their holdings. As can be seen from Table 4.9, Lord Clanmorris, in contrast to Lord Lucan, reserved his higher rent levels for his largest tenants. For example,

Table 4.9. *Average percentage by which
rents exceeded the government
valuation on the Clanmorris Estate,
County Mayo*

Size of holding (statute acres)	1877
Under 30	-24
30-100	-9
101–500	68

Sources: Sample of 23 farms, Clanmorris Estate
Rental, 1867–1888; *General Valuation, Unions of
Ballinrobe and Ballina.*

Garrett Nally, one of the largest graziers in Mayo, paid £480 rent for 443 acres of rich grazing land in the parishes of Pollawella and Knockalegan, which carried a valuation of £277.[135]

Lord Clanmorris' liberality and that of his son after 1876 was praised by *The Connaught Telegraph* when commenting on preparations by his tenants to present the young Lord Clanmorris and his new bride with an expensive service of plate and a pearl necklace on the occasion of their marriage. The newspaper referred to the recently deceased Lord Clanmorris as a "benign landlord" whose maxim in dealing with his tenants was "to let the tenants live by the land and live by it themselves."[136] Yet the good will generated by low rents and a "live-and-let-live" policy did not protect Lord Clanmorris from his politically active tenants during the Land War. In 1879, after the eviction of a woman and her five children for non-payment of rent on the Clanmorris estate, *The Connaught Telegraph* dropped the kind words of a year before and reported the eviction at length.[137] A few months later Lord Clanmorris' tenants joined with other Mayo farmers in demanding a 20 percent reduction of rents.[138] Nonetheless, Lord Clanmorris seems to have weathered the storm of 1879–81 and continued to profit from his estate without significant rises in his rents. In 1886 his Mayo lands yielded

---

[135] National Library of Ireland, Clanmorris Estate Rental, 1867–1888, MS 3120; *General Valuation, Unions of Ballinrobe and Ballina.*

[136] *The Connaught Telegraph*, 4 May and 20 July 1878. *The Telegraph or Connaught Ranger* was purchased in 1876 by James Daly and Alfred Hea and became *The Connaught Telegraph*. Hereafter *CT.*

[137] *Ibid.*, 14 June 1879.

[138] Dun, *Landlords and Tenants in Ireland*, p. 214.

£200 more in rental than they had in 1877 and his income from all his lands after taxes, expenses, wages and indentures had been subtracted rose from £1273 in 1877 to £1455 in 1886.[139]

The estate of the Earl of Erne at Lough Mask and Castlebar provides an example of a property where rents varied wildly and where moderate rents were no guarantee of immunity from the farmers' agitation during the Land War. Lord Erne's embattled agent, Captain Charles Boycott, told the Bessborough Commission that to the best of his memory the total rental on Lord Erne's Mayo estate was no more than £30 or £31 18s. 4d. over the government valuation.[140] This would place the rents at 3 percent above the valuation, which was the case in Killmor (Kilmore) townland whose residents were active in the famous "boycott" of Captain Boycott.[141] Yet Lord Erne had two townships in County Mayo, Kilkenny in the Castlebar union and Barna in the Ballinrobe union, where in 1879 the rents were on the average nearly 50 percent above the valuation.[142] One tenant on the highly rated Kilkenny property, James Daly, influential editor of *The Connaught Telegraph*, complained to the Bessborough Commission that his rent was 52 percent over the valuation for land that was "not worth more than the government valuation."[143] The inconsistency of rent levels on the Erne estate was in part the consequence of the often-praised "live and let live policy" of many landlords and their agents. Under this system old holdings that remained in a single family were moderately rented, with few if any rent increases, while newer lettings, especially those to graziers like Daly, were let at much higher rates in order to take advantage of the livestock economy.

During the Land War, tenant spokesmen often singled out for special sanction the owners of small or moderate-sized acreages. In his testimony before the Bessborough Commission, Daly called them the "curse of the country . . . white slave drivers."[144] Table 4.10 reveals that when the rental information presented to the Bessborough Commission is broken down by estate size, tenants on smaller estates paid higher rents relative to the valuation than did farmers on the largest estates. It is not surprising that owners of smaller estates charged higher rents. They

---

[139] Clanmorris Estate Rental, 1867–88.
[140] *Bessborough Commission, Vol. II, Minutes of Evidence, Pt. I*, p. 592.
[141] See Chapter 9 below.
[142] Public Record Office, Northern Ireland, Rental of the Earl of Erne's Mayo Estate, 1874–1879, D1939/10/3; *General Valuation, Unions of Ballinrobe and Castlebar*.
[143] *Bessborough Commission, Vol. II, Minutes of Evidence, Pt. I*, p. 570.
[144] *Ibid.*, p. 569.

Table 4.10. *Average percentage by which rents exceeded the government valuation on estates in County Mayo, calculated by estate size, 1881*

Size of estate in statute acres	Percentage above valuation
10,000 acres or above	42
5000–9999	74
1000–4999	72
Less than 1000	84

Notes and sources: Data taken from rents presented to the Bessborough Commission for County Mayo from 48 different estates with data on 142 individual farms and 24 townland summaries. Rather than attempt to adjudicate between the conflicting claims of landlords and tenants, I eliminated from these calculations those rents presented to the commissioners by tenant farmers or by James Daly that were challenged by their landlords. *Bessborough Commission, Minutes of Evidence, Pt. I,* pp. 522–70; *Pt. II, Appendices,* pp. 1323–5, 1366–7, 1392, 1398, 1439–43, 1474–7, 1485, 1506, 1516; *Returns of Owners of Land of One Acre and Upwards in the Several Counties, Counties of Cities and Counties of Towns in Ireland, Showing the Names of Such Owners Arranged Alphabetically in Each County; Their Addresses – As Far As Could Be Ascertained – the Extent in Statute Acres, and the Valuation in Each Case; Together With the Number of Owners in Each County of Less Than One Statute Acre in Extent; and the Total Area and Valuation of Such Proprietors; and the Grand Total of Area and Valuation for All Owners of Property in Each County, County of a City or County of a Town. To Which Is Added a Summary for Each Province and for All Ireland,* PP 1876 [C 1492], lxxx, pp. 307–13.

operated on a much narrower margin of profit than did the larger owners and could ill-afford generosity towards their tenants without seriously affecting their standard of living and putting their landownership in jeopardy. In addition, many owners of small or moderate-sized holdings had purchased or inherited neglected and unimproved land following the Famine. Consequently, they had to make extensive and expensive improvements on their land if they wanted them to turn a profit. Reimbursement for this outlay could only come from higher rents. One small landowner, Captain J. C. Sheffield, told the commissioners that he had spent £4000 on his 900 acre estate between 1864, when he purchased it from the Landed Estates Court, and 1870. Such an outlay, he claimed, nullified the use of government valuation as a criterion for a fair rent on his estate.[145]

A small extant rent ledger for the year 1878 allows for a more detailed picture of rents on a moderate-sized estate – that of Walter M. Bourke,

---

[145] *Ibid., Vol. III, Minutes of Evidence, Pt. III, Appendices,* pp. 1442–3.

owner of 4141 acres near Claremorris.[146] Bourke told the Bessborough Commission that his father had expended £7000 for houses, drains and fences, especially in the townland of Cultibo. Bourke went on:

> When the Poor Law valuation of Cultibo was made, a large portion of it was unoccupied, and a merely nominal value was assessed. Four times the valuation was offered at last year's lettings of land in the neighborhood of, but not on, my estate. Improvements were made at my father's expense; the lands were let at rents in no case exceeding, and in some instances less than the amounts proposed by the tenants, and these rents have not been increased, although the value of the lands has been enhanced from twenty to thirty percent by these improvements.[147]

In 1878 rents on the Bourke estate were on the average 57 percent above the government valuation. The rents in Cultibo, where, according to Bourke, the greatest amount of the improvements had been made, were 91 percent above the valuation.[148] Despite these improvements, Finlay Dun, traveling in Mayo in 1881, found the soil in Cultibo to be "poor and shallow, on a limestone conglomerate; a good deal of bog remains unreclaimed."[149] The Reverend Ulick Canon Bourke, parish priest of Claremorris, echoed this appraisal in a published letter to W. E. Gladstone following the eviction of fifty families from the Bourke estate in 1882. He described Cultibo as consisting "chiefly of a wet, marly mould, mixed with the refuse of peat which in centuries past had been used for fuel. This surface mixture of mud and marl degenerated in time into a broken swamp, half mire, half plash with an occasional knoll of arable soil on elevated sites."[150] Both Dun and Fr. Bourke noted that rents on the Bourke estate were not paid with money earned from the land, but with money earned from seasonal migration to England. The evictions of 1881 and 1882 occurred, according to Fr. Bourke, when the men of the

---

[146] This rent ledger was located by me in a County Mayo bank. I was given a photocopy of it by the bank manager only after promising that I would not reveal the bank or the source of my copy. The ledger was deposited in the bank by Surgeon General Bourke in 1888. A copy of my copy was made by the PROI, where it is cataloged as Business Records, Mayo 11.

[147] *Bessborough Commission, Vol. III, Minutes of Evidence, Pt. II, Appendices*, p. 1323. I assume that when Bourke refers to the "Poor Law valuation" that he means the government valuation of Mayo in 1857 and not the pre-Famine poor law valuation made under the Grand Jury Act method of valuation.

[148] Rent Ledger, Walter M. Bourke Estate.

[149] *Landlords and Tenants in Ireland*, p. 219.

[150] Rev. Ulick Canon Bourke, *A Plea For the Evicted Tenants of Mayo*, 3rd ed. (Dublin, 1883), pp. 6–7.

Bourke estate could no longer secure harvest employment in England and thus could not pay the "exorbitant rents."[151]

Yet, such high rents were uncharacteristic in Mayo, as was the case throughout Ireland. Nonetheless, the question of rents was foremost in the minds of most tenant activists during the early stages of the land agitation. The first tenant defense association to be formed in Mayo during the 1870s came in 1875 in response to the rent increase on the estate of the Marquis of Sligo.[152] Lord Sligo reportedly rebuffed delegates from the T.D.A. when told of his tenants' distress, by replying: "By heavens that is no matter to me. I must get the full value of my land."[153] As noted above, Lord Sligo believed that the increased rent on his estate was "fair and moderate," and apparently he had no qualms over offering the land to townsmen who could more easily meet the rent by establishing grazing farms on the land.[154] But his actions violated his tenants' sense of economic justice and jeopardized any slight gains his many smallholders may have made in the post-Famine economy.

For the larger farmers of Mayo who held grass farms and were most fully integrated into the livestock economy, the post-Famine rise in cattle prices had made them into producers for a cash economy, increased their incomes and expectations and made a valuable commodity of their land. However, it was a commodity over which they, the producers, had only limited control. In most instances, they could not buy the land, and had few assurances that they would be compensated for any improvements they had made to the land should they lose it. When cattle prices were booming, most large farmers were willing to share their earnings with their landlords, even though they resented the burden. The fall in cattle prices associated with the depression of 1877–80 reduced the farmers' income and transformed rents from a tolerable to an intolerable burden. In December 1879, Charles Stewart Parnell, MP, President of the Irish National Land League and leader of the agitation, summed up for an American reporter the economic doctrines of many Mayo farmers:

In a country like Ireland, where land is limited and the conditions of title are peculiar, a man should pay his just debts; but political economists established the maxim that rent is merely a fair share of the profits of the land, and that when there are no profits there is no rent.

---

[151] *Ibid.*
[152] Clark, *Social Origins of the Irish Land War*, p. 219.
[153] Reported by Fr. William Joyce, P. P. Louisburgh, *CT*, 6 Dec. 1879.
[154] *CT*, 1 Nov. 1879.

The shopkeeper has furnished the tenant with the necessaries of life, and should therefore be paid; but the landlord has only furnished land, which this year has not earned half a living, and he would therefore bear his share of the loss . . . We do not attach so much importance as you may think to mere reduction of rent. We do not consider the land question settled by the reduction of rents by any means. It is only a temporary assistance, but it establishes a principle . . . What I wish to do is create a natural state of affairs . . . Give the people the land and let it gradually distribute itself. Farmers would buy and sell, consolidate or subdivide, according to their inclination; and the size of farms would soon be regulated. The most profitable size would depend much on the locality and on the markets. Some lands are only fit for small farms, others are suitable for large. An increased demand for certain articles of produce or the decreased demand for others would have a great effect in determining the size of farms.[155]

This view of the land question, especially the desire to create a "natural state of affairs" on the land, was in keeping with the ideas of British political economists like John Stuart Mill, whose writings were often quoted from land agitation platforms. It appeared to many tenant farmers and their advocates that the primary obstacle to the establishment of free trade in Irish land was the grip that landlords had on the land. The depression of 1877–80 brought many Mayo farmers to the realization that in an agrarian capitalist economy, rents and landlords were an anachronism to be dispensed with if prosperity were to be established.

TOWNS, TOWNSMEN AND FARMERS FOLLOWING THE FAMINE

The post-Famine economic transformation of Mayo that was associated with the rapid growth of the livestock trade radically changed the nature and function of the county's towns. With the economic base of the county shifting to the countryside, towns became service centers for farmers who increasingly needed to purchase food and other supplies from shops. However, while the towns grew in importance for the rural community, they did not grow in population. As was the case elsewhere in Connacht, the urban population of County Mayo declined following the Famine. In 1851 Mayo had nine towns with populations of 1000

---

[155] Interview with Albert Chester Ives, *New York Herald*, 2 Jan. 1880, reprinted in *Special Commission . . . Proceedings . . .* , i, pp. 187–8.

persons or more, containing altogether 22,784 residents. By 1881 the county had only seven towns of this size, containing 18,668 people, and by 1901 there were only six towns of 1000 or more residents with a combined population of 16,011.[156] Despite this overall drop in population, the proportion of the residents of County Mayo that lived in towns of 1000 or more remained steady at roughly 8 percent between 1851 and 1901. This lack of urban growth is not surprising given the lack of industry or manufacturing around which an urban economy could be built. Rather than grow, the towns of Mayo changed their function from being centers of domestic linen manufacture and of the textile and grain trades to being commercial centers for the agricultural community.[157] According to Samuel Clark, "towns lost whatever status they had formerly enjoyed as viable economic entities in their own right. They became appendages to the farming population; and their main function was to serve its needs."[158]

The towns situated along the new railway lines were in the best position to profit from the livestock economy. The railroad, which arrived in Mayo by 1860, gave livestock farmers easier access to both the grazing farms of Leinster and Munster provinces, where their store cattle were fattened, and to the British market, where their fat cattle were sold for slaughter. The first line connected Ballyhaunis in eastern Mayo with the Galway to Dublin line at Athlone. Two years later the line was opened as far as Claremorris and by 1873 it stretched to Westport and Ballina. No additional lines were cut in the county until the 1890s, when lines were opened from Claremorris to Ballinrobe, from Claremorris to Tuam and Galway, and from Westport to Achill. These were the last rail lines built in the county despite efforts by the residents of Erris to have the track extended to Belmullet.[159]

The rail lines were the major arteries of the livestock trade, cutting through the rich grazing land of the central corridor of County Mayo. Trade was greatest during the fall when buyers from Munster, Leinster and Britain traveled west to purchase store cattle to replenish their herds and fat cattle for slaughter. Many of these buyers traveled to the October

---

[156] *Census of Ireland, 1881, Pt. I, Vol. III, No. 3*, pp. 285–353; *Census of Ireland, 1901, Pt. I, Vol. IV, No. 3*, pp. 3, 19, 59, 77. In 1898 the town of Ballaghaderreen (population about 1500) was transferred from County Mayo to County Roscommon.

[157] Cullen, *An Economic History of Ireland Since 1660*, pp. 121, 141.

[158] Clark, *Social Origins of the Irish Land War*, p. 135.

[159] E. R. Carter, *An Historical Geography of the Railways of the British Isles* (London, 1959), pp. 547, 563–5.

Fair at Ballinasloe, County Galway, which was the greatest fair in Ireland, although its importance was fading by the 1870s in the face of increasing competition from the fair towns opened up by the railroad.[160] One such fair, the largest annual cattle and sheep fair in Mayo, took place at Balla on 24 September. Even before the Famine the fairs at Balla had been important, but the arrival of the railroad combined with Balla's strategic location in the grazing lands of the Plains of Mayo and near the center of the county meant that by the 1860s it could attract sellers from all parts of Mayo.[161] Buyers of stock and wool came to Balla from all parts of Ireland, England and Scotland. No sales figures are extant from the Balla fair, but from reports in *The Connaught Telegraph* it appears that during the late 1870s as many as 1000–1500 cattle and sheep were sold at the September fair.[162] Other livestock fairs occurred throughout the summer and fall in south Mayo towns, the most important being at Keelogues and Hollymount. In north Mayo, Crossmolina was the "largest and most important of the annual fairs in the baronies of Tyrawley and Erris."[163]

Castlebar, Westport, Ballinrobe and Ballina, the four largest towns in the county, were the major market centers and became the commercial hubs of the county following the Famine. The occupational structure of these towns changed along with the needs of commerce. In 1841, 32 percent of the families residing in the towns of 1000 population or more were classified as being "chiefly employed" in agriculture. These were the casual agricultural laborers whose shacks dominated the outskirts of most towns. By 1861 the proportion of people in this classification had dropped to 10 percent. Changes in the way in which occupational statistics were presented in later censuses make exact comparisons with these percentages impossible. Nonetheless, by assuming that occupations of male urban dwellers over 20 years of age that were reported in the post-1861 censuses were roughly equivalent to the family occupational classification in the censuses of 1841–61, it is possible to make comparable estimates. Based on this assumption, the proportion of adult males living in Ballina, Ballinrobe, Castlebar and Westport who were engaged in agriculture had dropped to 7 percent by 1901. Conversely, the proportion of families classified as "chiefly

[160] *The Times*, 4–5 October 1876.
[161] Freeman, *Pre-Famine Ireland*, p. 262.
[162] *CT*, 30 Sept. 1876, 29 Sept. 1877, 28 Sept. 1878, 27 Sept. 1879.
[163] *CT*, 16 Sept. 1876.

employed" in manufacture or trade dropped from 47 percent to 32 percent between 1841 and 1861, but rose steadily afterwards; 50 percent of the males over 20 years of age living in the major towns of Mayo were classified as employed in commerce or industry in 1901.[164]

The economic vitality of the towns of Mayo in 1862 was commented on by Henry Coulter, traveling in the county as a correspondent for *Saunders' Newsletter*. He wrote: "Some twenty years ago, Ballinrobe did not contain a decent shop; now it has a good many large establishments, evincing by their thriving and prosperous appearance that there is an active and profitable trade carried on here." He found a "good deal of business transacted" at the "completely modern town" of Belmullet, but was most impressed with Ballina. It had "flourishing shops," "gas lights," "flagged streets," the "best appearing town in Mayo." Of the major towns only Castlebar, the center of the former linen trade but in 1862 having neither port nor railroad, was found wanting by Coulter. He reported that it had "not made any advance in prosperity" and as a consequence there was a "good deal of distress amongst artisan and labouring classes."[165]

As service centers for the farming community, towns in post-Famine Mayo depended for their prosperity upon farmers having money to spend. The growth of the livestock economy, encompassing both the large-scale graziers and the small farmers, produced an overall rise in agricultural income, which was supplemented in many instances by earnings from seasonal migration to Britain and by the sale of farm products. It has been estimated by Cormac O'Gráda that nationwide the per-capita annual income of farmers rose from less than £20 prior to the Famine to £32 in 1854 and £39 in 1876, with purchasing power rising at a somewhat slower rate due to inflation.[166] In addition, the farming population purchased a greater proportion of their food and other supplies from shops in towns than it had done previously. The diet of farm families was more varied, with indian meal (maize), bacon, herring, tea and sugar supplementing potatoes and milk. Rural people were also

[164] *Census of Ireland, 1841*, pp. 396–400; *Census of Ireland, 1861, Part V*, pp. 412–17; *Census of Ireland, 1901, Part I, Vol. IV, No. 3*, pp. 120–39.
[165] Coulter, *The West of Ireland*, pp. 165, 193, 204, 236.
[166] C. O'Gráda, *Ireland Before and After the Famine: Explorations in Economic History, 1800–1925* (Manchester, 1988), p. 130; O'Gráda "On Some Aspects of Productivity Change in Irish Agriculture, 1845–1926." Paper delivered at the Seventh International Economic History Congress, Edinburgh, August 1978. Reference from Clark, *Social Origins of the Irish Land War*, pp. 111–12.

more likely than before the Famine to buy rather than make their clothing. Coulter noted that the farming class "take their wages to shops to buy, instead of manufacturing for themselves. You will rarely see a suit of home manufacture worn by the peasantry, either male or female, particularly the latter, who spend their earnings in the neighbouring towns in the purchase of cotton dresses and striped petticoats, and have got quite out of the system of making their own clothes."[167]

The only available estimates of farm income and expenditure for Mayo were compiled in 1891–2 by inspectors for the newly formed Congested Districts Board. A particularly complete estimate of the cash economy of a "family in ordinary circumstances" at Pontoon north of Castlebar provides some indication of the variety of purchases made by a small farm family in 1892. As can be seen from Table 4.11, almost £23 or 61 percent of the family's annual purchases were for food to supplement the home-grown potatoes, cabbages and turnips in its diet. According to CDB estimates for twenty-nine families (nineteen in "ordinary circumstances" holding farms that rented for about £4 annually, and 10 in "poor circumstances" whose farms rented for less than £2) an average of 49 percent of family income went for store-bought food. For families in "ordinary circumstances" this represented about half of the food consumed.[168]

In the Islandeady district between Castlebar and Westport the inspector reported the typical diet as follows:

In autumn and winter –

Breakfast – Potatoes and milk or butter, followed by tea and flour bread is taken.

Dinner – Consists of potatoes, with eggs or fish (salt), generally herrings.

Supper – Potatoes and milk or butter is always taken, except by families in better circumstances, who use tea and flour bread.

In spring and summer –

The dietary is much the same, except that stirabout, made either of Indian or oaten meal, takes the place of potatoes. Indian meal is not much favoured except by very poor people, and oaten meal, the use of which at one time had almost died out, is now again being much used.[169]

---

[167] Coulter, *The West of Ireland*, p. 191.
[168] CDB, Base Line Reports, pp. 296–417.
[169] *Ibid.*, p. 364.

Table 4.11. *Estimated income and expenditure of a family in "ordinary circumstances" Pontoon district*

Income	£	s.	d.	Expenditure	£	s.	d.
Potato crop, consumed at home, cabbages and turnips the same				Potato manure, 1 cwt. guano, 12s. 6d.			
Oat crop, half a ton for sale at 7d. per 14 lbs. = 4s. 8d. per cwt.	2	7	6	1 cwt. bone manure, 7s. 6d.	1	0	0
				Seed oats	0	10	0
				Cabbage plants, 1000 at 3d. per 100	0	2	0
Sale of 1 three year old heifer or bullock, £6				10 stones of flour per month = 15 cwt. per annum, at £12 per ton	9	0	0
Sale of 3 sheep at 10s., £1 10s.							
Sale of 3 pigs, £10 (each 1½ cwt. at 45s. per cwt.) Less prime cost at 20s. each, £3 = £7	14	10	0	10 stones of Indian meal per month = 15 cwt. per annum, at £6 per ton	4	10	0
				Bran, 3 to 4 cwt. per annum	1	0	0
Sale of 10 hundreds of eggs at 6s., £3				Herrings or bacon, as "kitchen" to potatoes, 5s. per month	3	0	0
Sale of 10 chickens at 6d., 5s. Sale of 6 geese at 2s., 12s.	3	17	0	Tea, ¼ lb. per week = 13 lbs. per annum at 2s. 6d.	1	12	6
1 lb. butter sold weekly, 52 lbs., at 6½ per lb.	1	8	2	Sugar, 5 lbs. per week = 260 lbs. per annum at 2½d.	2	14	2
1 donkey load of turf sold weekly, 52 loads at 4d.	0	17	4	Tobacco, 2 oz. per week, 6d; malt liquor per week, 6d., or during the time spent by the wage earner in Ireland, for each item, 26s.	2	12	0
Migratory labour, 1 man	8	0	0	Paraffin oil, 10 gallons at 6d.	0	5	0
American money	5	0	0	Man's clothing – 2¼ yds. corduroy at 2s. = 4s. 6d.; 2½ yds. frieze at 5s. 6d. = 13s. 9d.; making suit, 8s.; trimmings, 6s. 6d.; shirt, 2s.; scarf, 2s.; boots, 7s. 6d; hat, 2s.	2	6	3
				Women's clothing – 3½ yds. flannel at 1s. = 3s. 6d.; 6 yds. cashmere at 1s. = 6s.; shawl, 7s. 6d.; handkerchief, 2s. 6d.; trimmings, 1s. 6d.; boots, 5s. 6d.,	1	6	6
				Children's clothing	1	16	1
				Donkeys' shoes	0	5	0
				Rent, road cess, and dog tax	4	0	0
	£36	0	0		£36	0	0

Table 4.12. *Proportion of houses in the four categories defined by census enumerators, County Mayo (percent)*

Year	First class	Second class	Third class	Fourth class
1841	0.6	6.0	33.7	59.7
1851	1.3	10.6	66.7	21.4
1861	1.5	14.7	65.4	15.3
1871	1.7	15.4	55.5	28.2
1881	2.2	18.4	73.6	8.0
1891	2.4	24.2	70.6	4.7
1901	2.8		95.7	2.1

Notes and sources: It is difficult to say whether the break in the pattern towards improved housing indicated by the 1871 figures for third and fourth class houses resulted from a statistical error on the part of the enumerators or from a temporary impoverishment caused by the agricultural depression of 1859–64. In 1901 the second and third class houses were combined in the statistics. *Census of Ireland, 1851, Pt. VI,* p. xxiv; *Census of Ireland, 1861, Pt. V,* p. 416; *Census of Ireland, 1871, Pt. I, Vol. IV, No. 3,* p. 354; *Census of Ireland, 1881, Pt. I, Vol. III, No. 3,* p. 354; *Census of Ireland, 1901, Pt. I, Vol. III, No. 3,* p. 469.

A significant aspect of this diet was the widespread adoption of indian or yellow meal made from American maize. Few of Mayo's smaller farmers could rely on their potato crop to feed their families for an entire year, as the last of the potatoes was often eaten late in the spring, leaving four months before the autumn harvest.[170] Indian meal, or oaten meal for the better-off families, filled the gap and most importantly reduced the family's vulnerability to a poor potato crop. Along with salted herring from England, bacon from America, tea, tobacco and sugar, indian meal could only be purchased from shops, increasing farm families' dependence on shopkeepers.[171] This dependence was furthered by the widespread adoption of bone manure and guano as fertilizers, stimulating a brisk business in these manures even for the small shops of Mayo.[172]

Additional signs of the growing post-Famine prosperity and the expansion of a cash based economy were the gradual rise in the quality of housing and the dramatic rise in the amount of money lodged in joint-stock banks. As can be seen from Table 4.12, the proportion of fourth-

[170] Coulter, *The West of Ireland,* p. 246.
[171] Cullen, *An Economic History of Ireland Since 1660,* p. 138.
[172] Bone Manure Book, 1895–1902 from shop at Park, near Turlough, County Mayo. The book is in the possession of Patrick J. Durkan of Westport, who kindly allowed me to read it.

class houses, described as windowless one room mud huts, declined steadily between 1841 and 1901, as did the number of third-class houses (two- to four-room mud huts with windows) after 1861. While a proportion of the decrease in poor houses was the result of emigration and eviction, it is clear that many farmers, occasionally with the aid of their landlords, upgraded the quality of their homes or moved to new, more commodious dwellings. This was not always done with the approval of the farmers, as Finlay Dun discovered while traveling in Mayo for *The Times* in 1880. He reported that tenants on the Cong property of Lord Ardilaun (Sir Arthur Guinness) found "too big," "too light" and hard to heat "the new substantial stone and slated houses, often of two storeys" to which they had been moved as part of a reorganization of the estate.[173]

Many farmers also accumulated a surplus of cash that could be deposited in joint-stock banks. These deposits, described by Cullen as "a sensitive barometer of agricultural incomes," rose nation-wide from about £8 million at the time of the Famine to £32,815,000 in 1876.[174] No comparable county figures exist. Between 1845 and 1847 the Mayo Savings Bank of Castlebar, founded in 1823, published annual reports in *The Telegraph or Connaught Ranger*. According to these reports, the number of depositors rose from 224 in 1823 to 1689 in 1846. Over the same years the amount deposited rose from £2553 to £53,850.[175] Table 4.13 provides a breakdown of who the depositors were in 1844. They came from a broad spectrum of Mayo society, including a significant number of small farmers and agricultural laborers. Unfortunately, the bank ceased to publish its annual report in *The Telegraph or Connaught Ranger* after 1847, so no comparable data is available after the Famine. However, we do know that the number of banks operating in Mayo rose from three in 1855 to nineteen in 1878, indicating a great increase in banking business after the Famine and no doubt reflective of the relative prosperity of the 1860s and 1870s.[176]

The primary beneficiaries of the increased wealth and trade in towns were the shopkeepers and publicans, whose numbers and prosperity

---

[173] Dun, *Landlords and Tenants in Ireland*, pp. 247–8.

[174] Cullen, *An Economic History of Ireland Since 1660*, pp. 137–8; J. S. Donnelly, Jr., *The Land and the People of Nineteenth Century Cork* (London and Boston, 1975), pp. 226, 377; *Thom's Irish Almanac and Official Directory, 1880* (Dublin, 1880), p. 716.

[175] *The Telegraph or Connaught Ranger*, 8 Jan. 1845, 7 Jan. 1846, 13 Jan. 1847.

[176] *Thom's Irish Almanac and Official Directory, 1855* (Dublin, 1855), pp. 632–4; *Thom's Irish Almanac and Official Directory, 1878* (Dublin, 1878), pp. 984–9.

Table 4.13. *Depositors, Mayo Savings Bank, 1844*

Occupation or status	Amount deposited		
	£	s.	d.
281 small farmers	8687	12	3
95 agricultural labourers	2167	12	7
37 shopkeepers	1903	14	7
81 journeymen, artificers and handimen	2250	2	10
144 domestic servants	3721	4	9
36 seafaring persons	1631	2	0
66 soldiers and police constables	2780	7	10
5 apprentices	89	4	7
21 teachers	1007	16	5
108 children	4996	7	8
191 spinsters	6666	13	2
56 clerks	2117	6	5
46 widows	1229	5	9
149 housekeepers	4657	15	10
17 charitable societies	958	4	2
1423	44,864	10	10

Of which there are	£		£
537 depositors whose balances do not exceed	20		
655 depositors whose balances are above	20	less than	50
167 depositors whose balances are above	50	less than	100
49 depositors whose balances are above	100	less than	150
14 depositors whose balances are above	150	less than	200
1 depositor whose balance is above	200		

Source: The Telegraph or Connaught Ranger, 8 January 1845.

increased significantly after the Famine. The censuses do not provide directly comparable categories for all the occupational groups that grew following the Famine, but an indication of the trend can be gained by looking at four occupational categories that remained roughly comparable in the seven censuses between 1841 and 1901. During those years the number of grocers rose from 14 to 267, the number of merchants in unspecified commodities from 55 to 109, the number of general shopkeepers from 433 to 1279 and the number of hotel, inn and tavern keepers from 185 to 405. As can be seen from Table 4.14, the growth of this small business class was even more dramatic when seen in relation to the size of the population of the county.

Clark has argued that small businessmen, especially shopkeepers and publicans, played a significant role within the agricultural community

Table 4.14. *Urban occupations per 10,000 population in County Mayo*

Year	Grocers	Merchants	Shopkeepers	Hotel, inn and tavern keepers
1841	0.4	1.4	11.1	4.7
1851	0.9	1.7	26.7	5.8
1881	10.8	3.4	41.0	12.1
1901	13.4	5.5	64.3	20.3

Sources: Census of Ireland, 1841, p. 404; *Census of Ireland, 1851, Pt. VI*, pp. 579–81; *Census of Ireland, 1881, Pt. I, Vol. III, No. 3*, pp. 365–85; *Census of Ireland, 1901, Pt. I, Vol. IV, No. 3*, pp. 112–19.

and as a consequence were able to capture an inordinate amount of political power and become prime movers in the agrarian agitation of 1879–82. He states that, following the Famine, members of the "small business class . . . came to rival landowners and clergymen as wielders of local power and patronage."[177] K. T. Hoppen suggests that this enhanced local power was especially significant in counties such as Mayo and Donegal, where the small businessman had less competition for power from the few large grazing farmers.[178]

The power of Irish shopkeepers to control urban and rural political and economic life is part of the folk tradition emanating from nineteenth-century Ireland. It has been the subject matter of novels such as Liam O'Flaherty's *House of Gold*, Patrick MacGill's *The Rat Pit* and *Children of the Dead End*, and John B. Keane's satirical *Letters*.[179] Clark, while cognizant of the tremendous gulf between the economic outlook and social position of the shopkeepers and that of the majority of farmers, builds his thesis around the view that the agitation of 1879–82 was conditioned by a convergence of interests among townsmen and farmers "based upon their mutual interdependence."[180] In effect, he argues that the Land War resulted from a lessening of class antagonism within the rural community. This view quite effectively explicates the political

[177] Clark, *Social Origins of the Irish Land War*, p. 128.
[178] K. T. Hoppen, "National Politics and Local Realities in Mid-Nineteenth Century Ireland," in A. Cosgrove and D. McCartney (eds.), *Studies in Irish History Presented to R. Dudley Edwards* (Dublin, 1979), p. 223.
[179] L. O'Flaherty, *House of Gold* (London, 1929); P. MacGill, *Children of the Dead End* (London, 1914), *The Rat Pit* (London, 1915); J. B. Keane, *Letters of a Successful T.D.* (Cork, 1967).
[180] Clark, "The Political Mobilization of Irish Farmers," *Canadian Review of Sociology and Anthropology*, 12 (1975), pp. 483–99.

union of the shopkeepers and large farmers, whose economic and political views coalesced to a great extent following the Famine. Yet the vast majority of Mayo farmers were smallholders who had reason to be suspicious of and antagonistic toward the large farmer–shopkeeper coalition. This ill will had a dual foundation. Small farmers were heavily indebted to shopkeepers and publicans for goods on credit and for cash loans. The rapacious attitude of some of these creditors tarnished the image of the merchant-lenders and became part of the Irish folk tradition. In addition, townsfolk were increasingly interested in using their profits to take up tracts of land for grazing stock, often at the expense of the smallholders whose land was amalgamated in order to form the grazing tracts.

While Mayo farmers of all classes had easier access to cash following the Famine, the demands on it for food, clothing, rent, fertilizers and dowries meant that frequently many farmers were in need of loans or goods on credit in order to survive until their stock or harvest could be sold or until income from seasonal migration could be earned.[181] They had three sources for these loans. They could go to the local shopkeeper for goods on credit or cash loans.[182] They could go to a "gombeen man" or usurer, who traditionally had been a farmer with a bit of capital to loan out. Or they could try the banks, which were often less willing to make loans to small farmers than were the other two sources. Furthermore, the banks required sureties and other guarantees that shopkeepers and "gombeen men" had no need for.

There is no way to draw a clear distinction between lending shopkeepers and "gombeen men." Peter Gibbon and Michael D. Higgins maintain that while prior to the Famine "gombeen men" had been farmers who engaged in usury, following the Famine "the term became transposed to shopkeepers either practicing usury as a sideline, or integrating orthodox commercial and usurious relations of exploitation."[183] Gibbon and Higgins make little distinction between money and credit lending when defining a "gombeen man," and this was

[181] Clark, *Social Origins of the Irish Land War*, p. 129.

[182] *Richmond Commission, Minutes of Evidence, Pt. I*, p. 89.

[183] Peter Gibbon and Michael D. Higgins, "Patronage, Tradition and Modernisation: The Case of the Irish Gombeen-man," *Economic and Social Review*, 6 (1974), p. 31. For the controversy that this article generated see: L. Kennedy, "A Skeptical View on the Reincarnation of the Irish 'Gombeenman,'" *Economic and Social Review*, 8 (1977), pp. 213–22; P. Gibbon and M. D. Higgins, "The Irish 'Gombeenman': Reincarnation or Rehabilitation?" *Economic and Social Review*, 8 (1977), pp. 313–20.

probably the case in the popular mind as well. Both money and credit lenders were in a position to exercise a powerful influence over their dependent clientage in the rural community that went beyond economic affairs to include political and cultural matters as well.[184] An unwritten social code, which Clark calls a "cooperative economic relationship," but which William O'Brien, reporter for the *Freeman's Journal* and future home rule and land reform agitator, called a "desperate partnership," bound the farmer to the creditor.[185]

Money and credit lenders had long been active in Mayo. The parish priests of Kilmore-Erris and Killeaden told the Devon Commission in 1845 of the activities of local usurers who charged 4s. to 5s. per pound in annual interest.[186] George Ormsby, agent to Lord Lucan, testified before the same panel that reliance on usurers for rent money was declining in Mayo just before the Famine due to the practice of borrowing from banks or taking bills for rent from estate agents or middlemen to be paid on return from seasonal migration to Britain. The rates charged by these lenders were no less severe than those demanded by the "gombeen men" and because they were due to banks or "gentlemen" they were if anything more "harassing" than debts to the usurious members of the agricultural community.[187]

Following the Famine, Irish tenant farmers had less need to go to money lenders for rent but more need to go to them for the consumer goods that were increasingly necessary in the cash-based economy. Coulter, writing from Castlebar in 1862, reported that "the system of borrowing money from loan officers and 'gombeen' men is universally practiced in this county; and as the rate of interest charged is enormously high, the unfortunate people who resort to this mode of obtaining money are constantly in a state of embarrassment . . . " Coulter made it clear that by "gombeen men" he was referring to "one of the peasant class who has contrived to accumulate some money, which he turns to account by lending to his poorer neighbours at usurious interest."[188] By the 1870s it appears that the lending activities of this class of usurers had been taken

---

184 M. D. Higgins, "The Gombeen Man in Fact and Fiction." Paper delivered to the Dublin History Workshop, Liberty Hall, Dublin, 11 Mar. 1978.
185 Clark, *Social Origins of the Irish Land War*, pp. 128–9; *The Freeman's Journal*, 12 Aug. 1879 (hereafter *FJ*); L. Kennedy, "Retail Markets in Rural Ireland at the End of the Nineteenth Century," *Irish Economic and Social History*, 5 (1978), pp. 54–5.
186 *Devon Commission, Minutes of Evidence, Pt. I*, pp. 162, 175; *Pt. II*, p. 381.
187 *Ibid., Pt. I*, p. 162; *Pt. II*, p. 435.
188 Coulter, *The West of Ireland*, p. 195.

over to a large degree by shopkeepers and bankers. In part, this was the consequence of their growing number and prosperity. However, a more significant factor encouraging their entry into the lending market was the Land Act of 1870, which gave tenants a degree of security on the land and thus made them better risks. The Land Act provided that an evicted tenant would be eligible for compensation from his or her landlord for improvements to the holding made by the tenant. Major Robertson, Assistant Commissioner to the Richmond Commission, testified in 1881 that the ease with which tenant farmers could secure credit during the 1870s "was attributed to the interest which tenants got in the passing of the Land Act. It gave them a greater stake in the land, and the shopkeepers, feeling that they had better security, gave the tenant more credit . . . "[189]

Dramatic changes in the county's economy during the two decades following the Famine brought in Mayo, as elsewhere in Ireland, a strong bond of economic interdependence between urban and rural society. The urban business class became to a much larger extent than previously reliant for its income on agricultural wealth, thus giving its members a major stake in the farmers' prosperity. As the editor of *The Connaught Telegraph* explained in 1879, the shopkeepers of Mayo know full well that "trade depends altogether on its agricultural class."[190] For the farmers, towns became essential for the markets and railway terminals that made possible the growing livestock trade with eastern Ireland and Britain and for essential supplies and credit. This bond between the two groups functioned amicably during the relatively prosperous years prior to 1877, but became a source of divisiveness during the bad economic years of 1877–80.

---

[189] *Richmond Commission, Minutes of Evidence, Pt. I*, p. 93; Solow, *The Land Question and the Irish Economy*, pp. 45–50, 85–8.
[190] *CT*, 9 Aug. 1879.

5. Post-Famine politics prior to the Land War

Mayo is in a very bad – in a most unsatisfactory state. No man can confidently state that either property or life is safe within the precincts. Terrorism has created throughout the county a widespread and very general sense of insecurity. Much of this feeling of insecurity is attributable to exaggerated reports and false rumours, but terrorism is the order of the day amongst us, and it is impossible to divest one's mind of the apprehension that attempts may be made, and successfully made, to carry out some of those threats with which we have become so familiar.

(N. R. Strich, RM, County Mayo, to Dublin Castle,
21 February 1870)[1]

During the 1860s and 1870s the merchants, tradesmen and substantial farmers of provincial Ireland, with their clientage of customers, debtors and sub-tenants, often became centers of patronage and power. Through a combination of wealth, prestige and intimidation they wielded considerable influence in both national and local politics, mounting a successful challenge to the near-monopoly of political power long enjoyed by the landed elite.[2] Few were in a position to stand for parliament, although they exercised increasing influence over those who did, but many members of this new elite found an outlet for their political ambitions in contests for the poor law boards of guardians, whose prestige and power over life in rural Ireland increased enormously between the Famine and the Land War. From the late 1860s, townsmen and substantial farmers, taking advantage of the liberal franchise for the

---

[1] SPO, Chief Secretary's Office, Registered Papers (CSORP), 1870, no. 3536.
[2] Hoppen, "National Politics and Local Realities in Mid-Nineteenth Century Ireland," pp. 190–3; J. H. Whyte, "Landlord Influence at Elections in Ireland, 1760–1885," *English Historical Review*, 80 (1965), pp. 740–55.

elected seats on the boards of guardians, brought a nationalist and occasionally pro-tenant component to Irish local government.[3]

However, by the late 1860s they were forced to share nationalist and pro-tenant political activity with Fenians and agrarian radicals who disrupted the county, often with attacks on the large grazing farmers who formed an essential component of the county's new elite. These radicals preached sedition, prepared for a violent rising against British rule, collected and distributed arms, issued threatening notices and carried out acts of agrarian outrage. In doing so they further developed the political consciousness of Mayo's small farmers, artisans and laborers and brought an organized immediacy to the struggle between landlord and tenant that Mayo had lacked heretofore.

MAYO POLITICS, 1846–1877

Parliamentary politics in County Mayo went through three distinctive phases between 1846 and 1879. The first, from 1846 to 1857, was marked by a struggle for power between conservative landlords, headed by the Marquis of Sligo, and a "popular" coalition of priests, tenant farmers and townsmen who supported Lord Sligo's cousin George Henry Moore. Moore was a liberal advocate of tenant rights and a leader of the Independent Irish Party in the House of Commons. The second phase, from 1857, when Moore was unseated due to charges of excessive clerical influence in his re-election, to 1874, was a period of political stability that resulted from an unofficial alliance between priests and landlords that was designed to avoid a contest for Mayo's two parliamentary seats. The third or nationalist phase began in 1874 when John O'Connor Power, a member of the Supreme Council of the Irish Republican Brotherhood (IRB or Fenians) defied both priests and landlords by contesting and winning one of Mayo's parliamentary seats. His victory demonstrated the degree to which the social and cultural transformation of post-Famine Mayo had eroded the base for landlord and clerical political dominance.

The elections of 1846, 1847, 1852 and 1857, in which Moore was a candidate, were spirited affairs prompting parliamentary inquiries in 1852 and 1857. Moore, a large landowner with an estate situated on the shores of Lough Carra, first stood for election to parliament in an 1846

---

[3] W. Feingold, *The Revolt of the Tenantry: The Transformation of Local Government in Ireland, 1872–1886* (Boston, 1984), pp. 11–90.

by-election. He stood as an independent candidate with no recognizable political principles, but with the backing of Mayo's foremost landlords who promised their tenant-electors' votes to him. Lord Sligo wrote to Moore on the day before the polling to report that his tenant-electors, "but one who has fever," had been assembled in Westport from where they would "be escorted" to vote for Moore.[4] Other landlords made similar arrangements, but they found themselves confronted by an equally effective electoral machine operated by the Archbishop of Tuam, John McHale, and the priests of Mayo. The clerical candidate, Joe McDonnell, was an advocate of the repeal of the union between Britain and Ireland and had the support of the aging but still popular leader of the repeal movement, Daniel O'Connell. The election was enlivened on both sides by the imprisonment of rival voters on election day, by mobs blocking voters' routes to the polls and by other acts of intimidation.[5] Only 60 votes out of 894 polled separated the two candidates, indicating the almost equal strength of the clerical and landlord influence in Mayo. Moore lost the election, but a year later in a general election, during which he attracted a segment of the popular vote with a spirited attack on the passivity of Irish MPs, topped the poll to join the repeal candidate R. D. Browne as member for Mayo.

As one of the 34 Catholics among the 105 Irish parliamentary delegates, Moore first came to prominence in the House of Commons and in Ireland through his leadership in the fight against the Ecclesiastical Titles Bill. Introduced in 1851 by the Whig Prime Minister, Lord John Russell, the Titles Bill was the government's response to the Pope's decision to assign territorial titles to Catholic bishops in Britain for the first time since the sixteenth century. The Pope's decision and the ensuing bill, which forbade Catholic clergy to assume territorial titles and outlawed the wearing of religious habits, prompted a wave of anti-Catholic riots in Britain. The most serious was at Stockport, Cheshire, on 28–29 February 1852, during which twenty-four Catholic homes were sacked and two chapels wrecked. Moore led the majority of Irish Liberal MPs away from support of the Whig government and suggested that they vote against the government on all issues until it and its Titles Bill were brought down.[6] The Irish Brigade (or Pope's Brass Band), as these

---

[4] Quoted in Hone, *The Moores of Moore Hall*, p. 134.

[5] *Ibid.*, pp. 134–5.

[6] Moore, *An Irish Gentleman: George Henry Moore*, pp. 172–5; J. H. Whyte, *The Independent Irish Party, 1850–9* (Oxford, 1958), pp. 21–2.

maverick liberals were called, joined with the Irish Catholic hierarchy in August 1851 to form the Catholic Defence Association, which in turn entered into an alliance with the Irish Tenant League that had been formed a year earlier to promote the rights of tenant farmers to fair rents, fixity of tenure on their holdings, and free sale of their interest in those holdings (the "Three Fs").[7]

Moore played an active role in these events so that when a general election was called in 1852, just months after the Stockport riots, he stood for re-election with the active and enthusiastic support of the clergy and tenant farmers of Mayo. A placard issued in Mayo during the election campaign demonstrates the intensity of Catholic feeling:

Massacre and Sacrilege at Stockport!
Irish Catholics murdered in their beds!!
Twenty-four houses wrecked and plundered.
The priest's house burnt!
The Chapel sacked and pillaged!!
The Tabernacle *broken open!!*
And the Holy of Holies Spilt on the Ground!!!
In consequence of Lord Derby's Proclamation
Catholics of Ireland! Whoever votes for a supporter of Lord
Derby's Government votes for the massacre of his countrymen!
The violation of the House of God; and
The pollution of the Body and Blood of His Redeemer!!
Down with Lord Derby and M'Alpine![8]

Moore's parliamentary activities had angered his former supporters among Mayo's landlords. His political patron during the first two campaigns, Lord Sligo, personally selected Lt. Col. James McAlpine to stand against Moore and George Gore Ouseley Higgins, the other sitting member from Mayo.[9] A Catholic, Higgins had been elected in a by-election in 1850 against the wishes of Lord Sligo, who supported Isaac Butt, the future home rule leader who was seeking his first parliamentary seat as a Conservative.[10] Higgins had been an early supporter of the Tenant League and was a member of the Irish Brigade, but was more

---

[7] Whyte, *The Independent Irish Party*, pp. 12, 28–9.
[8] Quoted in *ibid.*, p. 60. Lord Derby had become Tory Prime Minister in 1852; James McAlpine was the Conservative candidate in Mayo.
[9] Moore, *An Irish Gentleman*, p. 207.
[10] Hoppen, "National Politics and Local Realities in Mid-Nineteenth Century Ireland," p. 210.

moderate than Moore. His political base rested on Catholic landowners and substantial tenant farmers.[11] But the real contest in 1852 was between Moore, supported by the priests, and McAlpine, backed by large landlords. Lord Dillon, the second largest landowner in Mayo, gave "strict orders" to his tenants to vote for McAlpine, only to have his orders ignored by his agent, who escorted the voters to the polls.[12] Sir Roger Palmer, the third largest landowner in the county, took more drastic action, evicting fifteen tenants for voting against his wishes. In reply to a petition for reinstatement, Palmer expressed the belief of many Mayo landlords that they had the right to electoral supremacy over their tenants:

> Since receiving your petition I have enquired as to the cause for which you . . . received notice to quit your farms. I find that all of you (with one exception) voted directly against my wishes at the last election in Mayo, thereby disobliging me as much as it was in your power to do so. When tenants want favours or indulgences of any sort it is always to their landlord they apply and therefore I do think that tenants on their part [are] right to make a point of following their landlord's direction at elections in preference to those of any other person whatever.
>
> You . . . however did not do this; you not only refused to vote for the candidate I supported but you went dead against me and gave all your votes to the opposite party, in defiance of my known wishes and requests. Now you want me to overlook all this and to forgive the way in which you set me at defiance, but I consider such conduct deserves punishment; and therefore I shall not interfere with Mr. Ormsby's decision on the subject.
>
> I hope that on future occasions my tenants will consider, that those who refuse to comply with my reasonable requests, and who act in direct opposition to my wishes, can expect neither favours nor indulgences at my hands.[13]

Despite these actions by landlords, the electoral organization of the clergy again prevailed, with Moore and Higgins both topping McAlpine by almost two-to-one. The priests transported voters to the polls, arranged lodging and refreshments for them, instructed them from the

---

[11] Whyte, *The Independent Irish Party*, pp. 17, 29, 32–3.

[12] K. T. Hoppen, "Landlords, Society and Electoral Politics in Mid-Nineteenth Century Ireland," *Past and Present*, 75 (1977), p. 90.

[13] Quoted in Whyte, "Landlord Influence at Elections in Ireland," p. 749.

pulpit and lectured them from public platforms, all in Moore's interest.[14] In addition, Catholic mobs, mostly containing non-voters, expressed their political preference by harassing and intimidating voters being escorted to the polls by landlord representatives or police to vote for McAlpine.[15] However, organization rather than intimidation was the key to Moore's victory. The rival organizations employed similar methods to get their voters to the polls and ensure that they voted as instructed. Both had access to ample funds, but the organization put together by the priests proved more effective than that of the landlords because of its vast popular backing in a county where 97 percent of the population was Catholic.[16]

Five years later, at the next general election, Moore again stood for re-election in Mayo, but in an altered political environment. In 1857 he was the head of the near moribund Independent Irish Party and his chief opponent in Mayo was not the Conservative candidate but his former political ally (although personal antagonist) Ouseley Higgins. In a bizarre twist, Moore and his Catholic allies formed an election pact with the Conservative candidate Captain R. W. H. Palmer, son of the man who had evicted fifteen of his tenants for voting for Moore in 1852. The Independent Irish Party had disintegrated as a result of the defection to the Liberals of many of its MPs and the loss of support from most members of the Catholic hierarchy, who thought they had found in the Liberal Party the best hope for advancing Catholic interests.[17] One of those who defected was Higgins, who committed the arch sin in the eyes of the independents of accepting office from the Liberals in reward for breaking his pledge to remain "independent of and in opposition to" any government unwilling to introduce legislation furthering tenant rights in Ireland.[18] But Higgins was a Catholic whose drift to the Liberals was consistent with the political policy of the Catholic hierarchy as it had been developed by the Irish Primate, Paul Cullen, Archbishop of Dublin and Apostolic Delegate in Ireland. The sole dissenter within the hierarchy on the policy of accommodation with the Liberals was the

---

[14] *Minutes of Evidence Taken Before the Select Committee on the Mayo Election Petition, Together With the Proceedings of the Committee*, PP 1852–3 (415), xvi, pp. 57–84.

[15] *Ibid.*, pp. 5–37.

[16] Whyte, *The Irish Independent Party*, pp. 55, 70, 79; W. E. Vaughan and A. J. Fitzpatrick, eds., *Irish Historical Statistics: Population 1821–1971* (Dublin, 1978), p. 53.

[17] Whyte, *The Independent Irish Party*, pp. 93–141.

[18] Ibid., p. 147.

cantankerous Archbishop of Tuam, John McHale, Moore's major patron.[19] McHale's personal struggle with Cullen for power within the Irish church intensified his support for Moore, so that the battle in Mayo between Moore and Higgins was part of the larger struggle between the rival archbishops.

The county's clergy was split with the majority joining McHale, who nominated Moore. But a sizeable minority of the Catholic clergy supported Higgins, who had been nominated by the Dean of Tuam and Parish Priest of Westport, Bernard Burke.[20] To a large extent the Catholic electorate was split along class lines, reflecting the growing disparity of wealth and status produced within the Catholic community by the post-Famine rise in agricultural prices. As Cullen put it in a letter to Rome: "almost all the well-off Catholics were opposed to the candidate of the Archbishop, while those of the lower class favoured him."[21] Moore's supporters within the clergy were fervent and determined, as illustrated by this election manifesto issued by McHale and signed by three bishops:

People of Mayo! The voice of the Church calls upon you to do your duty! . . . All Ireland now expects your decision. With one combined effort elect your chosen candidates, G. H. Moore, Esq. and Captain R. W. Palmer, or by your apathy permit Mr. Ouseley Higgins to sneak in and be for ever disgraced! Hear the voices of your venerated bishops ever your guide in the day of trial. Resolved at a meeting of the bishops and several of the clergy connected with Mayo, held in Tuam, that all the energies of the people should be directed to the rejection of Mr. Ouseley Higgins, who has been unfaithful, and the return of Mr. Moore, who had been their honest, faithful and uncompromising friend in Parliament.[22]

One priest, speaking in Gaelic, even issued a curse on those who voted against Moore: "My curse as a priest, the curse of God, the curse of the church and people upon you if you vote for Colonel Higgins."[23]

These election techniques again proved effective, although Moore came in second with 75 votes less than Palmer. In addition, the Catholic

---

[19] E. Larkin, *The Making of the Roman Catholic Church in Ireland, 1850–1860* (Chapel Hill, North Carolina, 1980), pp. 370–87.

[20] *Ibid.*, p. 381; *CT*, 1 Apr. 1857.

[21] Quoted in Larkin, *The Making of the Roman Catholic Church in Ireland*, p. 384.

[22] *Minutes of Evidence Taken Before the Select Committee on the Mayo Election Petition, With the Proceedings of the Committee and Index*, PP 1857 (sess. 2) (182), vii, p. 3.

[23] Quoted in Hoppen, "National Politics and Local Realities in Mid-Nineteenth Century Ireland," p. 225.

gentry and larger farmers displayed their strength by overcoming intimidation from their co-religionists to register 1037 votes for Higgins, who lost Mayo's second seat to Moore by only 113 votes.[24] Moore's victory was short-lived as he was unseated on a petition filed in the House of Commons by Higgins alleging excessive clerical influence in the election. The unseating of Moore brought to an end eleven years of contentious politics in Mayo. His electoral alliance with the Conservative Palmer, forged to keep the "pledge breaker" Higgins from being re-elected, set the standard for the next seventeen years of parliamentary politics in Mayo. Following the unseating of Moore, Higgins, in the words of *The Telegraph or Connaught Ranger*, "dare not run again."[25] The seat was won by Lord John Browne, a Liberal who was unopposed. Between 1857 and 1874 there were no election contests in Mayo through three general and two by-elections. During these years Mayo returned one Liberal from the ranks of the gentry, who was formally selected by the Catholic clergy, and one Conservative, also a member of the gentry, who was selected by the landlords. This resurgence of landlord dominance of parliamentary politics in Mayo came at the expense of the priests, whose unity had been undermined and tactics discredited during the 1857 election. Archbishop Cullen was appalled at the clerical excesses during the 1857 election in Mayo and laid the blame for them, with considerable justification, on his rival, McHale. In a letter to Rome he called the conduct of the priests of Mayo "scandalous . . . very violent and wicked," and urged action against them. With renewed vigor he succeeded in isolating and containing McHale and curtailing the independent political activities of Irish priests.[26] By silencing the clergy in politics, Cullen gave the landlords a temporary ascendancy in Mayo politics, but also allowed for the emergence of a new political elite that would soon challenge successfully the political power of both landlords and clergy.

As can be seen from Table 5.1, the small electorate of Mayo grew by 132 percent between 1852 and 1862. This growth was the result of the zeal with which the rival election organizations of the 1850s registered tenants with holdings valued at £12 or more, who had been enfranchised by the Parliamentary Voters (Ireland) Act of 1850.[27] It also reflected the

---

[24] B. M. Walker (ed.), *Parliamentary Election Results in Ireland, 1801–1922* (Dublin, 1978), p. 302.

[25] *The Telegraph or Connaught Ranger*, 29 July 1857.

[26] Larkin, *The Making of the Roman Catholic Church in Ireland*, pp. 385, 461–6.

[27] 13 and 14 Vict., c. 69.

Table 5.1. *Size of electorate in County Mayo, 1852–1881*

Year	Number of electors	Percentage of electors to adult male population
1852	1738	3.6
1859	3779	7.4
1862	4033	7.9
1864	3679	7.2
1871	3703	7.3
1874	3632	7.2
1881	3087	6.7

Notes and sources: Male 25 years or older from nearest census. Walker (ed.), *Parliamentary Election Results in Ireland, 1801–1922*, p. 302; *Abstract Return of the Number of Electors on the Register of 1852 in Each County, City and Borough in Ireland, Distinguishing their Qualifications*, PP 1852–3 (957), lxxxiii, p. 2; *A Return of the Number of Electors in Every County, City, and Borough in Ireland, According to the Register Now in Force*, PP 1859 (sess. 1) (140–1), xxiii, p. 1; *Return in Tabular Form for the Year 1864 of the Number of Electors on the Register of Each County in Ireland*, PP 1865 (448), xliv, p. 5; *Return Relating to Constituencies (Ireland)*, PP 1874 (45), liii, pp. 5, 9, 11; Vaughan and Fitzpatrick (eds.), *Irish Historical Statistics: Population, 1821–1971*, pp. 126, 144; *Census of Ireland 1861, Pt. 1, Vol. IV, No. III*, p. 419; *Census of Ireland, 1871, Pt. 1, Vol. IV, No. III*, pp. 280, 362.

rising wealth of the county that enabled many men to qualify to vote for the first time. The available election statistics do not provide sufficient information to make possible a regional analysis of the electorate in Mayo, but given the rising economic importance of the central core, it is likely that a substantial proportion of the new voters resided in or near the towns of central Mayo. Some evidence to support this assertion can be extracted from extant 1856 voter lists for five of the nine Mayo baronies. Table 5.2 illustrates that the baronies of Clanmorris, Kilmaine and Tirawley, all of which contained portions of the central corridor, had electorates whose proportion of the total county electorate was roughly equivalent to the proportion of the baronies' population to the total population of the county. In contrast, the barony of Costello, which lies wholly in the eastern periphery of Mayo contained in 1861, 18 percent of the county's population but only 6.5 percent of its electors. Gallen, a transitional barony containing both core and peripheral land, displays a ratio of electorate to population that is midway between that of Clanmorris in the core, and Costello in the periphery. Unfortunately, comparable lists do not exist for later dates, but it seems certain that the political importance of the central core grew during the 1860s and 1870s.

Table 5.2. *Distribution of the electorate in selected baronies, County Mayo, 1856*

Barony and number of electors	% of electors to adult male heads of households	% of barony electorate to total county electorate	% of barony population to total county population
Clanmorris (289)	3.5	7.1	7.2
Kilmaine (370)	3.5	9.1	9.8
Tyrawley (535)	3.2	13.2	15.2
Costello (265)	1.2	6.5	18.1
Gallen (372)	2.2	9.2	14.8

Notes and sources: The 1861 Census does not contain age breakdown by baronies. PROI, Parliamentary Voters, County of Mayo, Baronies of Tyrawly, Kilmain, Gallen, Costello, Clanmorris; Copy of the Register of Persons Entitled to Vote at any Election of a Member of Members of Parliament for the County of Mayo, Between the 30th Day of November 1856 and the 1st Day of December 1857, M2782, M2783, M2784, M3447, M3448; *Census of Ireland, 1861, Pt. 1, Vol. IV, No. III*, pp. 412–14.

One major reason for the political development of the central core was the growing political ambitions of the post-Famine agrarian elite of large farmers and townsmen, who were clustered in the central lowlands of Mayo. The members of this elite turned to politics as a means of furthering their economic importance. In the rich grazing lands of eastern and central Ireland the large grazing farmers took the lead in securing political power, but in the west, where graziers were fewer in number, the townsmen who served the agricultural community often were the most dynamic political group.[28] During the 1860s and 1870s, in the absence of a strong national political movement, the agrarian elite turned to local politics, which offered easily exploitable opportunities for political advancement. The greatest opportunities for political position were provided by the elected seats on the boards of guardians that had been established to administer the poor laws.

The boards of guardians were established by the Poor Law Act of 1838 to administer workhouses, also established by the act, in a fashion similar to that set up in England four years earlier. In Ireland the boards had been barely constituted when the Famine put them to their greatest challenge, with many boards, including several in Mayo, collapsing under the weight of Famine responsibilities. Nonetheless, the Famine compelled the majority of boards of guardians to become efficient

[28] Feingold, *The Revolt of the Tenantry*, p. 214; Hoppen, "National Politics and Local Realities in Mid-Nineteenth Century Ireland," p. 223.

administrators of public money and programs. Following the Famine, parliament assigned to them myriad responsibilities in addition to poor relief. Many of these responsibilities had long been held by landlord-dominated grand juries. However, the grand juries' resistance to central direction and insistence upon local prerogatives had caused them to fall out of favor with the government with the result that by the 1870s much of their power was transferred to the boards of guardians. The 1872 Local Government Act completed this transfer by officially recognizing the boards as the chief agency of local government in Ireland.[29]

The growing power of the boards was only one feature of their attractiveness to the agrarian elite. Unlike the grand juries, whose members were all appointed by the high sheriff from among the county's gentry, the board of guardians contained an elected element with a franchise that included all but the poorest farmers and laborers. After 1847 roughly half of the seats on the boards were held by elected officers with the remaining held by ex-officio members chosen from the justices of the peace.[30] It was the elected seats that gave to farmers and townsmen an opportunity to challenge the landlord monopoly in local government that was manifest in the grand juries.

Following the reorganization of the unions in 1849, Mayo contained nine unions, with their workhouses and administrative centers situated in the towns of Ballinrobe, Claremorris, Castlebar, Westport, Ballina, Killala, Swinford and Belmullet. All but the last two of these towns are located in or on the fringe of the central corridor. They became the focal points of local political activity in post-Famine Mayo. The large landowners easily monopolized the ex-officio seats on the boards and until the 1880s retained control of many of the elected seats by arranging for the election of their agents and retainers.[31] In 1878 James Daly, a member of the Castlebar and Ballina boards, reported to a parliamentary committee the degree of landlord power on the boards in Mayo:

> In Castlebar, the Earl of Lucan is the Chairman, and his agent (Mr. Larminie) is on the board . . . His bailiff (Mr. Moran) is the poor rate collector; he has a tenant (Mr. O'Malley) to represent him [as] Deputy Vice-Chairman . . . We have as Vice-Chairman, Mr. Charles L. Fitzgerald, and then we have Mr. Robert Powell, his agent, and Edward Powell, his brother . . . There is a representative of Sir Roger

---

[29] Feingold, *The Revolt of the Tenantry*, pp. 12–13.

[30] *Ibid.*, pp. 13–26.

[31] *Ibid.*, pp. 39–40.

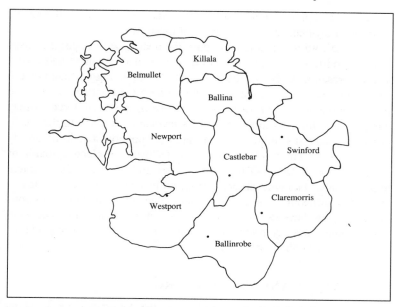

Map 5.1. Poor Law Unions, County Mayo. Source: Adapted from *First Report of the Commissioners Appointed to Inquire into the Number and Boundaries of the Poor Law Unions and Electoral Divisions in Ireland, with Appendix and Plans,* PP 1849 [1015], xxiii, p. 431.

Palmer, Mr. Francis O'Donnell on the board, his agent in Castlebar, and his tenant Andrew Walsh is there representing him. Then we have Sir Robert Lynch Blosse and his agent Mr. Tardy, as ex-officio guardians, and Francis Carty, his bailiff, is a guardian. There are other bailiffs and agents on the board.

In Ballina we have Sir C. Gore as Chairman, U. A. Knox, his brother-in-law as Vice-Chairman, Lieutenant-Colonel Gore, brother to the Chairman, E. C. Perry, another brother-in-law to the former gentleman, Henry Joynt, the Chairman's agent, and James Joynt, brother to the latter and agent to Mr. Perry, besides several tenants, their nominees and supporters on the board. In Westport we have the Marquis of Sligo as Chairman up to recently; his brother Lord J. T. Browne is the present Chairman; Hugh Wilbraham, their brother-in-law, as ex-officio; their agent J. S. Smith as elected guardian, besides two bailiffs, and a large number of their tenants as nominees on the board – all appointments from Clerk of the Union down to the lowest grade of official, are the favourites of these parties.[32]

Despite the ability of landlords to pack the boards with supporters, large farmers and townsmen (other than members of the gentry) had a substantial presence on the boards by the late 1870s. Feingold found that in 1873 there were at least ten tenant farmers on the Castlebar board and twelve on the Westport board. For the most part they were large farmers who, along with townsmen, brought a pro-tenant interest to the Mayo boards of guardians, although this alliance did not hold a majority on any board until the late 1880s. During the 1870s these elected guardians became agents in Mayo of Irish nationalism and leaders of the incipient tenant protest. Feingold argues persuasively that the elected poor law guardians formed the core of a new "rural elite" of "politically conscious and experienced men who were influential among the tenantry, and who, when called upon, were able to . . . perform the organizational chores required to make the Land League viable."[33]

FENIANISM AND POPULAR PROTEST

During the first two decades following the Famine, County Mayo experienced little if any agrarian agitation. The Tenant League of the 1850s was largely a movement of substantial farmers and was confined for the most part to the eastern and southern regions of the country. A branch was formed in Castlebar in 1850, a year that saw several large tenant right meetings in the county.[34] The largest was a gala affair at Trafalgar, the residence of Col. Ouseley Higgins, MP. *The Telegraph or Connaught Ranger* reported that 260 tents "exclusive of fruit and other stands" were set up on the lawn. "From almost every tent the sounds of the Irish bagpipe and violin were heard gladdening the year with strains of Irish music, while neatly attired lads and lasses – and of those the west can boast not a few – tripped it gaily on the light fantastic toe."[35] Thirteen resolutions were passed at the meeting. They ranged from condemning landlords for evictions and rack-rents, to praising the work of the Tenant League, to calling for a just settlement of the land question that could "only be effected by an act of parliament, framed in the spirit

---

[32] *CT*, 6 July 1878.
[33] Feingold, *The Revolt of the Tenantry*, p. 51.
[34] Whyte, *The Independent Irish Party*, p. 6; Clark, *Social Origins of the Irish Land War*, pp. 213–15.
[35] *The Telegraph or Connaught Ranger*, 4 Sept. 1850.

of fair play, and based on the strict principles of commutative justice, whereby relative 'rights and duties' shall be marked for Landlords as well as Tenants."[36] This and the handful of subsequent tenant right meetings in the county over the next few years were linked closely with the independent opposition in Parliament and its futile efforts to push for the adoption of legislation that would guarantee the "three Fs" of fair rents, fixity of tenure and free sale of a tenant's interest in the holding. The meetings generated little enthusiasm beyond that for the meetings themselves and spawned no agrarian movement in the county, violent or otherwise, during the 1850s and 1860s. In fact, the rate of agrarian crimes in post-Famine Mayo, per 1000 agrarian holdings above 1 acre, was below the average rate for both Ireland as a whole and for the province of Connacht.[37] In an editorial in 1854, *The Telegraph or Connaught Ranger* explained this passivity on the part of Mayo farmers as being a consequence of their improving condition:

> For months after months the enemies of the people have been exulting in an extraordinary lull of the Tenant Right agitation. The chief cause of this, as we believe, is not very mysterious or very deplorable. There has been a great deal of apathy in it, doubtless, and no wonder – the people have some reason to feel apathetic with a cause so vital yet so often betrayed . . . But the chief cause of this apparent apathy is, after all, not so gloomy . . . The farmers have, at last, got one season of low rents and high prices together; and console themselves in the absence of legislative protection by the natural barrier which a prosperous harvest has interposed between them and the crowbar.[38]

This apparent lack of interest in an agrarian movement lasted until the late 1860s when the county experienced a sharp increase in agrarian disorder.

A significant degree of responsibility for this surge of violence rests with members of the Irish Republican Brotherhood – the Fenians. Fenianism first surfaced in Mayo during the mid-1860s. By the end of the decade its influence among the small farmers, shopkeepers and artisans of the county was such that the Fenians were in a position to employ their organizational experience and political consciousness in support of an agrarian movement. Prior to this coming together of Fenianism and

---

[36] *Ibid.*
[37] SPO, Returns of Agrarian Outrages Specially Reported in Each County to the Constabulary, 1849–83, ref. from T. W. Moody, *Davitt and Irish Revolution, 1846–82* (Oxford, 1981), pp. 33, 566.
[38] *The Telegraph or Connaught Ranger*, 10 May 1854.

agrarianism in the west of Ireland, Fenianism throughout Ireland had been an urban-based political movement that appealed primarily to Ireland's Catholic bourgeoisie and petit bourgeoisie, "the alienated sons of commercial prosperity," in R. V. Comerford's words, and to urban and farm laborers.[39] The movement had little appeal to the nation's farmers, especially to the small farmers of the west, since it was unwilling to support a campaign for agrarian reform, fearing that a campaign for social reform would dilute the national struggle for Irish independence. Further, the Fenian leadership maintained that no social justice for Ireland could be expected from the British parliament and thus must wait until an independent Irish government was established. The Fenian plan was to have tenant farmers reject any form of constitutional struggle for land reform and embrace instead an armed campaign for national independence in defiance of both the clergy and moderate nationalists.

In this context, Mayo's first Fenians were townsmen rather than farmers, a group of whom were arrested in Castlebar in October 1865. By April 1866 twenty Fenian suspects were confined in the county gaol at Castlebar, the "great proportion" being natives of the town, according to *The Telegraph or Connaught Ranger*.[40] Those Fenian suspects arrested after February 1866 were gaoled under the provisions of an act of parliament suspending habeas corpus in Ireland.[41] During the first two months of the application of the act, thirty-four Fenian suspects were arrested in County Mayo without formal charges being levied against them. By early 1868 a total of forty-seven Fenian suspects had been arrested in the county under the terms of the act, representing roughly 4 percent of those arrested nationwide.[42] In addition to those arrested, between 1866 and 1871 local police reported the names of eighty-five additional Fenian suspects.[43]

These two lists, which record names, occupations and places of residence for the majority of the suspected Fenians, reveal the town-based, artisanal and small business character of Fenianism in County

---

[39] R. V. Comerford, *The Fenians in Context: Irish Politics and Society, 1848–82* (Dublin, 1985), p. 40; R. V. Comerford, "Patriotism as Pastime: The Appeal of Fenianism in the Mid-1860s," *Irish Historical Studies*, 22 (1981), pp. 239–42; Hoppen, "National Politics and Local Realities in Mid-Nineteenth Century Ireland," pp. 214–15; Clark, *Social Origins of the Irish Land War*, pp. 202–4.

[40] *The Telegraph or Connaught Ranger*, 25 Oct. 1865, 18 Apr. 1866.

[41] Habeas Corpus Suspension (Ireland) Act, 29 & 30 Vict., c. 1.

[42] SPO, Police and Crime Records, Fenian Papers, Abstract of Cases of Persons Arrested Under Habeas Corpus Suspension Act, 1866–8.

[43] SPO, Police and Crime Records, Fenian Papers, Fenianism: Index of Names.

Table 5.3. *Occupations of suspected Fenians, relative to the occupational distribution of the male labor force, County Mayo, 1866–1871*

Occupations	Percentage of suspects	Percentage arrested	Occupational class as a percentage of male labour force, County Mayo, 1871
Professional sector	8.3	8.1	4.3
Teachers	5.0	8.1	
Clergy	3.3		
Commercial and industrial sector	86.7	81.1	8.6
Tradesmen and artisans	70.0	64.9	
Clerks and commercial assistants	8.3	13.5	
Urban laborers	8.3	2.7	
Agricultural sector	5.0	10.8	70.4
Farmers and farmers' sons	1.7	5.4	
Farm laborers	3.3	2.7	
Other agricultural		2.7	
Total suspects	60		
Total arrested	37		

Notes and sources: Suspected Fenians are drawn from SPO, Police and Crime Reports, Fenian Papers, Fenianism: Index of Names 1866–71; arrested Fenians are drawn from SPO, Police and Crime Records, Fenian Papers, Abstract of Cases of Persons Arrested Under Habeas Corpus Suspension Act, 1866–8; *Census of Ireland, 1871, Pt. I, Vol. IV, No. III*, p. 363; a full list of the occupations appears in Appendix 2.

Mayo. As illustrated in Table 5.3, 86.7 percent of suspected Fenians and 81.1 percent of those arrested were from the commercial and industrial sector of the county's economy, the majority being tradesmen or artisans. Given that the 1871 census records only 8.6 percent of Mayo's male labor force as being occupied in the "commercial" or "industrial class," the high proportion of tradesmen and artisans among Fenians is particularly significant. At the other extreme is the farming sector which occupied 70.4 percent of Mayo's male labor force but only 5 percent of Fenian suspects and 10.8 percent of arrested Fenians. Not surprisingly, given their occupations, 54 percent of the suspects and 76 percent of those arrested resided in one of Mayo's seven towns with 1000 inhabitants or more, although only 8 percent of the county's population lived in these towns; 67 percent of the suspects and 76 percent of those arrested lived in the central corridor of the county.

From this base among townsmen, Fenianism established a firm

footing in Mayo from which it spread to the farming community. In 1938 a Ballintubber native told an Irish Folklore Commission archivist that during her youth in the late 1860s and early 1870s the countryside was "teeming" with young Fenians who drilled at night with wooden rifles and revolvers. She reported that they took up the farmers' cause by threatening landlords and "land grabbers" who took up land from which others had been evicted.[44] According to Fenian leader John Devoy, Mayo was the "best" organized county in Ireland by the 1870s, although by this time Fenianism was on the wane throughout Ireland.[45] Support for Devoy's assertion comes from a government report of 24 September 1871: "You will observe that Connaught is the best organized of the three [sic] provinces and during the past three years the leaders . . . have done more in the way of arming than I believe the other three put together."[46] Police reports reveal shipments of arms coming into the county in 1869 and 1870, many being shipped from Birmingham and Leeds by Fenian arms agent and Mayo native Michael Davitt. It appears that Mayo was quickly becoming the home of one of the best armed Fenian organiz-ations in Ireland.[47]

The reasons behind the late surge of Fenian activity in Mayo are difficult to trace, but a portion of the responsibility rests with Fenian organizers from County Galway. Prominent among them were Matthew Harris, a building contractor from Ballinasloe and "the most important man in the organisation in Connacht," and Mark Ryan, a student at St. Jarlath's, the diocesan college at Tuam.[48] Their success was determined by a new attitude towards an agrarian struggle on the part of many Fenians, especially those living among the small farmers of western Ireland. The failure of Ireland's farmers to respond during the Fenian rising of 1867, and the growing belief that the time was not ripe for an armed nationalist struggle brought many Fenians to eschew "pure" military nationalism and turn their attention to the land question. Many of those who made this transition were men of the lower social classes, a remarkable number of whom grew up in industrial Lancashire, the sons

---

44 Department of Irish Folklore Archives, University College, Dublin, Fenians, Ballintuber, MS 485, pp. 208–9.

45 J. Devoy, *Recollections of an Irish Rebel* (New York, 1929), p. 33.

46 SPO, Fenian Papers, Dublin Castle Report, 24 Sept. 1871. Quoted in Bew, *Land and the National Question in Ireland*, p. 43.

47 *Ibid.*, pp. 43–4; Moody, *Davitt and Irish Revolution*, p. 73; SPO, Fenian Files, 2 Dec., 5 Dec. 1869, MS 5191R, 4 Apr. 1870, MS 6114R/6246R, 21 Mar. 1871, MS 7303R.

48 M. Ryan, *Fenian Memories*, ed. with intro. by T. F. Sullivan, 2nd ed. (Dublin, 1946), pp. 20–41.

of emigrants from the west of Ireland.[49] Their burning resentment towards social injustice never fitted in with the passivity toward social issues that characterized the Fenians' middle-class leadership. Following the failed rising of 1867, the old leadership's grip on the movement slackened, allowing the lower-class militants a new importance.[50] Since many of them had roots deep in rural Ireland, they turned their attention naturally towards a renewed agrarian struggle.

In Mayo, that agrarian struggle began in earnest in 1869–70, when the reported instances of agrarian crime increased markedly.[51] Police reported instances of tenants being threatened if they paid rent in excess of the government valuation and of graziers being threatened and, in at least one instance, murdered.[52] Scottish graziers who had taken leases on large tracts of land following the Famine were particular targets of agrarian outrage. In January 1870 eighteen Scottish and English farmers holding land near Ballinrobe and Newport petitioned the Lord Lieutenant requesting protection in the wake of threatening notices. They said that they had come to Mayo "with skill and capital, after the year 1848, to occupy lands comparatively waste, giving employment and adding to the fruitfulness of the country." They were now, they explained, victims of "a deep and diabolical conspiracy . . . whose motto is 'Ireland for the Irish' having for its object the extermination of all English and Scotch residing in this part of Her Majesty's Kingdom, whether owners or cultivators of the land." The petitioners, whose annual rents ranged from £100 to £2300, were holders of large tracts of the grazing land, much of it in the rich central corridor, that they had occupied between 1848 and 1860.[53] They were targeted as "land jobbers," holding land from which Irish farmers had been evicted. Their prosperity was evidence of the growing disparity in the county between those profiting from rising cattle prices and the numerous small farmers who were not. But more importantly they were symbols of the link between the land and national questions that was essential for the union of agrarianism and nationalism. Irish farmers not only coveted the land held by Scots and English but saw

[49] Moody, *Davitt and Irish Revolution*, pp. 43–9.
[50] Clark, *Social Origins of the Irish Land War*, pp. 206–7; Bew, *Land and the National Question in Ireland*, p. 41.
[51] The degree of increase in agrarian crime is difficult to ascertain with certainty because of a new method of registering outrages on the part of the constabulary. See: Moody, *Davitt and Irish Revolution*, pp. 33, 566.
[52] Public Record Office, London, CAB 37/4/72, p. 13, ref. from *ibid.*, p. 33; SPO, CSORP, 6 Jan. 1870, MS 7015, 15 Jan. 1871, MS 9782.
[53] *Ibid.*, 15 Jan. 1870, MS 7015.

it as their rightful inheritance. This belief on the part of Irish farmers became a central feature of the ideology of the Land war. In the early 1870s it appears to have helped forge the connection between Fenians and small farmers. This was affirmed by the petitioners when they noted "the probable connection between the barbarous designs of those conspirators and the language which has been used at public meetings, ostensibly assembled to urge the liberation of [Fenian] 'political prisoners.'"[54]

Agrarian agitation subsided in the county during the mid-1870s but the influence of Fenianism continued. This influence was most dramatically revealed in the 1874 election of John O'Connor Power, a member of the Supreme Council of the IRB, to one of Mayo's parliamentary seats.[55] A native of Ballinasloe, County Galway but resident of England, Power had traveled to Mayo early in 1868, apparently as part of an effort by the Supreme Council to establish Fenian units in the county.[56] During the early 1870s he continued his Fenian activities while enrolled as a student at St. Jarlath's, the diocesan college of Tuam and a hotbed of Fenian activities in the west of Ireland.[57] In 1873 Power was influential in getting the Supreme Council of the IRB to drop its insistence upon insurrection and to endorse, cautiously, the constitutional efforts of the Home Rule League.[58] In effect, this fragile endorsement of constitutional nationalism was in the spirit of the alliance between Fenians and agrarian agitators that had been forged in County Mayo several years earlier.

Power was at the center of this new policy at both the national and local levels. By the time he announced his intention to stand for parliament in Mayo, he could claim the support of several prominent Irish members of parliament, Archbishop McHale, and the local Fenians, of whom he was the most notable.[59] He assembled an election committee composed of prominent Fenians who created what *The Ballinrobe Chronicle* called a "vast" organization in support of Power's candidacy.[60]

---

54 *Ibid.*
55 See: D. Jordan, "John O'Connor Power, Charles Stewart Parnell and the Centralisation of Popular Politics in Ireland," *Irish Historical Studies*, 25 (1986), pp. 49–53.
56 SPO, Fenian Files, 4 Jan. 1868, MS 242R.
57 Ryan, *Fenian Memories*, pp. 28–37; Moody, *Davitt and Irish Nationalism*, pp. 45–6, 124.
58 Jordan, "John O'Connor Power," pp. 48–9.
59 *Ibid.*, pp. 50–1; E. Larkin, *The Roman Catholic Church and the Home Rule Movement in Ireland, 1870–1874* (Chapel Hill, North Carolina, 1990), pp. 251–5.
60 *The Ballinrobe Chronicle and Mayo Advertiser*, 23 May 1874.

In addition to Fenians and their supporters, Power's candidacy was endorsed by townsmen, including twelve Castlebar merchants who signed his nomination papers. Among them was James Daly, a member of the Castlebar Board of Guardians and a grazier who, as editor of *The Connaught Telegraph* after 1876, was to become one of Mayo's most prominent nationalists and supporters of agrarian reform.[61] This potent alliance of Fenians and townsmen, when combined with Power's oratorical prowess and advanced views, proved successful despite the fierce opposition of many priests, although significantly not of Archbishop McHale.

In an effort to prevent the election of an advanced nationalist, who was also an outsider, the priests had put their rusty political machine to work for the first time since 1857. *The Times* reported that the Catholic clergy were leaving "no means . . . untried to influence popular feeling," while the nationalist newspaper, *Irishman,* contended that Power faced a "desperate struggle against the combined influence of the whole priest-hood of the county."[62] However, the days when the clergy and gentry could quietly control parliamentary politics in the county were past. The structural changes in Mayo society had created a new political environment, one in which militant nationalists, townsmen and farmers could ally to challenge successfully the influence of priests and landlords over local and national politics. It was this alliance, first forged during the 1874 election, that would provide the political consciousness, organizational experience and extensive influence among the farming classes that brought the Land War to County Mayo.

THE SOCIAL BASE OF THE LAND WAR IN COUNTY MAYO

The Land War, which began in County Mayo in April 1879, was fought to a large degree in the center of the county. As Map 5.2 illustrates, 76 percent of the land meetings held in the county between April 1879 and June 1881 took place in or on the borders of the lowland corridor, with 58 percent of the meetings occurring in south-central Mayo. This was in sharp contrast to the pattern of pre-Famine protest in the county in which protest activities were more evenly distributed between core and periphery. Moreover, by the time of the Land War approximately

---

[61] *Ibid.*; Feingold, *The Revolt of the Tenantry*, pp. 95–6.
[62] *The Times*, 1 June 1874.

55 percent of the county's population lived in the periphery, giving it a significantly lower rate of agrarianism per capita than the core, again in contrast with the situation prior to the Famine.[63] In addition, roughly 60 percent of the Mayo branches of the Land League were formed in the center of the county.[64] In part, this clustering of land movement activities in the core was a response to the relative ease of transportation and communication within the region. More significantly, it demonstrated the ability of the new farming and trading elite to structure politics in the county. Throughout Ireland the land agitation of the 1870s and 1880s was strongest in those regions where a dynamic livestock-based economy coexisted most closely with subsistence farming and rural poverty.[65] Mayo was no exception. Its central corridor was the hub of the county's livestock trade and of the wealth that accrued from it and, at the same time, the area where the lives, wealth and influence of the graziers contrasted most sharply with those of the small farmers.

Tension between graziers and small farmers stemmed from the post-Famine consolidation of smallholdings into grazing farms. The land clearances that wrenched many farm families from the land had been heaviest in the fertile center. Those clearances remained a source of great bitterness among the remaining small farmers and provided a contentious issue around which they could mobilize. The pace of land conversion had slackened considerably by the late 1870s, but "land grabbing" or "land jobbing" continued to reinforce the small farmers' sense of their vulnerability. Many "grabbers" were townsmen seeking grazing land that could be expected to turn a good profit with little effort on their part. James Simpson, a large grazier and one of the signatories of the 1870 petition from Scottish and English farmers to the Lord Lieutenant, told the Richmond Commission in 1880 that a "great many shopkeepers" were taking up newly converted grazing farms in his neighborhood near Ballinrobe. "These people," he testified, "hold shops in the county towns, and they hold grazing lands besides, and they give no

---

63 For list of Land League meetings, see Appendix 4.B. For distribution of pre-Famine protest see Map 3.1, p. 99 above. At the time of the 1831 census, approximately 45 percent of the county's population resided in the periphery. As a consequence of the thinning of the population in the core and the redistribution of the county's population discussed in Chapter 4, by the time of the 1881 census approximately 55 percent of the population resided in the periphery. The per capita level of Land War meetings is one meeting per 2255 people in the core and one meeting per 8873 people in the periphery.

64 Based on a list of forty local branches compiled from *The Connaught Telegraph*.

65 Clark, *Social Origins of the Irish Land War*, p. 255.

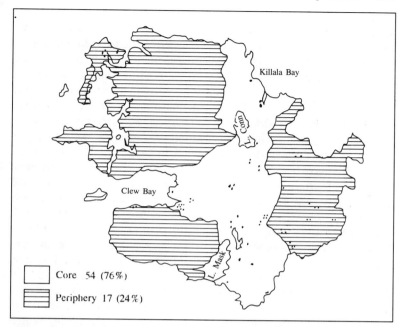

Map 5.2. Distribution of land meetings within the core and the periphery, 1879–1881

employment except to a shepherd to manage them."[66] Joseph McKenna, a tenant farmer, caricatured these ambitious shopkeepers at a land meeting held at Carrabawn near Westport in October 1879: "When a shopkeeper is twelve months in business he must have a cow to give him milk. After two years he must get a pony and trap and after three or four years he looks around for some holding of land, and by offering a high rent encourages the landlord to increase his rental."[67] As shopkeepers cast around for a piece of land, their economic interests began to compete with those of the small farmers whose land was most vulnerable to bids from townsmen with ready cash.

No doubt the indebtedness of many farmers to these same shopkeepers kept muted the farmers' anger over the townsmen's propensity to take up land. William O'Brien reported from Mayo to *The Freeman's Journal* that by the summer of 1879, after two years of disastrous harvests and

[66] *Richmond Commission, Minutes of Evidence*, I, p. 403.
[67] *CT*, 1 Nov. 1879.

low livestock prices, the farmers owed £200,000 to shopkeepers in the county.[68] Professor Baldwin and Major Robertson, Assistant Commissioners to the Richmond Commission investigating agriculture for the House of Commons, reported that "in many places they [farmers] owe on an average from three to five years' rent to shopkeepers alone. In some cases we . . . found they owed as much as eight to ten years' rent to shopkeepers." Baldwin went on to explain to the Commission how, in his opinion, this state of indebtedness had come about.

It has been going on increasing within the last eight to ten years. In some places a little further back than that.

People have been from a variety of remote causes deficient in thrift. Then came the great bound of modern prosperity. The growth of wealth led to the establishment of a great many banks; the banks gave money on easy terms to shopkeepers, and then the shopkeepers as it were, forced a system of credit upon the small farmers; and all of a sudden that has collapsed. The people got the goods on easy terms, and owing to their want of forethought and thrift, they accepted the goods so offered to them; and all of a sudden that has collapsed.[69]

Without doubt, the willingness of the shopkeepers to extend credit shielded many small farm families from acute distress. This was especially true during the economic crisis of 1877–80, during which investigators regularly credited shopkeepers with saving the farming population from destitution.[70]

The economic interdependence that developed between the urban traders and the agricultural community did not result in open tension between them. It seems that the terms of credit were not considered exorbitant by the standards of the day and were accepted by the majority of debtors. The majority of lenders did not need to resort to excessive demands for repayment until driven to financial collapse in 1880. Before that the economic bond between townsmen and farmers was to a large extent a congenial and stable one.[71]

Yet the tension was often right below the surface. While the economic bond was one of mutual interdependence, the upper hand belonged to the shopkeepers. As creditors, they could pressure the farmers to pay up

[68] *FJ*, 25 Aug. 1879.
[69] *Richmond Commission, Minutes of Evidence*, I, p. 89.
[70] *The Irish Crisis of 1879–80: Proceedings of the Mansion House Relief Committee, 1880* (Dublin, 1881), p. 8; *FJ*, 25 Aug. 1879.
[71] Clark, "The Political Mobilization of Irish Farmers," pp. 490–1.

by threatening to cut off credit. As respected members of the Catholic community, they were frequently on good terms with the local clergy, who apparently could be relied upon to use their influence to encourage recalcitrant debtors to meet their obligations.[72] When persuasion failed, the creditor could resort to legal action against the defaulter, although the relative rarity of this course of action before the economic distress of 1879–80 bears testimony to the ability of the majority of farmers to meet their obligations as well as to the ability of the shopkeepers to enforce a "moral economy" of their own making. Baldwin and Robertson, in their testimonies before the Richmond Commission, were quite insistent that even during the distress of 1879–80 the shopkeepers took "very good care of themselves." Baldwin believed that as a result of the high interest charged, shopkeepers had their principal repaid "over and over again." According to Robertson, shopkeepers exacted payments during the years of distress even though many landlords did not. As a consequence, he reported, "this [1880] has been a very good year for shopkeepers. The tenants have paid them, and they have not paid their landlords." Those tenants unwilling or unable to pay were liable, Baldwin and Robertson contended, to have their goods or stock seized by the shopkeeper in lieu of payment.[73]

The amicable nature during prosperous times of the bond between townsmen and small farmers should not be allowed to disguise the stresses created in rural Mayo by the economic and political authority exercised by small businessmen. The vast clientage of small farmers had little choice but to accept credit and borrowing as integral parts of the family economy, but with them came a complex system of obligations to the patron shopkeepers.

The degree to which townsmen and the more prosperous farmers shaped and controlled the land agitation is difficult to assess. As a consequence of their involvement with the poor law boards and the nationalist movement, they were the most politicized members of the community and were well-positioned to take a prominent role in the agitation. In the early stages of the agitation in Mayo, townsmen and large farmers played a pivotal role. The most important organizer of the land agitation, James Daly, was a poor law guardian with substantial business interests in Castlebar, including *The Connaught Telegraph*, of which he was proprietor and editor, and held in 1879 at least two grazing

[72] Gibbon and Higgins, "Patronage, Tradition and Modernisation," p. 33.
[73] *Richmond Commission, Minutes of Evidence*, I, p. 109.

farms totaling 380 acres.[74] Similarly, John J. Louden, whose importance to the early days of the agitation is second only to Daly's, was a Westport-based barrister and poor law guardian who held a 7000 acre farm from the Marquis of Sligo and the Earl of Lucan.[75] Both men joined with Fenians, farmers and other townsmen to organize the first land agitation mass meetings during the spring and summer of 1879. For example, the first meeting, at Irishtown on 20 April, was organized primarily by Daly, along with two farmers with holdings in excess of 100 acres, the son of one of the largest graziers in Mayo, two shopkeepers, a school teacher, and a commercial traveler.[76] All of these men had their farms or businesses located in the central heartland of Mayo.

Statistical evidence on the occupations of participants in the Land War is rare. The most nearly complete available record of occupations of Land War activists is contained in lists of men recommended by local constables for arrest and men actually arrested under provisions of the Protection of Persons and Property Act, 1881.[77] Clark compared the occupations of 845 men arrested nationwide with census data and found that 32.6 percent of those arrested could be classified in the "commercial and industrial sector" of the economy, although that sector represented only 23.3 percent of the labor force.[78]

Table 5.4 presents a similar analysis of the lists that include both the sixty-four Mayo men recommended for arrest and the thirteen of them actually arrested. The results do not differ significantly from those found by Clark. Men engaged in trade and commerce were far overrepresented relative to their numbers in the labor force, while farmers were underrepresented relative to their numbers in the county. Not surprisingly, 73 percent of the townsmen who were recommended for arrest resided in the central corridor, as did 71 percent of the entire list of suspects. Ninety-five percent of the farmers classified as being in "good" or "fair" circumstances lived in the core, while among the farmers in "poor" circumstances, half lived in the core and half in the periphery. Despite the possible biases on the part of the police towards the more visible town-

---

74 Feingold, *The Revolt of the Tenantry*, pp. 95–6; PROI, Householders' Returns, 1901 Census, Mayo, parcel 65, p. 31; SPO, Crime Branch Special (CBS) Papers, Biography of James Daly, Castlebar, 21 Apr. 1898, MS 16005/s; *Bessborough Commission, Vol. II, Minutes of Evidence, Pt. I*, p. 566.
75 Feingold, *The Revolt of the Tenantry*, pp. 67; Lucan Rent Ledger, 1848–73; PROI, Householders' Returns, 1901 Census, Mayo, parcel 150, p. 8.
76 See pp. 217–20 below.
77 44 Vict., c. 4.
78 Clark, *Social Origins of the Irish Land War*, pp. 250, 268.

Table 5.4. *Occupations of persons whose arrest was recommended and of those arrested under the Protection of Persons and Property Act, 1881, County Mayo*

Occupations	Percentage of suspects	Percentage of suspects arrested	Occupational class as a percentage of male labour force, County Mayo, 1881
Professional sector	0.0	0.0	0
Teachers			
Clergy			
Commercial and industrial sector	32.8	38.5	13
Tradesmen and artisans			
In "good circumstances"	10.9	15.4	
In "fair circumstances"	14.1	15.4	
In "poor circumstances"	4.7	7.7	
Clerks and commercial assistants	3.1	0.0	
Urban laborers	0.0	0.0	
Agricultural sector	60.9	30.8	80
Farmers and farmers' sons			
In "good circumstances"	21.9	23.1	
In "fair circumstances"	15.6	7.7	
In "poor circumstances"	17.2	0.0	
Farm laborers	4.7	0.0	
Other agricultural	1.6	0.0	
Other or no occupation given	6.3	30.8	
Total suspects	64		
Total arrested	14		

Sources: SPO, Police and Crime Reports, Protection of Persons and Property Act, 1881, List of Persons Whose Arrest Was Recommended and List of All Persons Arrested, Carton 1; *Census of Ireland, 1881, Pt. I, Vol. III, No. 3,* p. 363. The full list appears in Appendix 3.

based agitators, these lists reveal clearly that townsmen and the more prosperous farmers from the central lowlands played a preponderant role in the Land War in County Mayo.

These conclusions are reinforced by an analysis of the occupations of branch officers of the National Land League in Mayo. From a list of 166 officers compiled from *The Connaught Telegraph,* I was able to locate in commercial directories, newspapers, householder returns from the 1901 census, and other sources, occupational information on 73 (44 percent) of the officers. This method, which results in an overrepresentation of the more visible merchants, again points to the significant role taken in the agitation by traders and farmers from Mayo's central corridor. Seventy percent of the 166 branch officers resided in central Mayo, despite the fact that only 45 percent of the population resided there. In addition, of the 73 branch officers for whom occupational information could be found, 62 percent were traders and artisans while 38 percent were farmers.

The significant role of merchants and strong farmers in leading a movement that drew large numbers of small farmers into its ranks would appear to lend support to the thesis proposed by Samuel Clark and others that the post-Famine structural changes in Irish society had produced a substantial degree of solidarity within the farming and trading community by "increasing the economic and cultural integration of Irish society." This integration, Clark argues, had fostered the creation of a strong "rural–urban coalition" to challenge the political and economic power of the landed elite.[79] Without question, by the late 1870s County Mayo was characterized by a large, heterogeneous livestock-based farming community that was joined by vital economic ties to town-based merchants. Yet the degree to which this social and economic structure established the basis for political union is open to question. By the time of the Land War there was a significant division in Mayo between the farming structures and economic strategies of large and small farmers. In consequence, the social priorities and long-term goals of the two groups were quite different. The large landholders and merchants wanted the full extension of capitalism in the countryside through the abolition of the landlord monopoly on land ownership, and sought to seize political power from the landed gentry and, if necessary, from the clergy. In contrast, the small farmers, who had no objection to assaulting land-lordism, hoped for a more equitable distribution of the land at the expense of both landlords and large tenant graziers. For a brief moment in 1879 Mayo's large farmers and merchants joined with the county's small farmers, but in an alliance that could only last by focusing on toppling landlordism and obtaining relief from economic distress. The small farmers of Mayo played a substantial role during the early stages of the agitation and their willingness to participate added vastly to the agitation's power. However, they had little influence on its direction. Leadership came from the post-Famine elite, whose slow consolidation of political and economic power made the Land War possible. Yet, as the movement's early vitality began to fade after six months, the elite found its mass of supporters difficult to keep in line.

---

[79] *Ibid.*, pp. 138, 263.

Part 3

The Land War in County Mayo

6. *The West's Awake! The early months of the Land War*

The West's Asleep

When all beside a vigil keep
The West's asleep, the West's asleep
Alas and well may Erin weep
When Connacht lives in slumber deep
. . .
But hark some voice like thunder spake
The West's awake, the West's awake
Sing oh, hurrah, let England quake
We'll watch till death for Erin's sake!

Attributed to Thomas Davis

Now Alice, for goodness' sake don't begin. I am sick of that
Land League. From morning to night it is nothing but coercion and
Griffith's valuation.

George Moore, *A Drama in Muslin*[1]

The Irish Land War began at Irishtown in County Mayo on 20 April 1879.
By summer much of the county was enveloped in an agitation consisting
of Sunday rallies with fiery speeches and militant resolutions. It was a
heady time, when gaily dressed men and women marched to rallies in
military formation, following pike-carrying horsemen and local bands
playing patriotic airs. They cheered lustily the most inflammatory anti-
landlord speeches and listened attentively to balladeers lament their
plight and joyfully affirm their new militancy. Yet this air of festivity
could not mask the increased foreboding of Mayo people that the
economic distress of the previous two years would soon turn into a full-

---

[1] George Moore, *A Drama in Muslin* (Gerrards Cross, England, 1981), p. 107.

199

fledged famine. This fear about their economic and physical well-being provided the atmosphere in which the small farmers of Mayo could ally with large farmers, local townsmen and national political leaders to create a movement capable of challenging the political, economic and social foundations of Irish society. During the spring and summer of 1879, the small farmers were fearful but most were not yet hungry and the momentum, if not the organization, of the movement rested with them. Once the harvest of 1879 failed and starvation became a reality, the momentum of the movement was captured by larger farmers, townsmen, priests and national political leaders.

THE ECONOMIC CRISIS OF 1877–1880

An unforeseen confluence of bad weather, meager harvests and low livestock prices between 1877 and 1879 undermined the post-Famine prosperity of large farmers and shopkeepers while breaking the fragile pillars upholding the economy of small western farmers. Rain and cold weather diminished the grain crop, brought about shortages of fodder for stock, rotted potatoes and prevented the drying of turf for fuel. Coupled with the effects of bad weather, competition from American beef drove down prices in an English market already depressed by a downturn in the economy. To complete the devastation of the Mayo economy, wet weather and an agricultural depression in England and Scotland reduced the demand for seasonal workers, while in Mayo lack of feed and a cholera epidemic killed many chickens. In consequence of this multi-faceted economic crisis, many Mayo families had few sources of cash with which to pay the rent and purchase food.

To many observers the most alarming element of the crisis was the failure of the potato crop in those districts in western Ireland where the population remained most heavily dependent upon it. During the post-Famine period the small farmers had broadened their family economies to include cash-producing activities, but they still subsisted primarily on the potato. This was especially the case in the peripheral regions of Mayo where the land was not suitable for growing much but potatoes. The poor potato harvest of 1877 hurt them severely. In Mayo the yield was 1.8 tons per statute acre compared to 5.1 tons per acre the previous year and well below the 3.3 tons per acre average of the previous seven years.[2] By

---

[2] *Preliminary Report on the Returns of Agricultural Produce in Ireland in 1879; With Tables*, PP 1880 [C 2495], lxxvi, p. 37.

February 1878 the potatoes from this meager crop had been consumed in some districts and the first reports of starvation appeared in the press.[3] In May, Fr. William Joyce, PP of Louisburgh wrote to the Westport Board of Guardians expressing fear for many of his parishioners as a consequence of the failure of the potato crop. The guardians acknowledged that economic distress existed in the union, but denied Fr. Joyce's request for outdoor relief for the destitute, holding firm to their commitment not to grant relief to any able-bodied family outside of the workhouse.[4]

Widespread distress in 1878 was averted by an improved fall harvest. In the Westport union the potatoes were reported to be small but sound, and in the county as a whole the yield was a moderate 3 tons per statute acre.[5] The greatest distress was confined to the towns of Mayo where the weather and general depression of trade hurt laborers and small tradesmen. In late December 1878, Bishop Conway of Killala wrote to the *Ballina Herald* that the laboring poor in Ardnaree, adjacent to Ballina, "at no time . . . stand more in need of relief than during the last fortnight."[6] In January a committee was formed in Castlebar by Canon Magee PP to raise relief funds for the poor of that city who were unemployed due to the "unexampled and prolonged severity of the weather."[7]

Tenant farmers with a store of potatoes could avoid starvation during the winter and spring of 1879, although ceaseless rains and cold weather during planting time caused anxiety about the success of the fall crop. Of more immediate concern was cash with which to pay the rent and the shopkeeper-creditors. A substantial portion of the cash income of both large and small Mayo farmers came from the sale of cattle; however, between 1876 and 1877 prices for one to two year old cattle fell 12 percent, while the price for two to three year old cattle fell 4 percent. Seen as a percentage of the average prices of the previous six years, prices for one to two year old cattle in 1877 were down 5 percent, while prices for two to three year old cattle remained normal. In 1878 cattle prices stabilized, but in 1879 they again plummeted to the 1877 level for young cattle and to 8 percent below the 1871–76 average for two

---

[3] *CT*, 2 Feb. 1878.

[4] *Ibid.*, 1 June 1878.

[5] *Ibid.*, 24 Aug. 1878; *Preliminary Report on . . . Agricultural Produce . . . 1879 . . .*, p. 37.

[6] *CT*, 11 Jan. 1879.

[7] *Ibid*, 4 Jan. 1879.

to three year old cattle.[8] In March 1879 *The Connaught Telegraph* reported:

> nothing could be more calculated to discourage the graziers than the aspect of affairs as presented at the principal opening fair of the season. The Balla spring fair, held on Wednesday last, was fairly supplied with cattle in fair condition, but the prices that could be obtained were far from being remunerative to the seller. There was a fair attendance of buyers, but the majority left without buying a "tail" to use a jobbers' phrase.

In his editorial response to the fair, James Daly wrote:

> The depressed and disheartening state of affairs as presented at the Balla spring fair . . . is a rather gloomy foreboding that the price of cattle is still likely to come lower. The consequent result will be that the value of land must descend in the same ratio . . . There is no alternative left the grazier and the tiller of the soil but to call on the land owners to abate their rents.[9]

At the Balla May fair, "which is as a rule looked up to by the farmers of Mayo as a guide to the fairs of the season," prices were, according to *The Connaught Telegraph*, "fully 60 shillings per head under that obtained on May day 1878." It was reported that many graziers sold their cattle at a loss out of fear of not selling them at all.[10] At the June Balla fair cattle prices were reported to be 20–30s. lower than they had been in May, and by the time of the great September fair at Balla prices were reported to be 25 percent lower than during the previous year and the "most disheartening . . . since the Famine years."[11]

The decline in family income from the drop in cattle prices was compounded by the drop in earnings from seasonal migration. The "Great Depression" of the 1870s and 1880s in Britain brought a gradual shift away from grain tillage, which required the services of Irish harvest laborers, toward livestock production, which required far fewer imported laborers.[12] This trend, when combined with the extremely wet weather and poor British harvests of 1879, brought about a serious decline in

---

[8] Barrington, "A Review of Irish Agricultural Prices," p. 252; Clark, *Social Origins of the Irish Land War*, p. 229.

[9] *CT*, 22 Mar. 1879.

[10] *Ibid.*, 3 May 1879.

[11] *Ibid.*, 14 June and 27 Sept. 1879.

[12] E. J. Hobsbawm, *Industry and Empire* (Harmondsworth, 1969), p. 198; T. W. Fletcher, "The Great Depression of English Agriculture, 1873–1896," *Econ. Hist. Rev.*, 2nd series, 12 (1961), pp. 417–32.

the demand for migratory laborers. T. W. Grimshaw, in his report accompanying the first post-Famine enumeration of migratory laborers, wrote that migratory labor from Ireland to Britain "had been very unremunerative during the past years, especially during 1879, so much so, that the falling off in earnings of those who followed it was a material element in causing the distress which prevailed last winter [1880]."[13] While traveling in Mayo in August 1879 as special correspondent for *The Freeman's Journal*, William O'Brien was told in Ballyhaunis that the postal money orders coming from harvesters in England would not amount to one-third of the £22,000 received the previous year.[14] In Louisburgh he found that only a quarter of the usual average of remittances was coming into the post office from migratory laborers, many of whom were "sick or idle in the great English cities, applying at the workhouse gates for passages home."[15]

By the fall of 1879, with earnings from the sale of stock and from seasonal migration seriously reduced, many farm families were deeply in debt to shopkeepers for the indian meal on which they had survived since spring. In addition, their rents had gone unpaid while they and their landlords waited anxiously for the fall harvest. In August, O'Brien wrote from Mayo: "there is as yet no downright hunger among the small farmers. They are trusted with indian meal." Yet he added ominously, "it depends upon the state of the weather for the next fortnight whether they shall be precipitated into actual famine."[16] Eight days later he wrote from Ballyhaunis:

the prospect of an abundant harvest is at an end; the chance even of a tolerable one hangs dangerously in the balance. The lightnings of Sunday night, the rains and winds which have raged either daily or nightly ever since, have left the footprints of their vengeance deep behind them. The two props of the Mayo farmer's homestead have collapsed miserably upon his head. The potatoes are bad, the turf is worse.[17]

The potato harvest was a pitiful 1.4 tons per statute acre; less than half of what it had been in 1878 and the lowest yield in a decade.[18]

---

[13] *Agricultural Statistics . . . 1880 . . . Relating to Migratory Agricultural Labourers*, p. 6.
[14] *FJ*, 1 Sept. 1879.
[15] *Ibid.*, 28 Aug. 1879.
[16] *Ibid.*, 25 Aug. 1879.
[17] *Ibid.*, 1 Sept. 1879.
[18] *Preliminary Report on . . . Agricultural Produce . . . 1879*, p. 37.

To many observers the situation in Mayo following the fall harvest of 1879 was desperate and portended a famine as severe as that of 1846–9. In his Christmas editorial, James Daly wrote of the "fast approaching famine," and by early January letters to *The Connaught Telegraph* reported that the threatened famine had arrived in some parts of Mayo.[19] Within days of its founding in January 1880, at the insistence of the Lord Mayor of Dublin, the Mansion House Relief Committee received letters from several Mayo priests telling of extreme destitution and of the need for assistance for the starving tenantry.[20] By March, James H. Tuke, retracing a journey to Connacht that he had made during the Great Famine, found that 520 out of 800 families in the Louisburgh parish, 200 out of 276 families in Mulranny, and 70 percent of the people on Achill Island were on some sort of public relief.[21] The relief effort in Bangor-Erris, as related by the Parish Priest, James Durcan, probably paralleled that in many other parts of western Mayo. He reported that "there are 609 families in this parish, 150 of whom were relieved in March, 300 in April, 580 in May."[22]

Given the weakened state of the populace in Mayo, it is not surprising that by summer causes of typhus were surfacing in the most distressed regions. J. A. Fox, reporting to the Mansion House Committee on the condition of the poor in County Mayo, wrote of finding cases of typhus in eastern Mayo in July 1880. His findings were borne out by the Committee's medical commissioners, Dr. George Sigerson and Dr. Joseph Kenny, who also reported cases of typhus and extreme destitution in the county.[23]

To intensify the calamity, cholera decimated the chicken population of the county, thus removing the final prop of the small farm economy. The number of chickens in the county declined 20 percent between 1879 and 1880, with the greatest losses being sustained in the eastern parts of the county where 38 percent of the chickens were destroyed by disease.[24] Mr. Fox reported to the Mansion House Committee that "during the past ten months, but particularly since January last, the hens have been

---

[19] *CT*, 20 Dec. 1879 and 3 Jan. 1880.

[20] *The Irish Crisis of 1879–80*, pp. 232–4.

[21] J. H. Tuke, *Irish Distress and Its Remedies: The Land Question, A Visit to Donegal and Connaught in the Spring of 1880* (London, 1880), pp. 54, 58–9.

[22] *The Irish Crisis of 1879–80*, pp. 254–5.

[23] *Ibid.*, pp. 105–6, 143–50.

[24] *Preliminary Report on . . . Agricultural Produce . . . 1879*, pp. 66–9; *The Agricultural Statistics of Ireland for the Year 1880*, PP 1881 [C 2932], xciii, pp. 57–61.

seized with an epidemic like cholera, and fully 90 per cent of them have succumbed to the disease, which is fatal in a single night."[25] The importance of this loss was stressed by a special correspondent to *The Freeman's Journal*, who in a series of reports titled "Famine and Fever in the West" wrote from Attymas, County Mayo:

> None of these poor people had any means of supporting themselves whatsoever. The cholera had come and killed their hens, their greatest prop. This was the most melancholy thing and the hardest blow of all, this killing of the hens . . . which is as bad to thousands of people as the failure of the crop itself. All the cottiers of the West of Ireland kept hens – in fact it was they who were the greatest suppliers of the egg market . . . While they had these hens they had a treasure by which they could at least keep themselves alive. On all the hens a great epidemic has come.[26]

That this multitude of afflictions did not result in a full-scale famine was due in large part to the enormous efforts undertaken by a series of private relief committees and to the extensive credit given by many shopkeepers. The shopkeepers of Mayo maintained many of their customers during the winter and spring of 1879. O'Brien was told by a "gentleman of financial authority" that more than £200,000 was due to Mayo shopkeepers in August 1879. Many shopkeepers had been steadily accumulating debtors since the bad harvest of 1877, fully aware, in O'Brien's words, that "having staked their capital they had only to increase the stake; having trusted and ventured much, unless they would lose all, they had to trust and venture more. Had they closed their purse strings, had they abandoned or even greatly abridged their credit system, those who were already their heavy debtors must have been simply starved or beggard."[27] However, by the winter of 1879–80 many shopkeepers had no choice but to close "their purse strings" as they were having trouble securing credit themselves, and were too far extended to cope with the post-harvest destitution in Mayo. In its General Report for 1880 the Mansion House Relief Committee reported that "famine had been staved off from January to August 1879, by almost desperate credit" but following the disastrous harvest "the credit of the peasantry and shopkeepers alike had . . . touched bottom." The report concluded that with the "universal extinction of credit . . . nothing stood between the western peasants and

25 *The Irish Crisis of 1879–80*, p. 112.
26 *FJ*, 10 July 1880.
27 *Ibid.*, 25 Aug. 1879.

an unspeakable fate . . . except the power of the State or the charity of the world."[28]

Charity was funneled into County Mayo through the Mansion House Committee, the Duchess of Marlborough's Committee, *The New York Herald* Relief Committee, the Land League Fund, Archbishop McHale's Fund and innumerable small private donations.[29] It is quite likely that at least £100,000 worth of food, clothing, bedding and seeds was distributed in Mayo through the relief organizations during the first nine months of 1880, with an equal amount coming from private charity. The Mansion House Committee alone gave £31,105 to Mayo while the Land League distributed £50,000 worth of relief between December 1879 and April 1880, a substantial amount of which went to Mayo.[30]

By the time of the 1880 harvest these relief funds were nearly exhausted, but a return of mild weather brought a partial restoration of the potato crop and averted another winter of fuel famine. A good deal of the credit for the restoration of the potato crop rests with the relief committees, which distributed "champion" seed potatoes to replace the worn out old "white rock" seeds. The Royal Irish Constabulary reported that there was little failure of the champion seed potatoes, but that potatoes from the old seed were "small and blighted."[31] The yield for 1880 was 2.4 tons per statute acre, the heaviest harvests coming from the central regions where champion potatoes were in the widest use.[32] In addition, cattle prices rose 10 percent for one to two year old cattle and 6 percent for two to three year old cattle, while the decline in the number of chickens was arrested.[33] However, the crisis for Mayo farmers was far from over, especially since there were so many creditors with claims on the harvest and on proceeds from the sale of stock and eggs. Nonetheless, 1881 witnessed no repeat of the extreme destitution of 1880 as the Mayo economy slowly recovered.

The agricultural depression of 1877–80 had profound and far-reaching implications for County Mayo. Most significantly, it was a watershed in the fortunes of the small farm economy. Mayo's smallholders, especially

---

[28] *The Irish Crisis of 1879–80*, p. 8.

[29] N. B. Palmer, *The Irish Land League Crisis* (New Haven, 1940), pp. 83–105.

[30] *The Irish Crisis of 1879–80*, p. 311; M. Davitt, *The Fall of Feudalism in Ireland* (London and New York, 1904), p. 210; *FJ*, 18 Oct. 1882.

[31] *Agricultural Statistics . . . Ireland, 1880*, pp. 87–8.

[32] *Ibid.*, p. 71.

[33] Barrington, "A Review of Irish Agricultural Prices," p. 252; *The Agricultural Statistics of Ireland for the Year 1881*, PP 1882 [C 3332], lxxiv, p. 44.

those living in the peripheral areas of the county, appear to have lost faith in a family economy that revolved around a small potato patch, communal grazing, and earnings from the sale of a few cattle, eggs, and labor on the British market. This disillusionment is most dramatically illustrated by the emigration figures. Prior to the economic crisis of 1877–80, the west of Ireland, where the small farm economy prevailed, had the lowest rates of emigration in Ireland, yet following the crisis of 1877–80, the west experienced the highest rates, as an increased number of smallholders and their children abandoned their farms for America. As demonstrated on Figure 4.2 above, the number of emigrants from Mayo shot up dramatically in 1880 and again in 1883, remaining at a high level for the rest of the century. During the years following the agricultural crisis of 1877–80, the reduction in available seasonal work in Britain, the uncertainties of the cattle trade, and anxiety about another potato failure combined to undermine faith in the small farm economy and the culture that relied on it.

During the crisis some Mayo landlords sought to mitigate the distress of their tenants and avoid a confrontation with them over rent by granting rent abatements. This was especially the case following the commencement of the agitation, when tenants began to resist paying rents they thought were excessive. During the final six months of 1879 *The Connaught Telegraph* and *The Ballinrobe Chronicle* together reported seventy-six Mayo landlords as having granted rent abatements. Given the concern of James Daly with rent abatements and the number of his contacts and reporters throughout Mayo, this figure of seventy-six, taken mostly from *The Connaught Telegraph*, is probably a fairly accurate accounting of landlords who gave abatements. They represent 18 percent of the owners of 100 acres or more, owning roughly 21 percent of rural Mayo. The majority of them (71 percent) gave abatements of 20–25 percent of their 1879 rent, while eleven (14 percent) gave 50 percent or more; 88 percent of the landlords who gave abatements were small or middle-level land owners, with 5000 acres or less. Of the twenty landlords of 10,000 or more acres, who together owned 47 percent of County Mayo, only four are reported as having given abatements. Only one of the four, Viscount Dillon of Loughlynn House, who owned 83,749 acres, could be considered a large landlord.[34]

---

[34] *The Connaught Telegraph* and *The Ballinrobe Chronicle*, June–December 1879; *Return of Land . . . in Ireland . . .*, PP 1876 [C 1492], lxxx, pp. 307–13.

While these rent abatements represented a considerable concession, indeed sacrifice, on the part of many Mayo landlords, Clark has demonstrated that a rent reduction of 39 percent would only have reduced a farm family's expenditure by less than 5 percent; cold comfort in the face of the reduction of all sources of income.[35] Not surprisingly, these abatements did not quell the agitation, which was directed more at the existence of rents than at their level.

Also important for the strength of the land movement was the unwillingness of the major landlords to grant reductions. The Marquis of Sligo (114,881 acres) and Sir Roger Palmer (80,990 acres) both refused blatantly to grant abatements, while the Earl of Lucan (60,570 acres) curtly replied to a request for abatements, that rent reductions meant a "reduction of the proprietor's means."[36] No doubt many landlords agreed with Sir Robert Blosse (17,555 acres) and Captain Charles Knox (24,374 acres), who told their tenants that they refused to grant abatements because they were angered at the tenants' participation in land meetings.[37] These large landowners became symbols of oppression and injustice. Land meeting speakers often livened up their speeches with stories of the high living, debauchery and "oyster dinners" enjoyed by these often absentee landlords at the expense of their starving tenantry.

The depression of the late 1870s was an acute economic crisis that crumbled the pillars of the small farm economy. A decline in the demand for seasonal labor in Britain, the loss of easy credit, the potato failure, a depressed cattle market, and the decimation of the chicken population combined to raise the specter of famine. For the large farmers, the depression fostered a fuller awareness of the contradiction presented by landlordism in an agrarian capitalist economy, while for both large and small farmers, rents became the hated symbol of the weakness and vulnerability of the western economy. Large farmers resented sharing their farm earnings, and small farmers their seasonal wages, with their landlords. In this environment, rent reductions proved insufficient to mollify the anger of Mayo's farmers. For a few months the large graziers from the core of the county and the small farmers of the core and periphery put aside their differences in order to unite around demands for immediate relief from economic distress and for the eventual

---

[35] Clark, *Social Origins of the Irish Land War*, pp. 239–40.
[36] *CT*, 23 Aug., 20 Sept., 22 Nov. 1879.
[37] *Ibid.*, 27 Sept., 15 Nov. 1879.

end of landlordism and the establishment of peasant land ownership in Mayo. This alliance, forged as a result of the depression of the late 1870s, was capable of shaking the foundations of Irish landlordism.

THE AGITATION BEGINS

During the first months of the land agitation five men, two townsmen-graziers and three Fenians or former Fenians, played vital roles in shaping the direction of the movement in County Mayo: James Daly, editor of *The Connaught Telegraph* and grazier, John J. Louden, Westport barrister and extensive grazier, John O'Connor Power, MP and former Fenian, Matthew Harris, a member of the Supreme Council of the IRB, and Michael Davitt, a Mayo-born Fenian activist who had just been released from prison. The lead in publicly calling for an organized land movement in the west was taken by Daly in 1875.[38] In May 1876 the first tenant defense association in the region was formed in Ballinasloe, County Galway, by Harris. At the association's inaugural meeting, James Kilmartin, a Poor Law Guardian, identified the cause of the tenant farmers with the cause of Ireland, saying that the prosperity of one depended upon the prosperity of the other. He argued that a "united and persistent agitation" both inside and outside parliament would result in "the emancipation of the tenant farmers from the thraldom of landlord tyranny." At this meeting a special appeal was made to small farmers to become members of the Ballinasloe Tenants' Defence Association, indicating a break with the large farmer orientation of the Central Tenants' Defence Association, the only farmers' organization in Ireland at the time, but one with little support in Connacht.[39]

Harris was a familiar figure in Mayo. He was the leading Fenian organizer in the west of Ireland and had been Power's campaign manager in 1874. No doubt his involvement with the Ballinasloe TDA generated additional interest in the new organization in Mayo. Throughout the summer of 1876 *The Connaught Telegraph* reported the activities of the Ballinasloe TDA and in its 5 August editorial called for the establishment of a like organization in County Mayo.[40] As if to strengthen its call for the establishment of a TDA, Alfred Hea, co-editor of the newspaper,

[38] Clark, *Social Origins of the Irish Land War*, p. 273.
[39] *CT*, 13 May 1876.
[40] *Ibid.*, 5 Aug. 1876.

attended the next demonstration organized by the Ballinasloe TDA and was elected to its council.[41]

During the next two years *The Connaught Telegraph* continued to report on the activities of the Ballinasloe TDA and to call periodically for the establishment of one in Mayo. In October 1878 it could report that a TDA was "a good way of being established in the county."[42] During the previous week an organizing committee had been formed with the purpose of creating a TDA for the county. It was the hope of the committee, chaired by Louden, that the TDA would be inaugurated at a county meeting called for the following Sunday to hear Power address his constituents about his parliamentary activities during the previous session.[43] At the meeting Power endorsed the idea of a TDA for the county and raised a rousing cry of "the land of Ireland for the people of Ireland. Rack-renting and evictions must be stopped at all hazards." Daly, who was the prime mover behind the effort to found a TDA, followed Power. In his speech he outlined the purposes of a tenants' organization:

> The object of the league is to secure the tenant farmers of Mayo against capricious eviction and rack-renting in any place a landlord makes an attempt to evict, capriciously or without great cause; that the tenant's law expenses will be paid out of the general fund, and that he will be recouped in any loss he may sustain. In cases where landlords demand an exorbitant rent, the matter should be thoroughly investigated by the Executive Committee to see the poor tenant gets justice. In cases where a tenant refuses to pay the landlord a fair, just and equitable rent, the tenant could expect no protection from the proposed association.

Daly then read the names of ten priests and seventy-two "respectable farmers, merchants and traders" who had responded positively to a circular issued by the organizing committee requesting support for a TDA. The meeting ended with the passing of a resolution formally sanctioning the endeavors of the organizing committee to form a TDA for County Mayo.[44]

This meeting at Castlebar in October 1878 can be seen as the

---

[41] *Ibid.*, 19 Aug. 1876. Hea was co-editor until December 1878 when he severed his ties with the newspaper. He died several months later, leaving Daly as sole proprietor and editor until he sold it in 1892.

[42] *Ibid.*, 26 Oct. 1878.

[43] *Ibid.*, 19 Oct. 1878.

[44] *Ibid.*, 26 Oct. 1878.

beginning of the land agitation in the county, initiating a series of events and alliances that culminated in the first protest demonstration in April 1879. Its significance for the future land agitation was enhanced by the presence of Power. Since 1870 he had pioneered an alliance between those members and supporters of the IRB who were anxious to escape from the political isolation of orthodox Fenianism, and the most aggressive wing of the Irish parliamentary party, led first by Isaac Butt and from 1877 by Charles Stewart Parnell. Power's election as MP for Mayo in 1874 while he was still a member of the Supreme Council of the IRB had been a rousing endorsement of his efforts to align the two wings of the nationalist movement without undermining the principles of either. By promoting a Mayo TDA at a meeting convened to give Power an opportunity to speak to his constituents, Daly, Power's most resolute supporter in the county, consciously sought to link the nascent land movement with Power and the principles for which he stood. Daly understood the restiveness of Mayo's farmers probably sooner than any public man in the county and grasped the potential that an open and determined land agitation could have for the nationalist movement. Daly and Power saw that the land movement could mobilize the tenant farmers in defense of their economic interests while linking the struggle against landlordism with that for national independence.

Following the Castlebar meeting, Daly and Power toured the southern part of the county holding rallies at which they called for the formation of tenants' defense associations and stressed the value of an alliance between tenant farmers and aggressive parliamentarians like Power and Parnell.[45] Appropriately, this tour ended on 3 November in Ballinasloe, Power's home town and the site of the first TDA in the west of Ireland. It was especially significant that the tour was joined at Ballinasloe by Parnell, the recognized leader of the advanced faction within the Irish Parliamentary Party. During his first two years as a parliamentarian Parnell had skilfully cultivated nationalist support through his impassioned oratory and disruptive tactics within the House of Commons. By 1877 his ascendancy over Butt, the nominal head of Irish nationalist parliamentarians, was well established. In late 1877 he had been in County Mayo to speak at the unveiling of a monument commemorating the French soldiers who had died near Castlebar during the rising of 1798.[46] While there he received some valuable instruction

---

[45] *Ibid.*, 2 Nov. 1878.
[46] *Ibid.*, 8, 15 Dec. 1877.

from Daly and Power on the importance of the land question for western farmers, but at the time he returned to the west in November 1878 he was far from ready to commit himself to active involvement in a land movement.[47] Nonetheless, his presence on the stand with Power, Daly and Harris, the foremost men in the land movement in the west, could not but have been heartening to the movement's promoters. Harris opened with an aggressive and radical speech, during which he condemned Irish landlords and pointedly reminded his listeners, including Parnell, that the distinctions between "good" and "bad" landlords, which moderate land reformers generally insisted upon making, only weakened the movement. "This parleying in favour of the good landlord is your weak point. It does infinite honour to the goodness of your hearts but it enfeebles all your efforts . . . The exterminating laws of England do not spare the good any more than it [sic] does the bad tenant." Landlords, he went on, must be made to realize that when "the great law of retributive justice" arrives it would exempt no one.

Daly and Power followed Harris with speeches endorsing his strong words and calling for the formation of tenant associations to give strength and substance to the reform of the land system and, more immediately, to bring an end to evictions in Ireland. Both stressed the desirability of a union between the land and the nationalist movements. Power pressed this latter point most forcefully, putting both Parnell and the tenant farmers on the spot when he said that "they [tenant farmers] had no right to encourage Mr. Parnell to adopt a policy of energetic action in the House of Commons unless they on their part were prepared to adopt a policy of energetic action in Ireland." He then encouraged the formation of tenant associations to accomplish this end.

Parnell found himself in an awkward position. He had come to the meeting to seek support in his leadership battle with Butt and devoted most of his speech to encouraging the people to elect energetic members willing to follow the lead set by himself and Power. Although his ideas on land reform were far from set, he clearly felt bound to speak to the tenor of the meeting, even if ambiguously. He told those gathered that a bill for land reform was the solution, although he failed to offer any suggestions as to what such a bill should seek to do. Cautiously, he struck a middle ground between landlords, of whom he was one, and tenants by saying that the land movement should strive to "win the land and the right of living on the soil under the landlords, by paying rent or by

[47] *Ibid.*, 1 Apr. 1882; P. Bew, *C. S. Parnell* (Dublin, 1980), p. 23.

purchasing from the landlords and becoming possessors of their own farms." He hinted that he favored the latter system, which he said had worked in France and Prussia, and then concluded with a rousing call to end evictions and rent rises until a solution could be found.[48] The vigor of the nascent agitation had caught Parnell off guard, but he had yet to be convinced of its usefulness to his parliamentary campaign. In F. S. L. Lyons' words, at the time of the Ballinasloe meeting the land question was for Parnell "still incidental to the political struggle."[49]

During the bitter acrimony of 1881–2 that destroyed the Land League, Daly and Power suggested that it was they and the tenant farmers of the west who had taught Parnell the value of a land war as well as the principles on which it should be fought. While this may be overstating the case, it is quite likely that during his visit to Ballinasloe in 1878 Parnell became intrigued with the possibilities that a land movement might have for the nationalist struggle. Yet Parnell, hardly one to be swept up by popular enthusiasm, was clearly wary of a movement of tenant farmers and western-based radicals. He wanted two things from a rural movement: support for his claim to lead the Irish parliamentary party along new and aggressive lines and loyalty to him as leader of the nationalist movement. He was averse to aligning himself with a popular agitation that would be difficult to restrain and nearly impossible to direct as required by the exigencies of parliamentary politics. He was also wary of too close an association with Power. While the two men appeared to be comrades in arms in parliamentary obstruction and now in the campaign for agrarian reform, the mutual distrust and dislike that ultimately poisoned their relationship was already evident. Power, jealous because he thought that he rather than Parnell should be leader of the advanced wing of the parliamentary party, had dismissed Parnell as a "mediocrity" on their first meeting.[50] Parnell, for his part, was aware that Power was, as William O'Brien described him "a man of great resolution, with a merciless underjaw, a furious temper governed by a carefully studied urbanity of manner," who would never be a follower of any man.[51] Parnell shared with many Irish parliamentarians a distrust of Power and, furthermore, had little use for a strong politician who would

---

[48] *CT*, 9 Nov. 1878.
[49] F. S. L. Lyons, *Charles Stewart Parnell* (London, 1977), p. 85.
[50] R. B. O'Brien, *The Life of Charles Stewart Parnell, 1846–1891* (New York, 1898), I, p. 75.
[51] W. O'Brien, *Recollections* (New York and London, 1905), p. 140.

not follow loyally his lead. He realized that an alliance with Power could jeopardize his political prospects.[52]

However, Parnell had in Michael Davitt and John Devoy other suitors who conceivably could offer him firmer and more reliable support than could Power, Daly and Harris. Davitt had been born in Straide, County Mayo in 1846, but grew up in Lancashire after his family was evicted from their farm in 1852 and forced to migrate to England. In Lancashire he was a boyhood friend of Power's, whose family had also migrated to England after a spell in the Ballinasloe workhouse. As a youth Davitt, like Power, joined the IRB and was for a period a major procurer of guns for the organization. In 1870 he was sentenced to fifteen years of penal servitude and suffered through seven years of imprisonment before being released in December 1877, thanks in large part to the parliamentary efforts of Power.[53] Shortly after his release from prison Davitt toured Mayo, where he was greeted as a returning hero with torch-light parades and cheering crowds. While in Mayo he met with prominent Fenians, including J. W. Walshe and J. W. Nally. He also met with Daly who had organized Davitt's trip to the county.[54] While no record exists of the meetings between Davitt and Mayo's nationalists, there is little reason to doubt that he was given an appraisal of both the political and economic atmosphere of his native county. In his public speeches in Mayo he made no reference to the land question or to tenant organizations, preferring to speak of Fenian prisoners and of the efforts of Power to secure their release.[55] Nonetheless, it is significant that shortly after his tour of Mayo, while the impressions of what he saw and heard were fresh, he suggested to Parnell that "there must be more immediate issues put before the people, such as a war against landlordism for a root settlement of the land question."[56]

Davitt's views on the need for a more active policy on the part of Fenians towards the land question crystalized while he toured America during the fall of 1878. There he met John Devoy, a former member of the IRB who had had responsibility for swearing members of the British army into the organization. Arrested and imprisoned in 1866, Devoy had been released in 1871 on the condition that he not set foot in Britain or

---

[52] Lyons, *Charles Stewart Parnell*, p. 88; T. M. Healy, *Letters and Leaders of My Day* (London, n.d.), I, pp. 64–5.

[53] Moody, *Davitt and Irish Revolution*, pp. 1–185.

[54] *Ibid.*, pp. 190–4; *CT*, 26 Jan., 2 Feb. 1878.

[55] *CT*, 2 Feb. 1878.

[56] Davitt, *The Fall of Feudalism*, p. 112.

Ireland until the completion of his sentence in 1882. As a newspaperman and Irish activist in New York City, Devoy was the most dynamic member of Clan na Gael, the American wing of the IRB.[57] Davitt met with Devoy on 4 August, the day of his arrival in New York. During the next four months the two of them worked out a program, dubbed by Devoy the "new departure," that would result in cooperation between Parnell and the Fenians.[58] Thanks in large part to the work of Power, a working agreement between segments of the Fenian and constitutional nationalists had been operating since at least 1873. The new departure worked out by Davitt and Devoy focused this alliance on an open, aggressive campaign for land reform leading to the establishment of peasant propriety in Ireland. Their prestige within Ireland and America gave an immediate national character to the land agitation that might have been denied it had the western-based agitators gone it alone.

When news of the new departure first appeared in the press in October 1878, Daly could not resist some smug satisfaction on hearing that men who found it "easy to write or talk at a distance of three thousand miles" and who "had done much to dispirit earnest men in Ireland" through their unrelenting attacks on constitutional and agrarian agitation had finally come around to a position in keeping with Irish reality.[59] Two months later Daly returned to the subject, praising Devoy "and his friends [for] coming round to the programme before the public for the last seven years. They admit their past errors like honest men, and they should give dignity to their admission by joining heartily and unconditionally with those who have been all along working in the way they now so heartily commend."[60]

The precedent for constitutional agitation set by Power was not lost on orthodox Fenians such as Dr. Mark Ryan, who saw behind the new departure the nefarious influence of the member for Mayo.[61] However,

---

[57] O'Brien and Ryan (eds.), *Devoy's Post Bag, 1871–1829*, I, pp. xxxi–xxxii.

[58] Detailed discussions of the new departure appear in: T. W. Moody, "The New Departure in Irish Politics, 1878–9," in H. A. Croone, T. W. Moody, D. B. Quinn (eds.), *Essays in British and Irish History in Honour of James Eadie Todd* (London, 1949), pp. 303–33; Moody, *Davitt and Irish Revolution*, pp. 249–67; Lyons, *Charles Stewart Parnell*, pp. 77–83; Bew, *Land and the National Question in Ireland*, pp. 46–73; T. N. Brown, *Irish-American Nationalism, 1870–1890* (Philadelphia and New York, 1966), pp. 84–98.

[59] *CT*, 16 Nov. 1878.

[60] *Ibid.*, 11 Jan. 1879.

[61] Devoy, *Recollections of An Irish Rebel*, p. 313; John Devoy, "Davitt's Career, VII," *Gaelic American*, 21 July 1906; O'Brien and Ryan (eds.), *Devoy's Post Bag*, I, p. 348.

Power had not been alone among western Fenians in adopting years before the policies now embraced by Davitt and Devoy. They shared with the small farmers of the west an opposition to landlordism and the social injustices they felt came as a result of it. As Devoy later noted, one of Fenianism's major contributions to the Land League was to have given "the people habits of organization and of acting together" and to have helped train "a number of zealous, active, intelligent workers."[62] However, most of this training and organization had been underground and illegal, raising the question of whether such activity could be harnessed in the service of an open and, for the most part, legal movement. Devoy records that the Fenians' initial response to the economic crisis confronting Mayo's farmers was to hold secret meetings for the purpose of planning a campaign of agrarian outrages:

> Weeks before the first public land meeting was held at Irishtown (April 20, 1879) a land movement was in the air and the toss of a penny might decide whether it was to eventuate in a more or less peaceful agitation or work wholly with shotguns and revolvers.[63]

> Davitt saw the danger and determined to make a desperate effort to avert it. He hurried down to Mayo, pointed out the danger of the situation, and induced the young men to give other methods a trial. He succeeded, and after a few preliminary gatherings the first meeting of the Land Agitation was held at Irishtown in Mayo.[64]

Devoy's assertion that it was Davitt who talked the Fenians out of an illegal campaign is probably an accurate one, and this action may represent Davitt's most significant contribution to the early phase of the land agitation in Mayo. During his testimony before *The Times* Commission in 1889, Davitt was purposefully vague about his involvement with Fenians during the early stages of the Land War, but he did reveal that in January–February 1879 he toured Mayo to explain the land agitation to the "local leaders of the extreme party." He claimed that he could undertake such a task since "the extremists had confidence in me."[65] This access to the inner circles of the IRB in Mayo would have

---

[62] J. Devoy, *The Land of Eire: The Irish Land League, Its Origins, Progress and Consequences* (New York, 1882), p. 34.

[63] Devoy, "Davitt's Career, XII," *Gaelic American*, 8 Sept. 1906.

[64] Devoy, *The Land of Eire*, p. 38.

[65] Davitt and other Land League leaders who testified before the Commission attempted to play down the role of Fenians in the League in order to exonerate Parnell from involvement with violence. *Special Commission . . . Proceedings . . .* , iii, p. 597; Devoy may have been in Mayo at the same time as Davitt, preaching the same message,

been denied to Daly, who had never been a Fenian, and it is questionable whether Power still commanded sufficient loyalty within the organization to convince the Fenian leadership to enter the agitation. The task fell to Davitt and credit for the active participation of the local Fenians in the early stages of the Land War most likely rests with him.

THE IRISHTOWN MEETING, 20 APRIL 1879

The first mass rally of the Irish Land War, held at Irishtown, County Mayo, was the result of cooperation between local activists led by Daly and Dublin-based nationalists mobilized by Davitt. Together they planned and organized a precedent-setting land meeting at which the various farming classes came together with townsmen in a remarkable demonstration of solidarity. The meeting was all the more impressive given that the clergy took no part in planning it and refused to participate. Despite this refusal, a crowd estimated at between 7000 and 13,000 gathered from all parts of Mayo and from the neighboring counties of Galway and Roscommon to hear denunciations of landlordism with the accompanying slogan of "the land of Ireland for the people of Ireland." The meeting initiated a period in Irish history during which for the first time tenant farmers stood on "the political stage as leading players rather than as extras."[66]

The immediate issue around which the tenant farmers were mobilized was rent. Rents due on 1 November were normally not paid until February or March, but after two years of bad harvests and economic uncertainty many Mayo farmers were unable to pay. The number of ejectment decrees requested by Mayo landlords had increased 96 percent between 1877 and 1879, and while the number of decrees remained relatively small (560), the number of informal threats of evictions was undoubtedly high.[67]

It is not entirely clear why Irishtown was chosen as the site for the first meeting. In the standard account, presented by Davitt, the meeting was

---

although this would have been a violation of the terms of his release from prison. See: Devoy, "Michael Davitt's Career, XII," *Gaelic American*, 8 Sept. 1906.

[66] Lee, *Modernisation of Irish Society*, p. 72.

[67] *Return In Tabular Form, As Under the Civil Bill Ejectments On the Title From Those For Non-Payment of Rent, Tried and Determined In Each County In Ireland For Each of the Four Years Ending the 31st Day of December 1880, Exclusive of Ejectments For Premises Situated In Counties of Cities, Boroughs and Towns Under the Act 9, George 4, c. 82, Or "The Towns" Improvement (Ireland) Act 1854 or Any Local Act*, PP 1881 (90), lxxvii, pp. 2–5.

called to protest rents on a small estate in the County Galway townland of Quinaltagh near Irishtown. According to Davitt, the estate had been purchased in 1857 by Walter Bourke, who immediately doubled the rents. Bourke, the story goes, died early in 1879, leaving his brother Rev. Geoffrey Canon Bourke as executor of the arrears-ridden estate. Allegedly, Canon Bourke threatened the twenty tenants with eviction unless the rent was paid in full.[68] In January a delegation of tenants from the estate approached Daly to request that he print full particulars of rack-renting and threats of eviction on the estate. Daly later wrote that he declined to publish the details out of concern over libel action against *The Connaught Telegraph*, but after conferring with several prominent men from Irishtown and with John O'Keane, the former County Centre of the IRB in Mayo, suggested that a meeting be held "to expose the cruel treatment" of the tenants. Davitt later claimed that he, rather than Daly, was first contacted by the delegation regarding a protest meeting at Irishtown, but since Davitt's alleged meeting with the Irishtown tenants occurred in March, a month after *The Connaught Telegraph* announced and editorially supported the Irishtown meeting, Daly's account is more credible. This is not to say that Daly's account was not embroidered to enhance his importance.[69]

Davitt's biographer, T. W. Moody, has cast serious doubt on this traditional account of the origins of the Irishtown meeting. He points out that Canon Bourke's brother died in 1873, not 1879 as Davitt stated, and that the estate passed to Walter Bourke's son Joseph, not to his brother the canon. None of the contemporary accounts of the meeting or its origins mention the canon, who later took a minor but supportive role in the land movement. Furthermore, Canon Bourke and Daly later claimed that the canon had not been the owner or executor of the estate in 1879. Moody concludes that Davitt's account was based upon faulty knowledge of the situation and was colored by his feud with Daly. Moody argues that the grievances of the Bourke tenantry were probably the immediate cause of the meeting, but responsibility for those grievances rested with the absentee landlord Joseph Bourke and not with his uncle.[70]

Irishtown, or Dry Mills as it was sometimes called, lay in southeast

---

[68] Davitt, *The Fall of Feudalism*, pp. 146–7.

[69] *CT*, 15, 22 Feb. 1879, 21 Apr. 1879, 15 Jan. 1881. Davitt, *The Fall of Feudalism*, pp. 146–7; *Special Commission . . . Proceedings . . .* , iii, pp. 559–60. In his testimony before the Special Commission, John J. Louden said he "had the getting up of the meeting" himself, but gave no details. See: *ibid.*, iii, p. 642.

[70] Moody, *Davitt and Irish Revolution*, pp. 292–5.

Mayo where the rich central corridor and the infertile eastern periphery meet. It was thus an appropriate place to inaugurate a land movement that at first united the graziers of central Mayo with the small farmers of the periphery. In response to an appeal by the small farmers who approached him in January, Daly offered to make all the necessary arrangements in conjunction with his namesake, James Daly of Irishtown, and with Daniel O'Connor, both large graziers in the Irishtown area. He also offered to publicize the meeting in *The Connaught Telegraph*.[71]

As an influential nationalist with unparalleled contacts in Mayo, Daly could assure the attendance at the meeting of Mayo's leading constitutional nationalists as well as many tenant farmers. However, the extent of his contacts with local Fenians was probably quite limited, and recruiting them in aid of the meeting was Davitt's most important contribution to the success of the Irishtown rally. As noted above, Davitt was in Mayo in early 1879, attempting to convince the county's Fenians to take an active and open role in the pending land agitation. At one such meeting Davitt conferred with John Walshe, John O'Keane and P. W. Nally, the latter being Mayo's most prominent Fenian and the representative of Connacht province on the Supreme Council of the IRB. Davitt records that they all agreed to lend their influence and to collect an audience for the Irishtown meeting.[72] Their influence was considerable. Devoy later claimed that it was the local Fenians who "gathered the timid farmers and marshalled the crowds" at Irishtown and at other early land meetings. In the absence of parish priests to organize and lead them, the crowd that marched to the meeting was arranged into contingents and led to prearranged places by local Fenians.[73] A police sergeant who observed the Claremorris contingent leaving for Irishtown noted that the 1000 marchers "seemed to be looking up to P. W. Nally," who along with other prominent members of the Fenian organization led the marchers.[74] In his testimony before the Special Commission, Davitt contended that the Fenians of Mayo did not participate in the land movement as members of the IRB but as farmers and farmers' sons.[75] Strictly speaking, this was the case, since the Supreme Council had refused to sanction Fenian involvement in the land agitation. But, as Davitt later wrote, the "extreme men" brought to the land movement "an advanced nationalist spirit and

[71] *CT*, 15 Jan. 1881.
[72] Davitt, *Fall of Feudalism*, p. 147; Ryan, *Fenian Memories*, p. 63.
[73] Devoy, *The Land of Eire*, pp. 48, 51.
[74] *Special Commission . . . Proceedings . . .* , i, p. 628; *CT*, 21 Apr. 1879.
[75] *Special Commission . . . Proceedings . . .* , iii, p. 559.

revolutionary purpose" as well as organizational experience and an intact network of immeasurable value.[76]

Organized by the Fenians, a large crowd assembled at Irishtown on 20 April to hear rousing speeches from the principal speakers: John O'Connor Power, MP, Thomas Brennan, a Dublin-based Fenian, John Ferguson, a Glasgow nationalist, Michael M. O'Sullivan, a Fenian and member of the Ballinasloe TDA, John J. Louden and James Daly, who chaired the meeting. The crowd shouted its approval of several resolutions that had been prepared in advance by Davitt and the local leaders. As with everything else regarding the Irishtown meeting, there is controversy over who arranged for the speakers. Davitt claimed that it was he who did so, while Daly claimed to have arranged for Power and "other gentlemen" as speakers. Sorting out this controversy is impossible and serves little purpose, but it seems likely that Davitt arranged for the presence of the Fenians, O'Sullivan and Brennan, as well as for Ferguson, who Davitt had met in Glasgow. Daly's claim to have recruited Power is given credence by the fact that the MP's name as a potential speaker was published in *The Connaught Telegraph* prior to Davitt's entry into the planning of the meeting. Davitt did not attend the meeting. It has long been alleged that he meant to but missed the train from Dublin. However, Moody contends that Davitt stayed away so that his presence, as a felon on a ticket of leave from prison, would not compromise the meeting. It appears that two of the three resolutions were drafted by Davitt and sent to Mayo with Brennan, while the resolution on rent abatements was drafted locally. There is some evidence to suggest that the resolutions were submitted to Devoy for his approval.[77]

The first resolution declared cautiously the link between the land and national questions by calling on the people to express their determination "to resort to every lawful means whereby our inalienable rights – political and social – can be regained from our enemies."[78] But it was the second resolution that was the most significant of the day as it established the central issue of the Irish Land War:

That as the land of Ireland, like that of every other country, was intended by a just and all-providing God for the use and sustenance of

[76] Davitt, *Fall of Feudalism*, p. 125.

[77] *CT*, 22 Feb. 1879, 15 Jan. 1881; Davitt, *The Fall of Feudalism*, p. 147; *Special Commission . . . Proceedings . . .* , iii, pp. 559, 598, 642; Moody, *Davitt and Irish Revolution*, p. 291; H. James, *The Work of the Irish Leagues* (London, n.d.), p. 95.

[78] Accounts of the proceedings appear in *CT*, 21 Apr. 1879 and in Davitt, *The Fall of Feudalism*, pp. 147–51.

those of His people whom he gave inclination and energies to cultivate and improve it, any system which sanctions its monopoly by a privileged class, or assigns its ownership and control to a landlord caste, to be used as an instrument of usurious or political self-seeking, demands from every aggrieved Irishman an undying hostility, being flagrantly opposed to the first principles of their humanity – self preservation.

No mention was made at the meeting of the "three Fs" – fair rent, fixity of tenure and free sale of interest in the holding – the demand for which had sustained the moderate home rule and land reform movement since the Famine. Rather, following this resolution all of the speakers called in ringing terms for the establishment of peasant proprietorship in Ireland. As was to be customary throughout the Land War, vague references were made to France and Prussia as countries in which peasant proprietorship had been successfully introduced. In his speech, Brennan offered Irish landlords the choice of the French model of revolution or the Prussian model of reform and suggested that if landlords did not move quickly to bring about the latter, they would find themselves confronted with the former. Power, in a more constitutional vein, called for the abolition of landlordism but reminded his listeners that "some time must elapse before we can induce Parliament to adopt a solution of the question which commended itself so long ago to the ablest statesmen of Europe." In the meantime, he suggested that "an immediate remedy," the end of evictions, should be the primary object of the agitation.

The message that emerged from Irishtown was that Irish farmers would not be satisfied with partial victories that would give them only a degree of security in a landlord-dominated system. They now viewed immediate demands for the lowering of rent and the end of evictions as phases in an all-out attack on landlordism. Little note was taken of the meeting outside of Mayo, but Power understood its importance and passed the word along in London, reportedly telling William O'Brien that the meeting he had just attended would "make history."[79]

THE WESTPORT MEETING, 8 JUNE 1879

On the day following the Irishtown meeting *The Connaught Telegraph*, probably acting on the initiative of Louden, announced that "a monster

[79] O'Brien, *Recollections*, pp. 215–16.

meeting" would be held in Westport in early June.[80] Westport was an ideal location for transferring the impetus of the movement from an assault on a small landlord like Bourke to an attack on landlordism in general. The town was the seat of the Marquis of Sligo, whose 114,881 acre estate was the largest in Mayo and one of the largest in Ireland. His restive tenants considered their rents to be too high and estate regulations to be oppressive. In addition to being held in a town owned by one of Ireland's grandest absentee landlords, the Westport demonstration is significant for marking the occasion of Parnell's entry into the land movement. Furthermore, the Westport meeting provided the stage for a full confrontation between the Roman Catholic Church and the western agitation, in which the Church, embarrassingly, found itself the loser.

In the weeks following the Irishtown meeting Davitt secured the services of Parnell as a speaker for Westport.[81] Parnell's motives for agreeing to speak at Westport have remained something of a mystery. At the time his ideas on the land question were no clearer than they had been the previous November when he spoke at Ballinasloe and he was no closer to being willing to cast in his lot with the land movement. In the words of his biographer, F. S. L. Lyons, Parnell was anxious to "establish his personal ascendance in the country on a broader basis than any the Home Rule movement could offer," but had justifiable fears that the western land movement could not be sufficiently controlled to use it as the lever to catapult him into the national leadership.[82] Emmet Larkin's explanation that Parnell agreed to speak at Westport because he saw that "in the land agitation he had the possible means of forcing his leadership on a reluctant clergy" no doubt contains much truth.[83] Observing the hostility of the priests to the Irishtown meeting, Parnell understood that only by challenging the clergy could he hope to win its support in his struggle for political power in Ireland. Parnell reasoned, according to Larkin, that "only the Irish people could deliver them [priests] into his hands."[84]

Parnell accepted the invitation to speak at Westport in late May, before he could know that the venerable Archbishop of Tuam, John McHale,

---

[80] *CT*, 21 Apr. 1879.
[81] Davitt, *The Fall of Feudalism*, pp. 151–3; Lyons, *Charles Stewart Parnell*, pp. 87–92.
[82] Lyons, *Charles Stewart Parnell*, p. 87.
[83] Emmet Larkin, *The Roman Catholic Church and the Creation of the Modern Irish State, 1878–1886* (Philadelphia, 1975), pp. 22–3.
[84] *Ibid.*; Davitt, *The Fall of Feudalism*, p. 151; O'Brien, *The Life of Charles Stewart Parnell*, I, p. 191.

would make the confrontation at Westport dramatic and decisive. On 7 June, the day before the meeting, *The Freeman's Journal* published a letter from the Archbishop dated from Westport two days previously. In the letter, written in response to the receipt of Parnell's telegram of acceptance of the invitation to speak, the Archbishop attempted to prevent Parnell from coming and thus avoid a showdown with the clergy who remained officially opposed to the land movement. McHale pointed to an alleged connection between "night patrolling . . . with arms in hand" and the "lawless and occult association" which was connected with the land agitation. He warned Parnell that the Westport meeting had been organized in a "mysterious and disorderly manner" by "a few designing men, who, instead of the well-being of the community, seek only to promote their personal interests." He concluded by asserting the opposition of the clergy to the agitation.[85] Larkin argues that this letter "was written for Roman rather than Irish consumption" as part of a controversy with Propaganda over the 88-year-old Archbishop's ability to carry out his duties.[86] Popular opinion in Mayo, ever respectful of the beloved Archbishop, attributed the letter to Dr. Thomas McHale, the Archbishop's nephew and Vicar General, or to a "few clergymen who had evinced their indignation at not being consulted before the meeting was called."[87] Quite likely, McHale, the champion of Irish nationalism within the Catholic hierarchy for forty-five years, understood as well as Parnell the consequences of a struggle over political authority between the Catholic clergy and an ambitious Protestant landlord and sought to avoid such a confrontation. However, Parnell had no intention of avoiding the challenge posed by the clergy's hostility to the land movement.[88]

An additional consideration for Parnell was the increasingly active part taken in the agitation by Mayo's Fenians and the resulting stridency the new movement projected. During the six weeks that elapsed between the Irishtown and Westport meetings, *The Connaught Telegraph* reported two meetings in Mayo organized by the Fenians of Balla and

---

[85] *FJ*, 7 June 1879.

[86] Larkin, *The Roman Catholic Church and the Creation of the Modern Irish State*, p. 20.

[87] *CT*, 14 June, 12 July 1879; *Special Commission . . . Proceedings . . .* , iii, pp. 46–7. A discussion of the possible reasons for McHale's letter appears in C. J. Woods, "The Catholic Church and Irish Politics, 1879–92" (University of Nottingham, Ph.D. thesis, 1968), pp. 43–5. Also see: B. O'Reilly, *John McHale, Archbishop of Tuam: His Life and Correspondence* (New York & Cincinnati, 1890), pp. 669–70.

[88] Davitt, *The Fall of Feudalism*, p. 153.

Claremorris. The first occurred just outside Claremorris on 25 May. Fenian activists John O'Keane and P. J. Gordon assembled 200 people to call for the distribution among small farmers of land held in large grazing farms.[89] Despite the small number in attendance, this anti-grazier meeting, the first of the Land War, demonstrated the desire of the small farmers to see the agitation result in the distribution of grass farms among smallholders. It also publicly identified the county's Fenian leadership with the goals of the small farmers in an identification that was to last throughout the agitation.

The second Fenian-sponsored meeting took place on 1 June at Knock, where 20–30,000 people reportedly met to "enter a solemn and emphatic protest" against a condemnation of the land movement and its organizers issued by Archdeacon Kavanagh from the altar the previous Sunday. The Archdeacon had singled out O'Keane for special vilification. At the rally, seemingly organized by O'Keane and J. W. Nally of Balla, the priest was warned that malicious attacks on the leaders of the agitation would not dissuade the people from following them, but could "alter the cherished relations that have ever, through weal and woe, existed between the Irish peasant and his pastor."[90] This meeting, one of the largest of the entire movement, was the first to be held deep in the peripheral region of Mayo. The fact that it was organized by Fenians in defiance of a priest dramatized the degree to which the Fenians had captured a large share of the political initiative in Mayo and with it the ability to mobilize the small farmers.

For Parnell, this Fenian activity posed a number of threats. He must have realized that his hopes of leading the Irish people rested in part on his ability to bridge the gap between large and small farmers, and that such a bridge would not be possible if Mayo's Fenians took the movement to a level of radicalism that was unacceptable to the graziers. During the two years that had elapsed since Parnell rose to prominence as the leader of the Irish obstructionists in the House of Commons, his most unwavering support had come from the members of the Central Tenants' Defence Association, the organization of large grazing farmers in Ireland. As cattle rearers, its members had seen their incomes decline as a result of the fall in beef prices, but could not be expected to join a land reform movement in which the interest of small farmers in obtaining land at the expense of graziers was paramount. In a letter to *The*

[89] *CT*, 31 May 1879.
[90] *Ibid.*, 7 June 1879; *Special Commission . . . Proceedings*, i, p. 631.

Freeman's Journal in February 1879, following the conclusion of a land conference called by the CTDA, Matthew Harris had pointedly reminded the graziers that their interests and those of the small farmers were not the same and that the dominance of the tenant right movement by the "graziers' clubs" was causing some "uneasiness among the small farmers and their friends" in the west of Ireland.[91] Harris' association with the land movement, along with reports of Fenians holding anti-grazier meetings, caused great concern to the graziers and their representatives. Prior to deciding whether to attend the Westport meeting, Parnell met with A. J. Kettle, secretary of the CTDA and a man concerned about the impact of Fenianism on the new movement. Kettle advised Parnell to go to Westport, no doubt to see if he could curtail the anti-grazier militancy of the agitation.[92]

A second cause of concern for Parnell was the effect on the priests of unbridled Fenian involvement in the land movement. The hostility to Fenianism on the part of the Catholic hierarchy and most parish priests was long-standing and genuine. Archbishop McHale's pointed reference to a "lawless and occult association" in his letter of 7 June made it clear that Fenian involvement in the agitation was unacceptable to the clergy. At Irishtown and Knock, known Fenians had led invasions of tenant farmers into the parishes of two Mayo priests in order to condemn the clerics. To capture clerical support Parnell had to neutralize this confrontation between Fenians and priests, and appear as a leader who could keep the Fenian influence over the agitation within acceptable bounds. Parnell realized that he had to act quickly to seize the initiative before the anti-clericalism of many Fenian activists caused an irreparable rift between the clergy and the land movement.

Until the Westport meeting Parnell had stayed aloof but interested while Devoy and Davitt entreated him to agree to the new departure. Yet he had no wish to allow the Fenians of Mayo to embark upon a "new departure" of their own without his involvement. Many Fenians agreed with Harris, who saw the land agitation as part of a revolution that would bring about full national independence without recourse to parliament and without the aid of parliamentarians.[93] The achievement of independence for Ireland through revolutionary means had always been the goal

---

[91] *FJ*, 12 Feb. 1879.
[92] A. J. Kettle, *The Material for Victory*, ed. by L. J. Kettle (Dublin, 1958), pp. 21–2; Bew, *Land and the National Question in Ireland*, pp. 54–6.
[93] Bew, *Land and the National Question in Ireland*, pp. 59–60.

of the Fenian movement. For the western Fenians the new element, or the new departure, was their willingness to use the land agitation as a means to that goal. Parnell saw the link between the land and national questions in a different light. Whereas they saw a battle on the land question as part of a revolutionary struggle for national independence, Parnell saw the settlement of the land question as the removal of the final obstacle to a social unity in Ireland, which would create an environment conducive to securing home rule through constitutional means. For Parnell this desirable unity included not only large and small farmers, priests and townsmen, but ultimately landlords who, once freed from struggles over rent with disgruntled tenants, might join the national movement.[94] He came to Westport in an effort to arrest the divisive activities of the Fenians, to pave the way for clerical and grazier involvement in the movement and, above all, to secure for himself the leadership of the agitation on his own terms.

Eight thousand people defied Archbishop McHale's letter and the official disapproval of their priests to attend the meeting. Fr. Lavelle, curate at Louisburgh, later acknowledged that some priests "urged strongly on their flocks to attend the meeting" and had said Mass early that morning in order to enable their parishioners to attend.[95] No priests attended the meeting, although they had been invited in a circular issued on 12 May. Fr. Lavelle and Fr. Joyce of Louisburgh sent letters of apology for non-attendance. Parnell, noting in his speech that the assembled had come in their "thousands in the face of every difficulty," believed the meeting to have demonstrated that the momentum of the agitation could not be slowed by clerical condemnation. If the clergy wanted to regain their leadership of rural society they would have to do so by forging a role for themselves within the agitation.

Parnell had less success in gaining ascendance over the Fenian agitators. At the meeting they assumed their roles of leading contingents of marchers and controlling the vast crowd, while several prominent members of the Fenian brotherhood appeared on the platform along with Parnell, Louden, Daly and Davitt.[96] The first resolution passed at the meeting was written in order to accommodate Fenian sentiments. It called for the complete separation of Ireland from England and stressed the connection between "the legacy of English conquest" as the "cause

[94] *Ibid.*, pp. 56–65.
[95] *CT*, 20 Sept. 1879.
[96] Account of the meeting taken from *CT*, 14 June 1879.

of the woes of tenant farmers."[97] Davitt spoke to this resolution. In keeping with the principles he and Devoy had laid down for the new departure, Davitt refused to quibble publicly with Parnell on a definition of "self-government," although he reminded the crowd that they knew what his definition of it was. As he was to do throughout the agitation, he concentrated his attention on the land question, leveling an attack on both landlords and the Irish parliamentary politicians whose "legislative tinkering" would never produce a just settlement of the land question.

Davitt was followed by Michael M. O'Sullivan, a Fenian member of the Ballinasloe TDA, who had spoken at the Irishtown meeting and who was a close ally of Matt Harris. He trampled on the constitutionalism of Parnell by contending that complete separation from England could only be won when "moral force" was backed up by "the power of the sword." Underlying O'Sullivan's remarks on the agrarian question was the view, held by the militant Fenians, that no British government could be expected to do justice to Irish tenant farmers, who must inevitably rally to the national cause and seek redress from an Irish parliament. Harris concluded the Fenian portion of the proceedings by introducing the question of the relations between small and large farmers. He equated large grazing farmers with landlords and emphasized the growing militancy of the small farmers. "The people are beginning to revolt – to feel that if they did not stand up against such inequity, they would be almost as criminal as the landlords and graziers themselves." Thus Parnell was reminded of the potential for social revolution if the alliance between small farmers and Fenians was left unchecked.

The second and third resolutions at Westport focused on the land question. The first called for an end to eviction until a "permanent settlement" of the land question was obtained, while the second, introduced by Parnell, criticized previous land legislation and called for peasant proprietorship as the only solution guaranteed to "secure to the people of Ireland their national right to the soil of their country." No doubt understanding how much was at stake, Parnell followed with one of the most famous speeches of his career. In a revealing segment of it he outlined his thinking on the national question and on the link between it and the land question. He claimed that if the Irish people would send "men of determination or some sort of courage and energy" to the House of Commons, they would be able to wrest substantial concessions from

[97] Devoy, *The Land of Eire*, p. 50.

the British government. Then, in a statement opposed in spirit to that of the Fenians, Parnell said:

> I have always noticed that the breaking down of barriers between different classes has increased their self-respect and increased the spirit of nationality among our people. I am convinced that nothing would more effectively promote the cause of self-government for Ireland than the breaking down of these barriers between different classes. Nothing would be more effective for that than the obtaining of a good land bill – the planting of the people on the soil. If we had the farmers on the soil tomorrow, we would not be long getting an Irish parliament.

Parnell thus defined the connection he saw between the land and the national questions: a land settlement, achieved through an aggressive campaign in the House of Commons, backed up by an agitation in Ireland, was a prelude to the achievement of self-government. He maintained that this order of events was necessary if the independent Irish state were to be socially as well as politically unified. In contrast, the Fenian plan would pit class against class and could result in an Irish state that was unacceptable to many in Ireland, especially to the Anglo-Irish landlords. Parnell wished the land movement to be a means of a class alliance in Ireland and was to spend much of the next two years attempting to bring about social unity at the expense of the militancy that erupted in the west under Fenian auspices.[98]

Few in attendance at Westport understood the nuances of Parnell's remarks on the relationship between the land and national questions. Instead, they were anxious to hear him speak on the burning issues of rent and land ownership. He did not disappoint them. He affirmed his belief that a final settlement of the land question was the establishment of peasant proprietorship and he held up the examples of Belgium, Russia and Prussia as nations where this goal had been achieved. He said that prior to the final settlement tenants should not be required to pay more than a "fair rent," which he defined as "a rent the tenant can reasonably pay according to the times, but in bad times a tenant cannot be expected to pay as much as he did in good times." Parnell concluded by urging the people neither to allow themselves to be dispossessed nor "allow your small holdings to be turned into larger ones." In a statement which became the slogan of the agitation, he urged farmers "to keep a firm grip on your homesteads."

[98] Bew, *Land and the National Question in Ireland*, p. 59.

This electrifying speech somewhat overshadowed the sober calls of all the speakers for the tenant farmers of Mayo to organize themselves. Davitt urged the people not to simply "agitate, agitate" but to assume responsibility for their own fate and "organize, organize." He called on tenant farmers in Ireland to "organize themselves in one body" and "resolve to create a remedy where the evil is felt – in Ireland." Daly concluded the proceedings in a moderate but determined tone with the following homily:

> Let not the speeches you have heard here today be wasted on the desert air; let you hold meetings, but no night meetings; have your tenant right associations in every parish; be moderate but determined in your thousands; go home from this meeting respectfully and above all shun drink, for until the people of Ireland do so they can never expect to be free.

The Westport meeting, and especially Parnell's speech, was widely reported and commented on in the Dublin and London press. The meeting and the ensuing publicity added momentum to the movement and proved to the Catholic hierarchy of the west and to many local priests that clerical disapproval would not keep the people away from the agitation. In addition, in Parnell it brought a leader of enormous prestige and energy to the movement. His presence on the platform with known Fenians demonstrated to many that the new departure had been put into action. On the surface it looked as though "men of advanced nationalist spirit and revolutionary purpose" were participating with Parnell and his supporters "in a friendly rivalry . . . in the work of making English rule more difficult or impossible," as Davitt later described it.[99] The significance of a well-attended land meeting addressed by such a politically diverse group, along with the absence of the moderating presence of priests, was not lost on the press or politicians on either side of the Irish Sea. This was clearly a movement that could no longer be ignored.

---

[99] Davitt, *The Fall of Feudalism*, p. 25.

7. The centralization of the agitation, June 1879–April 1880

One morning, a few months ago, when my servant brought me some summer honey and a glass of milk to my bedside, she handed me an unpleasant letter. My agent's handwriting, even when I knew the envelope contained a cheque, has never quite failed to produce a sensation of repugnance in me; so hateful is any sort of account, that I avoid as much as possible even knowing how I stand at my banker's. Therefore the odour of honey and milk, so evocative of fresh flowers and fields, was spoilt that morning for me; and it was some time before I slipped on that beautiful Japanese dressing gown, which I shall never see again, and read the odious epistle.

That some wretched farmers and miners should refuse to starve, that I may not be deprived of my *demi-tasse* at Tortoni's; that I may not be forced to leave this beautiful retreat [Paris], my cat and my python – monstrous. And these wretched creatures will find moral support in England; they will find pity.

Pity, that most vile of all vile virtues, has never been known to me. The great pagan world I love knew it not. Now the world proposes to interrupt the terrible austere laws of nature which ordain that the weak shall be trampled upon, shall be ground into death and dust, that the strong shall be glorious, sublime. A little bourgeois comfort, a little bourgeois sense of right, cry the moderns.

George Moore, *Confessions of a Young Man*[1]

Meetings abounded in Mayo throughout the summer of 1879.[2] As Table 7.1 illustrates, the resolutions introduced at these meetings addressed the issues established at the Irishtown and Westport meetings.

---

[1] George Moore, *Confessions of a Young Man*, London, 1918; reprinted Harmondsworth, Middlesex, 1939, pp. 116–17.
[2] A list of land agitation meetings in the county appears in Appendix 4.

Table 7.1. *Content of resolutions proposed at 78 land meetings held in or near County Mayo, April 1879–June 1881*

Content of resolutions	Percentage of resolutions			
	4/79–9/79	10/79–4/80	5/80–12/80	1881
Resolutions containing demands				
An end to evictions	2.9	2.3	8.8	—
The "three Fs"	2.9	—	—	—
Reductions in rent	32.4	17.4	2.9	4.5
Peasant proprietorship	23.5	20.9	16.1	18.2
Self-government	14.7	1.2	1.5	—
Public works' jobs	2.9	14.0	1.5	—
Resolutions containing statements of policy				
Formation of tenant clubs	2.9	3.5	4.4	—
General support for the movement	8.8	1.1	1.5	4.5
Refusal to pay required rent	—	3.5	—	4.5
Censure of land grabbing	2.9	14.0	25.0	13.6
Censure of tenants who pay rent	—	2.3	—	—
General appeal to government for aid	—	2.3	1.5	
Opposition to government action (including arrest of leaders)	—	9.3	10.3	13.6
Adherence to the INLL and its national leadership	—	—	10.3	13.6
Division of large holdings into smaller ones	2.9	—	2.9	4.5
Other	2.9	8.1	13.2	18.2
Total number	34	86	68	22

Notes and sources: See Appendix 4. Some of the categories used above were adapted from Clark, *Social Origins of the Irish Land War*, p. 298. Resolutions that included two demands or statements were counted as two resolutions.

Demands for rent reductions and the establishment of peasant proprietorship dominated the meetings, comprising over half the resolutions. These were the issues around which all members of the rural community could agree, giving the appearance of a solid popular front of tenant farmers and their allies against landlordism. *The Connaught Telegraph* noted regularly that the meetings were attended by tenant farmers of "all classes." The meetings at Killala and Kilmeena attracted contingents of Protestant as well as Catholic tenant farmers.[3] This fragile class alliance barely survived the summer of 1879, but while it held, the land movement was at its most vigorous. The only discord

[3] *CT*, 12 July, 15 Nov. 1879.

during the summer resulted from the hesitancy of the priests to rally in support of the agitation. Their entry during the fall of 1879 marked a major victory for the movement, which had demonstrated to the Catholic clergy that the struggle against landlords would proceed despite clerical opposition.

THE LANDLORDS' REACTION

Few Mayo landlords were as perceptive as George Moore of the irony of their plight or literate enough to parody it, as Moore did in the excerpt from *Confessions of a Young Man* that opens this chapter. The most hysterical of Mayo landlords, Lord Oranmore and Browne and the Earl of Lucan, were convinced that there was a criminal conspiracy at work in the county. Lord Oranmore and Browne regularly entertained the House of Lords with lengthy monologues on the state of lawlessness in his native county.[4] In a letter dated 26 September 1879, the Earl of Lucan, Lord Lieutenant of the County, reported to the Conservative Chief Secretary for Ireland that "it is to communism alone [that] the present state of things in [Ireland] is to be attributed." He demanded more troops and police to be sent to Mayo "to arrest the conspiracy against all landed property."[5]

The more thoughtful landlords understood the magnitude of the threat to their economic and political power that was posed by the agitation. They saw it in the changed demeanor of their tenants towards them. This change was most evident in the rent office, where many landlords shared with George T. Shaen Carter, owner of an estate near Belmullet, the perception that in "their habits in the rent-room they were rather more independent."[6] William O'Brien reported in August 1879 that upon seeing a mob outside his office petitioning for a rent abatement, Lord Sligo's agent was "as much amazed at their boldness as if the mountain sheep had taken up arms to invade him."[7] The plight of many landlords was summed up by J. C. Sheffield, owner of an estate of 900 acres near Claremorris, who in a letter to the Chief Secretary reported:

---

[4] For example, see: *Hansard's Parliamentary Debates* (3rd ser.), ccxlvii (17 June–9 July 1879), cols. 1684–98.

[5] SPO, CSORP, the Earl of Lucan to J. Lowther, Chief Secretary for Ireland, 25 July 1879, no. 12933.

[6] *Special Commission . . . Proceedings . . .* , i, p. 594.

[7] O'Brien, *Recollections*, p. 225. The text of the petition appears in *CT*, 23 Aug. 1879.

I was considered a Good Landlord and the Tenants paid their rents most punctually. But in the last fortnight [July 1879] I have been calumniated by a priest of the Claremorris meeting and will be also by the Press of the Secret Society, and my tenants last Wednesday refused to pay their rents except at a reduction of 25 per cent and Rent Receipts altered to make it a permanent reduction. They do not assert poverty but one of them said they were combined to do it and the rest agreed.[8]

Captain Sheffield's statement that his tenants were not unable to pay, but unwilling, reflected a belief shared by most landlords. In many instances the question of whether the rent could or could not be paid was not one of the means, but one of how the resources available to the tenant family should be allocated. The landlords contended that rent payment should be the tenants' first priority. According to this view, a tenant farmer who possessed a cow, pig or a few acres of crops was not destitute and was thus able to pay the rent. But such an attitude fails to take into account the structural changes that had taken place in the economy of post-Famine Mayo. Most important of those was the widespread adoption of a cash-based economy, which meant that in times of economic distress rural people were faced with a variety of demands upon their means. They had become dependent upon cash purchases, and money or stock had to be kept in reserve to accommodate those expenditures, even if it meant withholding rent.[9] Furthermore, the farmers were regularly counseled at land meetings to pay the rent last. For example, at the Milltown meeting Davitt told the assembled farmers:

If . . . I were in possession of a farm . . . I would act as follows in reference to rental obligation: from the proceeds of what the cultivation of my farm and the industries in connection therewith would produce, I would first take care to feed myself and my family with good and substantial food similar to that which other classes deem essential to the proper nourishment of their bodies. . . . I would next insure my children being comfortably and respectably clothed, fairly and practically educated, and then see to the making of our home as snug and pleasant as our wants demanded. If, after putting aside a trifle each year towards the exigencies of helpless old age, there was sufficient left to pay the rent, I would pay it.[10]

---

[8] SPO, CSORP, J. C. Sheffield, JP to J. Lowther, Chief Secretary for Ireland, 25 July 1879, no. 12933.
[9] Clark, *Social Origins of the Irish Land War*, pp. 233–5.
[10] *CT*, 21 June 1879.

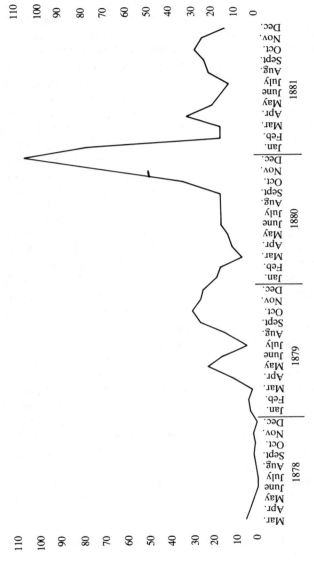

Figure 7.1. Cases of agrarian crime in County Mayo Reported by the Royal Irish Constabulary, March 1878–December 1881.
Source: see note 15

This advice was in keeping with Parnell's assertion the week before at the Westport meeting that a fair rent was "a rent the tenant can reasonably pay according to the times, but in bad times a tenant cannot be expected to pay as much as he did in good times."[11] Reinforcing the advice of Davitt was the image, fostered by agitation speakers and parodied by George Moore, of absentee landlords squandering the rent money. Together, these claims and the economic realities that gave them meaning resulted in a powerful combination against rents that left Mayo's landlords alarmed and virtually powerless since few felt in a position to embark upon wholesale evictions.

In addition to their concern over the unwillingness of their tenants to pay their rent, many landlords were anxious about the agrarian crime that accompanied the agitation and believed that the government was either unwilling or unable to protect them from acts of violence. In refusing to testify against Parnell and thirteen other Land League leaders in December 1880, Lord John Browne, chairman of the Mayo Grand Jury, summed up the feelings of many landlords:

> Most decidedly I am *not* willing to give evidence against Mr. Parnell for many reasons. If no other reason existed, I should refuse though I don't mind the risk of being shot, I do most decidedly object to having my hay burnt, my livestock maliciously injured, my herds prevented from acting for me and the public prohibited from purchasing my sheep and cattle: all of which I regard (to say the least) the possible result of giving offence to the only real government in the country – that of the Land League.[12]

While the number of agrarian offenses never reached the level that many landlords feared, there is no doubt that a wave of rural violence was a by-product of the land agitation and of the economic distress that sparked it. The number of cases of agrarian crime recorded by the Royal Irish Constabulary during the years of the Land War was higher than in any year since 1844, when the first published abstracts became available.[13] As can be seen from Figure 7.1, the number of agrarian crimes recorded by the RIC rose steadily following the commencement of the agitation from 81 in 1879 (91 percent of which occurred after the Irishtown meeting), to 343 in 1880 and 308 during 1881. Even more worrisome for

---

[11] *Ibid.*, 14 June 1879.
[12] SPO, Queen versus Parnell and Other Persons Papers, 1881, Lord John Browne to W. L. Omen, 21 Dec. 1880, carton vii. Seven other Mayo gentlemen refused to testify for similar reasons.
[13] Clark, *Social Origins of the Irish Land War*, p. 320.

landlords than the actual increased number of outrages, was the higher percentage of the crimes being committed against landlords and their employees.[14] But many of these outrages were acts of "intimidation by threatening letters," the great bulk of which never led to actual violence. If they are removed from the summaries presented by the RIC, the figures for outrages committed during the Land War is reduced to 66 in 1879, 207 in 1880, and 173 in 1881.[15]

The Land League regularly advised its followers, both from public platforms and in instructions issued to its local branches, not to participate in criminal activities.[16] Yet there is no doubt that the purposefully legal land movement stimulated the wave of agrarian crime that accompanied it. Clark argues that agrarian crime – attacks on property, stock and occasionally on people – was an important, if not entirely welcome, feature of the land movement. It aided in the enforcement of Land League laws, especially those against grabbing of land from which a tenant had been evicted, and silenced some of the movement's enemies.[17] Its effectiveness in these endeavors demonstrated the extent to which the Land League had become, as Lord Browne and other landlords alleged, "the only real government . . . in the county."

Many Mayo landlords, like those from other parts of Ireland, flooded the Chief Secretary's office with statements of alarm and pleas for police and military protection. In addition to these private appeals, Mayo gentlemen addressed two formal petitions to the Chief Secretary, one from the Mayo Grand Jury and the other from the Mayo County Magistrates. The first, dated 10 July 1879, was a call for "additional powers" to be "conferred on the Executive by Parliament" (i.e. a coercion act), while the second, passed on 30 December 1879, called for

---

14 Lee, *Modernisation of Irish Society*, pp. 89–90.

15 *Return Showing All Crimes . . . Reported by the Royal Irish Constabulary Between 1st March 1878 and 31st December 1879 . . .*, PP 1880 (6), lx, pp. 176–85; *Return of All Agrarian Outrages . . . Between the 1st January 1879 and the 31st January 1880 . . .*, PP 1880 (131), lx, p. 79; *Return of . . . Agrarian Offences in . . . 1880 . . .*, PP 1881 (12), lxxviii, pp. 2–15; *Return of . . . Agrarian Offences in . . . Ireland . . . 1881*, PP 1882 (8), lv, pp. 2–15.

16 For example, see Davitt's speech to the Newport meeting following the attempted shooting of Lord Sligo's agent. *CT*, 25 Oct. 1879. Also see: Trinity College, Dublin, Davitt Papers, J. J. Louden to M. Davitt, 14 Sept. 1888 (?), MS 3/H/182. I wish to thank Mr. William O'Sullivan, Keeper of Manuscripts, who, knowing that my time in Dublin was drawing to a close, allowed me to work with the Davitt papers shortly after they had been received from Professor T. W. Moody, and prior to their being fully processed and open to scholars.

17 Clark, *Social Origins of the Irish Land War*, pp. 320–6.

an increase in the number of police in the county and for the revocation of all gun licenses in the county with the "greatest care exercised in issuing new ones."[18] These appeals, in conjunction with numerous private ones, did result in more police being sent to the county and in many local gentlemen being provided with police bodyguards, but could do little to alter the precarious position in which Mayo landlords found themselves.

Many landlords realized a revolution was under way in Ireland that went far beyond refusals to pay the established rent and an increased willingness to assault landlords, their property and their employees. Their position at the political and economic helm of the county was being challenged on a number of fronts by the land movement and by the social and economic forces that had made the agitation so potent. On the economic front their position was seen increasingly by their tenants as incompatible with the agrarian capitalist economy that had been established in the county following the Famine. Politically they found their dominance of local government passing to farmers and townsmen. They perceived that their chief political prop, the Westminster government, was showing an alarming hesitancy to come to their aid. Probably most seriously, they saw their personal stature with their tenantry deteriorating. Those numerous landlords who had lived in harmony with their tenants with the appellation of being a "good landlord" found that charging a moderate rent and exercising leniently their legal rights over the land were no longer sufficient in the eyes of their tenants.[19] Even efforts by the priests, once they entered the movement, to gain tenant acknowledgment of the beneficent landlords in the county fell on deaf ears. By the fall of 1879 the destruction of the power of Irish landlordism, the long-term object of the land movement, was clearly under way.

THE PRIESTS JOIN THE AGITATION

The first hesitant move by a Mayo clergyman to regain control of his parishioners by asserting his leadership in the land movement occurred in July in Claremorris. The Rev. Ulick Canon Bourke, parish priest of Claremorris since November 1878, was a man long active in western

---

[18] SPO, CSORP, 1879, Resolution of the Mayo Grand Jury Relative To the State of that County, 10 July 1879, no. 12415; SPO, CSORP, 1880, Resolution of the Mayo Magistrates, no. 580.
[19] Clark, *Social Origins of the Irish Land War*, pp. 165–71.

politics. Prior to his appointment to Claremorris, Canon Bourke had been president of St. Jarlath's College, Tuam, where he was known as a man sympathetic to the Fenian movement.[20] In 1861 he had been one of the few priests in Ireland willing to defy Cardinal Cullen by sending a contribution to the obsequies fund to pay for the Fenian funeral of Terence Bellew McManus.[21] Despite his earlier sympathy with the Fenian movement, following his arrival in Claremorris, Canon Bourke convened a mission at which secret societies were denounced, and later had his crops and fences injured in retaliation for his initial opposition to the land movement.[22]

Thus, when Canon Bourke proposed that a land meeting be held in Claremorris in July 1879 his motives were immediately questioned by the agitation's leaders. Writing in the editorial column of his paper, James Daly claimed that Canon Bourke's views on the land question were highly suspect, that his true purpose in proposing the Claremorris meeting was to undermine the independence of the tenant movement and reassert the supremacy of those in "higher positions."[23] During the weeks before the meeting, Daly, in an editorial controversy with the editor of *The Tuam News*, the organ of the archdiocese, built through innuendo a case for Canon Bourke acting as the Mayo agent of the Archbishop and his Vicar General in their effort to take control of the land movement. He accused archdiocesan officials of taking the "rights of citizenship" from Mayo's priests so that they were "no longer free" to join the land movement.[24]

To complicate matters, during the week prior to the Claremorris meeting Archbishop McHale wrote his second letter attacking the land movement's leaders. After affirming his support for "beneficent legislation defining the rights of landlords and tenants" and for the "repeal of the disastrous union between Great Britain and Ireland," the Archbishop wrote:

> Let the tenant farmers of Mayo, as of all Ireland act judiciously, let them be guided as of old, by their faithful allies, the priests, who as a body in good report and in evil report, stood in the front ranks of the

20 See p. 188 above.
21 Ryan, *Fenian Memoirs*, pp. 28–9; T. O'Fiaich, "The Patriot Priest of Partry: Patrick Lavelle, 1825–1886," *Journal of the Galway Archaeological and Historical Society*, 35 (1976), p. 138.
22 *Special Commission . . . Proceedings . . .* , i, p. 631.
23 *CT*, 28 June 1879.
24 Quoted in *ibid.*, 28 June and 12 July 1879.

combat, sacrificing time and personal interests to the public welfare of society against the violence of their inveterate foes.

Let no attempt at dissevering so sacred a union fraught with blessings to the people be tolerated. In some parts of the country the people, in calmer moments, will not fail to be astonished at the circumstances of finding themselves at the tail of a few unknown strolling men who, with affected grief, deploring the condition of the tenantry, seek only to mount to place and preferment on the shoulders of the people; and should they succeed in their ambitious designs, they would not hesitate to shake aside at once the instruments of their advancement as an unprofitable incumbrance.[25]

This letter, along with Davitt's denial of the "strolling men" charge, was republished in *The Connaught Telegraph* on the eve of the Claremorris meeting. In his most rigorous attack to date on the Archbishop and the clergy, Daly accused McHale of preparing a Mayo agitation of his own around the "usual regulation talk and nothing beyond it, about 'rooting the people in the soil', and the 'disastrous union', and the 'trampled nation.' "[26]

Thus the morning of the meeting dawned under a heavy cloud resulting from McHale's letter and the responses it produced. But Canon Bourke's troubles were far from over. As if to purposely humiliate the embattled priest, Claremorris was full of Fenians from all over Connacht, who used the land meeting as a cover to convene a private meeting of their own in Henehan's public house to hear an explanation of the new departure from John Devoy, who was in Ireland illegally.[27] In addition, according to Devoy, Canon Bourke was under pressure from Rev. Thomas McHale, nephew and Vicar General to the Archbishop, to insist that the meeting include resolutions in favor of Catholic education and support for the temporal power of the Pope. Fr. Bourke found letters and a telegram from McHale to that effect when he arrived for the meeting. According to Devoy, Canon Bourke's efforts to include resolutions on these issues produced a sharp refusal from the speakers: "He was told that this was to be a land meeting, that they wanted to enlist Protestants

[25] *FJ*, 10 July 1879. The Archbishop was writing in response to an invitation to be present at a meeting in Ballyhaunis, Co. Mayo. Davitt wrote that the meeting was organized by "admirers" of the Archbishop "in rivalry with the new movement." *The Fall of Feudalism*, pp. 158–9.

[26] *CT*, 12 July 1879.

[27] *Special Commission . . . Proceedings . . .* , i, p. 268.

as well as Catholics in it, and therefore, there must be nothing sectarian in the resolutions." Canon Bourke reportedly pleaded and threatened not to take the chair at the meeting, "but it was all in vain . . . Wearied out and seeing that the men were immovable on that point, Canon Bourke at last yielded and agreed to preside."[28] The meeting called to "join the priests and tenant farmers to obtain lower rents" opened amidst considerable controversy and not under the control of the parish priest of Claremorris.

Canon Bourke opened the meeting on a platform that contained twelve priests, at least six prominent Fenians, and the agitation's leaders, Davitt, Daly and Louden. As *The Freeman's Journal* reporter commented, the significance of the resolutions introduced at Claremorris was enhanced by their "having been adopted at a gathering composed of speakers who on most other questions would, perhaps, be divided."[29] In his opening remarks Canon Bourke noted that the presence of the priests on the platform made the Claremorris meeting "something above the meetings hitherto held in favour of the tenants' cause." He went on to remind his listeners that "as dutiful Catholics you must be obedient to the laws; for social order rests on law." He argued that the most just settlement of the land question was the "three Fs" since they would allow for the retention of "a certain mutual attachment between the kind landlord and his tenantry." Canon Bourke concluded his remarks with a call for the establishment of a national legislature for Ireland.

This cautious opening speech, with its endorsement of land legislation that was considered inadequate by many of his hearers, was unusual at land meetings during the summer of 1879. Canon Bourke's position was not endorsed by the remainder of the speakers, although he did manage to have Louden read a resolution in support of the "three Fs." The other principal speakers all called for the establishment of peasant proprietorship and made no allowances for good landlords. Louden brought Canon Bourke to his feet in protest in response to his call to Irish voters to send no landlords to parliament and by his suggestion that the tenant movement in Ireland had "English democracy at [its] back." Canon Bourke retorted indignantly that the Irish were a "religious people" who have never "united with English people, particularly with the democracy and I hope we never shall." Eventually Louden calmed the Canon by saying

28   Devoy, "Michael Davitt's Career XVII," *Gaelic American*, 3 Nov. 1906; Woods, "The Catholic Church and Irish Politics," p. 37.
29   *FJ*, 14 July 1879.

that when referring to English democracy he meant the "Exiles of Erin," or Irish in England. The meeting ended with the call for the formation of a tenant club for Claremorris, the first to be formed since the commencement of the agitation.[30]

Canon Bourke's rough treatment at the meeting did not dissuade him from later asserting that it had been the "first great gathering" of the land movement since it had brought the "priests and the people under one banner."[31] Yet during the remainder of the summer the unity of "priests and people" that the Claremorris meeting was designed to bring about, failed to materialize. Undoubtedly, Canon Bourke's experiences at the Claremorris meeting alerted less politically committed priests to the sobering reality that the continuing presence of active Fenians in the movement and the hostility of Archbishop McHale made their participation in the land movement a difficult one. Many priests must have struggled with the vexing question of how to bridle the enthusiasm of their parishioners without jeopardizing their clerical authority. To make matters worse, there were no public invitations to the clergy of Mayo to join the movement and no resolutions lamenting their absence from the land meeting platforms.

This situation began to change shortly after the founding of the National Land League of Mayo on 16 August 1879.[32] While no documentation is available, it is quite likely that a decision to encourage clerical participation was arrived at in conjunction with the Mayo Land League's foundation. The first resolution encouraging the clerics to join the movement was introduced at a meeting at Balla on the eve of the foundation conference of the Mayo League. Yet the invitation was hardly one to give comfort to many priests. Speaking to the resolution, Matt Harris laid down harsh terms for the unity of "priest and people." "My resolution," he said, "is in favour of a closer union between the priests and the people. But it is well to understand the conditions upon which the union is possible or impossible." The proposed union, he asserted, must be one in which the people, not the priests, would determine the course of events. So long as the priests "show a firm front to the common enemy," the union with the people would last, but, he warned, if the priests "move towards that enemy . . . the people will not be with them . . . If there is to be a union let it be so intimate that the priests and the

[30] *CT*, 19 July 1879.
[31] *Ibid.*, 7 May 1881.
[32] See pp. 244–5 below.

people will sink or swim together."[33] Admittedly, as a Fenian leader, Harris was more hostile to the clergy than were many tenant farmers, but given the lack of a reported public call for clerical participation in the movement and the hostility shown to the clergy at meetings such as that at Knock, it seems safe to assume that Harris' views were shared, although in a more moderate form, by many of the agitation's participants.

According to Davitt, the agitation's leadership felt that a showdown with the Archbishop of Tuam was necessary before a union with the priests was possible. With this end in mind, a meeting was called for Tuam on 21 September to show Archbishop McHale the strength of the movement and the determination of its participants, even in the face of clerical hostility.[34] The meeting convened amidst considerable controversy as the town commissioners and the local clerics had not been consulted prior to the meeting.[35] The resolutions introduced and the speeches given by Davitt, Daly and Louden were all temperate, carefully avoiding mention of the primary reason for the meeting. No mention was made of the controversy with the Archbishop or of the failure of the priests to rally to the movement. Nonetheless, Davitt believed that the meeting had accomplished its purpose. He claimed it "put an end to the notion that . . . an Irish archbishop . . . was strong enough to frown down such a movement or turn its leaders from the objects upon which they had embarked. This was, for the time being, an end of clerical opposition."[36]

On the two Sundays following the Tuam meeting, rallies were held in Mayo that can be seen as the official welcoming of the priests into the movement. On the morning of the first meeting the Very Rev. Canon Magee, PP of Castlebar, spoke from the altar steps during the early Mass, supporting the agitation in forceful terms while at the same time cautioning the people to be peaceful and constitutional. Later the crowd of 10–15,000 paraded past the presbytery "cheering lustily" for Canon Magee. In a rousing speech at the meeting the Canon condemned land laws and landlords while the remaining speakers noted with pleasure the presence of six priests on the platform.[37]

[33] *CT*, 23 Aug. 1879.

[34] Davitt, *The Fall of Feudalism*, p. 159.

[35] Accounts of the meeting appear in *FJ*, 22 Sept. 1879 and *CT*, 19 Sept. 1879. Also see *FJ*, 11, 13, 16, 19 Sept. 1879 for letters and reports on the controversy surrounding the meeting.

[36] Davitt, *The Fall of Feudalism*, p. 159.

[37] *CT*, 4 Oct. 1879.

The following Sunday a similar meeting took place outside of Ballinrobe. Originally scheduled for Ballinrobe town, the meeting had to be moved into the adjoining parish because the parish priest of Ballinrobe remained hostile to the agitation.[38] This move, necessary to assure clerical participation in the meeting, put the platform in the parish of the Rev. John O'Malley, PP of The Neale, a man destined to play a major part in the land movement in Mayo. Also making his debut in the agitation was Fr. Patrick Lavelle, PP of Cong. Fr. Lavelle, by now failing in health and more temperate in his views, had been the "patriot priest of Partry," whose political activities as an open supporter of Fenianism had vexed popes, cardinals and English politicians for decades.[39] Fr. Lavelle was no longer "a turbulent priest and a speaker of seditious incentives," as Lord Oranmore had once called him, nor, as a hard line nationalist, was he entirely comfortable with the new movement. However, he was still remembered in Mayo for his spirited defense of Partry tenants evicted by their landlord, the Protestant Bishop of Tuam, because of their unwillingness to abandon their Catholic faith. Lavelle's presence at The Neale meeting undoubtedly lent it great prestige and contributed to its being the largest land meeting in the county to date. *The Connaught Telegraph* echoed the sentiments of most Mayo farmers when it congratulated Fr. O'Malley and Fr. Lavelle for not succumbing to "an exaggerated fear of the power of an emancipated democracy" as some of their colleagues had done, for not feeling the need to "cavil about nice points of etiquette as to who should have been consulted first or last," and for coming "full of hope and encouragement" for the people of Mayo.[40]

Following these fêtes to welcome the priests of County Mayo into the land movement, the clerics quickly moved to consolidate their position as community leaders in conjunction with the agitation. They presided at eighteen of the twenty-two land meetings held in Mayo during the remainder of 1879 and at 68 percent of the meetings held during 1880 and 1881. Clerical participation was far from benign, as many priests moved to divert the demands of "emancipated democracy" into the appeals of restricted democracy, but this was barely evident during the fall of 1879. Rather, as the economic situation deteriorated, the

---

[38] *Special Commission . . . Proceedings . . .* , i, p. 572.

[39] For Fr. Lavelle's career, see: O'Fiaich, "The Patriot Priest of Partry," and E. R. Norman, *The Catholic Church and Ireland in the Age of Rebellion, 1859–1873* (Ithaca, New York, 1965).

[40] *CT*, 11 Oct. 1879.

appearance of priests and people reunited brought great sighs of relief to the county.

THE FORMATION OF THE NATIONAL LAND LEAGUE OF MAYO

During the summer of 1879 Davitt revived the idea, first put forward by Daly in 1878, of forming an all-county tenant farmer organisation. Davitt's motives, by his own account, were five-fold. He wished to create "a permanent organization for the control and direction of the new movement" that would "supplant the tenants' defence associations" with "an aggressive movement which would try to rally the whole country in a fight against the whole land system." In addition, he hoped that the new organization would facilitate the establishment of several "root principles" upon which the land agitation could be expanded. However, his primary purpose was to use the Mayo League as "the nucleus for a national body" with Parnell at its head. He summed up this motive as follows: "An organized Mayo, where the people had already wrung reductions of rents from several landlords and silenced clerical opposition, was the vantage-ground from which the agitation was to operate for the capture of the land movement, with the moral certainty that success in this enterprise would mean the capture of Mr. Parnell, too, as the leader of the forces which were to be recruited for the contemplated struggle."[41] While Davitt and his colleagues accomplished all of these goals within six months, the National Land League of Mayo played little role in those successes. In fact, the organization met only once. The formation of the Mayo League was part of a stratagem by which Davitt hoped to lure Parnell into a formal alliance with the agitation. It is questionable whether Davitt ever intended the new organization to function.

The approximately fifty delegates who assembled at Daly's Hotel in Castlebar on 16 August were primarily men who had already taken an active role in the agitation and were representative only of the central corridor of the county. No priests attended, although Fr. William Joyce sent a letter of support. In well-orchestrated proceedings, Louden, Davitt's primary ally in Mayo, was voted into the chair, and later elected president of the new organization. The delegates heard and approved a lengthy document prepared by Davitt that declared that "the land of

---

[41] Davitt, *The Fall of Feudalism*, pp. 159–64.

Ireland belongs to the people of Ireland." It continued with a quote from J. S. Mill on the injustices of Irish land laws, which called for their replacement with "a system as will recognize and establish the cultivator of the said soil as its proprietor." In the interests of political expediency, Davitt included in the document a provision for landlords to be compensated for the loss of their land. The rules and objects of the new organization were set down. They included protecting tenant farmers from capricious eviction, rendering assistance to those evicted and struggling for the reform of the land laws.[42]

The formation of the Mayo Land League marked the beginning of a major change in the agitation. Davitt had given a form and structure to the movement that had begun at Irishtown, but he did so by wresting the initiative away from local activists.[43] From this point the focus of the land agitation became nationwide, paving the way for the movement's national leadership to try to direct the local agitation. Hitherto, there had been little visible animosity between the local activists, headed by Daly, and the Dublin-based radicals led by Davitt. But from August 1879 the needs of the national organization, as perceived by Davitt and his associates, began to clash with the requirements of the Mayo agitation, as perceived by Daly, Power and the Fenians. A month after the founding of the Mayo League, Power wrote to Fr. O'Malley of The Neale: "the half dozen gentlemen who have constituted themselves the 'Land League of Mayo' are determined to ride roughshod over the county."[44] However, by the time of the fall harvest, the divisions that later undermined the agitation were not yet evident.

THE EFFECT OF THE FALL HARVEST ON THE AGITATION

During the fall and winter of 1879–80 the pace of the agitation slowed as a result of significant alterations in the economic and political climate of the county. Paramount among them was the poor harvest of August–

---

[42] Accounts of the convention appear in: *CT*, 16 and 23 Aug. 1879; *FJ*, 18 Aug. 1879; Davitt, *The Fall of Feudalism*, pp. 160–4. Also see: Davitt to Devoy, 23 Aug. 1879 in O'Brien and Ryan (eds.), *Devoy's Post Bag*, I, p. 453, and Davitt's testimony before the Special Commission: *Special Commission Proceedings*, iii, pp. 560–3. The document approved at the convention is reproduced in full in: Curtis and McDowell (eds.), *Irish Historical Documents, 1172–1922*, pp. 254–9.

[43] Lee, *Modernisation of Irish Society*, p. 78.

[44] NLI, J. F. X. O'Brien Papers, J. O. Power to Fr. J. O'Malley, 26 Sept. 1879, MS 13,457.

September 1879. The fall harvest of the previous year had been a moderate one. Although it had not been sufficient to break the cycle of distress that Mayo had been locked into since 1877, it did enable most Mayo tenant farmers to put aside a store of potatoes to feed themselves and their families during the winter and spring of 1879. Yet continual rain and cold weather during the spring planting, combined with the weakness of the seed potatoes, caused considerable anxiety about the 1879 crop. It was in this environment of foreboding but not actual famine that the land agitation got its start. People could still obtain food, even though the decline in their cash incomes made payment of rents a hardship for many farmers. They could thus afford to participate in an aggressive campaign against their immediate enemies – rents and landlords – without having to resort to appeals for relief.

The fall harvest changed this picture so that by September Mayo was faced with the immediate prospect of a food and fuel famine. The effect on the agitation was profound, transforming many newly self-confident agitators into hungry mendicants forced on the charity of the world. That charity was forthcoming and prevented a full famine in Mayo during the winter and spring of 1880. As an institution, the Irish National Land League, formed at the height of the economic crisis, benefited from the new economic situation.[45] Its efficiency in raising and distributing £50,000 in relief during the winter increased its credibility in the eyes of Mayo farmers and demonstrated that it was more responsive and effective than was the Westminster government. Yet the near famine had a demoralizing effect on the agitation, transforming the tenor of the land meetings and altering the nature of the resolutions passed at them.

The failure of the fall harvest undoubtedly stimulated many heretofore hesitant clerics to join their parishioners in the land movement, using it as a vehicle to supply aid to their economically distressed flocks. Many priests, confident that they knew better than Fenian or Land League orators how best to aid the people, reasoned that the demands of "emancipated democracy" as *The Connaught Telegraph* continued to refer to the movement, were dangerous and potentially counter-productive, given the economic emergency in the county. The abolition of landlordism might be useful in the long run, but many priests felt that only appeals to the charity of the landlords and the English government had any hope of bringing immediate relief. Consequently, once priests began to take a prominent part in land meetings, they frequently called

45 See pp. 249–50 below.

on the assembled to be moderate in tone so as not to offend the local landlords or the government, and thus put relief from those sources in jeopardy.[46] Hugh Conway, Bishop of Killala, whose suspicion of the agitation contributed to its limited success in his diocese, set the pace, albeit in an extreme form, for clerical attempts to bring the movement into harmony with the charitable "good landlords." In a letter to the Killala meeting, the tone of which was the most moderate of any meeting held during the agitation, the bishop praised the conciliatory spirit of the resolutions:

These resolutions properly omit all references to the irrative question of the relations between landlords and tenants, for to select the occasion of asking favours and assistance from landlords as a time for expressing opinions subversive of their legal rights and hurtful to their feelings seems to me the most inopportune and foolish proceeding.[47]

Probably the majority of priests in the county were not as concerned with hurting the landlords' feelings as was Bishop Conway, and no doubt joined Fr. Joyce of Louisburgh in advising their parishioners to feed their families with the available money before they paid the rent.[48] Nonetheless, their overall impact on the land movement was to moderate its tone and begin to divert its goals away from those the priests felt to be unrealistic and in a direction more likely to produce immediate aid. As can be seen from Table 7.1 above, the number of resolutions calling for public works jobs from either the government or landlords rose markedly following the entry of the priests into the movement. Not surprisingly, the number of resolutions requesting aid rose at the expense of resolutions calling for self-government, of which there was only one introduced at meetings between September 1879 and April 1880. Demands for self-government were most clearly associated with Fenian participation in the agitation, participation that had presented the major obstacle to clerical involvement. While it is unlikely that the leaders of the agitation made a formal agreement to drop resolutions for self-government in return for clerical support, the priests' entry marked the beginning of the Fenians' slow drift away from a movement that was becoming too moderate and exclusively agrarian for them.

This moderation did not go unchallenged. At the Killala and Aughamore meetings in October, Davitt openly rejected the tone set by

---

[46] For examples, see: *CT*, 25 Oct., 1, 22 Nov. 1879.
[47] *CT*, 1 Nov. 1879.
[48] *Ibid.*, 8 Nov. 1879.

the clerics and struck out at landlordism with unbridled vigor. To the dismay of the meeting's organizers, he told the crowd at Killala, following the reading of the Bishop's letter, that he would respect the tenor of the meeting but stood before them "as an uncompromising enemy of landlordism in every shape and form." It was, he continued, "a system . . . responsible for every misery, for every affliction, for every wrong that had been perpetuated on a brave and industrious people." He concluded by condemning Irish landlordism as "nothing more or less than a system of gigantic robbery which would not be tolerated by the Irish people were they not so much under the influence of their holy religion and high moral training."[49]

In this and similar speeches given in Mayo during the winter of 1879–80, Davitt attempted to arrest the drift away from radical agrarianism that the priests were encouraging. In February 1880 he wrote to Devoy that counteracting the demoralizing effect of having to appeal for relief was the Land League's greatest challenge:

> Every effort is now made to turn the flank of the New Firm [Land League] by those who are dispensing charity and the greatest possible exertion and vigilance is required to prevent the work of the past year being undone through the demoralizing influences of meal and money.[50]

In the face of this potential demoralization, Davitt and the western radicals strove to keep the will to resist alive by preaching a gospel of no compromise and class warfare against landlords. Yet he also understood the dangers of collapse inherent in an agitation, isolated in the poorest regions of the country, which advocated a program that was too radical to allow for cooperation with moderate nationalists and land reformers. Consequently Davitt, in conjunction with Parnell, moved during the winter of 1879–80 to broaden the base of the agitation by attracting moderate opinion and by institutionalizing the land movement to gain more central control over its direction. In an attempt to transcend the rhetorical radicalism and rural resistance that had characterized the early stages of the land agitation, they formed a nationwide land-reform organization. This action prolonged the life of the movement at the expense of local initiative, paving the way for an eventual compromising of the interests of the small farmers of Mayo who had begun the agitation.

---

49 *Ibid.*, 1 Nov. 1879.
50 O'Brien and Ryan (eds.), *Devoy's Post Bag*, I, p. 483.

THE INSTITUTIONALIZATION OF THE AGITATION: THE IRISH NATIONAL LAND LEAGUE AND ITS BRANCHES

Davitt's successful effort to lure Parnell into the leadership of the land movement culminated with the founding of the Irish National Land League on 21 October 1879. Parnell had stayed away from the west of Ireland since his appearance at Westport in June, despite receiving numerous invitations to speak at land meetings. He understood better than Davitt the potential pitfalls of associating himself with an isolated radical movement, yet he also knew that the Irish nationalist party could not be effective in the world of British politics without a mass movement at its back. In addition, he was aware that in order to wrest control of the Irish parliamentary party away from the moderate old guard he needed a potentially revolutionary but malleable popular following that would support his leadership. The question in Parnell's mind during the fall of 1879 was whether the land agitation that had galvanized Mayo for six months would be durable enough to fulfill this function. Quite likely the failure of the harvest convinced him that the movement would last at least until the next general election, at which time Parnell hoped to employ the agitation to convince Ireland's electors to return to parliament men who were dedicated to fighting aggressively for Irish self-government under Parnell's leadership.[51] The movement proved durable but intractable. Parnell did not succeed in securing control of it until 1882, after much of its vitality had been sapped. Nonetheless, the founding of the Irish National Land League was Parnell's first step towards placing the agitation in the politically dependable hands of a small coterie of Dublin-based radicals willing to acknowledge Parnell's leadership, if not always to agree with his policies.

Despite their pioneering role in the land agitation, there were no Mayo representatives reported to have attended the founding conference of the Land League, although letters of support were read from Daly, Louden, Fr. Joyce, Canon Bourke and Power. At the convention, Parnell, voted president of the new organization, got his wish, a land program that could be advocated in the House of Commons. The program that emerged from the convention was a temperate version of the one formulated during the summer in Mayo. The demand for peasant proprietorship, a vital part of the Mayo platform, was relegated to the second of the new League's

[51] Larkin, *The Roman Catholic Church and the Creation of the Modern Irish State*, p. 23.

objectives. The first was "to bring out [sic] a reduction of rackrents," thus focusing on the acknowledged high rents rather than on rents in general. In a resolution proposed by Parnell, the conference approved a program of reform designed to canalize the rhetoric of the summer into a workable plan of action. The resolution read:

> That the objects of the league can be best attained by promoting organization among the tenant farmers, by defending those who may be threatened with eviction for refusing to pay unjust rents, by facilitating the working of the Bright clauses of the land act during the winter, and by obtaining such reform in the laws relating to land as will enable every tenant to become the owner of his holdings by paying a fair rent for a limited number of years.[52]

This was a moderate but ambitious program, especially the section that pledged the Land League to defend tenants threatened with eviction. This clause raised the expectations of the tenant farmers of Mayo and contributed to the early popularity of the League in the county.

Soon after the founding of the League, the new organization and its president were given an opportunity to demonstrate the extent of their commitment to defend those threatened with eviction. Appropriately, the opportunity came in central Mayo, the cradle of the agitation. In the first eviction attempted since the founding of the Land League, Sir Robert Bloose, an absentee landlord with 17,555 acres in central Mayo, moved to evict the Dempsey family of eight from their home at Loonamore, near Balla, for non-payment of rent. When word of the pending eviction reached Davitt, he organized a meeting to protest and, if possible, prevent the eviction.[53] His arrest on 19 November, along with the arrests of Daly and J. B. Killen, a Belfast barrister, for allegedly seditious speeches delivered at Gurteen, County Sligo, on 2 November, left the Loonamore rally without its principal speakers. Parnell, " 'with a falcon's eye for his chance' . . . swooped on Balla . . . winning spectacular publicity that concealed the essential moderation of his policy behind a romantic fighting facade."[54] Parnell's performance was captured by William O'Brien, who watched it:

---

52 An account of the proceedings appears in: *FJ*, 22 Oct. 1879. *The Freeman's Journal* report is reprinted in part in: Curtis and McDowell (eds.), *Irish Historical Documents, 1172–1922*, pp. 259–60 and in Davitt, *The Fall of Feudalism*, pp. 171–3. Also see: Lyons, *Charles Stewart Parnell*, pp. 97–8 and Bew, *Land and the National Question in Ireland*, pp. 69–72.

53 Davitt, *The Fall of Feudalism*, p. 178.

54 Lee, *Modernisation of Irish Society*, p. 78.

A vast column of young men, four deep, marched up the hill at the top of which the police were mustered around the tenant's house. All of a sudden the column divided into a huge crescent formation, Zulu fashion, spreading out at a rush to right and left, threatening to envelop the handful of police. Police rushed to their rifles and stood to arms in perfect panic. P[arnell] ran to one of the horns of the crescent and charged them furiously to fall back, striking at their hands with his umbrella and tumbling over one big countryman who had a stick and looked nasty. It was a dangerous moment. But Parnell and Brennan carried their point and beat back the column.[55]

It was indeed a "dangerous moment." A police inspector reported to Dublin castle that the rally was the "largest and most formidable gathering I have yet seen in this district." He went on to observe that "nearly all [marchers] were armed with blunt sticks," were "much more determined and earnest than on any former occasion," and were "much more under the control of persons directing their movements." In contrast to the impression given by O'Brien's account, Major Wise indicated that the marchers were under the command of P. W. Nally, leader of Mayo's Fenians who, prior to Parnell's furious umbrella charge, "rode to the point [of the hill] with a bugler also on horseback and ordered the halt to sound, which was done at once and obeyed with alacrity by the whole procession – at this moment Mr. Parnell appeared on the scene . . . "[56] The threatened evictions were called off, and the whole affray was celebrated with explosive speeches by Brennan and Parnell at the rally following the confrontation with the police. After the rally Parnell traveled to Sligo, where Davitt, Daly and Killen were being held. While there, he scorned the government for their arrests.[57] It was a highly charged few days during which Parnell almost singlehandedly humiliated and discredited the government while greatly enhancing the prestige and the number of adherents to the new League.

The sobering side of the Dempsey case came several weeks later, when, with the excitement past, Bloose quietly evicted the Dempsey family. It was soon revealed that the dramatic encounter between the

---

[55] O'Brien, *Recollections*, p. 232.
[56] SPO, CSORP, Report of Major Wise, No. 12061. For additional accounts of the confrontation and subsequent rally, see: *Report of the Special Commission, 1888, Appendix IV*, PP 1890 [C 5891], xxviii, pp. 127–31; *Special Commission . . . Proceedings . . .*, i, pp. 629–30; *CT*, 22 Nov. 1879; *FJ*, 24 Nov. 1879; Davitt, *The Fall of Feudalism*, pp. 178–80; Lyons, *Charles Stewart Parnell*, pp. 101–3.
[57] Davitt, *The Fall of Feudalism*, pp. 181–6.

League and the police had not prevented the eviction. Rather, the sheriff had postponed the eviction seven days before the famous meeting because the family was stricken with fever. When the fever passed, the eviction was carried out.[58] This eviction put the Land League leadership in a quandary. The eviction had demonstrated that rousing speeches and threatening rallies were not going to be enough to fulfill the plank in the League's program pledging the defense of tenant farmers threatened with eviction. The only option available was to admit defeat and use Land League funds, which were still quite slender, to pay the Dempseys' rent so they could be reinstated.[59] Accordingly, the £26 back rent was paid by the Land League while the £7 16s. 8d. for legal costs was raised by local subscription.[60] The saga of the Dempsey eviction, both its exhilarating and sobering moments, had given a clear message to the tenant farmers of Mayo. They realized that should they want protection from the evictions that everyone expected to occur during the winter, they had best join the Land League and form local branches of it.

From the time of the first land meetings in Mayo, Daly and other orators had called on the people to organize themselves into local tenant clubs. Yet despite this advice, the only tenants' defense associations reported as being formed by the end of 1879 were at Claremorris, where one was formed at the instigation of the local clergy, and at Westport.[61] However, during the early months of 1880 local TDAs and local branches of the Land League began to appear in rural Mayo. In part, the foundation of local tenant organizations was a consequence of the entry of the clergy into the agitation. While it was possible for local and national organizers to inaugurate a movement of mass meetings in the face of clerical opposition, it was unlikely that formal land reform organizations at the parish or townland level could be formed without clerical cooperation. Irish rural communities were socially organized around the parish, with Mass as the most important communal event of the week. The priest was at the center of this community. In most matters his advice was sought and his approval required before the community would act. Although at the county level some priests partially lost this authority, it remained intact at the parish level. In a letter to *The Connaught Telegraph*, Fr. Lavelle, CC, Louisburgh, reported that "the

---

[58] *CT*, 13 Dec. 1879.
[59] Bew, *Land and the National Question in Ireland*, pp. 91–2.
[60] SPO, CSORP, letters from Resident Magistrate, 12, 20, 27 Dec. 1879, No. 264.
[61] *CT*, 26 July, 15 Nov. 1879.

people always look for counsel from the clergy in all public matters of importance, and even they are very reluctant to do anything in the way of public business without the clergy."[62] The formation of local branches was possible only after the clergy were integrated into the movement and endorsed its goals. The importance of the clergy as promoters of local branches of the Land League and as the political center of their parishes is indicated by the frequency of their election to office in the branches. At least half of the branches of the Land League whose formation was reported in *The Connaught Telegraph* had priests as presidents, while numerous curates handled the duties of secretary or treasurer.[63]

Many priests were ready to join the movement by the fall of 1879, but local branches did not form with any regularity until the winter of 1880. No doubt the promise of Land League aid, not only for those threatened with eviction but for those threatened with starvation as well, determined the timing of branch formation in many instances. The last act of the founding convention of the Irish National Land League had been the request that Parnell travel to America "for the purpose of obtaining assistance from our exiled countrymen and other sympathisers" for the "sustainment of the movement."[64] Accordingly, on 21 December Parnell, accompanied by John Dillon, left for America. As the proceeds from his trip were sent to Ireland they were distributed to the needy through either the agency of the local branch of the League or through the offices of the parish priest. As Davitt put it:

> most of the opposition from that quarter [the priests] died out in the presence of the prompt and effective measures which were taken by the league executive to cope with the partial famine. Where no league organization existed the parish priest or curate was made the medium for the distribution of grants, the result being, in most instances of this kind, the formation of a branch of the movement, so that the work of combination kept pace with the relief operations among the people.[65]

In most instances the branch was formed to obtain relief and to promote the objects of the League in the parish, but there were cases of bogus branches being formed only to obtain the money and then disband once the distress had passed. For example, Fr. John Kelly, administrator of the parish of Crossmolina, told the Parnell Commission that "people joined

[62] *CT*, 20 Sept. 1879.
[63] Based on a survey of all Land League branches whose formation was reported in *The Connaught Telegraph* during 1880 and 1881.
[64] *FJ*, 22 Oct. 1879.
[65] Davitt, *The Fall of Feudalism*, p. 211.

the League solely for the purpose of getting relief from the National League in Dublin." His testimony was confirmed by the priest of a neighboring parish and by a prominent shopkeeper in Crossmolina who told the commissioners that the local branch did not hold regular meetings except to qualify for relief.[66] The Crossmolina branch was probably the exception rather than the rule, but the availability of relief money from the Land League Fund was a powerful stimulus to many parishes to form League branches, especially after it was learned that Mayo received 40 percent of the first installment of money that Parnell had collected in America.[67]

The League executive moved to capitalize on this eagerness to form branches by dispatching orators and organizers to Mayo, hoping to keep the spirit of the resistance alive in the face of the demoralizing effects of the near famine and appeals for aid. It was successful immediately in forming branches, many of which were created in conjunction with a League-sponsored land meeting in the vicinity. However, the League executive found that an equally rigorous campaign among the small farmers of central Mayo was being carried out by the county's Fenians. The campaign was directed against land "grabbers" (those who took land from which the previous tenant had been evicted) and against graziers. Fenian leadership of the anti-grazier struggle was longstanding in Mayo, but following the small rally outside Claremorris on 25 May, the vigor of the summer's anti-landlord campaign had temporarily silenced class conflicts within the farming community. The economic distress of the winter of 1880, which heightened the small farmers' feeling of vulnerability, brought a renewal of anti-grazier activity that was worrisome to those members of the Land League's central executive who were anxious to expand the movement to include the large farmers of the midlands and southeastern regions of Ireland.

As can be seen in Table 7.1 above, resolutions censuring persons who took land from which the previous tenant had been evicted were passed frequently at land meetings during the winter of 1879–80, after being virtually absent from land platforms during the first six months of the agitation. This increased censure of grabbers is not particularly surprising given the widespread belief that evictions were imminent. It was hoped that landlords would be reluctant to evict if they knew that they would have difficulty finding anyone to take the holding. P. J.

---

[66] *Special Commission . . . Proceedings . . .* , iii, pp. 529, 539, 709.
[67] *CT*, 17 Jan. 1880.

Gordon, a Claremorris Fenian, told a crowd in January that "if a farm from which a tenant had been evicted was left on the landlord's hands he would not evict many, for the landlord cannot live without his tenants."[68] At two meetings held in late December 1879 and early January 1880, and apparently organized by the Fenians of Balla and Claremorris, the small farmers gave vent to their concern over land grabbing and over the consolidation of holdings and the expansion of grazing farms at their expense. At Mayo Abbey on 28 December, during the first land meeting to be held in the county to denounce a specific grazier, James Daly, himself a grazier, joined with J. B. Walsh, a Castlebar publican, in calling for the subdivision of vacant grass farms into "ten to fifty acre" residential holdings.[69] A week later at Kilcolman, near Claremorris, a similar meeting was held at which no Land League leaders and, as had been the case at the Mayo Abbey meeting, no priests, were present. The meeting had been called to protest the action of a Claremorris shopkeeper-grazier who had taken a grass farm which the previous tenant had given up rather than pay an unabated rent. Resolutions were passed denouncing grabbing and graziers and calling for the subdivision of vacant grass farms. Gordon called grabbers traitors to their country who should be shunned and ostracized by the community. Local activists Daly and Louden were expected at this meeting but failed to appear and, curiously, no mention of the meeting appears in *The Connaught Telegraph*.[70]

The Fenians of Mayo were taking advantage of the economic distress to do more than organize an anti-grazier campaign. They were also building up their arsenal of weapons, apparently preparing for open warfare. In a letter to Devoy dated 11 February 1880, James J. O'Kelly, a Dublin-based Fenian activist, wrote that "the famine districts of the West of Ireland offer the best field now for our activity." He reported that during the previous weeks arms had been supplied to Fenians in the west and he requested $7000 from America to purchase and send 1500 additional weapons to the west of Ireland.[71] This request met with the approval of Dr. William Carrol, head of Clan na Gael, the American Fenian organization, who, in a letter to Devoy, said that the organization could not "stand idle without aiding in their last extremity the poor brave

---

[68] *FJ*, 7 Jan. 1880.
[69] *CT*, 3 Jan. 1880.
[70] *FJ*, 7 Jan. 1880; Bew, *Land and the National Question in Ireland*, p. 88.
[71] O'Brien and Ryan (eds.), *Devoy's Post Bag*, I, pp. 489–90.

people in Kyle's [Davitt's] immediate neighbourhood."[72] Davitt appears to have been privy to these arms shipments, and even claimed to have directed the uses to which they were put. He wrote to Devoy in February 1880 that there was "a great and general desire among the people to become possessed of material [arms]. Several of the successful attacks made upon the opposition were promoted by him [Davitt]."[73]

In one sense it appears that the Fenians and the Land Leaguers were operating at cross purposes. The former were pursuing an illegal policy among the small farmers leading toward insurrection, while the latter were promoting a legal movement designed to attract widespread support for a constitutional reform program. Yet in their own ways each organization had an appeal for the farmers of Mayo that differed in rhetoric and tactics, but complemented the other. The League could offer aid, organization and the hope for reform, while the Fenians could offer the thrill of class warfare and opportunities to seek revenge through agrarian violence. For as long as he was able, Davitt balanced both positions, knowing that together they provided the impetus needed to expand the land movement during the winter of great distress.

THE GENERAL ELECTION OF 1880

During the winter of 1879–80 it was widely expected in political circles that the Conservative Prime Minister, Benjamin Disraeli, would call a general election for the spring. Parnell viewed the election as an opportunity to increase his supporters in the House of Commons and to strengthen the alliance between the land agitation and radical parliamentarians.[74] When the election campaign came in March and April, the Land League remained officially aloof, as befitted an autonomous organization, many of whose members were steeped in Fenian hostility to electoral politics. In fact, two Mayo branches of the League requested that the organization deny publicly any involvement in the campaign.[75] Yet the association of Parnell with the land movement had brought great hope to tenant farmers, many of whom realized that their chance of

---

[72] *Ibid.*, pp. 495–6.

[73] *Ibid.*, I, p. 483.

[74] The importance of the general election for Parnell is discussed in: Lyons, *Charles Stewart Parnell*, pp. 116–29 and Conor Cruise O'Brien, *Parnell and His Party, 1880–90*, corrected ed. (Oxford, 1964), pp. 11–35.

[75] *FJ*, 12 Mar. 1880; Conor Cruise O'Brien, "The Machinery of the Irish Parliamentary Party, 1880–85," *Irish Historical Studies*, 5 (1946), pp. 56–7.

agrarian reform rested on the return of a Parnellite majority at the election. While in 1880 Parnell could not manipulate the land agitation for the benefit of parliamentary candidates as effectively as he would be able to do by the 1885 campaign, he had in the local branches a cadre of men on whom he could rely to pressure the electors to vote for his candidates.

In Mayo the general election marked the appearance of the first serious discord among the local League activists, and between them and the national leaders. The immediate issue that divided the movement's leaders was the candidacy of Power, but the underlying issue was the feeling on the part of many Mayo activists that they were being dictated to by the League central executive. The county's leadership divided into two camps, one led by Daly that supported Power and defended local control over candidate selection, and a second led by Louden that attempted to undermine Power's electoral strength and solicited outside direction for its efforts. This division was far from clear-cut by the time of the election, but it initiated a period of strife that during the nine months following the general election was to seriously weaken the land movement in Mayo.

Initially, it appeared that Mayo figured little in Parnell's election strategy. Its senior member, George Browne, was an ineffectual and frequently absent parliamentarian, but could be classified as a home ruler, albeit a meek one. Mayo's junior member, Power, was a towering figure both in and out of parliament, a man of great oratorical prowess who had been associated with Parnell in the parliamentary obstruction campaign of 1877–8, and whose participation in the land movement predated Parnell's by many months. The Catholic clergy in all three dioceses in Mayo, acting in accord with the wishes of the Archbishop of Tuam, took the lead in endorsing the two sitting members for re-election and passed resolutions deprecating the idea of a contest for either seat. At one clerical meeting in Swinford, presided over by the Bishop of Achonry, promises were obtained from Browne of "increased parliamentary attention and energy."[76]

Following a year of intense political activity, many people in Mayo were unwilling to accept the candidacy of Browne, a landlord holding 2809 acres in the county, and a man who was unwilling to throw his support behind either the land movement or Parnell. A "large deputation"

[76] TCD, Davitt Papers, F. MacCormack, Bishop of Achonry to Davitt, 2 Apr. 1880, MS 25/ALL/2611; *CT*, 3 Apr. 1880; *FJ*, 1 Apr. 1880.

of Mayo people called on Daly, requesting that he contact the Land League Executive or Parnell to solicit a candidate to run in conjunction with Power. Daly declined the request, suggesting that the delegation contact Parnell directly. At a rally held on 28 March at which Power addressed his constituents, Daly took the lead in denouncing Browne. He told those assembled that Power "should have an energetic colleague in Parliament . . . it was their duty to a man, to raise their voice against the man who would not adopt the Parnell policy . . . Let them get another Parnell, if possible for Mayo . . . If they sent landlords to Parliament they sent them to forge the chains of their slavery . . . "[77]

The first effort to field another candidate came the following Thursday when a contingent of electors and activists, including the leading Fenians in the county, met in Claremorris to select Thomas Brennan, a former Fenian and the most radical member of the Land League Executive, to stand for Mayo.[78] While the decision to ask Brennan to stand for Mayo appeared part of the movement to unseat Browne, there is some evidence that the real target of the meeting was Power. His entry into parliament in 1874 while he was still a member of the Supreme Council of the IRB remained a source of great bitterness among extreme Fenians, in particular Patrick Nally, the County Centre of the IRB.[79] In his letter to Devoy regarding arms for the west, James J. O'Kelly wrote that one reason for the increased arms supply was to "reassert the influence of the firm [IRB] with the view of bringing pressure to exclude a friend of Kyle's [Davitt] who is a Candidate."[80] This apparent reference to Power raises the possibility that the Fenian brotherhood was attempting to weaken Power's political base in Mayo. It is doubtful that they could have openly opposed him without jeopardizing Fenian support in Mayo, but they could have embarrassed him financially by forcing him into a costly canvass. As it turned out, Brennan declined to stand.[81]

The circumstances surrounding Parnell's last-minute decision to stand for Mayo are clouded by the bitter feelings that his decision produced among the county's political leaders. He had already been returned for Cork City and was assured of re-election in County Meath, so he was not in search of a seat. Despite his politically inspired pronouncements, he was never interested in actually occupying one of Mayo's seats in the

[77] *CT*, 27 Mar. 1880.
[78] *Ibid.*
[79] Moody, *Davitt and Irish Revolution*, p. 312.
[80] O'Brien and Ryan (eds.), *Devoy's Post Bag*, I, pp. 489–90.
[81] *CT*, 3 Apr. 1880.

House of Commons. It was Louden who wished to stand for Mayo in the Land League interest, but ran into the determined opposition of Power. He heard of Louden's intentions in September when he returned to Mayo following the parliamentary session. In a letter to Fr. John O'Malley of The Neale, Power made known his feelings on a Louden candidacy:

> You are evidently not aware that Parnell is determined to support *Louden*, well knowing that it is impossible for me as a Catholic to coalesce with him. Parnell hates the power of the clergy just as much as Louden himself, and he is personally jealous of me, and determined to thwart me covertly. However . . . I have declined to contest with Parnell, Louden, etc., and intend to forebear still further although a system of the most damnable lying has been set up against me.[82]

As an atheist who had a reputation for making slanderous attacks on religion and on the power of the clergy, Louden was an anathema to the local parties.[83] He was shunned by Power, who was anxious to maintain good relations with the clergy. According to Daly, Power had humiliated Louden back in 1876, "and from that period dates the cause of all the underhand, villainous attacks made upon him." Daly accused Louden of wishing to take revenge on Power by unseating him in Mayo.[84] The more likely scenario is that Louden hoped to run along with Power against Browne, but was rejected as a running mate by Power. In Daly's bitter words, Power "did not allow one of these political shams [Louden] to hang on to his coat-tails to drag him through an election contest in Mayo. Neither did Mr. O'Connor Power nor the priests of Mayo see the wisdom of tolerating such an insult to the people of a noble constituency."[85]

Louden's thwarted candidacy left his League supporters without a candidate to challenge Browne. They could not afford to further alienate the priests, who had by this time endorsed Browne and Power. The Bishop of Achonry appealed to Davitt "as a Mayo man, who I know on good authority, would not be party to lessen clerical influence even in political matters." He asked Davitt to prevent a contest that could "have the effect of alienating the clergy of Mayo from all connection and sympathy with the National Land League."[86] With less than two weeks remaining before the polling, only Parnell's candidacy might mollify the clergy, restore the image of the League, and defeat Browne. In these

[82] NLI, J. F. X. O'Brien Papers, Power to O'Malley, 26 Sept. 1879, MS 13457.
[83] *FJ*, 9 Apr. 1880.
[84] *CT*, 18 Mar. 1880.
[85] *Ibid.*, 29 May 1880.
[86] TCD, Davitt Papers, F. MacCormack to Davitt, 2 Apr. 1880, MS 25/All/2611.

circumstances, Davitt approached Parnell and secured his assent to stand for Mayo.[87]

Out of respect for Parnell's influence over the people of Mayo, the priests and bishops only mildly censured him for his decision to stand at such a late date.[88] Only the Bishop of Achonry lashed out at him for aspiring "to play the role of *universal* dictator" and warned that "the bubble of Mr. Parnell's popularity might at any moment burst before the indignant spirit of faith and fatherland."[89] Bishop MacCormack's warning was ten years premature, and Parnell was successfully able to contest Mayo without seriously alienating the priests or damaging his prestige.

Parnell's candidacy was announced in a letter to the electors of Mayo signed by Davitt and Brennan. On 5 April, the day of Parnell's return for Cork City, his nomination papers were signed.[90] P. J. B. Daly, a Ballinrobe solicitor, later said that he joined with Davitt and Louden in signing Parnell's nomination papers because no one in Daly's stronghold of Castlebar could be found to sign them.[91] Louden was hooted by a crowd as he approached the court house with Davitt to file the papers and soon rumors spread to the effect that Parnell's real motive was to oust Power, not Browne.[92]

These rumors received confirmation in the memoirs of Tim Healy, Parnell's campaign manager in Cork. He wrote that Parnell became a candidate in Mayo "nominally against George Browne, but in reality against O'Connor Power, on whom he wished to be revenged."[93] Parnell had sufficient reason to wish to oust Power, who had ambitions of his own to lead the Irish party, was jealous of Parnell's personal ascendancy, and was never going to be a loyal lieutenant to the Wicklow gentleman.[94] Furthermore, Power had displayed his independence by rejecting Parnell's apparent candidate, Louden, and in effect forcing Parnell to contest the seat himself. Nonetheless, if Parnell was part of a plot to oust Power from his seat, he did a masterful job of disguising his intentions. Repeatedly, he assured the electors of Mayo that his goal was to defeat

---

[87] *FJ*, 12 Apr. 1880.
[88] *Ibid.*, 8 Apr. 1880.
[89] *Ibid.*, 10 Apr. 1880.
[90] *CT*, 10 Apr. 1880.
[91] *Special Commission . . . Proceedings . . .* , ii, p. 122.
[92] *FJ*, 6 Apr. 1880; *CT*, 10 Apr. 1880; *The Times*, 12 Apr. 1880.
[93] Healy, *Letters and Leaders of My Day*, I, p. 92.
[94] Jordan, "John O'Connor Power," pp. 55–65.

Browne in alliance with Power and that in the event of Power being unseated, he [Parnell] would step down in Power's favor.[95] Somewhat to Parnell's chagrin, Power topped the poll, but Parnell had in a brief campaign demonstrated the power of his position in Ireland by winning a parliamentary seat in Mayo despite a short campaign and considerable opposition.[96]

Immediately on the publication of the election results, the various factions in Mayo politics scurried about to field a candidate for the seat they knew would soon be vacated by Parnell, who was certain to choose to represent Cork City despite being elected in counties Mayo and Meath as well. Louden, John Walsh of Balla and P. J. Monahan of Ballinrobe, working in concert with Parnell, hoped to put forward Andrew Kettle, the defeated Parnellite candidate for County Cork. To this end, Parnell and Kettle traveled to Ballaghaderreen to secure the blessing of Bishop MacCormack. Angered over Kettle's criticism of several priests during the Cork campaign, the Bishop refused his endorsement, killing Kettle's candidacy in the process.[97] The bishops and priests put forward Walter M. Bourke, an unpopular landlord who was later to fall victim to an assassin's bullet.[98] In an effort to thwart another Louden bid for the seat, Daly put forward the Rev. Isaac Nelson, a Presbyterian minister from Belfast and the recently defeated Parnellite candidate in County Leitrim.

The clergy of Mayo, finding that they had nominated an unpopular man who was abused by crowds as he attempted to canvass the county, were faced with a distasteful choice: to allow either a Presbyterian minister or a known anti-cleric to be elected for Catholic Mayo.[99] Determined to deny Louden the seat, the clergy agreed to secure Browne's retirement from the contest and remain neutral to a Nelson candidacy. With Parnell's and Louden's endorsement, Rev. Nelson was returned unopposed, to the satisfaction of no one. Six months later he alienated himself from Catholic Ireland by making some disparaging remarks about priests and became an embarrassment to all involved in his election.

The election of 1880 brought to a close the first phase of the land agitation. Superficially, the return of Power and Parnell appeared to be the triumphal consequence of a year of agrarian protest and political

[95] *CT*, 10 Apr. 1880.
[96] *Ibid.*, 17 Apr. 1880; Healy, *Letters and Leaders of My Day*, I, p. 92.
[97] Kettle, *Material for Victory*, pp. 33-4; *CT*, 29 May 1880.
[98] *CT*, 1 May 1880.
[99] *Ibid.*, 22 May 1880; *FJ*, 8 May 1880.

activity. Yet the outward harmony hid a series of fissures that had been under the surface for some time, but only burst out during and immediately following the election. During its first year the land movement in Mayo had radicalized a segment of the farming class, and had demonstrated to many farmers that their economic problems were the logical consequence of a system of land holding that was incompatible with the economic realities of post-Famine Mayo. The agitation had provided them with an open, legal vehicle for seeking short-term relief and for striving towards long-term solutions. In addition, it had furnished them with a cadre of capable leaders. However, the renewed economic distress during the winter of 1879–80 had put under serious strain the collaboration between large and small farmers, which had contributed greatly to the movement's early success. Many small farmers, especially those living in Mayo's central core in close proximity with the graziers, followed the lead of the Fenians in a campaign against land consolidation that was directed as much against grazing farmers as landlords. This campaign was never large, being characterized as much by sporadic acts of violence against graziers and their property as by public meetings. In part, this was an inevitable consequence of the Fenian leadership, which quickly grew impatient with public rallies. Also, it was hampered by not being able to effectively draw upon the numerous small farmers inhabiting the peripheral regions of Mayo. The small farmers of the periphery, especially those in the barren waste of western Mayo, lacked in 1880–1 the radical political leadership and experience necessary for an organized campaign against graziers. Furthermore, they remained to a larger extent than their central Mayo counterparts guided in political matters by their priests, who would not countenance class warfare. As will be shown in the next chapter, as the land movement weakened without having brought a noticeable improvement in the small farmers' condition, they gave up in despair, leaving Mayo in large numbers for England and America.

In contrast, the position of the large grazing farmers within the land movement strengthened during 1880. The centralization of the agitation that came with the establishment of the Irish National Land League in October 1879 facilitated the expansion of the movement into central and eastern Ireland. There the large farmers, with the political experience gained from the Tenant League and Central Tenants' Defence Association, were able to capture control of the Land League in their area and eventually to direct the policy of the League central executive away from support for the small farmers of western Ireland. The first year of the agitation was unique in that the political and economic forces that shaped post-Famine Mayo had created an environment in which an anti-landlord agitation could flash across Mayo and briefly inflame the rest of the country. But the combination of splits within the leadership and the collapse of class unity would soon quench the flames.

8. *Tensions within the Land League in County Mayo, 1880*

Each affiliated branch must communicate directly with the central executive in Dublin . . . in all matters relating to finances, reports, and organisation. County centralisation invites dangers and attacks which could not so easily affect a solid compact body under the complete guidance of a central executive council with the entire resources of the organization at its control.

Michael Davitt, December 1880[1]

Here we are, not alone in Castlebar but in every town in the West of Ireland, surrounded by those who have been evicted calling for assistance from the League without avail.

James Daly, August 1881[2]

Tension within the League leadership in Mayo and between it and the Land League central executive was rooted in a long-standing controversy over whether Irish grievances could best be redressed through a centralized political movement directed by professional revolutionaries (the United Irishman and Fenian tradition) or through a locally based agitation (the Whiteboy and Ribbonmen tradition). Unlike the earlier tactical controversies within Irish nationalism, the one that arose in Mayo in 1880 did not center around whether local or national grievances should be supreme. Rather, the issue was whether the Irish National Land League executive, which by the fall of 1880 was increasingly influenced by the more prosperous farmers of southern and eastern Ireland, could direct the agitation in Mayo more effectively than could local politicians

---

[1] Memorandum of Instructions to Organizers and Officers of the Branches of the Land League, 13 Dec. 1880. Reprinted in Sir Charles Russell, *The Parnell Commission, The Opening Speech for the Defence*, 3rd ed. (London, 1889), p. 231.

[2] *CT*, 20 Aug. 1881.

who could claim to be in closer accord with the county's small farmers. This question became particularly heated during 1880–1 as a result of a change in League policy away from the defensive strategy of thwarting the eviction of small farmers to a new offensive strategy that directed tenants to refuse to pay unjust rents, thus precipitating a duel between landlord and tenant for the farm. This policy, known as "rent at the point of the bayonet," favored large farmers who had the resources required for a prolonged skirmish with their landlords and who were able to pay their rents if necessary to preserve their farms. As a result, in Munster province, where there were large numbers of prosperous graziers, the number of evictions actually declined during 1881.[3] In contrast, the small farmers, clustered in western counties like Mayo, found that "rent at the point of the bayonet," coupled with the League's growing reluctance to defend them in court, left them increasingly vulnerable to eviction. In Mayo, the number of families evicted in 1881 was 130 percent higher than it had been in 1880 and 217 percent higher than in 1879.[4]

The most potent voices of Mayo's disenchantment with the Land League were those of James Daly, John O'Connor Power, MP, and the county's Fenian leadership, especially P. W. Nally and John O'Keane. All had been public advocates of the small farmers' rights to the land and on numerous occasions Daly and the Fenians had called for the redistribution of grazing farmers, despite the fact that Daly was himself a grazier, as was the father of Nally. These men were the small farmers' most articulate and steadfast supporters. Their public break with the League during 1880, when combined with the growing despair of Mayo's small farmers, undermined the Land League's authority in the county.[5]

THE DISAFFECTION OF JAMES DALY WITH THE LAND LEAGUE

Discord between local agrarian activists and the national Land League leadership was not confined to Mayo, but as a result of Daly's activities the antagonism between the two is best documented in the county. A querulous man who was distrusted and disliked by many of the Land League's leaders, Daly "typified," in Feingold's words, "the tendency

---

[3] Bew, *Land and the National Question in Ireland*, pp. 121–6, 188–9.
[4] See Table 4.1 above.
[5] For Power's break with the League, see: Jordan, "John O'Connor Power," pp. 59–65.

toward political parochialism and moderate politicians' growing distrust of the national administration . . . In his activities and writings . . . one finds all the elements that led to the deterioration of local confidence in the national movement among the constitutionalist supporters."[6] Throughout his career, Daly maintained that local leadership was the tenant farmers' only guarantee that their interests would not be compromised in the name of political expediency. Between 1880 and 1882 he fought against the centralization of the land movement, arguing that members of the League executive and their local agents had lost touch with the needs of Mayo's farmers. He once remarked that centralization of the land agitation put the direction of the movement in the hands of men who knew "as much about land as a crow does about Sunday."[7]

Daly was born sometime between 1838 and 1841 in Boghadoon, County Mayo, the son of a farmer and bailiff on the Elm Hall estate at Belcarra.[8] He was educated at the Errew monastery near Castlebar by the Franciscan Brothers and by the 1860s was tenant and bailiff of Harriet Gardiner on her estate near Breaghwy.[9] By 1880 he could boast before the Bessborough Commission: "I pay rent to four landlords. I am a newspaper proprietor by accident; farming is my forte."[10] In addition to the 120 acre grazing farm which Daly held from Harriet Gardiner, he held a 260 acre farm near Ballina from Sir Roger Palmer, a townpark in Kilkenny from the Earl of Erne, and his Castlebar home, offices and numerous outbuildings from the Earl of Lucan.[11] In Castlebar, Daly was a town councillor, a poor law guardian, the local agent for several Dublin-based firms, and most importantly, the editor and proprietor of

---

6 Feingold, *The Revolt of the Tenantry*, p. 142.

7 *CT*, 13 Aug. 1881.

8 The date of Daly's birth, like so much of his personal life, is obscure. Feingold reports it as 1838, presumably from family sources, but Daly told the census enumerator in 1901 that he was then 60 years old, which would have given him a birth date in 1840 or 1841. To muddle matters further, the police biography of Daly, supplied by Sergeant Thomas Clarke, lists Daly as being 64 in 1898, or born in 1833 or 1834. See: Feingold, *The Revolt of the Tenantry*, p. 95; PROI, Returns of 1901 Census, Householders' Returns, Mayo, parcel 65, p. 31; SPO, CBS, Biography of James Daly, Castlebar, 21 Apr. 1898, 16005/s. I wish to thank Mrs. Nolly Mongey of Castlebar for sharing with me her knowledge of her grandfather, James Daly.

9 Feingold, *The Revolt of the Tenantry*, p. 95.

10 *Bessborough Commission, Vol. II, Minutes of Evidence Pt. I*, p. 566.

11 *Ibid., Vol. III, Pt. II*, pp. 567, 570, and *Appendix C*, p. 1412; Feingold, *The Revolt of the Tenantry*, p. 96; *CT*, 11 Feb. 1882; PRONI, Rental on the Earl of Erne's Mayo Estate, 1874–79; PROI, Returns of 1901 Census, Householders' Returns, Mayo, parcel 65, p. 31.

The Connaught Telegraph. He was also a poor law guardian in Ballina, having first been elected there in 1874.[12]

The circumstances of Daly's entry into radical and national politics are obscure. Feingold relates a legend that Daly quarreled with Harriet Gardiner over the eviction of a tenant from her estate and either resigned or was dismissed from his agency as a result.[13] This may have launched his political career, although his election to the Castlebar Board of Guardians in 1869 appears to have been the result of a desire to represent the same division that his father had represented rather than the consequence of strong political commitment. Daly's first association with radical nationalism occurred in 1875, when he organized public meetings to raise funds to build a monument to the French soldiers who died near Castlebar during the rebellion of 1798.[14] In December of the same year Daly made his public debut as a land reformer at a speech in Louisburgh, calling for the formation of a tenants' association "to maintain our rights against the landlords."[15] At the Westport meeting in June 1879 Daly told the audience that it was "to advocate the cause of the poor struggling tenantry" that in 1876 he had purchased *The Telegraph or Connaught Ranger*, which had ceased publication in 1870.[16] He renamed it *The Connaught Telegraph* and quickly turned the newspaper into the herald of the land agitation, establishing himself, in his own words, as one of the major "sentinels on the watch towers of Mayo's politics."[17] As an educated and well-informed man who combined farming, business, journalism and politics, Daly became by the late 1870s the most influential man in Mayo.

Daly was a constitutional reformer. He had never been a Fenian and told the Bessborough Commission that he "would not be a Land Leaguer if it had anything behind it like Revolution," adding prophetically: "I would fight against it."[18] Regularly he cautioned against agrarian crime

---

[12] *CT*, 29 June 1878.

[13] Feingold, *The Revolt of the Tenantry*, p. 95.

[14] SPO, CBS, Biography of James Daly. It was at the unveiling of this monument in December 1877 that Daly, Power and Parnell first appeared together on a public platform, and was the occasion of Parnell's first visit to County Mayo.

[15] *Nation*, 18 Dec. 1875. Ref. from Feingold, *The Revolt of the Tenantry*, p. 96.

[16] *CT*, 14 June 1879.

[17] *Ibid.*, 1 Apr. 1882.

[18] *Bessborough Commission, Vol. III, Minutes of Evidence, Pt. II*, p. 571. The police biography of Daly describes him as an "ordinary member" of the IRB who was "never trusted," but this report is almost certainly in error regarding Daly's Fenian membership. SPO, CBS, Biography of James Daly.

and other illegal actions, which he claimed would "only have the effect of having coercive measures passed" and result in a "demoralized Ireland."[19] Yet, despite this moderation, Daly was an advocate of popular rather than parliamentary politics. During the 1870s he opposed the Home Rule movement, calling it a futile gesture that could only "appeal to sentiment which the average Englishman does not possess" and he periodically advised Irish MPs to withdraw from the House of Commons where they "would only expose [themselves] to fresh insults."[20] In 1880 he joined with Parnell and other constitutional nationalists to urge the people of Ireland to send resolute nationalists to parliament, but did so with little enthusiasm:

> The General Election of 1880 will be one of the utmost importance to these countries, although we have but very little faith in Parliamentary legislation, and while we know the Irish question must finally be settled outside the House of Commons, still we hold it is a duty incumbent on us to send the best men we can select to represent us there.[21]

Daly believed that no legislative tinkering with land laws could resolve the land question as long as landlords retained control over the land. A solution would only come about, he maintained, when an organized tenantry forced the government to abolish landlordism and establish peasant proprietorship throughout Ireland.

Although a grazier himself, Daly was a steadfast defender of Mayo's small farmers against the designs on their lands of avaricious grazing farmers. He shared with many subsequent Irish politicians an Arcadian vision of pre-Famine tillage farming and regularly called for grazing farms to be distributed into 10 to 50 acre tillage farms. In 1877 he wrote:

> If the vast grazing tracts of the country are broken up into small farms, the keenness of competition for land which at present prevails will be sensibly diminished. A good many graziers will go to the wall, but few will pity them. They have as a rule taken up the land over the heads of the deserving tenants, and have shown themselves completely indifferent to the conditions of their fellow farmers.[22]

Yet, despite these views, during the Land War Daly attempted to keep the farming class united against landlords, maintaining that it would be

---

[19] *CT*, 15 Jan. 1881.
[20] *Ibid.*, 15 July 1876.
[21] *Ibid.*, 13 Mar. 1880.
[22] *Ibid.*, 20 Jan. 1877; also see *Ibid.*, 3 Jan. 1880.

"injudicious to array the occupiers of grass farms against the claims of more deserving tenants."[23]

Daly's concern for unity against landlords within the land movement put him at odds with many radicals. Matt Harris, a Fenian and strident opponent of the grazing system, argued that grazing farmers should be kept out of the agitation, characterizing them as "a class of men who are more exacting and avaricious than the landlords themselves, and who, in the course of time, would become more cruel and tyrannical than the landlords are or ever have been."[24] Harris' remarks were part of a campaign to have large farmers excluded from the provisions of a land bill proposed by Isaac Butt. Daly's response was that by alienating the graziers, Harris' proposal would "exclude from the Tenant-right ranks a great many of the ablest men connected with the movement." Daly was seeking to avoid the political paralysis that he felt would be the conse-quence of class-based agitation and argued that "great public questions have to be fought out by practical means, and anything that could tend to weaken the unity of popular demand, by restricting the universality of its character, ought . . . to be carefully avoided."[25]

His interest in shoring up the unity of the land movement in Mayo was undermined during 1880 by his growing resentment at the policies of the Land League executive. At the Castlebar meeting of October 1878, Daly identified the purposes of a tenant league to be securing "tenant farmers . . . against capricious eviction and rack renting," paying legal expenses for tenant farmers threatened with eviction, and reimbursing evicted tenants for their financial losses.[26] By the summer of 1880 he became convinced that the Land League was not living up to these obligations and he launched a bitter assault against it. He charged that the League was aiding evicted tenants inadequately, that officers were profiting from League funds while promoting radical policies that could bring no immediate relief to Mayo farmers, and that the denunciation of John O'Connor Power by the League leadership displayed its contempt for the wishes of the people of Mayo.

Daly was concerned that those small farmers of Mayo who were threatened with eviction were not receiving the legal and material aid that the League had earlier promised them. Early in 1880 the League had

23 *Ibid.*, 26 Jan. 1878.
24 *Ibid.*, 20 Apr. 1878.
25 *Ibid.*, 6 Apr. 1878.
26 *Ibid.*, 26 Oct. 1878.

adopted a program of fighting ejectments in court, as proposed by its legal counsel John J. Louden. Basing his defense on a novel interpretation of a clause in the 1870 Land Act providing for compensation to tenants evicted without cause, Louden succeeded in winning substantial awards for tenants evicted for non-payment of exorbitant rent.[27] The success of this strategy enhanced the prestige of the League, but also resulted in its being flooded with requests for legal aid. At one meeting in Claremorris, 100 cases of ejectment were brought to the League for legal aid, but only one-fourth of them were selected as meriting League assistance. *The Freeman's Journal* reported that the tenants in attendance viewed the Land League as their "only real hope and shield."[28]

The surge in requests for legal aid were far from welcome to the Land League executive. Legal defenses were expensive. The Westport branch, for example, was charged £75 for just six cases. In the minds of the League leadership, the small farmers of the west were getting excessively litigious and were losing sight of the broad objectives of the movement. Despite these misgivings, the League executive understood that legal defenses were too popular with the small tenant farmers for it to refuse to pay them. The League continued to pay legal costs and support evicted tenants, but did so in a fashion that Daly felt to be begrudging and parsimonious.[29] He opened his attack on the League in a June 1880 editorial:

> Several struggling tenants have called on us during the week showing copies of their ejectments served upon them by their landlords invariably for two months' rent due May last . . . We read of Land meetings having been held after the process of eviction has taken place. Would it not be better to hold these meetings before the people are thrown adrift on the world? On the principle that prevention is better than cure, we would think the Land League would do their duty more consistently had they made preparations to defend these abject slaves to landlordism . . . We hold it would be the duty of the Dublin Branch to defend legally those poor serfs . . . The money expended in defending ejectments would be more judiciously and better spent than paying for first-class tickets and hotel expenses for attending meetings held on the ruins of devastated homesteads, after their occupants are driven homeless on the world . . . Such meetings do not mean much

---

27 Bew, *Land and the National Question in Ireland*, pp. 94–5.
28 *Ibid.*, pp. 113–14; *FJ*, 14 June 1880.
29 Bew, *Land and the National Question in Ireland*, pp. 110–14.

good for the benefit of Ireland or her people, particularly when held under the auspices of self-seeking, ambitious men for notoriety, which sounds more like crying after the funeral is gone.[30] Daly seized on the case of the Noonan family to prove the League's neglect of small farmers. During the summer of 1880, an elderly couple named Noonan abandoned their home at Cong Abbey, County Mayo, rather than await their pending eviction. Subsequently, William Burke, agent to Lord Ardilaun, took possession of the house and turned it over to a caretaker. When the Noonans attempted to retake possession of the house, they were arrested and sent for trial at the Winter Assizes in Castlebar. The Cong branch of the League retained Patrick Glynn, a Claremorris solicitor, to defend the Noonans with Fr. O'Malley of the Neale guaranteeing the £10 lawyer's fees. It is not clear when the League's central branch was first asked to pay the Noonans' legal costs, but in February 1881 Patrick J. Monahan, president of the Ballinrobe branch of the League, sent a series of letters to Dublin requesting legal expenses so that Fr. O'Malley would not have to make good his pledge to solicitor Glynn.[31] It appears that by October 1881 the League central branch had paid most of the expenses, but its delays had vexed some of the League's Mayo supporters.[32]

Daly's involvement with the case began when he paid £2 for the Noonans' lodging while they were in Castlebar for the Assizes. He immediately sought reimbursement from the League executive, only to be told that his request needed to be channeled through the Cong branch of the League. He eventually received his money, but not before using the case to widen his attack on the Land League executive:

Having not in their possession one farthing to pay for their lodgings in Castlebar during the Assizes, a benefactor [Daly] who made himself responsible for the amount of £2, made several ineffectual applications to that self-constituted body who doff themselves with being the Executive of the Irish National Land League – a body who receives close on £3000 weekly, and does not disperse as many shillings . . . We are sure that those benefactors of Ireland who subscribe their dollars intend them for a better purpose than that of lodging them in German banks while men of the Noonan type who brave the prison are allowed

---

[30] *CT*, 5 June 1880.
[31] NLI, Irish National Land League Papers, P. Higgins to the Irish National Land League, Dublin Office, 10 Feb. 1881, MS 8291 (9), Mayo.
[32] *Special Commission . . . Proceedings . . .*, i, p. 772.

to die in the Poorhouse. What is £5 to an evicted tenant, or to a family whose sole earner or protector is incarcerated? Yet £5, the maximum sum granted by this bogus ring in Sackville Street [the League offices in Dublin] cannot be wrung out of them to meet the destitution and want of those who are victimised between ruthless landlordism and faithless leadership in the ranks of the Land League . . . We reecho the voice of the manhood of Ireland when we say that 90 per cent of them are boiling over with rage and indignation at the apathy of the Land League Executive (self-appointed of course).[33]

Daly went on to accuse the League of failing to defend in the courts tenants threatened with eviction, suggesting to the League that it "purge [its] ranks of trimming and knavish politicians [in order to] keep on the good work initiated at Irishtown." As was his custom, Daly set himself up as the prototype of the poor tenant farmers' selfless defender who "dared the prison on behalf of Ireland's suffering poor, and stood on platforms before . . . those mercenary patriots . . . were known in Irish politics, and hopes, with God's assistance to do so again, when the memory of these mercenary patriots . . . will be as odious and detested in Ireland as that of Cromwell."[34]

No records exist that detail the extent of League contributions to evicted tenants, making it difficult to assess the accuracy of Daly's charges. One local League official, Patrick Higgins of the Cong branch, writing to *The Connaught Telegraph* "from personal knowledge of the facts," declared that Daly's attack on the League was "unsustainable," a view apparently shared by many branch members in Mayo.[35] After interviewing Daly in November 1881, a Canadian journalist remarked:

Mr. Daly as an original Land Leaguer, is certainly entitled to speak with some measure of authority as to that body, but I am bound to mention that he is the only Land Leaguer I have so far met who expresses any doubt of the bona fide character of the financial management of the affairs of the League. The people, whether educated or illiterate, seem to have every confidence in the integrity of the Executive of the League.[36]

However, existing Land League papers contain numerous letters from branch officials and priests revealing a widespread dissatisfaction with

---

[33] *CT*, 21 May 1881.
[34] *Ibid.*
[35] *Ibid.*, 28 May 1881.
[36] *Ibid.*, 27 Jan. 1882.

the League's aid program, which contributed to the weakening of League influence in Mayo during 1880–1.[37]

A more damaging charge made by Daly against the League was that its officials were profiting from League funds at a time when evicted tenants were left on the roadside with the odd contribution from Dublin. One deeply resented apparent form of profiteering came from the distribution of League relief in the form of vouchers redeemable for goods in local shops. During the summer of 1880, Daly charged that Joseph B. Walsh, a Castlebar publican and League activist, was using his position as chairman of the League's relief committee to increase the revenues in his pub. Daly, who regularly preached against drinking from Land League platforms and in the columns of *The Connaught Telegraph*, alleged that by distributing relief vouchers in his Old Harp pub, Walsh could induce the grateful recipients to spend some of the money in the pub.[38] Without mentioning Walsh by name, Daly editorialized:

Several complaints have reached us with regard to the distribution of Land League funds. We declined to accept the statements unless grounded on facts, but the persistent nature of the complaint so often repeated, we have reason to believe that they are not entirely vague or groundless . . . We . . . anticipated that bogus branches would start up which would collapse with the first stay of distribution. Well, not alone did bogus branches, but bogus leaders, crop up, who profess to be the "genuine article" since the American dollars glistened in the distance – fellows who were nonentities in politics until they found them a profitable game . . . We are of the opinion care should be taken to keep the movement out of the hands of hair-brained spirits, whose love of the movement appears to exist for the sake of gaining public house patronage . . . It was never anticipated by our exiled brothers and sisters in America, when subscribing their dollars . . . that it would be used as a sign board for attracting the attention of the public to assemble around establishments where they are tempted to patronize Jameson, Livingstone, or Guinness's XX, etc., for the sake of courting the favour of being handed a few miserable shillings, or a ticket for a few stone of meal.[39]

---

[37] For examples, see: NLI, Irish National Land League Papers, Mayo.

[38] Feingold, *The Revolt of the Tenantry*, p. 142; the selfish motives of the publican-Land Leaguer are portrayed in the figure of Paddy Heverin in George Birmingham's novel, *The Bad Times*, 3rd ed. (London, 1913). George Birmingham was the pseudonym of James Owen Hannay, a Protestant clergyman in County Mayo.

[39] *CT*, 7 Aug. 1880.

Daly's campaign against profiteering and political ambitions within the Land League leadership was eventually directed against John J. Louden, League legal counsel and County Mayo's highest-placed League official. Louden was an unpopular man in the Mayo, whose acceptance into the League's inner circle damaged the League's prestige in the county. His unpopularity was in part a consequence of his activities as a grazier. In 1877 he inherited the lease on 7000 acres in County Mayo from his father. Much of this land had been cleared of its tenants during and immediately after the Famine, creating a large grazing farm that was taken up by George Louden during the early 1850s. According to a statement released by the Louisburgh branch of the Land League, "in one week the Earl of Lucan levelled to the earth 269 human dwellings" in nine townlands near Louisburgh. "John J. Louden, Esq. B.L. now holds the above townlands in one vast grazing farm, and for miles around nothing is to be seen today but open fields trodden by bullocks and sheep on the very sites of many hundred once happy homes."[40] Louden's political vulnerability as a grazier whose land had been cleared of its tenants was heightened by accusations that he charged his subtenants "rack rents" in order to pay the excessive rents due by him to Lords Lucan and Sligo. Louden denied these charges, but was nonetheless regularly vilified by Daly as a "rack renting middleman" who was using the land movement for "feathering his nest."[41]

As discussed above, Louden's political position in Mayo was further undermined by his anti-clericalism, which made him "universally hated by the Priesthood of Mayo."[42] In September 1879, Power warned Fr. O'Malley of the Neale that Louden was planning to challenge clerical authority during the upcoming general election.[43] Apparently in keeping with this plan, Louden caused a near riot in Westport on 21 March 1880 by criticizing the clergy and, in the words of Eustace Lynch of Westport

[40] *CT*, 8 Jan. 1881.

[41] The charges against Louden were first publicly aired in a series of letters signed "Colonna" and posted from Louisburgh, which appeared in *The Connaught Telegraph* between 24 Jan. and 30 Apr. 1881. Detail on Louden's land holdings and the rent on them can be found in Lucan Rent Ledger, 1848–73. Biographical information on Louden appears in Feingold, *The Revolt of the Tenantry*, pp. 67, 98–100; *Special Commission . . . Proceedings . . .* , ii, pp. 639–57; Householders' Returns, Mayo, 1901 Census, parcel 150, p. 8. I wish to thank Erc MacBride of Westport for sharing with me his reminiscences of Louden.

[42] *CT*, 29 May 1880. For Louden's anti-clericalism and activities during the 1880 general election, see pp. 257–61 above.

[43] NLI, J. F. X. O'Brien papers, J. O'C. Power to Fr. J. O'Malley, 26 Sept. 1879.

in a letter to *The Freeman's Journal*, "outraged Catholic feeling by an eulogy from a window on such infamous miscreants as Garibaldi and Mazzini."[44] As a result, Louden was frequently booed and hooted when he appeared in public during the campaign, and found his plan to have himself rather than the Rev. Isaac Nelson placed in nomination for the seat vacated by Parnell blocked by the clergy. Immediately following the general election, Daly publicly broke with Louden, referring to him as a man "of no fixed principles or religion," part of a band of "lying ruffians [who] must be driven from the land movement."[45]

During the first year of the land agitation there were no public signs of rancor between Daly and Louden. They appeared side by side on numerous platforms, apparently in complete harmony of purpose. When Daly was arrested along with Davitt and Killen in November 1879, Louden acted as his counsel. In January, Daly praised Louden editorially for his defense of evicted tenants during the winter of 1879–80.[46] The breaking point in their relationship appears to have come when Daly determined that Louden had abandoned any commitment to the Mayo-based agitation in order to become one of the "salaried itinerant spouters of the Land League" executive. Louden had been a member of the League executive since its inception in 1879, when he arranged for the merger of the National Land League of Mayo, of which he was president, with the new Irish National Land League.[47] His partiality toward a centrally directed movement had become apparent in August 1879 when, at the founding convention of the Mayo League, he aligned with Davitt in what appears to have been an effort to wrest the initiative of the movement away from local men like Daly. Within months he was residing in Dublin, where he acted as League counsel and a member of its executive. In Mayo he was viewed by many local activists as a member of a coalition of League officials who were attempting to dictate to the local branches. For example, in March 1880, Louden was censured by the Islandeady branch of the League for directing that £25 of relief for Islandeady be distributed by the Westport rather than the Islandeady branch. The Islandeady branch president, the Rev. Thomas O'Malley, PP, charged that Louden was behind a campaign of defamation against the branch leadership and suggested that Islandeady regularly send

44 *FJ*, 8 May 1880.
45 *CT*, 29 May 1880.
46 *Ibid.*, 10 Jan. 1880.
47 *Special Commission . . . Proceedings . . .*, iii, p. 643.

delegates to the central branch meetings in order to monitor the activities of the executive and assure that local operations be represented accurately.[48]

By early 1880 Daly had become convinced that Louden, Davitt and other League leaders were determined to discredit him as part of their campaign to exert control over the agitation. In May he reported that they had attempted to take over control of *The Connaught Telegraph*, and when that plan failed, considered establishing a rival newspaper in Mayo.[49] The reasons for the League leadership's intense personal dislike for Daly are obscure. In the police biography of Daly, Sgt. Clarke reported that the "cause of the quarrel [between Daly and the League executive] was Daly held Land League funds which he refused to account for or give up." He also noted that "it was generally believed that [Daly] closed on a large portion" of the funds he collected in 1875–6 for the French Hill monument.[50] Daly refuted these charges of fiscal impropriety by turning on his accusers:

> Those noodles . . . gave it out that I closed on £300 of the Land League's money. Finding that this did not work . . . they reduced the figure to £6 or £7. That cock did not fight their battle . . . The parties used to circulate the reports are some low, dissipated fellows, who never lost a shilling by anything that would benefit Ireland – parties who appear very often in the law courts, not for any honourable cause, but for wife-beating . . . So far as the Land League is concerned, they owe me £5 to the 1 shilling I owe them.[51]

Mutual charges of profiteering from the Land League funds contributed to the estrangement between Daly and the League, as did the acrid debate between Daly and Davitt over rights to the title of "Father of the Land League." Yet, these squabbles alone would not have given rise to the acrimony between Daly and the League. That was rooted in Daly's outspoken independence, his willingness to criticize the League when he thought its policies were folly or counter to the interests of the tenant farmers of Mayo. He remarked to a land meeting in 1881:

> Some would insinuate [I] was opposed to the Land League. This was not so. [I] was a Land Leaguer as long as [I] considered Land Leagueism went right; but [I] was more than a Land Leaguer, and

[48] *CT*, 18 Mar. 1880.
[49] *Ibid.*, 29 May and 13 Nov. 1880.
[50] SPO, CBS papers, Biography of James Daly.
[51] *CT*, 13 Nov. 1880.

would be found so when required, when some of those who pretend
more, and when the test would be upon them, the shammers would be
known. [I] stood there a free lance, to give every man his merit; and as
a public journalist this was and could be [my] motto.[52]

Daly's outspoken independence alienated him from both radicals and
moderates within the League leadership. His major differences were with
the radicals, especially Davitt, Egan and Brennan, whom he accused of
fatuous militancy and self-serving actions. On many issues he was a
moderate, especially when he was convinced that moderation would
bring the greatest benefit to the small farmers. For tactical reasons, he
favored an alliance within the movement between large and small
farmers, welcomed priests into the agitation, and encouraged the farmers
of Mayo to exploit fully the provisions of the 1881 Land Act.[53] Yet
moderates within the land and national movements received little support
from the editor of *The Connaught Telegraph*, who rejected the conditions
which Parnell gradually placed on moderation between 1880 and 1882.
Parnell insisted upon: loyalty to himself as leader of the agrarian and
parliamentary struggles; subordination of the local branches of the land
and national movements to central control, which by 1882 meant control
by the Parnellite wing of the Irish parliamentary party; abandonment of
radical agrarianism except as a tool of a constitutional struggle in which
home rule, rather than peasant propriety, was the primary object. During
these years Daly generally refrained from criticizing Parnell directly,
preferring to direct his barbs against "the chief's" lieutenants. He
distrusted parliamentary action, of which Parnell was a master, and
steadfastly refused to endorse a campaign for home rule rather than
complete national independence. By standing on these principles and
breaking with both the Land League and Parnellite politicians, Daly
found himself in harmony with the county's Fenians, although he had
never been a supporter of radical nationalism.

MAYO FENIANS BREAK WITH THE LEAGUE

Fenian opposition to the Land League in Mayo developed simul-
taneously with that of Daly and John O'Connor Power. Yet, while Daly
and Power were concerned over what they perceived as the erratic
militancy of the League executive, the Fenians were angered that the

---

[52] *Ibid.*, 16 Apr. 1881.
[53] See pp. 306–11 below.

League was not militant enough. Furthermore, Daly and Power were more willing than the Fenians to compromise temporarily the ultimate goals of peasant proprietorship and national independence if they thought the tenant farmers would benefit from moderate measures of reform or relief. Yet despite these differences, the Fenians shared with Daly and Power an antagonism to self-serving within the League.

The early participation of Mayo's Fenians in the land movement had been qualified by their belief that the British parliament would never accede to the establishment of peasant propriety in Ireland. Consequently, they believed that the tenant farmers would soon abandon an agrarian campaign in favor of a nationalist one to create an Irish parliament willing to abolish landlordism.[54] The Fenian rank and file bothered little with this political analysis, preferring to see the land agitation as an extension of the local agrarian conflict with landlords that had been going on intermittently throughout the century. In many districts of the county the IRB and the Land League shared many members and, indeed, often the local Fenian organization functioned as the League's branch during 1880 and 1881. It appeared that the League had temporarily replaced the IRB, but in effect they were virtually the same body with two different names.[55] Davitt noted that this was especially the case when the parish priest was hostile to the agitation, leaving the way open for Fenian leadership of the League's local branch.[56]

The willingness of the Fenian leadership in Mayo to employ its network and leadership experience in the service of the agrarian campaign depended upon the land movement retaining its early commitment to radical land reform and to an aggressive, non-parliamentary campaign for peasant propriety.[57] Within a year of the Irishtown meeting Mayo's Fenian leadership was becoming restive with what is perceived to be the Land League's moderation and its close ties with the Irish parliamentary party.[58] When in June 1880 Power introduced in parliament for the Irish party a bill to compensate evicted tenants rather than one to stop evictions altogether, Fenian fears of a parliamentary compromise were realized.[59] Breaking with the wishes of the League leadership, the Fenians of Mayo held a demonstration at Irishtown on June 27 to

54 Bew, *Land and the National Question in Ireland*, p. 73.
55 *Special Commission . . . Proceedings . . .* , ii, pp. 478–99, 527.
56 Davitt, *The Fall of Feudalism*, p. 311.
57 Bew, *Land and the National Question in Ireland*, p. 40.
58 M. Harris to J. Dillon, 4 Apr. 1880, *Special Commission . . . Proceedings . . .* , i, p. 72.
59 Jordan, "John O'Connor Power," p. 60.

denounce parliamentarianism. The symbolism was not lost on Daly of an "anti-agitation meeting" being held "in the same locality that some eighteen months ago the great land agitation was inaugurated." Daly reminded his readers that the principal Fenians in attendance, P. W. Nally, John O'Keane and Daniel O'Connor, "were prominently connected with the agitation in its earliest stages."[60]

By the fall of 1880 Fenian displeasure with the Land League was increasingly evident in Mayo. On September 26 at Clonbur, County Galway, near where Lord Mountmorris had been assassinated the previous day, P. J. Gordon of Claremorris expressed the frustrations of many Mayo Fenians when he told a land meeting audience: "In this agitation I have taken a most active part . . . I am not here as a Land Leaguer but an Irish nationalist; and if the Land League does not go far enough for the tenant farmers, and if you are prepared to take a better stand – to take the field – I am prepared to take the sword with you."[61] A fortnight later, at a "nationalist" land meeting held in Ballyhaunis to which representatives of the Land League were not invited, Matt Harris reminded his listeners of his belief "that the liberty and independence of our country is to be gained by fighting, not by talking," and urged them to use "every means within their power, to keep first and foremost the great national question."[62] Apparently, this militant talk was accompanied by a demand to the Land League executive for money with which to purchase arms. When this demand was refused in September 1880, a segment of Mayo's Fenians threatened to break up Land League meetings in the Claremorris area.[63] This Fenian combativeness coincided with the arrival of troops and Orange laborers to harvest the crops of the beleaguered Captain Charles Boycott. William O'Brien later told the Special Commission that when he arrived in Mayo to report on the "Boycott Affair" he found the "young men" of the Lough Mask area "talking in a terribly wild way."[64]

Shared fears that the interests of the small farmers of the west of Ireland would be compromised by League officials further united Daly and the Fenians in opposition to the League. In December 1880, the Fenians launched a campaign for the redistribution of grazing farms into

---

[60] *CT*, 3 July 1880; Bew, *Land and the National Question in Ireland*, pp. 110–11, 132.
[61] *CT*, 2 Oct. 1880.
[62] *Ibid.*, 16 Oct. 1880.
[63] J. Redpath, *Talks About Ireland* (New York, 1881), p. 44.
[64] *Special Commission . . . Proceedings . . .* , iii, p. 202. For the Boycott Affair see pp. 285–93 below.

15 acre residential holdings. At a meeting in Kilbree, near Westport, J. B. Walsh claimed that this campaign was "a new phase of the land agitation" in keeping with the nationalists' commitment to land reform and that its purpose was to "replace the people who were evicted in '47 and '48 in their holdings."[65] During the ensuing weeks, similar meetings were held in Mayo with the support of Daly, until the introduction of Gladstone's long-awaited land bill and the arrest of Daly and several Fenians in the spring of 1881 under provisions of a new Coercion Bill slowed the movement for radical land redistribution.[66]

The degree to which Mayo's Fenians had rejected the Land League was demonstrated in the fall of 1881 when P. W. Nally joined with Daly and Power in encouraging Mayo's tenant farmers to take full advantage of the terms of the new land bill, despite the League's instructions to the contrary. In a letter dated 12 October 1881, Nally, after criticizing the League executive for squandering the "principal part" of the League funds, wrote:

> The tenants should avail themselves of the Land Act, not such fools as to trust themselves to the mercy of landlords or Land Leaguers. Resolutions should be passed expressing confidence in J. Daly and O'C. Power, and calling on Parnell to purge the Executive of such men as Louden and a lot of other greedy vultures.[67]

Parnell later told the Special Commission that "the branches of [the Land League in] Mayo, according to the information I received at the time ceased to exist during 1881 . . . In the beginning of that year, I always heard that the physical force part had driven the Land League out of Mayo."[68]

The crisis of the League in Mayo was in sharp contrast to its fortunes elsewhere in Ireland. The defeat in the House of Lords of the Compensation for Disturbances Bill in August 1880 demonstrated to many of Ireland's more prosperous tenant farmers the need to link up their fortunes with those of the League. The bill would have allowed tenants with holdings valued at £30 or under to claim compensation when

---

65 *CT*, 1 Jan. 1881.

66 *Ibid.*, 8, 15 Jan., 12, 19 Mar., 16, 23 Apr. 1881. For the land and coercion bills see pp. 303–11 below.

67 This letter, signed P. O'Dowd, was introduced at Nally's trial in the Crossmolina Conspiracy Case as being in Nally's handwriting. It was reintroduced as Nally's before the Special Commission in 1888. *Special Commission . . . Proceedings . . .* , ii, pp. 486–7.

68 Quoted in Bew, *Land and the National Question in Ireland*, p. 134.

evicted for non-payment of rent, if they could establish that their inability to pay was the result of the previous two years' bad harvests. Farmers holding tenancies valued at over £30 and those living in the relatively prosperous regions of Ireland had been excluded from the provisions of the bill at the very time when their worsening economic situation was pushing them towards an accommodation with the Land League. Parnellite MPs and members of the League executive moved quickly to take advantage of the farmers' discontent, stressing to the large farmers that only by joining the agitation could they expect to benefit from land reform. In late September, Parnell presented the League's case clearly to the large farmers in a speech at New Ross, County Wexford:

> When the Compensation for Disturbance Bill was brought forward in the last session to the House of Commons, the counties and the people whom I am now addressing, namely the four counties of Waterford, Wexford, Kildare and Carlow were excluded with the exception of a small portion of the county of Waterford. The whole county of Mayo was included in the bill . . . but you were left out. Now, why were you left out? It was because you had not raised your voices; had not organized yourselves and shown the determination and the power of the thousands of people who live in these counties. But I think that after today . . . there will be no fear that the people of these counties will be left out of the coming Land Bill.[69]

The success of the league in expanding its base beyond Connacht was also a result of the decline in evictions, which the League could point to as a result of the agitation. During the last quarter of 1880, the number of evictions declined nationwide by 72 percent, and in Mayo by 70 percent, when compared to the previous quarter.[70] It appeared that the Land League was winning the war against landlords, and its members and strength increased as a result. In a letter to Devoy, written in December 1880, Davitt expressed the League's confidence:

> It would take me a week to give you anything like an account of the immense growth and power of the Land League. It now virtually rules

---

[69] *FJ*, 27 Sept. 1880.
[70] *Return Compiled From Returns Made To the Inspector General, Royal Irish Constabulary, of Cases of Eviction Which Have Come To the Knowledge of the Constabulary in Each Quarter of the Year Ended the 31st Day of December 1880, Showing the Number of Families Evicted in Each County in Ireland During Each Quarter, the Number Readmitted as Tenants and the Number Readmitted as Caretakers*, PP 1881 (2), lxxvii, pp. 4–6.

the country . . . There are branches now in every county in Ireland, and the total number of members throughout the country will top 200,000! . . . On the whole the outlook is splendid. The people are beginning to recognize their own power . . . [71]

Despite the optimistic tone of this letter, Davitt and the League leadership were aware of the danger that the disaffected Fenians and local activists posed for the movement. He was further aware that the danger was most extreme in Mayo, where militancy against the League was on the rise, and where those dissatisfied with the League were in a position to lead many farmers out of the organization. In an October letter to Devoy, Davitt had singled out Nally as a driving force behind a plan to break up the Land League. In the letter quoted above he reported that all of the League's opponents had been silenced – "Nationalist *Leaders* excepted."[72] In an effort to counter the divisive influence of the Fenians in Mayo, a League representative, R. D. Walsh, pleaded with Mayo farmers at a meeting in Shrule in October 1880 not to allow the movement to be split into "two parties, the National Land League and the Fenians," but to little avail.[73] In effect, the compromise between the interests of the small and large farmers, which had been vital for the League to survive, had been broken up. The policy of "rent at the point of the bayonet" and the eagerness with which the League executive solicited grazier support in the south and east during the fall of 1880 left Mayo with little role to play in the Land League and left the county's small farmers with little option but to abandon protest in favor of emigration, which they did in unprecedented numbers during 1881.

---

[71] O'Brien and Ryan (eds.), *Devoy's Post Bag*, II, pp. 22-4. This letter is analyzed in Moody, *Davitt and Irish Revolution*, pp. 440–2.

[72] O'Brien and Ryan (eds.), *Devoy's Post Bag*, I, p. 555 and II, p. 24.

[73] SPO, Irish National Land League and Irish National League papers (hereafter INLL and INL), Reports of Speeches, 1879–86, Shrule, 31 Oct. 1880, carton 1, no. 315.

9. The collapse of the land agitation, 1880–1881

The final year of the land agitation was a period of great despair in Mayo. The harvest of 1880, while improved over the previous years in the core, had not improved in the periphery. The sharp rise in emigration during the year demonstrated the degree to which Mayo people had lost faith in the land system, but it also reflected their distrust in the ability of the Land League to reform that system. Reporting for *The Daily News* on a land meeting held at Tiernaur, County Mayo in October 1880, Bernard Becker found the people "rather tired than excited by the proceedings."[1] While there was no decline in the number of land meetings during 1880, there was a noticeable reduction in enthusiasm for the League, with Fenians rather than Land Leaguers often dominating the proceedings. At several meetings in October, including the one attended by Becker, *The Connaught Telegraph* noted that the League failed to send promised delegations to Mayo meetings, thus contributing to the decline in its support among Mayo farmers.[2]

A further indication of the League's loss of influence in Mayo was the dramatic increase in agrarian crime during the fall of 1880.[3] The murder in late September 1880 of Lord Mountmorris, an unpopular landlord and magistrate, near Clonbur, County Galway, a few miles from the Mayo border, highlighted the serious nature of the new wave of agrarian crime. Consistently, the League leadership counseled against agrarian outrage and claimed with considerable justice that it was responsible for the relatively low level of agrarian crime during the first year of the agitation.[4] However, during the last three months of 1880 the number of

---

[1] Bernard Becker, *Disturbed Ireland* (London, 1881), p. 36.
[2] *CT*, 9, 30 Oct. 1880.
[3] See: Figure 7.1 above.
[4] For example, see Louden's speech to a land meeting held near Westport on 31 Oct. 1880. *CT*, 6 Nov. 1880.

agrarian crimes in Mayo was 300 percent higher than the three-month average for the first year and a half of the Land War. Ominously, the percentage of offenses against persons and property rose, while the percentage of relatively harmless "threatening letters and notices" dropped from 63 percent of the total agrarian crimes recorded in 1879 to 39.7 percent in 1880.[5]

During the fall of 1880 an increasing number of Mayo people were ignoring the advice of the Land League to organize peacefully, while others were emigrating from the country. These signs of despair, when combined with the effect of the intense disputes within the League leadership and the restiveness of the county's Fenians, resulted in the League having little power in Mayo by the winter of 1880–1. Ironically, this disintegration of the League within Mayo was occurring at the time of the famous "Boycott affair," when it appeared to the outside world that the Land League in Mayo was at its most potent.

THE HARVEST OF 1880

Countywide, thanks to the distribution by relief organizations of healthy "champion" seed potatoes in some districts, the potato harvest of 1880 was 2.4 tons per acre, up from 1.4 tons the previous year, although well below the 5.1 tons per acre harvested in 1876, the last year before the outset of the economic crisis.[6] Yet, while the overall harvest in Mayo was improved, there remained large pockets of poverty, concentrated in the peripheral areas where champion seed had either not been distributed by the boards of guardians or had been distributed in small quantities. *The Connaught Telegraph* reported that with the exception of the "champions" the county's potato harvest was "many degrees worse" than it had been in 1879, leaving whole districts without potatoes.[7] One such district was Addergoole, northwest of Castlebar. The Castlebar Board of Guardians had refused to supply champion seeds, supplying inferior ones instead, prompting the parish priest to report that the "seed supplied was of the very worst description . . . The potatoes were a complete failure . . . the people are now in a far worse position than they were twelve

---

[5] *Return of All Agrarian Outrages Reported by the Royal Irish Constabulary Between the 1st January 1879 and the 31st January 1880* . . . , p. 79; *Return of . . . Agrarian Outrages in . . . 1880*, pp. 2–15.

[6] *Preliminary Report on the Returns of Agricultural Produce in Ireland in 1879*, p. 37; *The Agricultural Statistics of Ireland for the year 1880*, PP 1881 [C 2932], xciii, p. 71.

[7] *CT*, 18, 25 Sept. 1880.

months ago."[8] A Poor Law Inspector reported that in the Swinford Union he found "greater misery than I ever saw in my life. The poor people cannot be said to be living at all. They are simply dragging out a miserable existence under the most painful circumstances. I found they had almost eaten the champions already." Similar scenes were reported from the Claremorris Union.[9]

The distress, compounded in many districts by typhus, "famine fever," and cholera among pigs and chickens, left large sections of Mayo destitute.[10] The number of families on relief during the summer and fall of 1880 was up dramatically over the previous year. In the Belmullet Union 2398 persons were on outdoor relief in July 1880, up from 74 in July 1879. The Bishop of Anchonry reported that 82 percent of the families in his east Mayo parishes were on relief.[11] For many people the only option was to flee the country. During 1880, 5816 emigrated from County Mayo, up 26 percent from 1879 and the highest number of emigrants to leave in one year since 1852.[12] This continuing economic distress only accentuated the failure of the Land League to fulfill the expectations it had raised among the small farmers during 1879. Yet, for a few weeks in October in 1880, the attention of the press and public in Ireland, Britain and America was focused not on the crisis facing the county's small farmers, but on the plight of Captain Charles Boycott.

THE BOYCOTT AFFAIR

The practice of social and economic ostracism for violators of rural codes of conduct did not originate during the Land War, although prior to the fall of 1880 landlords and their agents, presumably immune to such community pressure, were generally exempted from the tactic. Davitt claimed that the "programme adopted at the convention of the Mayo Land League, in August 1879 . . . clearly defined this policy of social ostracism against grabbers and others who should help landlords," and in December 1879 he advised the members of the Land League branches to shun the land grabber as a "traitor to the interests of his fellow tenant

---

[8] *Ibid.*, 9 Oct. 1880.

[9] *Ibid.*

[10] J. A. Fox, "Reports on the Condition of the Peasantry of the County of Mayo During the Famine Crisis of 1880," in *The Irish Crisis of 1879–80*, pp. 105–22.

[11] SPO, CSORP, 1880, Report of H. A. Robinson, Inspector, Belmullet Union, 12 July 1880 and letter from Dr. F. J. MacCormack, Bishop of Anchonry, 15617.

[12] See Figure 4.2 above.

farmers and an enemy to the welfare of his country."[13] In this spirit, during 1879–80 numerous League speakers advocated a policy of social ostracism against land grabbers. In September 1880, Parnell, in a famous speech at Ennis, County Clare, lent his enormous prestige to the doctrine by telling the crowd:

> When a man takes a farm from which another has been evicted, you must show him on the roadside when you meet him, you must show him in the streets of the town, you must show him at the shop-counter, you must show him in the fair and at the marketplace, and even in the house of worship, by leaving him severely alone, by putting him into a sort of moral Coventry, by isolating him from the rest of his kind as if he were a leper of old, you must show him your detestation of the crime he has committed, and you may depend upon it if the population of a county in Ireland carry out this doctrine, that there will be no man so full of avarice, so lost to shame, as to dare the public opinion of all right-thinking men within the county and to transgress your unwritten code of laws.[14]

Less than a week after Parnell's speech the policy of "moral Coventry" was put into practice in County Mayo and given a new name, "boycotting," after its victim, Captain Charles Boycott. However, there is no evidence linking Parnell's speech or the Land League executive with the action against Boycott, which began as and remained a locally organized operation.[15]

Boycott, an arrogant, aloof man, had become agent and principal tenant on the Earl of Erne's Lough Mask estate near Ballinrobe in 1873, after eighteen years farming on Achill Island, County Mayo. In an evaluation shared by most of the tenant farmers and laborers of the

---

[13] Davitt, *The Fall of Feudalism*, p. 270; Moody, *Davitt and Irish Revolution*, p. 345. Davitt's assertion regarding the advocacy of social ostracism in the program of the Mayo League apparently rests on the following statement: "Pending a final and satisfactory settlement of the land question, the duty of this body will be to expose the injustice, wrong, or injury which may be inflicted upon any farmer in Mayo . . . by giving all such . . . acts the widest possible publicity, and meeting their perpetration with all the opposition which the laws for the preservation of the peace will permit of. In furtherance of which the following plan will be adopted: . . . The publication of the names of all persons who shall rent or occupy land or farms, from which others have been dispossessed . . . or shall offer a higher rent for land or farms than that paid by the previous occupier." *CT*, 23 Aug. 1879.

[14] Quoted in Lyons, *Charles Stewart Parnell*, p. 134.

[15] A popular account of the Boycott affair appears in: J. Marlow, *Captain Boycott and the Irish* (London, 1973). Also see: Davitt, *The Fall of Feudalism*, pp. 266–79 and Palmer, *The Irish Land League Crisis*, pp. 195–217.

Lough Mask region, Connor Maguire, MD of Claremorris, described Boycott, whom he knew "personally and met . . . frequently," as a "surly, cranky man ready to snap at anybody, friend or foe."[16] During the brief period of Boycott's notoriety, numerous stories surfaced among the tenantry telling of Boycott's brusque, often tyrannical treatment of his laborers and tenants, both on Achill Island and at Lough Mask. The stories told of petty regulations, rigorously enforced with fines for everything from allowing a hen to stray onto his property to tardiness at work or the accidental breakage of farm implements.[17]

Boycott's troubles with his tenants began in August 1879 when he, like many other Mayo landlords and agents, found attached to his gate a notice demanding a rent abatement of 20–25 percent and illustrated with a coffin. This threat, which came a few days after the Earl of Erne had authorized Boycott to give a 10 percent abatement, appears to have been the result of a widely held belief that it was on his agent's advice that Lord Erne authorized a 10 rather than a 20 percent rent reduction.[18] As was the case with most threatening notices and letters, that which Boycott received in August 1879 came to nothing, but a year later, in August 1880, he found himself again in trouble, this time in a wage dispute with his farm laborers. On 17 August, the day Boycott set to commence cutting his corn, his farm laborers struck for higher wages and, according to Boycott, for the right to stay in his employ until 1 November, rather than be laid off at the conclusion of the corn harvest. After a day during which Boycott, his wife and two young nieces cut and bound the corn, the Captain met his laborers' demands, raising wages from a rate of 7s. to 11s. per week to a rate of 9s. to 15s.[19]

In late September, Boycott was faced with an unwillingness on the part of all but two of the sixty tenants on the Lough Mask estate to pay the rents then due unless the previously demanded 25 percent abatement was granted. The agent responded with ejectment proceedings against eleven of the tenants, but on 22 September only three of the ejectment

[16] University College Dublin, Department of Irish Folklore, Transcript of a small notebook written by Connor Maguire, MD of the Claremorris District of County Mayo, MS 1304, pp. 135–6.

[17] *FJ*, 11 Nov. 1880; Marlow, *Captain Boycott and the Irish*, p. 101. Many of these stories were still being circulated in the Lough Mask area in 1946, at the time of the filming of "Captain Boycott." See: Department of Irish Folklore, Traditions of Captain Boycott collected by Mrs. Liam Redmond, 1946, MS 1131, pp. 290–324.

[18] *CT*, 1 Aug. 1879; *FJ*, 11 Nov. 1880; *Bessborough Commission, Vol. II, Minutes of Evidence, Pt. I*, pp. 592–3.

[19] *CT*, 21 Aug. 1880; *Bessborough Commission, Vol. II, Minutes of Evidence, Pt. I*, p. 595.

processes could be served before the process server and his constabulary escort were driven off by a rock and mud-throwing crowd of women and children. *The Connaught Telegraph*'s correspondent described colorfully what followed the driving off of the process server:

During the night of Wednesday [22 September], and during the morning of Thursday the "word" was sent round, and at an early hour on the latter day thousands of human beings, including every age and sex, might be seen swarming on the hill sides that surrounded the picturesque valley of Loughmask. On one of these eminences was planted a huge pole bearing aloft a green flat that fluttered gaily in the morning breeze, and that gave courage and hope to the high souled and manly youths that surrounded it. While awaiting the expected arrival of the police a curious scene was enacted. As if by one sudden impulse every man in that vast throng rushed down towards Loughmask House – the residence of the very unpopular agent – and at once hunted away every labourer, follower, and servant in and around the place, so that the Captain will find it rather difficult to find help to work his huge farm . . . Ultimately it was resolved to starve the agent out of the place.[20]

For the next two months until his departure from Mayo, Captain Boycott was "boycotted," the term coined by the Rev. John O'Malley, PP of the neighboring parish of The Neale during a conversation with the American journalist James Redpath.[21] Boycott was unable to hire farm laborers, herds or servants, mail and telegraph services were cut off to Lough Mask House, and Boycott and his family were unable to obtain goods and services in southern Mayo. Only as a result of a subterfuge carried out by a sympathetic doctor did the Boycotts receive bread, while they had to import servants from distant counties.[22] Boycott told the Bessborough Commission on 22 October that he was "subjected to terrible injuries by every possible mode of malice that ingenuity could devise" and *The Times*, editorializing on a letter from Boycott that it published on 18 October, claimed that "a more frightful picture of triumphant anarchy has never been presented in any community pretending to be civilized and subjected to law."[23]

The final phase of the Boycott affair came on 10 November when fifty

[20] *CT*, 25 Sept. 1880.
[21] Redpath, *Talks About Ireland*, p. 81.
[22] Typescript of a small notebook written by Connor Maguire, p. 132; *FJ*, 11 Nov. 1880.
[23] *Bessborough Commission, Vol. II, Minutes of Evidence, Pt. I*, p. 592; *The Times*, 18 Oct. 1880.

laborers recruited in counties Cavan and Monaghan by ambitious Orange politicians "invaded" Lough Mask to harvest the Captain's root crops and thresh his wheat. The laborers were protected by 1000 troops and several hundred police, costing the government an estimated £3500 to harvest £350 worth of crops during a driving rain. As *The Freeman's Journal* reporter put it: "it is only Mayo that can produce rain in its perfection as an instrument of torture." Or, in Davitt's words: "'The Lough Mask Expedition' . . . was left to the tender mercies of a Connaught rainy season, and never in all the climatic records of that province did the Celtic Pluvius indulge more copiously in a pitiless downpour than during 'the famous diggin' of Boycott's prayties.'"[24] In the popular phrase, "the weather had joined the Land League," leaving its human members to ridicule the harvesters but, under strict orders from local leaders, not to molest or attack them. The episode concluded on 26 November when the Boycott family and the northern laborers left County Mayo for good.

Boycott and the conservative press were convinced that the Captain's troubles were part of a Land League plot. Boycott told the Bessborough Commission that he had been "picked out as a victim to show the power of the Land League," while *The Times* informed its readers that Boycott was being persecuted for committing "some offence against the Land League's code."[25] In actuality, the initial impulse to lay siege to the inhabitants of Lough Mask House came from the tenants themselves. The local League branch quickly harnessed this impulse into an effective, enforceable, and non-violent plan of action. Yet the League's national executive remained throughout the affray indifferent, if not hostile, to the actions of the tenant farmers.

The man generally credited with leading the tenant farmers during the boycott was Fr. John O'Malley, PP of The Neale. Described by Davitt as a man who "enjoyed great popularity for his kindly nature, his devotion to the poor, and jovial disposition," Fr. O'Malley was a close political ally and friend of John O'Connor Power and James Daly and had been one of the first Mayo priests to rally to the land agitation.[26] According to James Redpath, Fr. O'Malley had been told of a speech that Redpath had given in Claremorris on 14 September in which the American journalist

---

[24] *Bessborough Commission, Vol. II, Minutes of Evidence, Pt. I*, p. 592; Davitt, *The Fall of Feudalism*, p. 277; *FJ*, 13, 15 Nov. 1880.

[25] *Bessborough Commission, Vol. II, Minutes of Evidence, Pt. I*, p. 593; *The Times*, 18 Oct. 1880.

[26] Davitt, *The Fall of Feudalism*, p. 275.

had called for ostracism of land grabbers and landlords as a way of satisfying the League's American supporters that their money was being well-spent. Apparently, O'Malley took this advice to heart and urged the tenant farmers to try the tactic on Captain Boycott.[27] His advice seems to have been first offered the day after the tenant farmers had occupied the grounds of Lough Mask House. O'Malley, who was the president of The Neale branch of the Land League, joined with Patrick Monaghan, president of the Ballinrobe branch, in journeying to Lough Mask where they assembled the crowd into a "vast" process that marched the three miles to The Neale. During the march "the sustained cheering and the music of the band attracted the villagers for miles around so that on arriving at The Neale quite a monster meeting was assembled." Fr. O'Malley addressed the crowd "at some length" from the steps of the sacristy door of the parish church offering the tenant farmers the congratulations and support of the local League and presumably suggesting social ostracism as the way to deal with Captain Boycott.[28]

Fr. O'Malley, local League leaders, and the Fenian leadership were all anxious that the campaign against Boycott remain non-violent. The reporter for *The Freeman's Journal* wrote that on the day the Orange laborers arrived in Mayo, "representatives of the Nationalists from the different parts of the country have come by the early trains, and I am able to state that the result of their deliberations has been the adoption of a placard which has been published counselling the people to remain at their homes and 'let the British Government display its despotism unheededly.'"[29] Constrained by both the Fenian and local League leadership, the tenant farmers and their supporters scoffed at the northern harvesters but made no attempt to attack or molest them, while rigorously maintaining the boycott of anyone who had any dealings with the residents of Lough Mask House.

From 22 September when the Boycott affair began to 15 November, five days after the arrival in Mayo of the northern laborers, the Land League's central executive avoided any public statements on the events taking place in Mayo and offered neither aid nor advice to the

---

27 *Ibid.*, pp. 267–8; Redpath, *Talks About Ireland*, p. 81.
28 No verbatim account of Fr. O'Malley's remarks exists. *CT*, 25 Sept. 1880.
29 12 Nov. 1880. Bew asserts that "the organisation of large-scale passive resistance against the Orange labourers and their military guard . . . must be seen . . . as a pre-emptive intervention led by Father O'Malley . . . and James Daly against a Fenian outbreak." However, he does not document this assertion, which does not seem sustained by the available evidence. *Land and the National Question in Ireland*, p. 133.

participants. The executive was compelled to become involved when a telegram arrived from Fr. O'Malley on 15 November requesting its opinion on a proposed excursion by the Lough Mask tenants to Crom Castle, the home of Lord Erne at Newtownbutler, County Fermanagh. The tenants hoped to present their case against Captain Boycott directly to their landlord, with whom Fr. O'Malley contended the tenants had no grievance. They hoped that Lord Erne would dismiss his agent once he understood "Captain Boycott's tyranny is intolerable," thus clearing the way for the tenants to pay their rents.[30] Moreover, according to a placard posted throughout Ballinrobe, the trip was designed to "appeal to our sturdy brother farmers of Ulster, be they Orange or Green, Protestant or Catholic, to say whether they will allow our struggle, which is their struggle, to be defeated."[31] In his telegram to the League executive Fr. O'Malley explained that the campaign against Captain Boycott "is not a question of rents. It is a question whether Captain Boycott or the people shall win. If we succeed in displacing him, victory is complete. If Lord Erne remain obdurate we will have the credit of having unarmed done in the North of Ireland what Orangemen have done in Mayo under the protection of the army."[32] *The Freeman's Journal* correspondent in Ballinrobe wrote:

> The proceedings of the Northern labourers at Lough Mask have sunk into insignificance and contempt compared with the preparations for the approaching visit of Lord Erne's Mayo tenantry to Fermanagh . . . All interest has suddenly turned from Lough Mask to Lough Erne. The project of an appeal to Lord Erne, and . . . for appeal to public opinion in the North, has excited the most extraordinary enthusiasm.[33]

This enthusiasm was not shared by members of the League executive when they met in Dublin on 16 November to consider Fr. O'Malley's telegram. With Davitt in America, probably an unfortunate circumstance for the Lough Mask tenants, League radical Thomas Brennan took the initiative in discussing the proposed trip. In a remark that set the tone for the discussion, Brennan said: "I don't think it is their [the Lough Mask tenants'] business to go to pay any rent. It is the business of the landlords to come and ask for their rents."[34] The idea of tenants paying rents without a prolonged struggle violated the principle of the "rent at the

[30] *FJ*, 17 Nov. 1880.
[31] *Ibid.*, 16 Nov. 1880.
[32] *Ibid.*, 17 Nov. 1880.
[33] *Ibid.*, 16 Nov. 1880.
[34] *FJ*, 17 Nov. 1880.

point of a bayonet" strategy that the League had recently adopted.[35] In keeping with this policy, the League could not sanction an excursion by Lord Erne's tenants that might result in their handing over the rent without further struggle. Despite Fr. O'Malley's assertion that Lord Erne's rents, which were in general quite moderate, were not the issue, the members of the executive focused exclusively on the possibility that while at Crom Castle the tenant farmers might pay their rents.[36]

In effect, the dispute between Lord Erne's tenants and the League executive was a product of the widening split between the small western farmers who had begun the land movement and the Land League, which was moving to accommodate the interests of the larger eastern farmers. "Rent at the point of the bayonet," which favored those tenants who could afford a lengthy struggle over rents, implied a turning away on the part of the League from a policy of defending small farmers from eviction and high rents. The new League strategy was an offensive one of direct, legal confrontation between landlords and tenants that was designed to permanently reduce rents.[37] The Boycott affair and the proposed journey of the Lough Mask tenants to Crom castle were thus seen by the League executive as a retrogressive step in the prosecution of the Land War. As T. P. O'Connor put it during the executive's discussion of Fr. O'Malley's telegram: "They [the members of the League executive] could have nothing to do with a compromise of this kind."[38]

The League executive had several other reasons for hostility towards the proposed excursion to County Fermanagh. Since August, the League, anxious to establish itself in the north of Ireland, had sponsored land meetings in Ulster. The effort was given a major boost on 9 November when Parnell, John Dillon and James J. O'Kelly inaugurated what Parnell called "the land campaign in the north of Ireland" during a rally at Belleck, Co. Fermanagh.[39] Belleck was only about 30 miles from Crom Castle. Although Fr. O'Malley was convinced that the appearance in Fermanagh of fifty orderly, unarmed Mayo farmers would strengthen the bond between the Protestant and and Catholic tenants of Ireland, the League was fearful that an "invasion" of Fermanagh would jeopardize its northern initiative. Moreover, on 2 November the government announced that it would prosecute Parnell and thirteen other League

[35] See pp. 265, 282 above.
[36] For Lord Erne's rents, see p. 153 above.
[37] Bew, *Land and the National Question in Ireland*, pp. 121–4.
[38] *FJ*, 17 Nov. 1880.
[39] *Ibid.*, 10 Nov. 1880.

leaders for conspiracy to prevent the payment of rents and for creating tension between tenants and landlords.[40] When members of the executive met on 16 November to consider Fr. O'Malley's request for advice and assistance, the impending state prosecutions were foremost in their minds. The non-violent character of the events at Lough Mask House was making the government look foolish for sending thousands of troops to Mayo and for threatening to prosecute the movement's leaders for promoting violence. The prospect, no matter how remote, of a League-sanctioned trip to Fermanagh erupting into a bloody confrontation between Protestant and Catholic farmers, and thus lending credence to the government's accusations, prejudiced the executive against the trip. Brennan wired the League's disapproval to Fr. O'Malley who, with great reluctance, abandoned the project.[41]

In his telegram to protest the executive's action, Fr. O'Malley warned that "abandonment of the project, now that we are pledged, would involve imputations which there would be no answering."[42] Writing after the League executive's telegram of disapproval had been received in Ballinrobe, *The Freeman's Journal* correspondent reported that "an extraordinary change in the aspect of affairs here was caused by the action of the Land League . . . The announcement [of its disapproval] was a complete surprise."[43] Disappointment with the executive's action furthered the disillusionment with the League in Mayo, prompting William O'Brien to report to the Special Commission in 1888: "I don't believe the Land League ever had great power here [in Mayo] after the Lough Mask expedition."[44]

THE LADIES' LAND LEAGUE IN MAYO

The decision by the government to prosecute fourteen leaders of the Land League prompted Davitt, in January 1881, to suggest to the League executive that a women's organization, modeled after the Ladies' Land League of America, be established in Ireland that could continue the agitation should arrests cripple the existing Land League. The American Ladies' Land League had been founded in New York on 15 October 1880 by Parnell's younger sister Fanny as a fund-raising organization for the

---

[40] Lyon, *Charles Stewart Parnell*, p. 139.
[41] *FJ*, 17 Nov. 1880.
[42] *Ibid.*, 17 Nov. 1880.
[43] *Ibid.*, 17 Nov. 1880.
[44] *Special Commission . . . Proceedings . . .*, iii, p. 202.

Land League. By November, Ladies' Land League branches had been formed in County Limerick and an unauthorized national Ladies' Land League had been attempted in Dublin.[45] Davitt's suggestion that a women's organization be formed in Ireland, this one to be headed by another of Parnell's younger sisters, Anna, "was laughed at by all" the members of the League executive except Patrick Egan, and was "vehemently opposed by . . . Parnell, Dillon and Brennan who feared we would invite public ridicule in appearing to put women forward in places of danger." Despite this initial opposition, Davitt persevered, obtaining from the members of the League executive "a passive assent to what they dreaded would be a most dangerous experiment."[46] A provisional committee, which included two women from Mayo, was duly formed and on 31 July 1881 the Ladies' National Land League came into existence.[47] This organization, later dubbed by Katherine O'Shea as a "wild army of mercenaries" and by William O'Brien as a band of "devoted women," who combined the "modesty of a Sister of Charity and the heroism of a Boadicea," played an eventful part in League affairs, beginning in County Mayo.[48]

Before the Land War women had not challenged the male monopoly on participation in the land and nationalist movements. Previous organizations had been dominated to a large degree by parliamentarians, priests, or militarists, none of whom countenanced women in their organizations. The secret societies that flourished in rural Ireland during the eighteenth and nineteenth centuries admitted no women, nor did the Irish Republican Brotherhood, the largest and most broadly based nationalist organization prior to the Land League. Recalling the Fenians of Ballintubber, Co. Mayo, an elderly woman told an Irish Folklore Commission collector in 1938 that "the Fenians did not take their mothers or sisters into their confidence. They did not tell them when, or where, they drilled. 'Women were gabbey' was the opinion held by

---

[45] Moody, *Davitt and Irish Revolution*, p. 433.
[46] Davitt, *The Fall of Feudalism*, p. 299.
[47] *FJ*, 27, 31 Jan. 1881; Moody, *Davitt and Irish Revolution*, p. 457; T. W. Moody, "Anna Parnell and the Land League," *Hermathena*, 117 (1974), pp. 8–15; R. F. Foster, *Charles Stewart Parnell: The Man and His Family* (Hassocks, Sussex, 1976), pp. 264–6.
[48] K. O'Shea, *Charles Stewart Parnell: His Love Story and Political Life*, 2 vols. (London, 1914), I, p. 261; O'Brien, *Recollections*, p. 377. Boadicea (Boudicca) was a first century AD Celtic queen of the Iceni tribe of Norfolk. In 61 Boadicea, described by the Roman historian Dio Cassius as "huge of frame, terrifying of aspect, and with a harsh voice," led a rebellion against the Romans that was defeated only after the rebels had sacked and burned much of East Anglia and London.

Fenians. If their sisters, through curiosity, followed them or tried to find out anything concerning their movements, the younger men drove the girls home, threatening the fate of an informer on them."[49]

As an open, constitutional mass movement, the Land War provided opportunities for women to participate. Its open air meetings were open to all, with women often attending in large numbers. James Daly, commenting on the presence of a "large sprinkling of the fairer sex" at a meeting in Mayo Abbey, noted approvingly that "they appeared to be as enthusiastic as ever, and listened to the different speeches with rapt attention."[50] However, women undertook more important and active roles in the agitation than merely "gracing" land meetings for the pleasure of men like Daly. For example, they organized the defense of their homes against process servers armed with eviction notices. The American reporter James Redpath provided a colorful account of what was for the women of Mayo a serious and well-organized business:

> In some parts of the West of Ireland the peasantry have a secret code of signals. By waving a flat (you may call it a petticoat if you like) of a certain color, the neighbors come to a cabin to assist the signaling party. . . . If I remember rightly, the red flag means that the process-server has come. These signals caused all the women and girls in the neighborhood to assemble. . . . The women won't allow the men to resist the process-server because they are sent to jail so long for doing so, and, besides, these women think they can take care of the process-server themselves.[51]

Employing these tactics, the women of Mayo were often successful in thwarting process-servers. It was the women of Lough Mask who prevented the process-serving on Lord Erne's estate, thus inaugurating the "Boycott Affair," while during the same week women on George Moore's estate prevented all but four of twenty processes from being served.[52] Not infrequently, the women and girls tormented the process-servers and their police escorts with abusive language and drove them from the area with scalding water, rocks and sticks. In one case at Newton Clogher, *The Connaught Telegraph* reported that a process-server "had a narrow escape" after being chased by "about one hundred" women armed with "tongs, sticks, stones, etc." In another the land agent

[49] Department of Irish Folklore, Fenians, Ballintubber: taken down from a woman born in 1861, MS 485, pp. 208–9.
[50] *CT*, 3 Jan. 1880.
[51] *Talks About Ireland*, pp. 70–80.
[52] *CT*, 25 Sept. 1880.

of Sir Arthur Guinness was "doused with scalding water" by a young woman whose parents had recently been served with an eviction notice.[53] This was dangerous work as the women were not immune from arrest or assault by the police.[54] Nonetheless, they defended their homes, often mere hovels, out of a deeply felt belief that they had a legitimate right to their homes regardless of their ability to pay rent. By thwarting the work of the process-servers and evicting landlords they challenged the rights of landlordism and the legal system that supported it, giving additional force to the legitimacy of the tenant farmers' claim to the land.

Occasionally the women of Mayo adopted tactics first developed in the county during the 1830s and enforced a type of "moral economy" by preventing the export of food from the county during the economic crisis that coincided with the Land War. In one incident in Westport, Redpath came across a crowd of poor women who had stormed the cart of a potato broker and cut open his bags of potatoes. When he inquired whether the women had proceeded to steal the potatoes, Redpath was told: "We're not got down so far as that yet; we don't want to stale [sic]; all the wimmen [sic] wanted was to stop the potato from going out of the county." According to Redpath's informant, the women were motivated by a desire to prevent a profiteer from shipping the potatoes out of Mayo where they were needed, and out of concern that if "the Dublin folks hear we're sending potatoes out of the county, they'll stop sending us relafe [sic]."[55] By preventing the shipment of the potatoes, the women attempted to interrupt the working of the free market economy of post-Famine Mayo. They were willing to exploit fully that economy for the sale of eggs and other farm products that helped pay the rent, but when the free market was applied to the potato, their primary food source, it violated their moral assumptions and threatened the precarious subsistence of their families.[56]

Redpath described the crowd as consisting of "mostly barefooted" women, "all poorly clad with blue lips and hungry looks."[57] These women were from small farm families, eking out a marginal existence with near-total reliance on the potato for food. To a large extent it was this class of women who harassed process-servers, disrupted evictions

[53] *CT*, 21, 29 June 1879.
[54] *Ibid.*, 8 Jan. 1881.
[55] *Ibid.*, 15 May 1880.
[56] E. P. Thompson, "The Moral Economy of the English Crowd in the Eighteenth Century," *Past and Present*, 50 (1971), pp. 76–136.
[57] *CT*, 15 May 1880.

and defended the moral economy of the community. However, such riotous activities were not seen as suitable to the women of better-off farm and merchant families, women whose economic status in the community carried with it pretensions of gentility. It was these women who joined the Ladies' Land League of Mayo, making it a league not of women, but of ladies, and of those who aspired to be.[58]

Women's status in rural Ireland had been reduced by the commercialization of farming in post-Famine Ireland. This was especially the case for women from large farm families who, with no means of economic independence, were subjected to the restrictive marriage and inheritance policies that developed among the rural bourgeoisie in order to protect and advance the family's land and wealth.[59] The one dowered daughter was often married to an older man who had just come into his farm and who, as the sole wage earner in the family, dominated his economically powerless wife. The unmarried daughters found few opportunities for employment in rural Ireland, having almost no options but to remain on the farm at the mercy of their brothers or to flee Ireland, which many did. As Joseph Lee concludes: "Economic circumstances . . . conspired to make Ireland an increasingly male dominated society after the Famine."[60] With that domination came an ethos, found most often in large farm families, which idealized women as fixtures of home and family. Again to quote Lee, whose pioneering essays have broken through the longstanding taboos against serious study of the role of women in Irish society: "Just at the moment when women were losing a good deal of such independence as they enjoyed, their role came to be idealized."[61] This idealization of women was far advanced by the time of the Land War and limited the role that middle-class women could play in the agitation.

The Ladies' Land League, which gave women a formal role in the movement for the first time, was sharply criticized for bringing women out of the home and into the world of politics. Possibly the classic statement of opposition to women in the land agitation came in a pastoral

---

[58] Katharine Tynan, an early Ladies' Land League volunteer in Dublin, said that at an early meeting she asked "Why not Women's Land League?" and was told that such a name was "too democratic." *Twenty-five Years: Reminiscences* (London, 1913), p. 75.

[59] See pp. 124–30 above.

[60] "Women and the Church Since the Famine," in M. MacCurtain and D. O'Corrain (eds.), *Women in Irish Society: The Historical Dimension* (Dublin, 1978), p. 38.

[61] Lee, "Continuity and Change in Ireland, 1945–70," in J. Lee (ed.), *Ireland 1945–70* (Dublin, 1979), p. 168.

letter from Dr. Edward McCabe, Archbishop of Dublin. He was a fierce opponent of the Land League whose views on the land movement and its leaders were not universally shared by members of the Catholic hierarchy. Nonetheless, his idealized vision of women in the home and his strictures against women in the agitation were ardently promoted by the Catholic clergy, the bulk of whom came from the families of large farmers.[62] Writing six weeks after the formation of the Ladies' Land League, the Archbishop told his clergy:

> The modesty of her daughters was the ancient glory of Ireland. The splendour of the purity of St. Brigid won for her the sublime title of the Mary of Ireland. Her spiritual children were worthy of their mother's fame, and Ireland shone out more brightly by the chastity of her daughters than even by the learning or labours of her most distinguished sons. Like Mary, their place was the seclusion of home. If charity drew them out of doors, their work was done with speed and their voices were not heard in the world's thoroughfares . . . But all this is now to be laid aside, and the daughters of our Catholic people, be they matrons or virgins, are called forth, under the pretext of charity, to take their stand in the noisy arena of public life . . . They are asked to forget the modesty of their sex and the high dignity of their womanhood by leaders who seem utterly reckless of consequences . . .
>
> Very Reverend dear Fathers, set your faces against this dishonourable attempt, and do not tolerate in your sodalities the woman who so far disavows her birthright of modesty as to parade herself before the public gaze in a character so unworthy a child of Mary.[63]

In Mayo, where the Ladies' Land League held its inaugural public meeting, James Daly greeted the organization with a blast similar in spirit to that of Archbishop McCabe, saying that "God or nature never intended woman to take the advanced position in fighting for the emancipation of any nation."[64] Yet, underlying Daly's unrelenting opposition to the Ladies' Land League was his concern that Ireland's Celtic manhood would be jeopardized if women assumed an important role in the land and national movements. In October 1879 he had chided the men of Ballina that if they did not quickly take the initiative in

[62] Lee, "Women and the Church Since the Famine," pp. 39–41.

[63] *FJ*, 12 Mar. 1881. This view was not shared by all members of the Catholic hierarchy. See Archbishop Croke's letter to A. M. Sullivan reprinted in Davitt, *The Fall of Feudalism*, p. 315.

[64] *CT*, 12 Feb. 1881.

beginning a land agitation in northern Mayo, "there is every danger of their [the men] being driven out of the political world by the fairer sex."[65] In his editorial response to the founding of the Ladies' Land League, Daly graphically returned to this theme:

God or nature never intended . . . that the manhood of any nation could be so cowardly and demoralized as to intrench themselves behind the fair sex . . . We do not see how any man or body of men having Celtic blood coursing in their veins can be found to descend to or condescend to female leadership in Irish constitutional warfare . . . We . . . enter our solemn protest against having the responsibility of Irish affairs vested in women.[66]

It was evident from the time of its founding that despite the ethos of home and family within the rural middle class, the Ladies' Land League in Mayo was going to be composed of middle-class farm women. The two women from Mayo who were appointed to the provisional committee of the Ladies' National Land League in January 1881 were both prominent members of the new rural elite. Anne Dean of Ballaghaderreen was a prosperous businesswoman, the cousin of nationalist MP John Dillon, and for a time national president of the new league.[67] Beatrice Walshe of Balla was almost certainly the daughter of a substantial farmer, sister of Land League organizer John W. Walshe, and a cousin of Davitt, with whom she may have had a brief flirtation.[68] Katharine Tynan described Beatrice Walshe as having "a beautiful dark face, the face of a Muse." She was "steeped to the lips in an ideal patriotism, which had very little to do with a movement *a servir*, such as the Land League was. She had read much poetry. I can remember her . . . reading English ballad poetry to me with an ecstasy which forgot the flight of time. She was very religious, yet she had endured . . . the denunciations of the priests." According to Tynan, Walshe, her sister Margaret and her cousin May Nally, all active in the Ladies' Land League, had grown up in a world that was "romantic, high-minded, full of poetry and ideals. They had lived amid the making of history, their own men, and the men who were their friends and lovers, already engaged in the making . . . They had a singular refinement, even elegance. I cannot imagine that the hard times had pinched them very seriously. If they had known poverty, it had

---

[65] *Ibid.*, 11 Oct. 1879.
[66] *Ibid.*, 12 Feb. 1881.
[67] F. S. L. Lyons, *John Dillon: A Biography* (Chicago, 1968), pp. 2, 64; W. S. Blunt, *The Land War in Ireland* (London, 1912), pp. 59–60.
[68] Moody, *Davitt and Irish Revolution*, pp. 190, 327.

left no dreary traces on them."[69] This picture of the lives of the rural elite is no doubt a highly romanticized one, but gives a clear sense of the class of women initially drawn to the Ladies' Land League.

Beatrice Walshe was one of twenty-one Mayo women who joined Anna Parnell on the platform at Claremorris on 13 February 1881 for the first open air meeting held by the Ladies' Land League.[70] Of the twenty-one women, it has been possible to identify with some certainty the social position of nine. Seven were the daughters, sisters or wives of merchants, one was a hotel proprietor, and one, Beatrice Walshe, was the daughter of a strong farmer. It is highly likely that most of the remaining women on the platform were also from the strong farmer-merchant class of Mayo.

At the meeting Miss Parnell made it clear that the Ladies' Land League was not going to be simply an alms-giving organization, a women's version of the St. Vincent De Paul Society, as some members of the League executive wished, but was going to be a "relief movement."[71] As explained by Davitt, the special responsibilities of the Ladies' Land League were to monitor eviction proceedings, aid the evicted, organize resistance to land grabbing, support the families of imprisoned League members and "keep up a semblance of organization during the attempted repression that I saw was coming."[72] At the Claremorris meeting Anna Parnell called upon the women of every parish in Mayo to form a branch of the Ladies' Land League in order to prosecute this active program. It is unclear how effective her call for branches was since Daly ceased publishing reports of the Ladies' League branches after February 1881 and no contemporary papers exist that document the number and activities of the Ladies' League branches in Mayo. Documenting the activities of the new league is compounded by Anna Parnell's belief that the quiet organization of resistance to paying rents and to evictions was more effective than were mass meetings.[73] Consequently, the branches rarely commanded the attention of the press, especially given Daly's hostility to the Ladies' Land League.

During February 1881 the formation of five Mayo branches of the Ladies' League was reported in *The Connaught Telegraph*. Three of

---

[69] Tynan, *Twenty-five Years*, pp. 75–6.

[70] *CT*, 19 Feb. 1881.

[71] *Ibid.*, 19 Feb. 1881; Foster, *Parnell and His Family*, pp. 265–6.

[72] *Special Commission . . . Proceedings . . .*, iv, p. 152; Davitt, *The Fall of Feudalism*, p. 300.

[73] Foster, *Parnell and His Family*, p. 267.

them were in townlands close to Westport (Kilmeena, Kilmaclasser, Coislough), one was in Claremorris and one in Swinford.[74] The initial membership of these five branches was approximately 250, with 17 branch officers, all but one of whom were unmarried, probably young, women. Although no documentation is available, it seems likely that most of the members and officers of these branches were the daughters and sisters of middle and large-sized farmers who were anxious to find a role for themselves in the land movement. That role, as it turned out, was above all to attend and file reports on evictions, send subscriptions to the central executive and distribute relief to evicted tenants in the form of cash or the provision of wooden huts "for shelter, but also to enable the evicted family to keep a vigilant watch over their interests in the vacant farm."[75]

During 1881 the number of evictions rose by 130 percent over the previous year, or to 244, the highest number of annual evictions in the county since 1855.[76] This wave of evictions was prompted by a desire on the part of landlords to take advantage of the weakness of the Land League, with its local and national leaders arrested under terms of the coercion bill, and to be rid of their arrears-laden tenants before the soon-to-be introduced land bill went into effect.[77] Neither the Land League nor the Ladies' Land League was prepared to deal with this surge in the number of evictions, although the Ladies' League proved to be much better organized and more systematic in providing assistance than were the men.[78] The problem of providing relief to so many evicted tenants was compounded by the issuance from the recently imprisoned League leadership of a "No Rent Manifesto" on 18 October 1881. The manifesto called upon the tenant farmers of Ireland "to pay no rents under any circumstances to their landlords until the government relinquishes the existing system of terrorism and restores the constitutional rights of the people." Further, it promised that "the funds of the National Land League will be poured out unstintedly for the support of all who may endure eviction in the course of the struggle."[79] Two days following the publication of the No Rent Manifesto, the government proclaimed the

---

[74] *CT*, 5, 12, 26b Feb. 1881.
[75] Davitt, *The Fall of Feudalism*, p. 300.
[76] See Table 4.1 above.
[77] See pp. 306–11 below.
[78] *Special Commission . . . Proceedings . . .* , iv, p. 152; Moody, "Anna Parnell and the Land League," pp. 13–14; Foster, *Parnell and His Family*, p. 267.
[79] *FJ*, 19 Oct. 1881; Davitt, *The Fall of Feudalism*, pp. 335–6.

Land League an illegal organization. With its leaders in prison and its activities now illegal, the Land League ceased to exist, leaving to the Ladies' League full responsibility for carrying out the spirit and the promises of the manifesto.

In many ways the No Rent Manifesto was the logical continuation of the "rent at the point of the bayonet" policy, and as such favored those tenants who could best afford to make a political stand by withholding rents. The notion of a strike against rents had first been proposed by Davitt in February 1881, when the League appeared at the height of its powers and resources. When it was finally adopted as League policy in October the League had been in disarray for months, demoralization was widespread and its leadership was in prison. Davitt later concluded that a "true revolutionary opportunity" had been lost in February. In contrast, the October manifesto was "an act of desperation" that "would only demoralize . . . not explode."[80]

As it turned out, many League leaders, including Parnell, shared Davitt's anxiety about a no rent campaign and supported it luke warmly at best.[81] However, an ardent believer in the campaign was Anna Parnell, who pledged the Ladies' Land League to the task of convincing the tenant farmers of Ireland to withhold their rents. She found little resolve to do so on the part of the tenant farmers and later claimed there had been little support from the "Land League [that] had by no means the same objection to rent being paid as we [the Ladies' Land League] had."[82] She found that most applications for relief to the Ladies' League came from impoverished tenants evicted because they were unable to pay rents, rather than from those who refused to do so out of principle. Moreover, she feared that relief money often went to pay rents rather than assist the evicted family with food, shelter and legal fees.[83]

It is not clear how Anna Parnell's commitment to the radical spirit of the No Rent Manifesto affected the work of the Ladies' Land League in County Mayo. Nor is it clear the degree to which the Ladies' League continued to function in the county after the heady early days of its founding. In May 1881, Anna Parnell came to Bohola for an outdoor meeting of the Ladies' Land League. In the spirit of female solidarity that was her hallmark, she refused to speak until the men "who were pressing

---

80 Davitt, *Fall of Feudalism*, pp. 337–8; Moody, *Davitt and Irish Revolution*, pp. 458–9.
81 Lyons, *Charles Stewart Parnell*, pp. 171–5.
82 NLI, Anna Parnell Papers, "Tale of a Great Sham," MS 12,144, p. 188, quoted in Foster, *Parnell and His Family*, p. 267.
83 *Ibid.*, p. 268; Moody, "Anna Parnell and the Land League," pp. 13–14.

forward . . . and preventing the women from hearing me" stepped to the back. "I came down on purpose to speak to the women" she retorted. However, once the women were allowed to come forward she implied that the women of Mayo had not been holding up the spirit of the Ladies' Land League.[84] Given the high rate of evictions in the county during 1881 and the fact that most of those evicted had no resources with which to pay their rents, it is quite likely that despite the relief that the Ladies' Land League distributed in the county, Ms. Parnell's irritation with the impoverished tenants' willingness to pay rent if they could, when combined with earlier League accusations that Mayo small farmers were failing to fight off eviction with sufficient vigor, furthered the deterioration of support for both Leagues in Mayo.[85] It appears that in October 1881, when the No Rent Manifesto was issued and the Land League suppressed, the attention of most tenants in Mayo was directed towards the workings of the land courts established under the new land bill. The demise of the League and the militancy of Anna Parnell and her associates had become of little interest or consequence to most tenant farmers in Mayo.

THE COERCION AND LAND REFORM BILLS OF 1881

By November 1880 the Liberal government of William Gladstone had concluded reluctantly that a coercion bill allowing for discretionary arrest and the suspension of habeas corpus would have to be enacted in order to mollify Conservatives and landlords before a land reform bill could be introduced in parliament. In late October the government had announced its intention to prosecute Parnell and other League leaders for conspiracy to prevent the payment of rents. This move was taken not out of any hope of actually gaining a conviction, but as a means of demonstrating the ineffectiveness of ordinary law for dealing with Irish agitators and thus providing the justification for a coercion measure.[86] However, by the time the prosecution of Parnell and the other League

---

[84] *FJ*, 23 May 1881.

[85] According to an account prepared by Anna Parnell, more evictions were reported to the Ladies' Land League from Mayo than from any other county. However, it is not clear the degree to which the Ladies' Land League was able to respond to those reports by attending the evictions and supplying the evicted with huts, relief and legal assistance. See: D. B. Cashman, *The Life of Michael Davitt to Which Is Added the Secret History of the Land League by Michael Davitt* (Glasgow, n.d.), p. 232.

[86] O'Brien, *Parnell and His Party*, p. 55.

leaders opened on 28 December, the sharp increase in agrarian crime in Ireland during the last three months of 1880 had provided sufficient justification for the introduction of a coercion measure. In the Queen's Speech, delivered 6 January 1881, the government announced its intention to submit a coercion bill to parliament, which it did on 24 January, the day after the collapse of the state trials against the League's leaders. On 3 February, to demonstrate its determination to break the League, the cabinet revoked Davitt's ticket of leave from prison and arrested him the next day in Dublin. Three weeks later, the bill giving the government the power to arbitrarily arrest and imprison Irish activists and the right to abolish trials by jury was passed into law. It remained in effect for fourteen months.[87]

The passing of the coercion bill posed a serious threat to the League, as noted by Davitt in December when he predicted to Devoy that "if the H.C. [habeas corpus] is suspended the whole movement would be crushed in a month and universal confusion would reign."[88] The League leadership was divided over how to respond to the imposition of coercion. A small radical section within the leadership wanted the Irish parliamentary party to withdraw from parliament in order to lead an all-out rent strike in Ireland, while others proposed sending Parnell to America to raise funds and to leave the radicals free to fight coercion. However, following the arrest of Davitt, which made immediate the need for action, Parnell called on members of the parliamentary party to remain in the House of Commons and cautioned the League's membership in Ireland to exercise restraint in response to the forthcoming arrests.[89]

Parnell's decision not to take the fight against coercion back to Ireland left the local branches of the League, in Davitt's words: "the centres of active opposition."[90] In Mayo these branches, already weakened by splits within the local leadership, neglect from the League executive, and the disaffection of many local Fenians, were ill-equipped to respond aggressively to the crescendo of evictions and arrests that occurred in the county during the spring and summer of 1881. The first arrests in the county under the Protection of Persons and Property Act, as the coercion

87 Bew, *Land and the National Question in Ireland*, pp. 145–52; Moody, *Davitt and Irish Revolution*, pp. 427–30, 454–6.

88 O'Brien and Ryan (eds.), *Devoy's Post Bag*, II, p. 23.

89 Bew, *Land and the National Question in Ireland*, pp. 152–5; Lyons, *Charles Stewart Parnell*, pp. 146–9.

90 Davitt, *The Fall of Feudalism*, p. 311.

Table 9.1. *Offenses charged for those arrested and those recommended for arrest under the Protection of Persons and Property Act, 1881, County Mayo*

	Total arrested	Offenses against persons		Offenses against property		Offenses against public peace		Treasonable activities	
	Number	Number	%	Number	%	Number	%	Number	%
Persons arrested									
League officers and activists	9			1	11.0	8	88.0		
Others	26	7	26.9	4	15.4	15	57.7		
Persons recommended for arrest but not arrested									
League officers and activists	16	1	6.3	1	6.3	11	68.8	3	18.8
Others	36	3	8.3	5	13.9	12	33.3	16	44.4

Notes: This division of agrarian crime into three categories is made in the constabulary reports on agrarian offenses. "Treasonable activities" includes Fenian membership or activities. Percentages are per category of those arrested ("League officers and activists" or "Other"). League officers and activists were identified by comparing lists of those arrested and those recommended for arrest with lists of branch officers and activists compiled from reports in *The Connaught Telegraph*. Most of those listed in the "Other" category were League members.

bill was called, came during the second week of March, when five persons, including county League activists Joseph B. Walsh of Castlebar and John W. Nally of Balla, were arrested. In all, thirty-five Mayo men were arrested under the terms of the coercion bill of 1881, although the arrest of fifty-two others was recommended by the local constabulary.[91] Of those arrested, 26 percent were either local League branch officials or prominent League activists. As illustrated in Table 9.1, there was a sharp contrast between the degree of crimes with which League officials were charged and those with which other detainees were charged. Only one League official, as opposed to fourteen (53.8 percent) of the other detainees, was charged with a crime against persons or property. Most League leaders were charged with intimidation, inciting or boycotting, all non-violent crimes associated with League meetings and activities. Despite the wide powers at their disposal, the police failed in Mayo to arrest people for Fenian activities. The constabulary recommended the

[91] See Appendix 3.

arrest of sixteen people for Fenian membership, night drilling, administering secret oaths, or gun smuggling, including the county's Fenian leaders, P. W. Nally and John O'Keane, but only two prominent Fenians were arrested. Rather, the government concentrated on arresting League activists on the mistaken assumption that doing so would reduce agrarian crime as well as weaken the League. This, it was hoped, would ensure public acceptance of the land bill that Gladstone introduced on 7 April.

The measure guaranteed to Irish tenant farmers the "three Fs": fixity of tenure so long as the rent was paid, and the landlord–tenant covenants were observed; free sale of the tenant's interest in the holdings; fair rent fixed by an independent land court. The bill fell far short of meeting the principal demand of the land movement for the abolition of landlordism, but it did recognize the principle of dual ownership of the soil, shared in unequal proportions by the landlord and tenant.[92] Its most attractive feature from the tenant farmers' point of view was the establishment of an Irish Land Commission whose commissioners, holding court around the country, could arbitrate rent disputes and fix fair rents, which would stand for fifteen years. During those years the tenant could not be evicted so long as the rent was paid and the land was not abused. Gladstone later conceded that the bill was a direct response to the actions of the Land League, without which "the Act of 1881 would not now be upon the Statute Book."[93] As Solow argues: "the Land Act of 1881 reflected no principle, no hypothesis, and thus there was no shaping of legislation to correct a situation or fill a need. There was no policy framed, only demands granted – and hastily."[94] The bill was a political act, designed in Davitt's assessment as "a bribe to the tenants to throw over the league."[95]

As early as December 1880 Davitt had predicted in a letter to Devoy that the land bill would "satisfy a great number inside the league," creating "a serious split within its ranks."[96] The League had endeavored to prepare the tenants to reject such a compromise measure and was, following the bill's introduction, faced with a serious challenge.[97] The left wing of the League leadership, without the aid of the jailed Davitt,

---

92 Solow, *The Land Question and the Irish Economy*, pp. 147–67.
93 Quoted in *ibid.*, p. 156.
94 *Ibid.*, p. 157.
95 Davitt, *The Fall of Feudalism*, p. 319.
96 O'Brien and Ryan (eds.), *Devoy's Post Bag*, II, p. 23.
97 Moody, *Davitt and the Irish Revolution*, p. 483.

condemned the bill, but at a League convention to consider the bill, held in late April, the militants' position was defeated. The convention, called on a suffrage basis of 1 representative for every 500 League members, reflected the unwillingness of tenant farmers to reject outright such a far-reaching measure. Guided by Parnell, the convention delegates refused to either sanction or condemn the bill. Rather, they resolved to allow the parliamentary party to attempt to improve the bill through amendments. Parnell, supported by the majority of delegates, was buying time, trying to keep his militant and moderate supporters from splitting into two camps, while he conducted what T. W. Moody calls a "subtle and devious parliamentary campaign . . . on the bill."[98]

In Mayo, James Daly greeted the land bill in an editorial as "a step in the right direction and no more."[99] It was in this spirit that a county meeting was called for 17 April to consider the bill. At the meeting, held six days after the arrest of Daly under the provisions of the coercion bill, John O'Connor Power explained the details of the measure from a platform full of priests and Mayo notables. Those assembled (and Power later assured the House of Commons that admission to the meeting was open to all) passed a resolution on the bill that was in the spirit of that passed a week later by the national League convention held in Dublin. It affirmed "that the only final solution of the Land Question" was the establishment of peasant propriety, but nonetheless encouraged Mayo's parliamentary representatives "to make strenuous efforts . . . to improve its [the land bill's] provisions that . . . it may become a measure of real protection to the tenant farmers of Ireland."[100] The bill was not without its detractors in Mayo. Louden, who denounced the bill before the League executive, spoke against it to a land meeting at Kilbree, Islandeady on 10 April.[101] Three weeks later Thomas Brennan, who since Davitt's arrest had been the leader of the League's militant wing and the land bill's most ardent opponent within the League executive, criticized the bill in "a no compromise with the enemy" speech before a disruptive land meeting at Claremorris.[102] However, the deterioration of League influence in Mayo was far advanced, while the moderating voice of the county's clergy was becoming more pronounced. In this environment

---

[98] *Ibid.*, p. 484; Bew, *Land and the National Question in Ireland*, pp. 161–5; O'Brien, *Parnell and His Party*, pp. 65–7.
[99] *CT*, 9 Apr. 1881.
[100] *Ibid.*, 23 Apr. 1881; Jordan, "John O'Connor Power," p. 62.
[101] *Ibid.*, 16 Apr. 1881.
[102] *Ibid.*, 7 May 1881.

acceptance of the land bill by the majority of Mayo's tenant farmers was never in doubt.

During the land bill's passage through parliamentary committees the League's supporters within the Irish parliamentary party "settled down" in Conor Cruise O'Brien's words, "in earnest, and in good faith, to the business of amending the act, and defending the government text against amendments from the right."[103] However, only one League-endorsed amendment of any substance was included in the land bill when it became law on 22 August 1881. The amendment, introduced by Tim Healy, prohibited rent raises based upon improvements to the holding made by tenants. The Healy clause, in its author's view, "put millions in the pockets of tenants" who now had an additional legal foundation for contesting increases in rent.[104] Its inclusion in the bill made it all the more likely that the League would be unable to restrain the tenant farmers from seeking rent reductions under the provisions of the bill, thus exploding any possibility of a no rent campaign. Overall, the measure was widely acclaimed by moderates and clergy in Ireland as a substantial move forward. Davitt, who remained in prison at the time of the bill's passage, later acknowledged that it was a "semi-revolutionary scheme . . . which struck a mortal blow at Irish landlordism and doomed it to abolition."[105] However, at the time, League militants and its Irish–American supporters denounced the measure, calling upon tenant farmers to reject it. In Mayo, Daly gave the bill a mixed review in the editorial columns of his newspaper, but did not condemn it outright.[106]

In an effort to resolve the differences over the bill between the League's moderate and militant wings, Parnell called a national convention in Dublin for 15–17 September. Amid rancorous debates and inflammatory telegrams from America, Parnell secured passage of a compromise policy for testing the act.[107] Parnell hoped that tenant farmers might be prevented from abandoning the League and flocking "indiscriminately" to the rent arbitration courts "until they have seen the results of the decisions upon test cases."[108] This equivocal policy reinforced Daly's belief in the irresponsibility of the League executive and drove him to take a stronger stand than previously in support of the

---

[103] O'Brien, *Parnell and His Party*, p. 68.
[104] O'Connor, *Memoirs of an Old Parliamentarian*, I, p. 179.
[105] Davitt, *Fall of Feudalism*, p. 317.
[106] *CT*, 27 Aug. 1881.
[107] *FJ*, 16, 17, 19 Sept. 1881.
[108] Quoted in Lyons, *Charles Stewart Parnell*, p. 164.

land bill. In a blistering editorial, he accused the League leadership of orchestrating the rejection of the bill solely to keep the dollars coming in from America:

But despite this superficial opposition, the tenant farmers are cunning enough to see their way to take the Land Act for what it is worth, in fact to take it as an installment of their long lost rights, and look for more. The bulk of the Irish tenant farmers keenly see that what has been obtained under such difficulties as the Land Act was not to be thrown away to satisfy the whims of those who have been feathering their nests by the agitation.[109]

Daly's assessment of the tenant farmers' eagerness "to take the Land Act for what it is worth" was fully justified. During the first week of the land courts' sessions, Castlebar was full of people seeking information on how to take advantage of the land act.[110] On 26 October "over one thousand tenant farmers from different parts of Mayo poured into Castlebar" to initiate rent arbitration proceedings. According to *The Freeman's Journal* correspondent, the crush of applicants caught the authorities ill-supplied with the necessary forms, but Daly aided the applicants by printing the forms on his presses and distributing them "up to a late hour."[111] Joseph B. Walsh, who returned to Castlebar at this time after serving eight months in Kilmainham jail for his League activities, wrote to his imprisoned brother that "the people are coming in [to the land courts] with a hiss," adding that in their excitement the tenant farmers of Mayo had forgotten that anyone was in jail.[112] During the first three weeks of the operation of the land courts, over 7000 Mayo farmers applied to have their rents judicially fixed.[113]

The eagerness of the tenants to enter the land courts appeared fully justified by the results of the first cases to be decided in Mayo. A Canadian journalist in Mayo during mid-November reported that "the rush to the Land Court had been hastened and intensified . . . by recent decisions given by the Sub-Commission sitting at Ballina." Tenants on the estate of Florence Knox had their rents reduced by an average of 53 percent, which:

decided the minds of many who were wavering between adhering to the League programme and going into the Courts in favour of the

---

[109] *CT*, 24 Sept. 1881.
[110] *Ibid.*, 29 Oct. 1881.
[111] *FJ*, 28 Oct. 1881.
[112] NLI, INLL Papers, Mayo, J. B. Walsh to M. Walsh, 31 Oct. 1881, MS 8291 (9).
[113] *CT*, 8 Apr. 1882.

latter . . . Nothing but the Ballina decisions was talked of for some days; the news went round at fairs and markets, and League or no League, the bulk of the people in this county intend to go into the Court. It is the same story everywhere, the Ballina decisions have tipped the wavering balance in favour of the Government scheme.[114]

Many priests encouraged their parishioners to defy the League and seek reductions in the land courts. Those priests who had never accepted the loss of influence to League activists no doubt agreed with Laurence Gillooly, Bishop of Elphin, that the land bill, given the League's rejection of it, gave "us [Catholic clergy] an opportunity of asserting our proper influence and authority in this Land Question – and of taking the tenant farmers of the Country from under the ruinous and tyrannical control of the L. League."[115] However, the majority of priests viewed the measure as an honest response by the Liberal government to Irish distress and the land agitation – the produce of the "seed down in [Mayo] soil," according to Canon Bourke of Claremorris.[116] The priests supported the bill from its introduction in parliament and most likely engineered the county meeting of 17 April, at which the bill was given conditional approval.

During 1881, as disillusionment with the League's lay leadership intensified in Mayo, the Catholic clergy attempted to step into the leadership vacuum in order to prevent its being filled by secret societies and violence-prone men.[117] In late October, in the wake of the suppression of the League, several Mayo priests seized the initiative and formed tenant defense associations "to aid and instruct the tenant farmers in use of the Land Bill and other constitutional means."[118] This move, part of a nationwide trend, was sufficiently worrisome to Parnell that he wrote from Kilmainham jail calling the newly formed organizations "mongrel revolutionary associations" in the service of the government.[119] These associations, warmly welcomed in Mayo by Daly, never got off the ground in the county. In contrast to the national pattern, League branches in Mayo had collapsed long before the suppression of the League and there was little enthusiasm for new tenant organizations.

114 *CT*, 7 Jan. 1882.
115 Quoted in Larkin, *The Roman Catholic Church and the Creation of the Modern Irish State*, p. 93.
116 *CT*, 7 May 1881.
117 Larkin, *The Roman Catholic Church and the Creation of the Modern Irish State*, p. 130.
118 *CT*, 15 Nov. 1881.
119 *FJ*, 29 Oct. 1881.

Instead, there was the growing belief that with the Land League having failed in Mayo, the farmers should take what they could from the new land bill rather than form new combinations.

THE COLLAPSE OF HOPE FOR THE COUNTY'S SMALL FARMERS

With their hopes for land ownership dashed and the movement they had founded in disarray, those Mayo farmers who were eligible to do so sought rent reductions through the land courts. It is appropriate that given the early weakening of League authority in the county, more farmers from Mayo went into the land courts than did farmers from other counties in Ireland. This is particularly surprising given that as many as two-thirds of Mayo's small farmers were not even eligible to apply to the land courts because they were in arrears on their rent.[120] During the first year of the courts' operation, 9171 Mayo farmers applied to the land courts to have their rents fixed. This was 2567 more than from the next highest county (Galway) and represented 12 percent of the total applicants in the country.[121] Those who benefited most from the land bill were the more substantial farmers whose rents were above the Griffith's valuation and who had made improvements on their holdings, the value of which was now exempt from rent calculations. Smallholders, who constituted the vast majority of Mayo farmers, benefited least from the legislation.

The exemption from the land bill of the arrears-laden tenants – approximately one-third of all tenant farmers in the country – had been a major defeat for the Irish parliamentary party during the committee stage of the bill's passage through parliament. This defeat demonstrated the failure of the Land League to fulfil for the small farmers even the minimal goal of rent reduction that had been set during the early days of the agitation. This realization was particularly bitter for the small farmers of Mayo, who had been the first in the field during the spring of 1879. But their pressing need for a defense against eviction and their coveting of the grassland of the large farmers who became the backbone

---

[120] Lee, *Modernisation of Irish Society*, p. 86.
[121] *Return Showing for Each County in Ireland For the Year Ending 22 August 1882 and For Each Month From September 1882 to April 1883, the Number of Applicants for Fair Rents Lodged in the Land Commission Court, Those Fixed, Dismissed, Struck Out and Withdrawn, the Number of Agreements Out of Court, and of Appeals Lodged, Heard and Withdrawn*, PP 1883 (352), lvii, pp. 2–15.

of the Land League proved their undoing. When during 1880 the League opted for an offensive war against landlordism in alliance with the strong farmers, the small western farmers were doomed to become the victims, not the victors, of the "Land League revolution."

After the "Boycott affair" in October 1880, the small farmers of Mayo played little role in the land movement. There were few land meetings in 1881 and few mass protests, despite the increased evictions. The Land War had moved away from Mayo, leaving the small farmers to find their own solution to the land agitation – emigration. During 1881, 5437 people emigrated from Mayo. In 1882 the number was 4881 and in 1883, 7831, the highest number since the Famine. When, belatedly, an Arrears Act was passed in August 1882 that eventually resulted in the state paying £800,000 in arrears for Irish tenants, the small farmers of Mayo responded apathetically.[122] Many of them had lost faith in the small farm economy. This faith had been temporarily bolstered during the heady days of the Land War, when it appeared that they, as well as the large farmers, would benefit from the abolition of landlordism. But the shift in the League's allegiance from the small western farmers to the large eastern and southern graziers demonstrated that the capitalization of Irish agriculture after the Famine was not going to be interrupted by a social revolution of the type envisioned by the small farmers and their Fenian allies. Ultimately, the land agitation proved another vehicle for the post-Famine consolidation of the political and economic power of the new rural elite.

Without additional local studies of the land agitation, it is difficult to determine how unique the Mayo experience was. League officials seemed to think it unique as far as the disruptive potential of the Fenians was concerned, and certainly in contrast to its early days, the land agitation died away faster in Mayo than elsewhere in Ireland. It is significant that the Irish National League, Parnell's tightly organized and highly centralized successor to the Land League, never got a firm foothold in Mayo. Reporting in June 1886, a police inspector noted that "in Mayo the [National League] has never been a success owing . . . to the opposition of the Fenian party there."[123] Two years later William O'Brien told the Special Commission that he and Davitt attempted "to revive the League" in Mayo in 1883, "but the meeting was a dead failure," after which the League leadership "practically abandoned

---

[122] *Ibid.*, p. 88; *CT*, 9 Sept., 7 Oct. 1882.
[123] SPO, INLL and INL papers, Progress Report, 1 Jan. to 30 June 1886, carton 7.

Mayo" for four years before again organizing the League there "with the greatest difficulty."[124] It may be that the memory of the Land League's failure in Mayo remained too vivid for the small farmers to enroll in an organization that was often little more than the local election machine for the Irish parliamentary party.

However, in 1898 Mayo was again the cauldron in which a major land agitation was brewed, the final one in Irish history. As had been the case with the Land League, the agitation that brought into being the United Irish League began in County Mayo, where it was confined for over a year. This agrarian movement was a fitting sequel to the Land War of 1879–81 for the small farmers in that it was from the beginning an anti-grazier campaign, carried out in opposition to the wishes of the parliamentary leadership. With a new crop of local leaders, many of whom had gained their first political experience during the earlier land agitation, the United Irish League organized around the doctrine "that the grazing industry is the curse and ruination of the west of Ireland and must, at all cost, be got rid of . . . "[125] It ultimately failed in this object, as once again the land agitation was eventually moderated and made an agent of the Irish parliamentary party, but its early vitality demonstrated that the conflicts between the farming classes of Mayo that had appeared so clearly during the Land War remained unresolved and volatile.

---

[124] *Special Commission . . . Proceedings . . .* , iii, p. 202.
[125] SPO, CBS papers, United Irish League: Its Origins and History, 10 Oct. 1898, 17425/s.

Appendix 1: *Mayo evictions: explanation of calculations and sources for Table 4.1 and Figure 4.1*

A. METHODS FOR ESTIMATING MISSING DATA

Evictions were not recorded before 1849. Consequently, estimates of the number of evictions between 1846 and 1848 must be derived from judicial records that only record the number of ejectment decrees issued. These figures do not reveal how many of the decrees were actually carried out or how many of the evicted tenants were reinstated, either as tenants or as caretakers. I have dismissed the first deficiency in the data as insignificant for calculating evictions during the Famine. Clark has argued that following the Famine landlords often used ejectment decrees as a means of compelling recalcitrant tenants to pay their rents or abide by estate rules.[1] This argument is effective for conditions after the Famine, but would seem to have little relevance during the Famine since most landlords realized that such tactics would not work on a destitute population. Consequently, I have assumed that all of the ejectment decrees were carried out, although no doubt such an assumptions results in overestimating the number of legal ejectments. This is probably compensated for by those incidents where tenants were thrown off their holdings without the niceties of legal decrees and by those tenants who fled the country rather than stay to be evicted.

The problem of reinstated tenants cannot be so easily dismissed. During the years 1849–53, when the number of evictions remained high, 26.8 percent of the recorded evictions resulted in the reinstatement of the tenants. Yet this average masks considerable variations from year to year. The chief variable for the number of reinstatements seems to be the number of evicted tenants who emigrated. For example, in 1852 when only 15.6 percent of the evicted tenants were reinstated, the number of

[1] Clark, *Social Origins of the Irish Land War*, pp. 168–70.

recorded emigrants from Mayo was 7133, approximately 80 percent more than the number who emigrated in 1849, when 37.8 percent were reinstated. While yearly emigration figures for the years 1846–8 were not collected, the estimated number of Famine emigrants for Mayo indicates that many more evicted tenants left Ireland per year during the Famine than was the case after 1851, when emigration figures became available.[2] Consequently, I have adopted the low figure of 15 percent to estimate the number of tenants who were reinstated on their holdings between 1846 and 1848.[3] These figures are given in parentheses in Table 4.1.

The reinstatement figures given in the parliamentary returns for 1870–9 only include tenants reinstated as tenants, whereas the previous figures include tenants reinstated as caretakers as well. In order to produce comparable data on families reinstated, I have adopted a method employed by Solow for estimating the number of tenants reinstated as caretakers during the years 1870–9.[4] From 1880 onwards the annual eviction statistics divide reinstated tenants into categories for those reinstated as tenants and those reinstated as caretakers. I have taken the figures for 1880 and for the first two quarters of 1881 and have calculated that in County Mayo 43 percent of those tenants evicted were reinstated as caretakers. Using this average, I estimated the number of evicted tenants who were reinstated as caretakers for the years 1870–9. I added this estimate to the actual figure for tenants reinstated as tenants and provide the total figure in parentheses in Table 4.1.

B. SOURCES

RETURNS OF CASES OF EVICTION (IN CHRONOLOGICAL ORDER)

Returns From the Courts of the Queen's Bench, Common Pleas and Exchequer in Ireland, Of the Number of Ejectments Brought In Those Courts Respectively For the Last Three Years Beginning With Hilary Term 1846 and Ending With Hilary Term 1849, Both Included; Specifying the Number In Each Term and Year and the Counties In Which They Have Been Brought, and the Number of Persons Served In Each Ejectment, According To the Affidavits Of Service, Distinguishing the Number Brought For Non-Payment Of Rent and the

---

[2] See pp. 108–10, 122 above.

[3] Donnelly adopts the high estimate of 40 percent, although he acknowledges that the figure was probably 20 percent or less. See: *The Land and the People of Nineteenth Century Cork*, pp. 112–13.

[4] Solow, *The Land Question and the Irish Economy*, pp. 54–7.

Number Brought For Over-Holding; and From the Assistant Barrister's Court of Each County In Ireland, Of the Number of Civil Bill Ejectments Entered In Each Of Such Courts For A Similar Period, Together With the Number Of Defendants In Each Civil Bill Ejectment and Distinguishing the Number Sued For Non-Payment Of Rent, and the Number For Over-Holding and the Number For Desertion, PP 1849 (315), xlix, 235.

Return By Provinces and Counties (Compiled From Returns Made To the Inspector General, Royal Irish Constabulary) Of Cases of Evictions Which Have Come To the Knowledge of the Constabulary In Each of the Years From 1849–1880 Inclusive, PP 1881 (185), lxxvii, 725.

Return (Compiled From Returns To the Inspector General, Royal Irish Constabulary) of Cases of Evictions Which Have Come To the Knowledge of the Constabulary In Each Quarter of the Year Ended 31st Day of December 1880, Showing the Number of Families Evicted In Each County in Ireland During Each Quarter, the Number Readmitted As Tenants and the Number Readmitted As Caretakers, PP 1881 (2), lxxvii, 713.

Return . . . In Each Quarter of the Year Ended 31st Day of December 1881 . . ., PP 1882 (9), lv, 229.

Return . . . In Each Quarter of the Year Ended 31st Day of December 1882 . . ., PP 1882 [C 3465], lvi, 99.

Return of Cases of Eviction Which Have Come To the Knowledge of the Constabulary In the Quarter Ended 31st Day of March 1883 . . . In Each County . . ., PP 1883 [C 3579], lvi, 107.

Return . . . In Each Quarter Ending the 30th Day of June 1883 . . ., PP 1883 [C 3770], liv, 111.

Return . . . In Each Quarter Ending the 30th Day of September 1883 . . ., PP 1884 [C 3893], lxiv, 407.

Return . . . In Each Quarter Ending the 31st Day of December 1883 . . ., PP 1884 [C 3892], lxiv, 411.

Return . . . In Each Quarter Ending the 31st Day of March 1884 . . ., PP 1884 [C 3994], lxiv, 415.

Return . . . In Each Quarter Ending the 30th Day of June 1884 . . ., PP 1884 [C 4089], lxiv, 419.

Return . . . In Each Quarter Ending the 30th Day of September 1884 . . ., PP 1884–5 [C 4102], lxv, 29.

Return . . . In Each Quarter Ending the 31st Day of December 1884 . . ., PP 1884–5 [C 4300], lxv, 33.

Return . . . In Each Quarter Ending the 31st Day of March 1885 . . ., PP 1884–5 [C 4394], lxv, 37.

Return . . . In Each Quarter Ending the 30th Day of June 1885 . . ., PP 1884–5 [C 4485], lxv, 41.

Return . . . In Each Quarter Ending the 30th Day of September 1885 . . ., PP 1886 [C 4618], liv, 29.

Return . . . In Each Quarter Ending the 31st Day of December 1885 . . ., PP 1886 [C 4619], liv, 33.

Return . . . In Each Quarter Ending the 31st Day of March 1886 . . ., PP 1886 [C 4720], liv, 37.

Return . . . In Each Quarter Ending the 30th Day of June 1886 . . ., PP 1886 [C 4875], liv, 41.

Return . . . In Each Quarter Ending the 30th Day of September 1886 . . ., PP 1887 [C 4946], lxviii, 41.

Return . . . In Each Quarter Ending the 31st Day of December 1886 . . ., PP 1887 [C 4947], lxviii, 55.

Return . . . In Each Quarter Ending the 31st Day of March 1887 . . ., PP 1887 [C 5037], lxviii, 59.

Return . . . In Each Quarter Ending the 30th Day of June 1887 . . ., PP 1887 [C 5095], lxviii, 63.

Return . . . In Each Quarter Ending the 30th Day of September 1887 . . ., PP 1888 [C 5289], lxxxiii, 433.

Return . . . In Each Quarter Ending the 31st Day of December 1887 . . ., PP 1888 [C 5290], lxxxiii, 437.

Return of the Number of Evictions From Agricultural Holdings Which Have Come to the Knowledge of the Constabulary, and Also the Number of Tenancies Determined in the Quarter Ended the 31st Day of March 1888, Showing: Actual Evictions Under the Provisions of the Land Law Act, 1887, and Under Other Processes of Law, the Number of Evictions, Not At Suit of Landlord for Debt, Foreclosure of Mortgage, etc., PP 1888 [C 5405], lxxxiii, 441.

Return . . . in the Quarter Ended the 30th Day of June 1888 . . ., PP 1888 [C 5498], lxxxiii, 447.

Return . . . in the Quarter Ended the 30th Day of September 1888 . . ., PP 1888 [C 5583], lxxxiii, 453.

Return . . . in the Quarter Ended the 31st Day of December 1888 . . ., PP 1889 [C 5642], lxi, 545.

Return . . . in the Quarter Ended the 31st Day of March 1889 . . ., PP 1889 [C 5700], lxi, 551.

Return . . . in the Quarter Ended the 30th Day of June 1889 . . ., PP 1889 [C 5784], lxi, 557.

Return . . . in the Quarter Ended the 30th Day of September 1889 . . ., PP 1890 [C 5935], lx, I.

Return . . . in the Quarter Ended the 31st Day of December 1889 . . ., PP 1890 [C 5936], lx, 7.

Return . . . in the Quarter Ended the 31st Day of March 1890 . . ., PP 1890 [C 6018], lx, 13.

Return . . . in the Quarter Ended the 31st Day of June 1890 . . ., PP 1890 [C 6093], lx, 19.

Return . . . in the Quarter Ended the 30th Day of September 1890 . . ., PP 1890–1 [C 6231], lxv, I.

Return . . . in the Quarter Ended the 31st Day of December 1890 . . ., PP 1890–1 [C 6262], lxv, 7.

Return . . . in the Quarter Ended the 31st Day of March 1891 . . ., PP 1890–1 [C 6345], lxv, 13.

Return . . . in the Quarter Ended the 30th Day of June 1891 . . ., PP 1890–1 [C 6481], lxv, 19.

Return . . . in the Quarter Ended the 30th Day of September 1891 . . . , PP 1892 [C 6580], lxv, 447.

Return . . . in the Quarter Ended the 31st Day of December 1891 . . . , PP 1892 [C 6581], lxv, 483.

Return . . . in the Quarter Ended the 31st Day of March 1892 . . . , PP 1892 [C 6667], lxv, 489.

Return . . . in the Quarter Ended the 30th Day of June 1892 . . . , PP 1892 [C 6784], lxv, 495.

Return . . . in the Quarter Ended the 30th Day of September 1892 . . . , PP 1893–4 [C 6872], lxxiv, pt. II, 451.

Return . . . in the Quarter Ended the 31st Day of December 1892 . . . , PP 1893–4 [C 6882], lxxiv, pt. II, 457.

Return . . . in the Quarter Ended the 31st Day of March 1893 . . . , PP 1893–4 [C 6995], lxxiv, pt. II, 463.

Return . . . in the Quarter Ended the 30th Day of June 1893 . . . , PP 1893–4 [C 7099], lxxiv, pt. II, 469.

Return . . . in the Quarter Ended the 30th Day of September 1893 . . . , PP 1893–4 [C 7210], lxxiv, pt. II, 475.

Return . . . in the Quarter Ended the 31st Day of December 1893 . . . , PP 1893–4 [C 7273], lxxiv, pt. II, 481.

Return . . . in the Quarter Ended the 31st Day of March 1894 . . . , PP 1894 [C 7364], lxxii, 63.

Return . . . in the Quarter Ended the 30th Day of June 1894 . . . , PP 1894 [C 7462], lxxii, 69.

Return . . . in the Quarter Ended the 30th Day of September 1894 . . . , PP 1895 [C 7617], lxxxii, 129.

Return . . . in the Quarter Ended the 31st Day of December 1894 . . . , PP 1895 [C 7618], lxxxii, 135.

Return . . . in the Quarter Ended the 31st Day of March 1895 . . . , PP 1895 [C 7724], lxxxii, 141.

Return . . . in the Quarter Ended the 30th Day of June 1895 . . . , PP 1895 [C 7850], lxxxii, 147.

Return . . . in the Quarter Ended the 30th Day of September 1895 . . . , PP 1896 [C 7965], lxix, 615.

Return . . . in the Quarter Ended the 31st Day of December 1895 . . . , PP 1896 [C 7966], lxix, 621.

Return . . . in the Quarter Ended the 31st Day of March 1896 . . . , PP 1896 [C 8058], lxix, 627.

Return . . . in the Quarter Ended the 30th Day of June 1896 . . . , PP 1896 [C 8166], lxix, 633.

Return . . . in the Quarter Ended the 30th Day of September 1896 . . . , PP 1897 [C 8293], lxxxiii, 315.

Return . . . in the Quarter Ended the 31st Day of December 1896 . . . , PP 1897 [C 8321], lxxxiii, 321.

Return . . . in the Quarter Ended the 31st Day of March 1897 . . . , PP 1897 [C 8467], lxxxiii, 327.

Return . . . in the Quarter Ended the 30th Day of June 1897 . . ., PP 1897 [C 8556], lxxxiii, 333.

Return . . . in the Quarter Ended the 30th Day of September 1897 . . ., PP 1898 [C 8689], lxxiv, 171.

Return . . . in the Quarter Ended the 31st Day of December 1897 . . ., PP 1898 [C 8726], lxxiv, 177.

Return . . . in the Quarter Ended the 31st Day of March 1898 . . ., PP 1898 [C 8878], lxxiv, 183.

Return . . . in the Quarter Ended the 30th Day of June 1898 . . ., PP 1898 [C 8969], lxxiv, 189.

Return . . . in the Quarter Ended the 30th Day of September 1898 . . ., PP 1899 [C 9099], lxxix, 679.

Return . . . in the Quarter Ended the 31st Day of December 1898 . . ., PP 1899 [C 9168], lxxix, 685.

Return . . . in the Quarter Ended the 31st Day of March 1899 . . ., PP 1899 [C 9274], lxxix, 691.

Return . . . in the Quarter Ended the 30th Day of June 1899 . . ., PP 1899 [C 9447], lxxix, 697.

Return . . . in the Quarter Ended the 30th Day of September 1899 . . ., PP 1900 [Cd 11], lxix, 657.

Return . . . in the Quarter Ended the 31st Day of December 1899 . . ., PP 1900 [Cd 51], lxix, 663.

Return . . . in the Quarter Ended the 31st Day of March 1900 . . ., PP 1900 [Cd 163], lxix, 669.

Return . . . in the Quarter Ended the 30th Day of June 1900 . . ., PP 1900 [Cd 298], lxix, 675.

Return . . . in the Quarter Ended the 30th Day of September 1900 . . ., PP 1900 [Cd 400], lxix, 681.

Return . . . in the Quarter Ended the 31st Day of December 1900 . . ., PP 1901 [Cd 472], lxi, 535.

RETURNS OF AGRICULTURAL PRODUCE IN IRELAND (IN CHRONOLOGICAL ORDER)

Returns of Agricultural Produce in Ireland in the Year 1847, Pt. I: Crops, PP 1847–8 [923], lvii, I.

Returns of Agricultural Produce in Ireland in the Year 1847, Pt. II: Stock, PP 1847–8 [1000], lvii, 109.

Returns of Agricultural Produce . . . 1848, PP 1849 [1116], xlix, I.

Returns of Agricultural Produce . . . 1849, PP 1850 [1245], li, 39.

Returns of Agricultural Produce . . . 1850, PP 1851 [1404], l, I.

The Census of Ireland For the Year 1851, Pt. II: Returns of Agricultural Produce in 1851, PP 1852–3 [1589], xciii, I.

Returns of Agricultural Produce . . . 1852, PP 1854 [1714], lvii, I.

Returns of Agricultural Produce . . . 1853, PP 1854–5 [1865], xlvii, I.

Returns of Agricultural Produce . . . 1854, PP 1856 [2017], liii, I.
Returns of Agricultural Produce . . . 1855, PP 1857 (sess. I) [2174], xv, 81.
Returns of Agricultural Produce . . . 1856, PP 1857–8 [2289], lvi, I.

THE AGRICULTURAL STATISTICS OF IRELAND (IN CHRONOLOGICAL ORDER)

The Agricultural Statistics of Ireland For the Year 1857, PP 1859 (sess. 2) [2641], xxvi, 57.
The Agricultural Statistics . . . 1858, PP 1860 [2599], lxvi, 55.
The Agricultural Statistics . . . 1859, PP 1861 [2763], lxii, 73.
The Agricultural Statistics . . . 1860, PP 1862 [2997], lx, 137.
The Agricultural Statistics . . . 1861, PP 1863 [3156], lxix, 547.
The Agricultural Statistics . . . 1862, PP 1864 [3286], lix, 327.
The Agricultural Statistics . . . 1863, PP 1865 [3456], lv, 125.
The Agricultural Statistics . . . 1864, PP 1867 [3766], lxxi, 201.
The Agricultural Statistics . . . 1865, PP 1867 [3929], lxxi, 491.
The Agricultural Statistics . . . 1866, PP 1867–8 [3958-II], lxxi, 255.
The Agricultural Statistics . . . 1867, PP 1868–9 [4113-II], lxii, 645.
The Agricultural Statistics . . . 1868, PP 1870 [C 3], lxviii, 439.
The Agricultural Statistics . . . 1869, PP 1871 [C 239], lxix, 347.
The Agricultural Statistics . . . 1870, PP 1872 [C 463], lxiii, 299.
The Agricultural Statistics . . . 1871, PP 1873 [C 762], lxix, 375.
The Agricultural Statistics . . . 1872, PP 1874 [C 880], lxix, 199.
The Agricultural Statistics . . . 1873, PP 1875 [C 1125], lxxix, 131.
The Agricultural Statistics . . . 1874, PP 1876 [C 1380], lxxviii, 131.
The Agricultural Statistics . . . 1875, PP 1876 [C 1568], lxxviii, 413.
The Agricultural Statistics . . . 1876, PP 1877 [C 1749], lxxxv, 529.
The Agricultural Statistics . . . 1877, PP 1878 [C 1938], lxxvii, 511.
The Agricultural Statistics . . . 1878, PP 1878–9 [C 2347], lxxv, 587.
The Agricultural Statistics . . . 1879, PP 1880 [C 2534], lxxvi, 815.
The Agricultural Statistics . . . 1880, PP 1881 [C 2932], xciii, 685.
The Agricultural Statistics . . . 1881, PP 1882 [C 3332], lxxiv, 93.
The Agricultural Statistics . . . 1882, PP 1883 [C 3677], lxxvi, 825.
The Agricultural Statistics . . . 1883, PP 1884 [C 4069], lxxxv, 313.
The Agricultural Statistics . . . 1884, PP 1884–5 [C 4489], lxxxv, I.
The Agricultural Statistics . . . 1885, PP 1886 [C 4802], lxxi, I.
The Agricultural Statistics . . . 1886, PP 1887 [C 5084], lxxxix, I.
The Agricultural Statistics . . . 1887, PP 1888 [C 5477], cvi, 415.
The Agricultural Statistics . . . 1888, PP 1889 [C 5785], lxxxiii, 215.
The Agricultural Statistics . . . 1889, PP 1890 [C 6099], lxxix, 371.
The Agricultural Statistics . . . 1890, PP 1890–1 [C 6518], xci, 277.
The Agricultural Statistics . . . 1891, PP 1892 [C 6777], lxxxviii, 285.
Agricultural Statistics of Ireland, With Detailed Report on Agriculture, For the Year 1892, PP 1893–4 [C 7187], ci, 285.
Agricultural Statistics . . . 1893, PP 1894 [C 7531], xciii, 173.

Agricultural Statistics . . . *1894*, PP 1895 [C 7763], cvi, 315.
Agricultural Statistics . . . *1895*, PP 1896 [C 8126], xcii, 309.
Agricultural Statistics . . . *1896*, PP 1897 [C 8510], xcviii, 359.
Agricultural Statistics . . . *1897*, PP 1898 [C 8885], cii, 321.
Agricultural Statistics . . . *1898*, PP 1899 [C 9389], cvi, 325.
Agricultural Statistics . . . *1899*, PP 1900 [Cd 143], ci, 311.
Agricultural Statistics . . . *1900*, PP 1901 [Cd 577], lxxxviii, 313.

Appendix 2: *Occupations of suspected Fenians, County Mayo, as recorded in police files, 1866–71*

Occupations	Number of suspects	Number arrested
Professional sector		
Teachers		
National school teacher	3	2
Schoolmaster		1
Clergy		
Parish priest	1	
Curate	1	
Commercial and industrial sector		
Tradesmen and artisans		
Baker	1	5
Blacksmith	2	
Butcher	2	
Cabinet maker	1	1
Carpenter	1	3
Coachman		1
Cooper	1	1
Corn buyer	1	
Draper	1	
Grocer	1	
Hardware dealer	1	
Mason	1	2
Nailor	2	1
Painter	1	
Plasterer		1
Peddler	3	
Portrait painter	1	
Presser of friezes	1	
Publican	1	
Saddler	4	
Shoemaker	4	6
Shopkeeper	6	1
Slater		1
Stonecutter	1	
Tailor	3	
Tinker		1

Occupations	Number of suspects	Number arrested
Tinsmith	1	
Trader/newsagent	1	
Clerks and commercial assistants		
Assistant postman	1	
Assistant shopman	1	
Clerk		1
Draper's assistant		2
Grocer's assistant	2	1
Postboy		1
Son of canteen keeper	1	
Urban laborers		
Journeyman baker		1
Journeyman nailor	1	
Journeyman stonecutter	1	
Laborer	3	
Agricultural sector		
Farmers and farmers' sons		
Farmer	1	1
Farmer's son		1
Farm laborers	2	1
Other agricultural		
Gamekeeper		1
Total	60	37

Notes and sources: Suspected Fenians are drawn from SPO, Police and Crime Records, Fenian Papers, Fenianism: Index of Names 1866–71; arrested Fenians are drawn from SPO, Police and Crime Records, Fenian Papers, Abstract of Cases of Persons Arrested Under Habeas Corpus Suspension Act, 1866–8.

Appendix 3: *List of persons whose arrest is recommended under the Protection of Persons and Property Act, 1881, County Mayo[a]*

Name	Residence	Occupation circumstances	Suspected crimes and evidence
Ballaghaderreen District			
Thomas Kelly[b]	Ballyhaunis	Commercial traveler, poor circumstances, small salary	Inciting acts of violence, strongly suspected of being a Fenian agent, secretly importing arms, organized indignation meeting and recommended boycott.
Michael Shiel	Carralacta, Kilmovee	Small farmer, assistant secretary to Kilmovee branch, poor circumstances	Suspected Fenian agent, prominent Fenian 1867–73, now associates with advanced, violent Land Leaguers, may be involved with illegal nighttime drilling.
Ballina District			
Arthur Muffney[b]	Ballina	Hardware merchant, circumstances, fair	Was principally instrumental in establishing various branches of the Land League in the neighborhood, intimidating car owners who supplied cars to the police.
Michael Kavanagh	Knockanello	Laborer, fair	Inciting crowd to free prisoner from police.
Michael Gallagher	Ballina	Publican and baker, fair	Old Fenian, active Land Leaguer, may be smuggling arms.
Patrick Gallagher	Ballina	Draper, good	Fenian and Land Leaguer, may be smuggling arms.
Michael Garden	Rusheens	Lives with father, farmer, good	Arrested drunk, in pocket found paper with pass words and sign believed to be of a secret society.

Name	Residence	Occupation circumstances	Suspected crimes and evidence
Mathew Melvin	Ballybroney	Lives with father, farmer, good	Active local Land Leaguer, believed to be active Fenian.
Cormac Flanagan	Ballybroney	Cartwright and farmer, fair	Active local Land Leaguer, believed to be active Fenian.
David Walsh	Catthrorathroe	Farmer, bad	Secretary of local branch, believed to have written a threatening letter.
Patrick Sweeney	Smithstown	Lives with father, farmer, fair	President of local branch.
Ballinrobe District James Mannian	Brownstown	Laborer	Firing at David Feerick, agent who had evicted Mannian for non-payment.
Patrick Macken	Coolyloughrarre	Small farmer	Murder of David Feerick, suspected accessory, active member of Land League.
John Hennelly	Glencorrib	Small farmer's son	Treasurer Shrule branch, suspected of sending threatening letters.
Patrick Hughes	Cregduff	Small farmer's son	Threatening notices warning parishioners against paying dues to priest who spoke from altar against secret societies.
Thomas Dungan	Hundredacres	Strong farmer's son, good	Same as Patrick Hughes
Patrick Burke	Caherivicklawn	Small farmer's son	Suspected of taking part in driving Captain Boycott's stock off grass farm.
William Burke	Ardkill	Small farmer's son	Suspect of participating in burning of nine cocks of hay to enforce reduction of rent.
Patrick J. Monaghan	Ballinrobe	Hotel and shopkeeper, fair	Unlawful assembly, breaking windows not illuminated in support of Parnell.
Hubert Monaghan	Ballinrobe	Shop assistant	Brother of Patrick, Secretary of Ballinrobe branch.

Name	Residence	Occupation circumstances	Suspected crimes and evidence
Castlebar District			
James Daly[b]	Castlebar	Newspaper proprietor, farmer, good	Intimidation and meeting to crime in various ways.
J. B. Walsh[b]	Castlebar	Publican, good	Same as James Daly.
Richard McDonnell	Turlough	Blacksmith, fair	Intimidating and meeting to many acts of outrage.
James Winterscahill[b]	Ballybreane	Small farmer, fair	Several agrarian outrages, "one of the worst characters in . . . district."
Thomas Madden[b]	Maherfadda	Farmer and herd, good	Several outrages and intimidations.
John King	Clonfert	Farmer, fair	Several outrages and intimidations.
John Hynes	Carrouclougher	Farmer, fair	Several outrages and intimidations.
Michael Morahan	Mount Daisy	Farmer, fair	Several outrages and intimidations.
Patrick Moran[b]	Killadeer	Farmer, good	Several outrages and intimidations.
Anthony Clarke	Ballinamarogue	Farmer, good	Several outrages and intimidations.
Denis Duffy	Ballinamarogue	Farmer good	Several outrages and intimidations.
John J. Walsh	Balla	Agitator, good	General disloyal character.
John W. Nally[b]	Balla		Recommended shooting landlords and boycotting.
John McEllin	Balla	Hotel keeper, good	Suspected of organizing for revolutionary purposes and supplying arms.
Richard Walsh[b]	Craggagh, Balla	Farmer and cattle jobber, good	Intimidation and boycotting, agrarian outrage.
Patrick W. Nally	Balla	Farmer, good	Suspected of organizing revolution and supplying arms.
Thomas O'Reilly	Balla	Shopkeeper, good	Suspected of organizing revolution and supplying arms.
Claremorris District			
Patrick J. Gordon[b]	Claremorris	Shopkeeper, fair, supposedly paid by Land League	Inciting through speeches, possible Fenian.

Name	Residence	Occupation circumstances	Suspected crimes and evidence
Thomas Quinn	Claremorris	Clerk to local poor law board, gardener's son, fair	Suspected of being one of David Ferrick's murderers, believed to be a Fenian, most active member of the Land League, bad character, feared by the respectable.
John O'Kane	Claremorris	Shopman and partner in public house	District master in Fenian society, importing arms.
Daniel O'Connor[b]	Knockadoon	Farmer, good	Leading Fenian and Ribbonman, inciting people to outrage, prominent Land League organizer.
Dominick Costello	Murneen	Keeper of a stallion, poor	Administration of unlawful oaths.
James Daly	Boleby	Farmer, good	Clearing farms and other agrarian offenses.
Patrick Murphy		Carpenter, good	Suspected Fenian and Ribbonman, intimidation and threats.
Crossmolina District			
Thomas McCawley[b]	Grange	No occupation, son of a steward	Believed to be master of a secret society.
Thomas Daly[b]	Crossmolina	Shopkeeper, and dealer, and small farmer, middling	Believed to be member of treasonable society.
W. J. Cormack	Crossmolina	Publican, grocer and extensive dealer, very good	Chief manager of Land League, intimidation, threatening letter.
Michael O'Hara	Crossmolina		Believed to be parish master of treasonable society.
Anthony Daly	Letterbrick	Son of small farmer, poor	Believed to be member of secret society.
Michael Daly	Bohadoon	Sub-post master, son of farmer, very good	President of Keenagh branch, intimidation, organization.
Patrick Hegarty	Shrahyconagaun	Son of small farmer, poor	Intimidation and violence against grabber.
John Gallagher		Publican, middling	Intimidation

Name	Residence	Occupation circumstances	Suspected crimes and evidence
Michael Bourke	Knockmore	Publican, poor	Treasurer, Knockmore branch, Lane League court held in pub.
Michael Walsh	Knockmore	Small farmer, former national school teacher	Secretary Knockmore branch, present at court.
Richard Hymn	Kisaniska	Farmer and dealer in meal, good	Member Knockmore branch, present at court.
James Duffy	Backwansha	Small farmer, fair	Active and overbearing member of Knockmore branch.
Richard McHugh	Crossmolina	Laborer	Inciting
Hollymount District			
Edward Slevin	Thomastown	Land steward, formerly plough-man, very fair (a "spoiled priest")	Member of Land League, suspected of arranging intimidation and writing threatening notices.
Thomas Casey	Knocknadlinna	Small farmer, fair, returned from US	Suspected organizer of secret societies.
Michael Hughes	Curracrow	Small farmer, fair, returned from US	Violent outrages, member of Land League, suspected Fenian.
Patrick Ferrick	Kiltrore	Small farmer, fair	Suspected murderer of Peter Mullin, a Fenian.
Swinford District			
Patrick White	Ashbrook	Small farmer	Intimidation of grabber.
Westport District			
John Sweeny	Louisburgh	Small shopkeeper, fair	Posting inflammatory notices.
Thomas Hastings	Louisburgh	Small shopkeeper, middling	Fenian

Notes:

[a] SPO, Police and Crime Reports, Protection of Persons and Property Act, 1881, carton 1.

[b] Denotes persons actually arrested.

Appendix 4: *Explanation of categories and list of Land League meetings for Map 5.2 and Table 7.1*

EXPLANATION OF CATEGORIES

"Three Fs" – fair rents, fixity of tenure and free sale of interest in the holding were the land reform objectives of the Tenant League during the 1850s and of the Irish parliamentary party at the beginning of the Land War.

"Self-government" – this was a neutral term that could refer to Home Rule or to complete independence for Ireland. The term was often left purposely undefined in order to bring the widest spectrum of nationalists into the land movement.

"Public works' jobs" – these were either government or landlord funded projects, usually for land reclamation or road building.

"Censure of land grabbing" – this refers to censuring farmers or shop-keepers who took up holdings from which the previous tenant had been evicted.

"Centure of tenants who pay rent" – this refers to cases where tenants on a given estate or parish had resolved not to pay rent until an abatement or other concession was granted by the landlord.

"Opposition to government" – these resolutions began following the arrest of James Daly, Michael Davitt and J. B. Kileen in November 1879 and are in opposition to those arrests.

LAND MEETINGS HELD IN OR NEAR COUNTY
MAYO, APRIL 1879–DECEMBER 1881. REPORTED IN
THE CONNAUGHT TELEGRAPH OR *THE FREEMAN'S
JOURNAL*

1879[a]

20 April	Irishtown
25 May	Claremorris
1 June	Knock
8 June	Westport
15 June	Milltown, Co. Galway[b]
22 June	Mayo
29 June	Carnacon, Ballintubber
6 July	Kilcommon, Hollymount
13 July	Claremorris
27 July	Shrule
15 August	Balla
31 August	Ballyhaunis
21 September	Tuam, Co. Galway[b]
29 September	Castlebar
6 October	The Neale
12 October	Ballinvoy, Westport
19 October	Newport
25 October	Killala
26 October	Carrabawn, Westport
26 October	Aughamore
2 November	Lecanvy, Westport
2 November	Gurteen, Co. Sligo[b]
9 November	Kilmaine
9 November	Kilmeena
16 November	Islandeady
16 November	Keltimagh
22 November	Loonamore, Balla
23 November	Aughagower
23 November	Swinford
30 November	Louisburgh
30 November	Ballaghadereen[b]
7 December	French Hill, Castlebar
14 December	Fahey, Kilmeena, Westport
14 December	Mount Partry
14 December	Ballina
21 December	Kilmeena, Westport
28 December	Mayo Abbey

1880[a]

18 January	Curry, Co. Sligo[b]
1 February	Straide
15 February	Knock
7 March	Ballindine
1 May	Balla
2 May	Irishtown
13 June	Drumanor, Killasser, Swinford

13 June	Ballyglass
27 June	Irishtown
4 July	Bohola
11 July	Cong
18 July	Islandeady
22 August	Louisburgh
5 September	Ballycroy
26 September	Clonbur, Co. Galway[b]
3 October	Glencastle, Belmullet
10 October	Ballyhaunis
16 October	Westport
24 October	Tiernaur, Newport
31 October	Knockmore, Ballina
31 October	Shrule
31 October	Sheeane Hill, Westport
7 November	Ballyhean
14 November	Aughagower
21 November	Newport
21 November	Ballaghaderreen[b]
28 November	Keltimagh
1 December	Gurtnasella, Swinford
12 December	Foxford
19 December	Ranacreeva, Balla
19 December	Kilkelly
26 December	Kilbree, Westport

1881

2 January	Straide
9 January	Sarnaght, Castlebar
16 January	Lahardane
30 January	Rosslahan, Belcarra
13 February	Claremorris
10 April	Kilbree, Islandeady
1 May	Claremorris
22 May	Bohola
12 June	Ballycroy

Notes:

[a] 1879 = Total of 37 meetings
 1880 = Total of 32 meetings
 1881 = Total of 9 meetings
[b] Not included on Map 5.2, p. 192.

Bibliography

I. CONTEMPORARY SOURCES

MANUSCRIPT MATERIAL

Department of Irish Folklore, University College, Dublin

Fenians, Ballintuber, MS 485.

Traditions of Captain Boycott Collected by Mrs. Liam Redmond, 1946, MS 1131.

Typescript of a Small Notebook Written by Connor Maguire, MD, of the Claremorris District of County Mayo, MS 1304.

National Library of Ireland

Clanmorris Estate Rental, 1867–1888, MS 3120.

Irish National Land League Papers, Mayo, MS 9291 (9).

J. F. X. O'Brien Papers: Letters To Very Rev. Father John O'Malley and J. F. X. O'Brien Regarding Tenant Difficulties in Mayo, 1879–1883, MS 13,457.

Public Record Office, Ireland

Householders' Returns, 1901 Census.

Lucan Rent Ledgers, 1848–73, Business Records, Mayo 13.

Parliamentary Voters, County of Mayo, Barony of Tyrawly, Barony of Kilmain, Barony of Gallen, Barony of Costello, Barony of Clanmorris; Copy of the Register of Persons Entitled To Vote At Any Election of a Member or Members of Parliament for the County of Mayo, Between the 30th Day of November 1856 and the 1st Day of December, 1857, MS 2782, 2783, 2784, 3447, 3448.

Rent Ledger, Walter M. Bourke Estate, Business Records, Mayo 11.

Public Record Office, Northern Ireland

Charles O'Hara of Nymphsfield, "A Survey of the Economic Development of County Sligo in the Eighteenth Century," (typed manuscript), T.2812/19/1.

Rental of the Earl of Erne's Mayo Estate, 1848–53, D1939/10/2.
Rental of the Earl of Erne's Mayo Estate, 1874–9, D1939/10/3.

State Paper Office, Dublin Castle

State of the Country Papers, 1802–19, 1821–8.
Outrage Papers, 1830–4.
Outrage Reports, 1846–7.
Police and Crime Records, Fenian Papers: Abstract of Cases of Persons Arrested Under the Habeas Corpus Suspension Act, 1866–8 (3 vols.); Fenianism, Index of Names, 1866–71; Fenian Photographs, 1866–70; Fenian Files (R), 1866–70.
Irish Crime Records: Descriptions of Fenian Suspects, 1866–72.
Chief Secretary's Office, Registered Papers, 1867–82.
Irish National Land League and Irish National League Papers, 1879–88: Cartons 1, 8, 9, 10.
Police and Crime Reports: No. 5: Protection of Persons and Property Act (Ireland), 1881. Carton 1, List of Persons Whose Arrest Is Recommended Under the Protection of Persons and Property Act (Ireland), 1881, Mayo. List of Persons Arrested Under the Protection of Persons and Property Act (Ireland), 1881, Mayo.
Queen versus Parnell and Other Persons Papers, 1880–1: Cartons 1, 4, 6, 8; Crime Branch Special Papers, 1890–1904.

Trinity College Library, University of Dublin

Base-Line Reports to the Congested Districts Board, 1892–8.
Davitt Papers: Letters from John J. Louden, 1889–90, 3/H/182–6; Miscellaneous Letters to Davitt, 1879–93, 5/V/468–84; Letters from Davitt to John Dillon, 1880–92, 17/BC/1554–74; Miscellaneous Letters and Papers, 1878–98, 25/A11/2607–92;Western Relief Fund, April 1886–July 1886, 27/A14/2856–2929; Miscellaneous Letters, 33/A26 (i)/3586–3612.

PUBLISHED MATERIAL

Parliamentary Papers, Ireland

Journals of the Honourable House of Commons, Ireland, 1613–1800, 19 vols., Dublin 1796–1800.

Parliamentary Papers, Britain

a. Returns of Agricultural Produce in Ireland (in chronological order)
   Returns of Agricultural Produce in Ireland in the Year 1847, Pt. I: Crops, PP 1847–8 [923], lvii, I.
   Returns of Agricultural Produce in Ireland in the Year 1847, Pt. II: Stock, PP 1847–8 [1000], lvii, 109.

Returns of Agricultural Produce . . . 1848, PP 1849 [1116], xlix, I.

Returns of Agricultural Produce . . . 1849, PP 1850 [1245], li, 39.

Returns of Agricultural Produce . . . 1850, PP 1851 [1404], 1, I.

The Census of Ireland For the Year 1851, Pt. II: Returns of Agricultural Produce in 1851, PP 1852–3 [1589], xciii, I.

Returns of Agricultural Produce . . . 1852, PP 1854 [1714], lvii, I.

Returns of Agricultural Produce . . . 1853, PP 1854–5 [1865], xlvii, I.

Returns of Agricultural Produce . . . 1854, PP 1856 [2017], liii, I.

Returns of Agricultural Produce . . . 1855, PP 1857 (sess. I) [2174], xv, 81.

Returns of Agricultural Produce . . . 1856, PP 1857–8 [2289[, lvi, I.

b. The Agricultural Statistics of Ireland (in chronological order)

The Agricultural Statistics of Ireland For the Year 1857, PP 1859 (sess. 2) [2641], xxvi, 57.

The Agricultural Statistics . . . 1858, PP 1860 [2599], lxvi, 55.

The Agricultural Statistics . . . 1859, PP 1861 [2763], lxii, 73.

The Agricultural Statistics . . . 1860, PP 1862 [2997], lx, 137.

The Agricultural Statistics . . . 1861, PP 1863 [3156], lxix, 547.

The Agricultural Statistics . . . 1862, PP 1864 [3286], lix, 327.

The Agricultural Statistics . . . 1863, PP 1865 [3456], lv, 125.

The Agricultural Statistics . . . 1864, PP 1867 [3766], lxxi, 201.

The Agricultural Statistics . . . 1865, PP 1867 [3929], lxxi, 491.

The Agricultural Statistics . . . 1866, PP 1867–8 [3958-II], lxxi, 255.

The Agricultural Statistics . . . 1867, PP 1868–9 [4113-II], lxii, 645.

The Agricultural Statistics . . . 1868, PP 1870 [C 3], lxviii, 439.

The Agricultural Statistics . . . 1869, PP 1871 [C 239], lxix, 347.

The Agricultural Statistics . . . 1870, PP 1872 [C 463], lxiii, 299.

The Agricultural Statistics . . . 1871, PP 1873 [C 762], lxix, 375.

The Agricultural Statistics . . . 1872, PP 1874 [C 880], lxix, 199.

The Agricultural Statistics . . . 1873, PP 1875 [C 1125], lxxix, 131.

The Agricultural Statistics . . . 1874, PP 1876 [C 1380], lxxviii, 131.

The Agricultural Statistics . . . 1875, PP 1876 [C 1568], lxxviii, 413.

The Agricultural Statistics . . . 1876, PP 1877 [C 1749], lxxxv, 529.

The Agricultural Statistics . . . 1877, PP 1878 [C 1938], lxxvii, 511.

The Agricultural Statistics . . . 1878, PP 1878–9 [C 2347], lxxv, 587.

The Agricultural Statistics . . . 1879, PP 1880 [C 2534], lxxvi, 815.

The Agricultural Statistics . . . 1880, PP 1881 [C 2932], xciii, 685.

The Agricultural Statistics . . . 1881, PP 1882 [C 3332], lxxiv, 93.

The Agricultural Statistics . . . 1882, PP 1883 [C 3677], lxxvi, 825.

The Agricultural Statistics . . . 1883, PP 1884 [C 4069], lxxxv, 313.

The Agricultural Statistics . . . 1884, PP 1884–5 [C 4489], lxxxv, I.

The Agricultural Statistics . . . 1885, PP 1886 [C 4802], lxxi, I.

The Agricultural Statistics . . . 1886, PP 1887 [C 5084], lxxxix, I.

The Agricultural Statistics . . . 1887, PP 1888 [C 5477], cvi, 415.

The Agricultural Statistics . . . 1888, PP 1889 [C 5785], lxxxiii, 215.

The Agricultural Statistics . . . 1889, PP 1890 [C 6099], lxxix, 371.

The Agricultural Statistics . . . 1890, PP 1890–1 [C 6518], xci, 277.

The Agricultural Statistics . . . 1891, PP 1892 [C 6777], lxxxviii, 285.

Agricultural Statistics of Ireland, With Detailed Report on Agriculture, For the Year 1892, PP 1893–4 [C 7187], ci, 285.

Agricultural Statistics . . . 1893, PP 1894 [C 7531], xciii, 173.

Agricultural Statistics . . . 1894, PP 1895 [C 7763], cvi, 315.

Agricultural Statistics . . . 1895, PP 1896 [C 8126], xcii, 309.

Agricultural Statistics . . . 1896, PP 1897 [C 8510], xcviii, 359.

Agricultural Statistics . . . 1897, PP 1898 [C 8885], cii, 321.

Agricultural Statistics . . . 1898, PP 1899 [C 9389], cvi, 325.

Agricultural Statistics . . . 1899, PP 1900 [Cd 143], ci, 311.

Agricultural Statistics . . . 1900, PP 1901 [Cd 577], lxxxviii, 313.

c. Returns of Cases of Eviction (in chronological order)

Returns From the Courts of the Queen's Bench, Common Pleas and Exchequer in Ireland, Of the Number of Ejectments Brought In Those Courts Respectively For the Last Three Years Beginning With Hilary Term 1846 and Ending With Hilary Term 1849, Both Included; Specifying the Number In Each Term and Year and the Counties In Which They Have Been Brought, and the Number of Persons Served In Each Ejectment, According To the Affidavits Of Service, Distinguishing the Number Brought For Non-Payment of Rent and the Number Brought For Over-Holding; and From the Assistant Barrister's Court of Each County in Ireland, Of the Number of Civil Bill Ejectments Entered In Each Of Such Courts For a Similar Period, Together With the Number of Defendants In Each Civil Bill Ejectment and Distinguishing the Number Sued For Non-Payment Of Rent, and the Number For Over-Holding and the Number for Desertion, PP 1849 (315), xlix, 235.

Return By Provinces and Counties (Compiled From Returns Made To the Inspector General, Royal Irish Constabulary) Of Cases of Evictions Which Have Come To the Knowledge of the Constabulary In Each of the Years From 1849–1880 Inclusive, PP 1881 (185), lxxvii, 725.

Return (Compiled From Returns To the Inspector General, Royal Irish Constabulary) of Cases of Evictions Which Have Come To the Knowledge of the Constabulary In Each Quarter of the Year Ended 31st Day of December 1880, Showing the Number of Families Evicted In Each County in Ireland During Each Quarter, the Number Readmitted As Tenants and the Number Readmitted As Caretakers, PP 1881 (2), lxxvii, 713.

Return . . . In Each Quarter of the Year Ended 31st Day of December 1881 . . ., PP 1882 (9), lv, 229.

Return . . . In Each Quarter of the Year Ended 31st Day of December 1882 . . ., PP 1882 [C 3465], lvi, 99.

Return of Cases of Eviction Which Have Come To the Knowledge of the Constabulary In the Quarter Ended 31st Day of March 1883 . . . In Each County . . ., PP 1883 [C 3579], lvi, 107.

Return . . . In Each Quarter Ending the 30th Day of June 1883 . . ., PP 1883 [C 3770], liv, 111.

Return . . . In Each Quarter Ending the 30th Day of September 1883 . . ., PP 1884 [C 3893], lxiv, 407.

Return . . . In Each Quarter Ending the 31st Day of December 1883 . . . , PP 1884 [C 3892], lxiv, 411.

Return . . . In Each Quarter Ending the 31st Day of March 1884 . . . , PP 1884 [C 3994], lxiv, 415.

Return . . . In Each Quarter Ending the 30th Day of June 1884 . . . , PP 1884 [C 4089], lxiv, 419.

Return . . . In Each Quarter Ending the 30th Day of September 1884 . . . , PP 1884–5 [C 4102], lxv, 29.

Return . . . In Each Quarter Ending the 31st Day of December 1884 . . . , PP 1884–5 [C 4300], lxv, 33.

Return . . . In Each Quarter Ending the 31st Day of March 1885 . . . , PP 1884–5 [C 4394], lxv, 37.

Return . . . In Each Quarter Ending the 30th Day of June 1885 . . . , PP 1884–5 [C 4485], lxv, 41.

Return . . . In Each Quarter Ending the 30th Day of September 1885 . . . , PP 1886 [C 4618], liv, 29.

Return . . . In Each Quarter Ending the 31st Day of December 1885 . . . , PP 1886 [C 4619], liv, 33.

Return . . . In Each Quarter Ending the 31st Day of March 1886 . . . , PP 1886 [C 4720], liv, 37.

Return . . . In Each Quarter Ending the 30th Day of June 1886 . . . , PP 1886 [C 4875], liv, 41.

Return . . . In Each Quarter Ending the 30th Day of September 1886 . . . , PP 1887 [C 4946], lxviii, 41.

Return . . . In Each Quarter Ending the 31st Day of December 1886 . . . , PP 1887 [C 4947], lxviii, 55.

Return . . . In Each Quarter Ending the 31st Day of March 1887 . . . , PP 1887 [C 5037], lxviii, 59.

Return . . . In Each Quarter Ending the 30th Day of June 1887 . . . , PP 1887 [C 5095], lxviii, 63.

Return . . . In Each Quarter Ending the 30th Day of September 1887 . . . , PP 1888 [C 5289], lxxxiii, 433.

Return . . . In Each Quarter Ending the 31st Day of December 1887 . . . , PP 1888 [C 5290], lxxxiii, 437.

Return of the Number of Evictions From Agricultural Holdings Which Have Come to the Knowledge of the Constabulary, and Also the Number of Tenancies Determined in the Quarter Ended the 31st Day of March 1888, Showing: Actual Evictions Under the Provisions of the Land Law Act, 1887, and Under Other Processes of Law, the Number of Evictions, Not At Suit of Landlord for Debt, Foreclosure of Mortgage, etc., PP 1888 [C 5405], lxxxiii, 441.

Return . . . in the Quarter Ended the 30th Day of June 1888 . . . , PP 1888 [C 5498], lxxxiii, 447.

Return . . . in the Quarter Ended the 30th Day of September 1888 . . . , PP 1888 [C 5583], lxxxiii, 453.

Return . . . in the Quarter Ended the 31st Day of December 1888 . . . , PP 1889 [C 5642], lxi, 545.

Return . . . in the Quarter Ended the 31st Day of March 1889 . . ., PP 1889 [C 5700], lxi, 551.

Return . . . in the Quarter Ended the 30th Day of June 1889 . . ., PP 1889 [C 5784], lxi, 557.

Return . . . in the Quarter Ended the 30th Day of September 1889 . . ., PP 1890 [C 5935], lx, I.

Return . . . in the Quarter Ended the 31st Day of December 1889 . . ., PP 1890 [C 5936], lx, 7.

Return . . . in the Quarter Ended the 31st Day of March 1890 . . ., PP 1890 [C 6018], lx, 13.

Return . . . in the Quarter Ended the 31st Day of June 1890 . . ., PP 1890 [C6093], lx, 19.

Return . . . in the Quarter Ended the 30th Day of September 1890 . . ., PP 1890–1 [C 6231], lxv, I.

Return . . . in the Quarter Ended the 31st Day of December 1890 . . ., PP 1890–1 [C 6262], lxv, 7.

Return . . . in the Quarter Ended the 31st Day of March 1891 . . ., PP 1890–1 [C 6345], lxv, 13.

Return . . . in the Quarter Ended the 30th Day of June 1891 . . ., PP 1890–1 [C 6481], lxv, 19.

Return . . . in the Quarter Ended the 30th Day of September 1891 . . ., PP 1892 [C 6580], lxv, 447.

Return . . . in the Quarter Ended the 31st Day of December 1891 . . ., PP 1892 [C 6581], lxv, 483.

Return . . . in the Quarter Ended the 31st Day of March 1892 . . ., PP 1892 [C 6667], lxv, 489.

Return . . . in the Quarter Ended the 30th Day of June 1892 . . ., PP 1892 [C 6784], lxv, 495.

Return . . . in the Quarter Ended the 30th Day of September 1892 . . ., PP 1893–4 [C 6872], lxxiv, pt. II, 451.

Return . . . in the Quarter Ended the 31st Day of December 1892 . . ., PP 1893–4 [C 6882], lxxiv, pt. II, 457.

Return . . . in the Quarter Ended the 31st Day of March 1893 . . ., PP 1893–4 [C 6995], lxxiv, pt. II, 463.

Return . . . in the Quarter Ended the 30th Day of June 1893 . . ., PP 1893–4 [C 7099], lxxiv, pt. II, 469.

Return . . . in the Quarter Ended the 30th Day of September 1893 . . ., PP 1893–4 [C 7210], lxxiv, pt. II, 475.

Return . . . in the Quarter Ended the 31st Day of December 1893 . . ., PP 1893–4 [C 7273], lxxiv, pt. II, 481.

Return . . . in the Quarter Ended the 31st Day of March 1894 . . ., PP 1894 [C 7364], lxxii, 63.

Return . . . in the Quarter Ended the 30th Day of June 1894 . . ., PP 1894 [C 7462], lxxii, 69.

Return . . . in the Quarter Ended the 30th Day of September 1894 . . ., PP 1895 [C 7617], lxxxii, 129.

Return . . . in the Quarter Ended the 31st Day of December 1894 . . ., PP 1895 [C 7618], lxxxii, 135.

Return . . . in the Quarter Ended the 31st Day of March 1895 . . ., PP 1895 [C 7724], lxxxii, 141.

Return . . . in the Quarter Ended the 30th Day of June 1895 . . ., PP 1895 [C 7850], lxxxii, 147.

Return . . . in the Quarter Ended the 30th Day of September 1895 . . ., PP 1896 [C 7965], lxix, 615.

Return . . . in the Quarter Ended the 31st Day of December 1895 . . ., PP 1896 [C 7966], lxix, 621.

Return . . . in the Quarter Ended the 31st Day of March 1896, PP 1896 [C 8058], lxix, 627.

Return . . . in the Quarter Ended the 30th Day of June 1896 . . ., PP 1896 [C 8166], lxix, 633.

Return . . . in the Quarter Ended the 30th Day of September 1896 . . ., PP 1897 [C 8293], lxxxiii, 315.

Return . . . in the Quarter Ended the 31st Day of December 1896 . . ., PP 1897 [C 8321], lxxxiii, 321.

Return . . . in the Quarter Ended the 31st Day of March 1897 . . ., PP 1897 [C 8467], lxxxiii, 327.

Return . . . in the Quarter Ended the 30th Day of June 1897 . . ., PP 1897 [C 8556], lxxxiii, 333.

Return . . . in the Quarter Ended the 30th Day of September 1897 . . ., PP 1898 [C 8689], lxxiv, 171.

Return . . . in the Quarter Ended the 31st Day of December 1897 . . ., PP 1898 [C 8726], lxxiv, 177.

Return . . . in the Quarter Ended the 31st Day of March 1898 . . ., PP 1898 [C 8878], lxxiv, 183.

Return . . . in the Quarter Ended the 30th Day of June 1898 . . ., PP 1898 [C 8969], lxxiv, 189.

Return . . . in the Quarter Ended the 30th Day of September 1898 . . ., PP 1899 [C 9099], lxxix, 679.

Return . . . in the Quarter Ended the 31st Day of December 1898 . . ., PP 1899 [C 9168], lxxix, 685.

Return . . . in the Quarter Ended the 31st Day of March 1899 . . ., PP 1899 [C 9274], lxxix, 691.

Return . . . in the Quarter Ended the 30th Day of June 1899 . . ., PP 1899 [C 9447], lxxix, 697.

Return . . . in the Quarter Ended the 30th Day of September 1899 . . ., PP 1900 [Cd 11], lxix, 657.

Return . . . in the Quarter Ended the 31st Day of December 1899 . . ., PP 1900 [Cd 51], lxix, 663.

Return . . . in the Quarter Ended the 31st Day of March 1900 . . ., PP 1900 [Cd 163], lxix, 669.

Return . . . in the Quarter Ended the 30th Day of June 1900 . . ., PP 1900 [Cd 298], lxix, 675.

Return ... in the Quarter Ended the 30th Day of September 1900 ..., PP 1900 [Cd 400], lxix, 681.

Return ... in the Quarter Ended the 31st Day of December 1900 ..., PP 1901 [Cd 472], lxi, 535.

d. Other Parliamentary Papers (in chronological order)

Report from the Select Committee on the Employment of the Poor in Ireland, PP 1823 (561), vi, 331.

Abstract of Answers and Returns Pursuant to Act 55. Geo. 3, For Taking an Account of the Population of Ireland in 1821: Part IV, Province of Connaught, PP 1824 (577), xxii, 411.

Minutes of Evidence Taken Before the Select Committee of the House of Lords Appointed to Inquire into the State of Ireland, More Particularly With Reference to the Circumstances Which May Have Led to Disturbances in That Part of the United Kingdom, PP 1825 (521), ix, 249.

First Report from the Select Committee on the State of Ireland, PP 1825 (129), viii, I.

Second Report from the Select Committee on the State of Ireland, PP 1825 (129 continued), viii, 173.

Abstract of the Population Returns, 1831: Part VI, Province of Connaught, PP 1833 (634), xxxix, 59.

First Report From His Majesty's Commissioners for Inquiring Into the Condition of the Poorer Classes in Ireland, Appendix (A) and Supplement, PP 1835 (369), xxxii, pt. 1, I.

Poor Inquiry (Ireland): Appendix (E) Containing Baronial Examinations Relative to Food, Cottages and Cabins, Clothing and Furniture, Pawnbroking and Savings Banks, Drinking and Supplement Containing Answers to Questions 13 to 22 Circulated by the Commissioners, PP 1836 [37], xxxii, I.

Poor Inquiry (Ireland): Appendix (F) Containing Baronial Examinations Relative to Con-Acre, Quarter or Score Ground, Small Tenantry, Consolidation of Farms and Dislodged Tenantry, Emigration, Landlord and Tenant, Nature and State of Agriculture, Taxation, Roads, Observations on the Nature and State of Agriculture: and Supplement, PP 1836 [38], xxxiii, I.

Report of the Commissioners Appointed to Take the Census of Ireland for the Year 1841, PP 1843 (504), xxiv, I.

Report from Her Majesty's Commissioners of Inquiry into the State of Law and Practice in Respect to the Occupation of Land in Ireland, PP 1845 [605], xix, I.

Evidence Taken Before Her Majesty's Commissioners of Inquiry into the State of the Law and Practice in Respect to the Occupation of Land in Ireland, Pt. I, PP 1845 [606], xix, 57.

Evidence Taken Before Her Majesty's Commissioners of Inquiry into the State of the Law and Practice in Respect to the Occupation of Land in Ireland, Pt. II, PP 1845 [616], xx, I.

Evidence Taken Before Her Majesty's Commissioners of Inquiry into the State of the Law and Practice in Respect to the Occupation of Land in Ireland, Pt. III, PP 1845 [657], xxi, I.

Evidence Taken Before Her Majesty's Commissioners of Inquiry into the State of the Law and Practice in Respect to the Occupation of Land in Ireland, Pt. IV, PP 1845 [672], xxii, I.

A Return from the Poor Law Commissioners, Showing the Name of Each Union in Ireland; the Name of the County in Which Situated; the Name of Each Electoral Division in Each Union; the Total Numbers of Occupiers in Each Electoral Division on Whom the Rate is Made; the Total Estimated Extent of Statute Acres in Each Electoral Division, the Rate for Which Is Made on the Occupier; the Total Number of Hereditaments Not Exceeding £4 in Each Electoral Division, for Which the Rate is Made on the Immediate Lessor; the Total Estimated Extent, Statute Acres, in Each Electoral Division, the Rate for Which is Made on the Immediate Lessor; the Total Estimated Extent of Bog or Waste not Rated in Each Electoral Division, PP 1846 (262), xxxvi, 469.

Copies or Extracts of Correspondence Relating to the State of Union Workhouses in Ireland, PP 1847 [766], lv, 27.

Papers Relating to Proceedings for the Relief of the Distress and State of Unions and Workhouses, Fourth Series, 1847, PP 1847–8 [896], liv, I.

Papers Relating to Proceedings for the Relief of the Distress and State of Unions and Workhouses, Fifth Series, 1848, PP 1847–8 [919], lv, I.

Papers Relating to Proceedings for the Relief of the Distress and State of Unions and Workhouses, Sixth Series, 1848, PP 1847–8 [955], lvi, I.

Papers Relating to Proceedings for the Relief of the Distress and State of Unions and Workhouses, Seventh Series, 1848, PP 1847–8 [999], liv, 313.

Papers Relating to Proceedings for the Relief of the Distress and State of Unions and Workhouses, Eighth Series, 1849, PP 1849 [1042], xlviii, I.

First Report of the Commissioners Appointed to Inquire Into the Number and Boundaries of the Poor Law Unions and Electoral Divisions in Ireland, With Appendix and Plans, PP 1849 [1015], xxiii, 369.

A Return in Continuation of Parliamentary Papers No. 311, of the Session of 1848, and in the Same Tabular Form, of the Valuation of Each Electoral Division in Ireland, With Its Population in 1841, and the Total Poundage Directed To Be Raised By Any Rate or Rates Made Upon Every Such Electoral Division During the Years Ending the 31st Day of December 1848; Distinguishing the Unions in Which Out-Door Relief Has Been Administered for the Able-Bodied Poor, Made Under the Order to the Poor Law Commissioners, and Specifying the Date of Such Order, PP 1849 (198), xlix, 243.

Minutes of Evidence Taken Before the Select Committee on the Mayo Election Petition, Together With the Proceedings of the Committee, PP 1852–3 (415), xvi, 221.

Abstract Return of the Number of Electors on the Register of 1852–3 in Each County, City and Borough in Ireland, Distinguishing their Qualifications, PP 1852–3 (957), lxxxiii, 413.

Report of the Commissioners Appointed to Inquire into the State of the Fairs and Markets in Ireland, PP 1852–3 [1674], xli, 79.

The Census of Ireland for the Year 1851, Pt. I: Showing the Area, Population and the Number of Houses, By Townlands and Electoral Divisions, Vol. IV, Province of Connaught, County of Mayo, PP 1852–3 [1542], xcii, 453.

The Census of Ireland for the Year 1851, Part V: Tables of Deaths, Vol. I, PP 1856 [2078-I], xxix, 261.

The Census of Ireland for the Year 1851, Part VI: General Report, PP 1856 [2134], xxxi, I.

Minutes of Evidence Taken Before the Select Committee on the Mayo Election Petition, With the Proceedings of The Committee and Index, PP 1857 (session 2) (182), vii, 357.

A Return of the Number of Electors in Every County, City and Borough in Ireland, According to the Register Now in Force, PP 1859 (sess. 1) (140-I), xxiii, 145.

Census of Ireland for the Year 1861, Pt. V: General Report, PP 1863 [3204-IV], lxi, I.

Return in Tabular Form for the Year 1864 of the Number of Electors on the Register of Each County in Ireland, PP 1865 (448), xliv, 549.

Report From the Select Committee on General Valuation (Ireland), Together With the Proceedings of the Committee, Minutes of Evidence, Appendix, and Index, PP 1868–9 (362), ix, I.

First Annual Report of the Registrar General of Marriages, Births, and Deaths in Ireland, 1864, PP 1868–9 [4137], xvi, 665.

Return Relating to Constituencies (Ireland), PP 1874 (45), liii, 557.

Copy of the Special Case and of the Shorthand Writer's Notes of the Judgement of Each of the Judges for the Court of Common Pleas in Ireland, in the Matter of the County Mayo Election Petition, PP 1874 (165), liii, 747.

The Census of Ireland for the Year 1871, Pt. I: Area, Houses and Population; Also the Ages, Civil Condition, Occupations, Birthplaces, Religion, and Education of the People, Vol. IV, Province of Connaught, No. 3, County of Mayo, PP 1874 [C 1106-III], lxxiv, 273.

Return of Owners of Land of One Acre and Upwards In the Several Counties, Counties of Cities and Counties of Towns in Ireland, Showing the Names of Such Owners Arranged Alphabetically In Each County; Their Addresses – As Far As Could Be Ascertained – The Extent In Statute Acres, and the Valuation In Each Case; Together With the Number of Owners in Each County of Less Than One Statute Acre in Extent; and the Total Area and Valuation of Such Proprietors; and the Grand Total of Area and Valuation for All Owners of Property in Each County, County of a City or County of a Town, To Which Is Added a Summary For Each Province and For All Ireland, PP 1876 [C 1492], lxxx, 61.

Return Showing All Crimes Against Human Life, Firing Into Dwelling Houses, Administering Unlawful Oaths, Demands of Money, Threatening Letters, or Other Intimidation, Incendiary Fires, Robbery of Arms, etc., Reported by the Royal Irish Constabulary Between 1st March 1878 and 31st December 1879; Both Dates Inclusive: Distinguishing As Far As Possible

Agrarian Crimes, and Showing: Number of Names of Persons Convicted; Number and Names of Persons Made Amenable, but Not Convicted; Number of Cases in Which No Person Was Made Amenable, PP 1880 (6), lx, I.

Return of All Agrarian Outrages Reported by the Royal Irish Constabulary Between the 1st January 1879 and the 31st January 1880, Giving Particulars of Crime, Arrests, and Results of Proceedings, PP 1880 (131), lx, 199.

Return of All Agrarian Crimes and Outrages Reported by The Royal Irish Constabulary in the Counties of Galway, Mayo, Sligo, and Donegal From 1st February 1880 to 30th June 1880; Number of Meetings Promoting the Land Agitation Reported by the Constabulary Within the Same Counties Since 30th June 1879; Number of Cases Reported by the Constabulary in Which Resistance Was Offered to the Police When Protecting Process Servers, Bailiffs, and Others in the Execution of Their Duty, etc., PP 1880 (327), lx, 291.

Return in Numbers in Receipt of Relief in the Several Unions in Ireland on the 1st Day of January, the 1st Day of March and the 1st Day of June in 1878, 1879, and 1880, PP 1880 (sess. 2) (420-II), lxii, 289.

Preliminary Report on the Returns of Agricultural Produce in Ireland in 1879; With Tables, PP 1880 [C 2495], lxxvi, 893.

Royal Commission on the Depressed Condition of the Agricultural Interest: Minutes of Evidence, Vol. I, PP 1881 [C 2778-I], xv, 25.

Royal Commission on the Depressed Condition of the Agricultural Interest: Minutes of Evidence, Vol. II, PP 1881 [C 3069], xvii, I.

Preliminary Report of the Assistant Commissioners for Ireland, PP 1881 [C 2951], xvi, 841.

Report of Her Majesty's Commissioners of Inquiry Into the Working of the Landlord and Tenant (Ireland) Act, 1870, and the Acts Amending the Same, PP 1881 [C 2779], xviii, I.

Report of Her Majesty's Commissioners of Inquiry Into the Working of the Landlord and Tenant (Ireland) Act, 1870, and the Acts Amending the Same, Vol. II: Digest of Evidence, Minutes of Evidence, Pt. I, PP 1881 [C 2779-I], xviii, 73.

Report of Her Majesty's Commissioners of Inquiry Into the Working of the Landlord and Tenant (Ireland) Act, 1870, and the Acts Amending the Same, Vol. III: Minutes of Evidence, Pt. II; Appendices, PP 1881 [C 2779-II], xix, I.

Return In Tabular Form, As Under the Civil Bill Ejectments On the Title From Those For Non-Payment of Rent, Tried and Determined In Each County In Ireland For Each of the Four Years Ending the 31st Day of December 1880, Exclusive of Ejectments For Premises Situated In Counties of Cities, Boroughs and Towns Under the Act 9, George 4, c. 82, Or, "The Towns" Improvement (Ireland) Act 1854 or Any Local Act, PP 1881 (90), lxxvii, 685.

Return Showing For Each Month of 1879 and 1880 the Number of Land League Meetings Held and Agrarian Crimes Reported to the Inspector

General of the Royal Irish Constabulary, in Each County Throughout Ireland, PP 1881 (5), lxxvii, 793.

Return of the Number of Agrarian Offences in Each County in Ireland Reported to the Constabulary Office in Each Month of 1880, Distinguishing Offences Against Person, Offences Against Property, and Offences Against the Public Peace, With Summary for Each County for the Year, PP 1881 (12), lxxviii, 619.

Agricultural Statistics, Ireland, 1880, Report and Tables Relating to Migratory Agricultural Labourers, PP 1881 [C 2809], xciii, 813.

Return of the Number of Agrarian Offences in Each County in Ireland Reported to the Constabulary Office in Each Month of 1881, Distinguishing Offences Against Person, Offences Against Property, and Offences Against the Public Peace, With Summary for Each County for the Year, PP 1882 (8), lv, I.

Return By Provinces of Agrarian Offences Throughout Ireland Reported to the Inspector General of the Royal Irish Constabulary Between the 1st Day of January 1881 and the 31st Day of December 1881, Showing the Number of Cases in Which Offenders Were Convicted; the Number of Cases in Which Persons Were Made Amenable But Not Convicted; the Number of Cases in Which Accused are Awaiting Trial; and the Number of Cases in Which Offenders Were Neither Convicted Nor Made Amenable, PP 1882 (72), lv, 17.

The Census of Ireland for the Year 1881, Part I: Area, Houses and Population, Vol. III, Province of Connaught, No. 3, County of Mayo, PP 1882 [C 3268-III], lxxix, 273.

Return By Province of Agrarian Offences Throughout Ireland Reported to the Inspector General of the Royal Irish Constabulary Between the 1st Day of January 1882 and the 31st Day of December 1882, Showing the Number of Cases in Which Offenders Were Convicted; the Number of Cases in Which Persons Were Made Amenable But Not Convicted; the Number of Cases in Which Accused Are Awaiting Trial; and the Number of Cases in Which Offenders Were Neither Convicted Nor Made Amenable, PP 1883 (12), lvi, I.

Return Showing for Each County in Ireland For the Year Ending 22 August 1882 and For Each Month From September 1882 to April 1883, the Number of Applicants for Fair Rents Lodged in the Land Commission Court, Those Fixed, Dismissed, Struck Out and Withdrawn, the Number of Agreements Out of Court, and of Appeals Lodged, Heard and Withdrawn, PP 1883 (352), lvii, 977.

Report of the Special Commission, 1881, Appendix IV, PP 1890 [C 5891], xxviii, 477.

The Census of Ireland for the Year 1891, Part I: Area, Houses and Population: Also the Ages, Civil or Conjugal Condition, Occupations, Birthplaces, Religion and Education of the People, Vol. IV, Province of Connaught, No. 3, County of Mayo, PP 1892 [C 6685-II], xciii, 277.

The Census of Ireland for the Year 1901, Part I: Area, Houses and Population: Also the Ages, Civil or Conjugal Condition, Occupations, Birthplaces,

Religion and Education of the People, Vol. IV, Province of Connaught, No. 3, County of Mayo, PP 1902 [Cd 1059-II] cxxviii, 365.

Thirty-Eighth Detailed Annual Report of the Registrar General (Ireland), Containing a General Abstract of the Number of Marriages, Births and Deaths Registered in Ireland During the Year 1901, PP 1902 [Cd 1902], xviii, 501.

Newspapers

Ballinrobe Chronicle and Mayo Advertiser (Ballinrobe)
The Connaught Telegraph (Castlebar)
The Freeman's Journal (Dublin)
Gaelic American (New York)
The Telegraph or Connaught Ranger (Castlebar)
The Times (London)

Other contemporary records

Calendar of State Papers Relating to Ireland, 1509–1670, 24 vols., London, 1860–1912.

Dunlop, Robert (ed.), *Ireland Under the Commonwealth: Being A Selection of Documents Relating to the Government of Ireland from 1651–1659,* 2 vols., Manchester, 1913.

Firth, C. H. and R. S. Riat (eds.), *Acts and Ordinances of the Interregnum, 1642–1660,* 3 vols., London, 1911.

Freeman, A. M. (ed.), *The Compossicion Booke of Conought,* Dublin, 1936.

General Valuation of Rateable Property in Ireland, County Mayo, Dublin, 1857.

Historical Manuscript Commission, *The Manuscripts of the Marquis of Ormonde,* 2 vols., London, 1899.

MacParlan, James, *Statistical Survey of the County of Mayo,* Dublin, 1802.

O'Brien, William and Desmond Ryan (eds.), *Devoy's Post Bag, 1871–1928,* 2 vols., Dublin, 1948.

O'Sullivan, W. O. (ed.), *The Strafford Inquisition of County Mayo,* Dublin, 1958.

Ridgeway, William, *A Report of the Proceedings Under A Special Commission, of Oyer and Terminer, and Gaol Delivery for the Counties of Sligo, Mayo, Leitrim, Longford and Cavan, in the Month of December 1806,* Dublin, 1807.

Simington, R. C. (ed.), *Books of Survey and Distribution,* 4 vols., Dublin, 1949–67.

(ed.), *The Transplantation to Connacht, 1654–58,* Shannon, Ireland, 1970.

Special Commission Act, 1888: Report of the Proceedings Before the Commissioners Appointed By the Act, Reprinted From The Times, 4 vols., London, 1890.

The Irish Crisis of 1879–80: Proceedings of the Mansion House Relief Committee, 1880, Dublin, 1881.

Wakefield, Edward, *An Account of Ireland: Statistical and Political,* 2 vols., London, 1812.

Other contemporary works

Becker, Bernard, *Disturbed Ireland*, London, 1881.

Bede, *A History of the English Church and People*, rev. ed., Harmondsworth, Middlesex, 1965.

Blake, H. and Family (attributed), *Letters from the Irish Highlands*, London, 1825.

Blunt, Wilfrid Scawen, *The Land War in Ireland*, London, 1912.

Bourke, Rev. Ulick Canon, *A Plea For the Evicted Tenants of Mayo*, 3rd ed., Dublin, 1883.

Cashman, D. B., *The Life of Michael Davitt to Which Is Added the Secret History of the Land League by Michael Davitt*, Glasgow, n.d.

Coulter, Henry, *The West of Ireland: Its Existing Condition and Prospects*, Dublin, 1862.

Davitt, Michael, *The Fall of Feudalism in Ireland*, London and New York, 1904.

Devoy, John, *The Land of Eire: The Irish Land League, Its Origins, Progress and Consequences*, New York, 1882.

"Davitt's Career, I–XVII," *Gaelic American*, New York, 9 June–3 November 1906.

Recollections of an Irish Rebel, New York, 1929.

Dun, Finlay, *Landlords and Tenants in Ireland*, London, 1881.

Foster, Thomas Campbell, *Letters on the Condition of the People of Ireland*, London, 1846.

Healy, Timothy M., *Letters and Leaders of My Day*, 2 vols., London, n.d.

James, Henry, *The Work of the Irish Leagues: The Speech of the Right Hon. Sir Henry James, QC, MP, Replying in the Parnell Commission Inquiry*, London, n.d.

Jobit, J. L., "Journal de l'expedition d'Irlande suivi de notes sur le Général Humber qui l'a commandé," *Analecta Hibernica*, no. 11 (1941), Nuala Costello (ed.), pp. 7–55.

Kettle, A. J., *The Material for Victory*, L. J. Kettle (ed.), Dublin, 1958.

Knight, P., *Erris in the Irish Highlands and the Atlantic Railway*, Dublin, 1836.

Lavelle, Patrick, *The Irish Landlord Since the Revolution*, Boston, 1870.

Lecky, W. E. H., *A History of Ireland in the Eighteenth Century*, 8 vols., London, 1906.

Little, James, "Little's Diary of the French Landing in 1798," *Analecta Hibernica*, no. 11 (1941), Nuala Costello (ed.), pp. 59–168.

Musgrave, Richard, *Memoirs of the Different Rebellions in Ireland*, Dublin, 1801.

O'Brien, R. Barry, *The Life of Charles Stewart Parnell, 1846–1891*, 2 vols., New York, 1898.

O'Brien, William, *Recollections*, New York and London, 1905.

O'Connor, T. P., *Memoirs of an Old Parliamentarian*, 2 vols., London and New York, 1929.

O'Reilly, Bernard, *John McHale, Archbishop of Tuam: His Life and Correspondence*, New York and Cincinnati, 1890.

O'Shea, Katherine, *Charles Stewart Parnell: His Love Story and Political Life*, 2 vols., London, 1914.

Otway, Caesar, *Sketches in Erris and Tyrawly*, Dublin, 1841.

Power, John O'Connor, "Fallacies About Home Rule," *Fortnightly Review*, new series, 26 (1879), pp. 224–35.

"The Irish Land Agitation," *The Nineteenth Century*, 6 (1879), pp. 953–67.

"The Irish in England," *Fortnightly Review*, new series, 27 (1880), pp. 410–21.

"The New Reform," *The Nineteenth Century*, 17 (1885), pp. 15–24.

Redpath, James, *Talks About Ireland*, New York, 1881.

Russell, Sir Charles, *The Parnell Commission, The Opening Speech for the Defence*, 3rd ed., London, 1889.

Ryan, Mark, *Fenian Memories*, ed. with intro. by T. F. Sullivan, 2nd ed., Dublin, 1946.

Stock, Joseph, *A Narrative of What Passed at Killala in the County of Mayo and the Parts Adjacent During the French Invasion in the Summer of 1798, by an Eye-Witness*, Dublin, 1800; reprinted Ballina, Ireland, 1982, G. Freyer (ed.).

Thackeray, William Makepeace, *The Irish Sketchbook*, London and Glasgow, n.d.

Tuke, James H., *Irish Distress and Its Remedies: The Land Question, A Visit to Donegal and Connaught in the Spring of 1880*, London, 1880.

Tynan, Katherine, *Twenty-five Years: Reminiscences*, London, 1913.

Young, Arthur, *A Tour in Ireland: With General Observations on the Present State of that Kingdom, Made in the Years 1776, 1777, 1778 and Brought Down to the End of 1779*, 2 vols., London, 1780; 4th ed., A. W. Hutton, 2 vols., London, 1892.

LATER WORKS

PUBLISHED WORKS

Aalen, F. H. A., *Man and the Landscape in Ireland*, London, 1978.

Andrews, J. H., "Land and People, c. 1780," in T. W. Moody and W. E. Vaughan (eds.), *A New History of Ireland, Vol. IV: Eighteenth Century Ireland, 1691–1800*, Oxford, 1986, pp. 236–64.

Bagwell, Richard, *Ireland Under the Stuarts and During the Interregnum*, 3 vols., London, 1909–16.

Baker, A. R. H. and R. A. Butlin, *Studies of Field Systems in the British Isles*, Cambridge, 1973.

Barrington, Richard M., *Notes on the Prices of Irish Agricultural Produce: A Paper Read Before the Statistical and Social Inquiry Society of Ireland, Wednesday 1st March 1893*, Dublin, 1893.

Barrington, Thomas, "A Review of Irish Agricultural Prices," *Journal of the Statistical and Social Inquiry Society of Ireland*, 15 (1927), pp. 249–80.

Bartlett, Thomas, "Select Documents XXXVIII: Defenders and Defenderism in 1795," *Irish Historical Studies*, 24 (1985), pp. 373–94.

"An End to Moral Economy: The Irish Militia Disturbances of 1793," in C. H. E. Philpin (ed.), *Nationalism and Popular Protest in Ireland*, Cambridge, 1987, pp. 191–218.

Beames, Michael R., *Peasants and Power: The Whiteboy Movements and their Control in Pre-Famine Ireland*, Brighton and New York, 1983.

"The Ribbon Societies: Lower Class Nationalism in Pre-Famine Ireland," in C. H. E. Philpin (ed.), *Nationalism and Popular Protest in Ireland*, Cambridge, 1987, pp. 245–63.

Bew, Paul, *Land and the National Question in Ireland, 1858–82*, Dublin, 1978.

C. S. Parnell, Dublin, 1980.

Bieler, L., *History of Irish Catholicism, Vol. I: St. Patrick and the Coming of Christianity*, Dublin and Melbourne, 1967.

Bottigheimer, Karl S., *English Money and Irish Land: The "Adventurers" in the Cromwellian Settlement of Ireland*, Oxford, 1971.

Bowen, Desmond, *The Protestant Crusade in Ireland, 1800–70*, Dublin, 1978.

Bric, Maurice, "Priests, Parsons and Politics: The Rightboy Protest in County Cork, 1785–1788," in C. H. E. Philpin (ed.), *Nationalism and Popular Protest in Ireland*, Cambridge, 1987, pp. 163–90.

Brown, Thomas, N., *Irish-American Nationalism, 1870–1890*, Philadelphia and New York, 1966.

Buckley, Barbara, "The Geology of Mayo," in Bernard O'Hara (ed.), *Mayo: Aspects of Its Heritage*, Galway, 1982, pp. 201–6.

Butler, W. F. T., *Confiscation in Irish History*, Port Washington, New York, 1970. Reprinted, Dublin, 1917.

Carroll, Kenneth L., "Quaker Weavers at Newport, Ireland, 1720–1740," *Journal of the Friends' Historical Society*, 54 (1976), pp. 15–27.

Carter, Ernest R., *An Historical Geography of the Railways of the British Isles*, London, 1959.

Clark, Samuel, "The Social Composition of the Land League," *Irish Historical Studies*, 17 (1971), pp. 447–69.

"The Political Mobilization of Irish Farmers," *Canadian Review of Sociology and Anthropology*, 12 (1975), pp. 483–99.

"The Importance of Agrarian Classes: Agrarian Class Structure and Collective Action in Nineteenth-Century Ireland," *The British Journal of Sociology*, 29 (1978), pp. 22–40.

Social Origins of the Irish Land War, Princeton, 1979.

Clarke, Aidan, "Pacification, Plantation and the Catholic Question, 1603–23," in T. W. Moody, F. X. Martin, F. J. Byrne (eds.), *A New History of Ireland, Vol. III: Early Modern Ireland, 1534–1691*, Oxford, 1976, pp. 187–232.

"The Government of Wentworth, 1632–40," in T. W. Moody, F. X. Martin, F. J. Byrne (eds.), *A New History of Ireland, Vol. III: Early Modern Ireland, 1534–1691*, Oxford, 1976, pp. 243–69.

Comerford, R. V., "Patriotism as Pastime: The Appeal of Fenianism in the Mid-1860s," *Irish Historical Studies*, 22 (1981), pp. 239–50.

The Fenians in Context: Irish Politics and Society, 1848–82, Dublin, 1985.

Connell, K. H., "The Colonization of Waste Land in Ireland, 1780–1845," *Economic History Review*, 2nd series, 2 (1950), pp. 44–71.

"Land and Population in Ireland, 1780–1845," *Economic History Review*, 2nd series, 2 (1950), pp. 278–89.

The Population of Ireland, Oxford, 1950.

"Peasant Marriage in Ireland After the Great Famine," *Past and Present*, 12 (1957), pp. 76–91.

"The Land Legislation and Irish Social Life," *Economic History Review*, 2nd series, 11 (1958), pp. 1–7.

"Peasant Marriage in Ireland: Its Structure and Development Since the Famine," *Economic History Review*, 2nd series, 14 (1962), pp. 502–23.

Connolly, S. J., "Law, Order and Popular Protest in Early Eighteenth Century Ireland: The Case of the Houghers," in P. J. Cornish (ed.), *Historical Studies XV: Radicals, Rebels and Establishments*, Belfast, 1985, pp. 51–68.

"Marriage in Pre-Famine Ireland," in Art Cosgrove (ed.), *Marriage in Ireland*, Dublin, 1985, pp. 78–98.

"The Houghers: Agrarian Protest in Early Eighteenth Century Connacht," in C. H. E. Philpin (ed.), *Nationalism and Popular Protest in Ireland*, Cambridge, 1987, pp. 139–62.

Conroy, J. C., *A History of Railways in Ireland*, London, 1928.

Corkery, Daniel, *The Hidden Ireland*, Dublin, 1924; paperback ed., Dublin, 1967.

Cousens, S. H., "Regional Death Rates in Ireland During the Great Famine, from 1846–1851," *Population Studies*, 14 (1960), pp. 55–74.

"The Regional Pattern of Emigration During the Great Irish Famine, 1846–51," *Transactions and Papers of the Institute of British Geographers*, 28 (1960), pp. 119–34.

"Emigration and Demographic Change in Ireland, 1851–1861," *Economic History Review*, 2nd series, 14 (1961), pp. 275–88.

"The Regional Variation in Mortality During the Great Irish Famine," *Proceedings of the Royal Irish Academy*, 63: C (1963), pp. 127–49.

"The Regional Variations in Population Changes in Ireland, 1861–1881," *Economic History Review*, 2nd series, 17 (1964), pp. 301–21.

Cresswell, Robert, *Une Communaute rurale de l'Irelande*, Paris, 1969.

Crotty, Raymond D., *Irish Agricultural Production: Its Volume and Structure*, Cork, 1966.

Cullen, L. M., "Problems in the Interpretation and Revision of Eighteenth Century Irish Economic History," *Transactions of the Royal Historical Society*, 5th series, 17 (1967), pp. 1–22.

"The Hidden Ireland: Re-Assessment of a Concept," *Studia Hibernica*, 9 (1969), pp. 7–47.

An Economic History of Ireland Since 1660, London, 1976; paperback ed., London, 1972.

"Economic Development, 1691–1750," in T. W. Moody and W. E. Vaughan (eds.), *A New History of Ireland, Vol. IV: Eighteenth Century Ireland, 1691–1800*, Oxford, 1986, pp. 123–58.

Cunningham, Bernadette, "The Composition of Connacht in the Lordships of Clanricarde and Thomond, 1577–1641," *Irish Historical Studies*, 24 (1984), pp. 1–14.

Curtis, L. Perry, *Coercion and Conciliation in Ireland, 1880–1892*, Princeton, 1963.

Danaher, Kevin, *The Year in Ireland*, Cork, 1972.

Daultrey, Stuart, David Dickson, Cormac O'Gráda, "Eighteenth-Century Irish Population: New Perspectives from Old Sources," *Journal of Economic History*, 41 (1981), pp. 601–28.

deValera, Ruaidhri and Sean O'Nuallain, *Survey of Megalithic Tombs of Ireland, Vol. II: County Mayo*, Dublin, 1964.

Dickson, David, Cormac O'Gráda, Stuart Daultrey, "Hearth Tax, Household Size and Irish Population Change, 1672–1821," *Proceedings of the Royal Irish Academy*, 82: C: 6 (1982), pp. 125–81.

Dillon, Michael and Nora Chadwick, *Celtic Realms*, London, 1967.

Dolley, Michael, *Anglo-Norman Ireland*, Dublin, 1972.

Donnelly, James S., Jr., *Landlord and Tenant in Nineteenth Century Ireland*, Dublin, 1973.

The Land and the People of Nineteenth Century Cork, London and Boston, 1975.

"The Agricultural Depression of 1859–64," *Irish Economic and Social History*, 3 (1976), pp. 33–54.

"The Rightboy Movement, 1785–8," *Studia Hibernica*, 17–18 (1977–8), pp. 120–202.

"The Whiteboy Movement, 1761–5," *Irish Historical Studies*, 21 (1978–9), pp. 20–54.

"Propagating the Cause of the United Irishmen," *Studies: An Irish Quarterly*, 69 (1980), pp. 5–23.

"Irish Agrarian Rebellion: The Whiteboys of 1769–96," *Proceedings of the Royal Irish Academy*, 83: C (1983), pp. 293–331.

"Pastorini and Captain Rock: Millenarianism and Sectarianism in the Rockite Movement of 1821–4," in Samuel Clark and James S. Donnelly, Jr. (eds.), *Irish Peasants: Violence and Political Unrest, 1780–1914*, Madison, Wisconsin, 1983, pp. 102–39.

"The Social Composition of Agrarian Rebellions in Early Nineteenth-Century Ireland: The Case of the Carders and Caravets, 1813–16," in Patrick J. Cornish (ed.), *Radicals, Rebels and Establishments*, Belfast, 1985, pp. 151–69.

"Famine and Government Response, 1845–6," in W. E. Vaughan (ed.), *A New History of Ireland V: Ireland Under the Union, I, 1801–70*, Oxford, 1989, pp. 272–85.

"The Administration of Relief, 1846–7," in W. E. Vaughan (ed.), *A New History of Ireland: V: Ireland Under the Union, I, 1801–70*, Oxford, 1989, pp. 294–306.

"The Soup Kitchens," in W. E. Vaughan (ed.), *A New History of Ireland: V: Ireland Under the Union, I, 1801–70*, Oxford, 1989, pp. 307–14.

"The Administration of Relief, 1847–51," in W. E. Vaughan (ed.), *A New History of Ireland: V: Ireland Under the Union, I, 1801–70*, Oxford, 1989, pp. 316–29.

"Excess Mortality and Emigration," in W. E. Vaughan (ed.), *A New History of*

Ireland: V: Ireland Under the Union, I, 1801–70, Oxford, 1989, pp. 350–6.

Drake, Michael, "Marriage and Population Growth in Ireland, 1750–1845," *Economic History Review*, 2nd series, 16 (1963), pp. 301–12.

"The Irish Demographic Crisis of 1740–41," in T. W. Moody (ed.), *Historical Studies VI*, London, 1968, pp. 101–24.

Elliott, Marianne, "The Origins and Transformation of Early Irish Republicanism," *International Review of Social History*, 23 (1978), pp. 405–28.

Partners in Revolution: The United Irishmen and France, New Haven and London, 1982.

Falkiner, C. Litton, *Studies in Irish History and Biography*, London, 1902.

Feingold, William, *The Revolt of the Tenantry: The Transformation of Local Government in Ireland, 1872–1886*, Boston, 1984.

Fitzpatrick, David, "The Disappearance of the Irish Agricultural Labourer, 1841–1912," *Irish Economic and Social History*, 7 (1980), pp. 66–92.

"Marriage in Post-Famine Ireland," in Art Cosgrove (ed.), *Marriage in Ireland*, Dublin, 1985, pp. 116–31.

Fletcher, T. W., "The Great Depression of English Agriculture, 1873–1896," *Economic History Review*, 2nd series, 12 (1961), pp. 417–32.

Foster, Roy F., *Charles Stewart Parnell: The Man and His Family*, Hassocks, Sussex, 1976.

Modern Ireland, 1600–1972, London, 1988.

Freeman, T. W., *Pre-Famine Ireland: A Study in Historical Geography*, Manchester, 1957.

Ireland: A General and Regional Geography, 4th ed., London, 1969.

Gardiner, Samuel R., "The Transplantation to Connaught," *English Historical Review*, 14 (1899), pp. 700–31.

Garvin, Tom, "Defenders, Ribbonmen and Others: Underground Political Networks in Pre-Famine Ireland," in C. H. E. Philpin (ed.), *Nationalism and Popular Protest in Ireland*, Cambridge, 1987, pp. 219–44.

Gibbon, Peter and Chris Curtin, "The Stem Family in Ireland," *Comparative Studies in Society and History*, 20 (1978), pp. 429–53.

Gibbon, Peter and Michael D. Higgins, "Patronage, Tradition and Modernisation: The Case of the Irish Gombeen-Man," *Economic and Social Review*, 6 (1974), pp. 27–44.

"The Irish 'Gombeenman': Reincarnation or Rehabilitation?" *Economic and Social Review*, 8 (1977), pp. 313–20.

Graham, Jean M., "Rural Society in Connacht 1600–1640," in Nicholas Stephens and Robin E. Glasscock (eds.), *Irish Geographic Studies in Honour of E. Estyn Evans*, Belfast, 1970, pp. 192–208.

Haughton, J. P., "The Mullet of Mayo," *Irish Geography*, 4 (1959), pp. 1–15.

Hayes, Richard, "Priests in the Independence Movement of '98," *Irish Ecclesiastical Record*, 5th series, 66 (1945), pp. 258–70.

"Gaelic Society in Ireland in the Late Sixteenth Century," in G. A. Hayes-McCoy (ed.), *Historical Studies*, IV, London, 1963, pp. 45–61.

The Last Invasion of Ireland, Dublin, 1937; reprinted, 1979.

Hayes-McCoy, G. A., "The Completion of the Tudor Conquest and the Advance of the Counter-Reformation, 1571–1603," in T. W. Moody, F. X. Martin, F. J. Byrne (eds.), *A New History of Ireland, Vol. III: Early Modern Ireland, 1534–1691*, Oxford, 1976, pp. 94–141.

"The Royal Supremacy and Ecclesiastical Revolution, 1534–47," in T. W. Moody, F. X. Martin, F. J. Byrne (eds.), *A New History of Ireland, Vol. III: Early Modern Ireland, 1534–1691*, Oxford, 1976, pp. 39–68.

Hechter, Michael, *Internal Colonialism: The Celtic Fringe in British National Development, 1536–1966*, Berkeley and Los Angeles, 1975.

"Internal Colonialism Revisited," in Edward Tiryankian and Ronald Rogowski (eds.), *New Nationalism of the Developed West: Toward Explanation*, Boston, 1985, pp. 17–26.

Hoban, Brendan, "Dominick Bellew, 1745–1812: Parish Priest of Dundalk and Bishop of Killala," *Seanchas Ardmhacha*, 6 (1972), pp. 333–71.

Hobsbawm, Eric J., *Industry and Empire*, Harmondsworth, Middlesex, 1969.

Hoffman, Elizabeth and Joel Mokyr, "Peasants, Potatoes and Poverty: Transaction Costs in PreFamine Ireland," in Gary Saxonhouse and Gavin Wright (eds.), *Research in Economic History, Supplement 3: Technique, Spirit and Form in the Making of Modern Economics: Essays in Honor of William N. Parker*, Greenwich, Conn., 1984, pp. 115–45.

Hogan, Patrick, "The Migration of Ulster Catholics to Connaught, 1795–96," *Seanchas Ardmhacha*, 9 (1979), pp. 286–301.

Hone, Joseph, *The Life of George Moore*, New York, 1936.

The Moores of Moore Hall, London, 1939.

Hoppen, K. Theodore, "Tories, Catholics, and the General Election of 1859," *Historical Journal*, 13 (1970), pp. 47–67.

"Landlords, Society and Electoral Politics in Mid-Nineteenth Century Ireland," *Past and Present*, 75 (1977), pp. 62–93.

"National Politics and Local Realities in Mid-Nineteenth Century Ireland," in Art Cosgrove and Donal McCartney (eds.), *Studies in Irish History Presented to R. Dudley Edwards*, Dublin, 1979, pp. 190–227.

Hughes, K., *The Church in Early Irish Society*, London, 1966.

Hurst, Michael, *Parnell and Irish Nationalism*, London, 1968.

Johnson, J. H., "The Two 'Irelands' at the Beginning of the Nineteenth Century," in Nicholas Stephens and Robin E. Glasscock (eds.), *Irish Geographic Studies in Honour of E. Estyn Evans*, Belfast, 1970, pp. 224–43.

Jordan, Donald, "John O'Connor Power, Charles Stewart Parnell and the Centralisation of Popular Politics in Ireland," *Irish Historical Studies*, 25 (1986), pp. 46–66.

Kennedy, Liam, "A Skeptical View on the Reincarnation of the Irish 'Gombeen-man,'" *Economic and Social Review*, 8 (1977), pp. 213–22.

"Retail Markets in Rural Ireland At the End of the Nineteenth Century," *Irish Economic and Social History*, 5 (1978), pp. 46–63.

Kennedy, Robert E., *The Irish: Emigration, Marriage and Fertility*, Berkeley and Los Angeles, 1973.

Knox, Hubert T., *The History of the County of Mayo to the Close of the Sixteenth Century*, Dublin, 1908.

Lane, Padraig, "An Attempt At Commercial Farming in Ireland After the Famine," *Studies*, 61 (1972), pp. 54–66.

"The Encumbered Estates Court, Ireland, 1848–49," *Economic and Social Review*, 3 (1972), pp. 413–53.

"The General Impact of the Encumbered Estates Act of 1849 on Counties Galway and Mayo," *Journal of the Galway Archaeological and Historical Society*, 33 (1972–3), pp. 44–74.

Larkin, Emmet, *The Roman Catholic Church and the Creation of the Modern Irish State, 1878–1886*, Philadelphia, 1975.

The Historical Dimensions of Irish Catholicism, New York, 1976.

The Making of the Roman Catholic Church in Ireland, 1850–1860, Chapel Hill, North Carolina, 1980.

The Roman Catholic Church and the Home Rule Movement in Ireland, 1870–1874, Chapel Hill, North Carolina, 1990.

Lee, Joseph, "The Dual Economy in Ireland, 1800–1850," in T. W. Williams (ed.), *Historical Studies VIII*, Dublin, 1971, pp. 191-201.

The Modernisation of Irish Society, Dublin, 1973.

"The Ribbonmen," in T. D. Williams (ed.), *Secret Societies in Ireland*, Dublin and New York, 1973, pp. 26–35.

"Women and the Church Since the Famine," in Margaret MacCurtain and Donncha O'Corrain (eds.), *Women in Irish Society: The Historical Dimension*, Dublin, 1978, pp. 37–45.

"Continuity and Change in Ireland, 1945–70," in Joseph Lee (ed.), *Ireland 1945–70*, Dublin, 1979, pp. 166–77.

"On the Accuracy of the Pre-Famine Irish Censuses," in J. M. Goldstrom and L. A. Clarkson (eds.), *Irish Population, Economy and Society: Essays in Honour of the late K. H. O'Connell*, Oxford, 1981, pp. 37–56.

Lynch, P. and J. Vaizey, *Guinness's Brewery in the Irish Economy, 1756–1876*, Cambridge, 1960.

Lyons, F. S. L., *John Dillon: A Biography*, Chicago, 1968.

Ireland Since the Famine, New York, 1971.

Charles Stewart Parnell, London, 1977.

McCaffrey, P. R., *The White Friars: An Outline Carmelite History*, Dublin, 1926.

McCracken, J. L., "The Ecclesiastical Structure, 1714–60," in T. W. Moody and W. E. Vaughan (eds.), *A New History of Ireland, Vol. IV: Eighteenth Century Ireland, 1691–1800*, Oxford, 1986, pp. 84–104.

MacDonagh, Michael, *The Home Rule Movement*, Dublin, 1920.

MacDonagh, Oliver, "Irish Emigration to the United States of America and the British Colonies During the Famine," in R. E. Edwards and T. D. Williams (eds.), *The Great Famine*, New York, 1957, pp. 319–88.

McDowell, R. B., *The Irish Administration, 1801–1914*, London, 1964.

Ireland in the Age of Imperialism and Revolution, 1760–1801, Oxford, 1979.

MacIntyre, Angus, *The Liberator: Daniel O'Connell and the Irish Party, 1830–1847*, London, 1965.

McNeill, J. T., *The Celtic Churches: A History, A.D. 200–1200*, Chicago, 1972.

Marlow, Joyce, *Captain Boycott and the Irish*, London, 1973.

Maxwell, W. H., *History of the Irish Rebellion in 1798*, London, 1903.

Micks, W. L., *An Account of the Constitution, Administration and Dissolution of the Congested Districts Board for Ireland from 1891–1923*, Dublin, 1925.

Miller, David W., "Irish Catholicism and the Great Famine," *Journal of Social History*, 9 (1975), pp. 81–98.

"The Armagh Troubles, 1784–95," in Samuel Clark and James S. Donnelly, Jr. (eds.), *Irish Peasants: Violence and Political Unrest, 1780–1914*, Madison, Wisconsin, 1983, pp. 155–91.

Miller, Kerby, *Emigrants and Exiles: Ireland and the Irish Exodus to North America*, New York, 1985.

Mokyr, Joel, "The Deadly Fungus: An Econometric Investigation into the Short-Term Demographic Impact of the Irish Famine, 1846–1851," *Research in Popular Economics*, 2 (1980), pp. 237–77.

"Irish History With the Potato," *Irish Economic and Social History*, 8 (1981), pp. 8–29.

Why Ireland Starved, London, 1983.

Mokyr, Joel, and Cormac O'Gráda, "Poor and Getting Poorer? Living Standards in Ireland Before the Famine," *Economic History Review*, 2nd series, 41 (1988), pp. 209–35.

Moody, T. W., "The New Departure in Irish Politics, 1878–9," in H. A. Cronne, T. W. Moody, D. B. Quinn (eds.), *Essays in British and Irish History in Honour of James Eadie Todd*, London, 1949, pp. 303–33.

"Anna Parnell and the Land League," *Hermathena*, 117 (1974), pp. 5–17.

Davitt and Irish Revolution, 1846–82, Oxford, 1981.

Moody, T. W. (ed.), *The Fenian Movement*, Cork, 1968.

Moody, T. W., and Leon O'Broin, "Selected Documents: XXXII. The I.R.B. Supreme Council, 1868–78," *Irish Historical Studies*, 19 (1975), pp. 286–332.

Moore, Barrington, Jr., *Social Origins of Dictatorship and Democracy: Lord and Peasant in the Making of the Modern World*, Boston, 1966.

Moore, Maurice G., *An Irish Gentleman: George Henry Moore, His Travels, His Racing, His Politics*, London, n.d.

Murphy, John A., "The Support of the Catholic Clergy in Ireland," in J. L. McCracken (ed.), *Historical Studies, V*, London, 1965, pp. 103-21.

Nicholls, Kenneth, *Gaelic and Gaelicised Ireland in the Middle Ages*, Dublin, 1972.

Norman, Edward R., *The Catholic Church and Ireland in the Age of Rebellion, 1859–1873*, Ithaca, New York, 1965.

O'Brien, Conor Cruise, *Parnell and His Party, 1880–90*, corrected ed., Oxford, 1964.

"The Machinery of the Irish Parliamentary Party, 1880–85," *Irish Historical Studies*, 5 (1946), pp. 55–85.

O'Brien, George, *The Economic History of Ireland in the Eighteenth Century*, Dublin and London, 1918.

O'Brien, R. Barry (ed.), *The Autobiography of Theobald Wolfe Tone, 1763–1798*, 2 vols., Dublin, 1910.

O'Broin, Leon, *Revolutionary Underground: The Story of the Irish Republican Brotherhood, 1858–1924*, Dublin, 1976.

O'Corrain, Donncha, *Ireland Before the Normans*, Dublin, 1972.

O'Donovan, John, *The Economic History of Livestock in Ireland*, Cork, 1940.

O'Dowd, Mary, "Land Inheritance in Early Modern Sligo," *Irish Economic and Social History*, 10 (1983), pp. 5–18.

O'Farrell, Patrick, "Millenialism, Messianism, and Utopianism in Irish History," *Anglo-Irish Studies*, 2 (1976), pp. 45–68.

O'Fiaich, Tomás, "The Clergy and Fenianism, 1860–70," *Irish Ecclesiastical Record*, 109 (1968), pp. 94–9.

"The Patriot Priest of Partry: Patrick Lavelle, 1825–1886," *Journal of the Galway Archaeological and Historical Society*, 35 (1976), pp. 129–48.

O'Gráda, Cormac, "Seasonal Migration and Post-Famine Adjustment in the West of Ireland," *Studia Hibernica*, 13 (1973), pp. 48–76.

"Agricultural Head Rents, Pre-Famine and Post-Famine," *Economic and Social Review*, 5 (1974), pp. 385–92.

"The Investment Behavior of Irish Landlords, 1850–75: Some Preliminary Findings," *Agricultural History Review*, 23 (1975), pp. 139–55.

"Demographic Adjustment and Seasonal Migration in Nineteenth Century Ireland," in L. M. Cullen and F. Furet (eds.), *Ireland and France, 17th–20th Centuries: Towards a Comparative Study of Rural History*, Ann Arbor, Michigan and Paris, 1980, pp. 181–93.

Ireland Before and After the Famine: Explorations in Economic History, 1800–1925, Manchester, 1988.

"Some Aspects of Nineteenth Century Irish Emigration," in L. M. Cullen and T. C. Smout (eds.), *Comparative Aspects of Scottish and Irish Economic and Social History*, Edinburgh, n.d.

O'Muraile, Nollaig, "An Outline History of County Mayo," in Bernard O'Hara (ed.), *Mayo: Aspects of Its Heritage*, Galway, 1982, pp. 10–35.

O'Neill, Kevin, *Family and Farm in Pre-Famine Ireland: The Parish of Killashandra*, Madison, Wisconsin, 1984.

O'Neill, T. P., "The Organization and Administration of Relief, 1845–52," in R. D. Edwards and T. D. Williams (eds.), *The Great Famine*, New York, 1957, pp. 209–60.

"From Famine to Near Famine, 1845–1879," *Studia Hibernica*, 1 (1961), pp. 161–71.

Palmer, Norman D., *The Irish Land League Crisis*, New Haven, 1940.

Raymond, R. J., "A Reinterpretation of Irish Economic History (1730–1850)," *Journal of European Economic History*, 2 (1982), pp. 651–64.

Roberts, Paul E. W., "Caravats and Shanvests: Whiteboyism and Faction Fighting in East Munster, 1802-11," in Samuel Clark and James S. Donnelly, Jr. (eds.), *Irish Peasants: Violence and Political Unrest, 1780–1914*, Madison, Wisconsin, 1983, pp. 64–101.

Sheehy-Skeffington, F., *Michael Davitt: Revolutionary, Agitator and Labour Leader*, Boston, 1909.

Simms, J. G., "Connacht in the Eighteenth Century," *Irish Historical Studies*, II (1958), pp. 116–33.

"The Restoration, 1660–85," in T. W. Moody, F., X. Martin, F. J. Byrne (eds.), *A New History of Ireland, Vol. III: Early Modern Ireland, 1534–1691*, Oxford, 1976, pp. 420–53.

The Williamite Confiscation in Ireland, 1690–1703, Westport, Connecticut, 1976. Reprint of original edition, London, 1956.

"The Establishment of the Protestant Ascendancy, 1691–1714," in T. W. Moody and W. E. Vaughan (eds.), *A New History of Ireland, Vol. IV: Eighteenth Century Ireland, 1691–1800*, Oxford, 1986, pp. 1–30.

Skinner, William, "Regional Urbanization in Nineteenth Century China," in William Skinner (ed.), *The City in Late Imperial China*, Stanford, 1977, pp. 211–49.

"Cities and the Hierarchy of Local Systems," in *The City in Late Imperial China*, Stanford, 1977, pp. 275–351.

Solow, Barbara, *The Land Question and the Irish Economy*, Cambridge, Mass., 1971.

Steele, E. D., *Irish Land and British Politics: Tenant Right and Nationality, 1865–1870*, Cambridge, 1974.

Thompson, E. P. "The Moral Economy of the English Crowd in the Eighteenth Century," *Past and Present*, 50 (1971), pp. 76–136.

Thornley, David, *Isaac Butt and Home Rule*, London, 1964.

Tohall, Patrick, "The Diamond Fight of 1795 and the Resultant Expulsions," *Seanchas Ardmhacha*, 3 (1958), pp. 17–50.

Vaughan, W. D., "Landlord and Tenant Relations in Ireland Between the Famine and the Land War, 1850–1878," in L. M. Cullen and T. C. Smout (eds.), *Comparative Aspects of Scottish and Irish Economic and Social History*, Edinburgh, n.d., pp. 216–26.

"Agricultural Output, Rents and Wages in Ireland, 1850–1880," in L. M. Cullen and F. Furet (eds.), *Ireland and France, 17th–20th Centuries: Towards a Comparative Study of Rural History*, Ann Arbor, Michigan and Paris, 1980, pp. 85–96.

"An Assessment of the Economic Performance of Irish Landlords," in F. S. L. Lyons and R. A. J. Hawkins (eds.), *Ireland Under the Union, Varieties of Tension: Essays in Honour of T. W. Moody*, Oxford, 1980, pp. 173–99.

Walsh, Brendan M., "A Perspective on Irish Population Patterns," *Eire–Ireland*, 4 (1969), pp. 3–21.

"Marriage Rates and Population Pressure: Ireland 1871 and 1911," *Economic History Review*, second series, 23 (1970), pp. 148–62.

Watt, John, *The Church in Medieval Ireland*, Dublin, 1972.

Whyte, J. H., *The Independent Irish Party, 1850–9*, Oxford, 1958.

"The Influence of the Catholic Clergy on Elections in Nineteenth Century Ireland," *English Historical Review*, 75 (1960), pp. 239–59.

"Landlord Influence at Elections in Ireland, 1760–1885," *English Historical Review*, 80 (1965), pp. 740–60.

Woodham-Smith, Cecil, *The Reason Why*, London, 1953.

The Great Hunger, London, 1962.

UNPUBLISHED WORKS

Almquist, Eric L., "Mayo and Beyond: Land, Domestic Industry and Rural Transformation in the Irish West," Boston University, Ph.D. thesis, 1977.

Hochberg, Leonard and David Miller, "Regional Boundaries and Urban Hierarchy in Prefamine Ireland: A Preliminary Assessment," unpublished paper presented to the Annual Meeting of the Social Science History Association, Washington, DC, October 1989.

"Ireland on the Eve of the Famine: A Geographic Perspective," unpublished paper presented at the National Center for Geographic Information and Analysis, Santa Barbara, California, March 1991.

"Internal Colonialism in Geographic Perspective: The Case of Pre-Famine Ireland," forthcoming in L. Hochberg and G. Earle, *The Geography of Social Change*, Stanford.

Jordan, Donald, "Land and Politics in the West of Ireland: County Mayo, 1846–82," University of California, Davis, Ph.D. thesis, 1982.

McCourt, Desmond, "The Rundale System in Ireland: A Study of Its Geographical Distribution and Social Relations," The Queen's University, Belfast, Ph.D. thesis, 1950.

Vaughan, W. E., "A Study of Landlord and Tenant Relations in Ireland Between the Famine and the Land War, 1850–78," Trinity College, University of Dublin, Ph.D. thesis, 1974.

Woods, Christopher J., "The Catholic Church and Irish Politics, 1879–92," University of Nottingham, Ph.D. thesis, 1968.

WORKS OF REFERENCE

CONTEMPORARY WORKS

Dublin, Leinster and Connaught Trades Directories, 1903, Edinburgh, 1903.

Hansard's Parliamentary Debates.

Lewis, Samuel, *A Topographical Dictionary of Ireland*, 2nd ed., 2 vols., London, 1840.

The Parliamentary Gazetteer of Ireland, 2 vols., Dublin, London and Edinburgh, 1846.

Slater, Isaac, *Slater's Royal National Commercial Directory of Ireland*, Manchester, 1881.

Thom's Irish Almanac and Official Directory of the United Kingdom of Great Britain and Ireland, Dublin, 1884–1930.

LATER WORKS

Curtis, Edmund and R. B. McDowell (eds.), *Irish Historical Documents, 1172–1922*, London and New York, 1968.

The Irish National Committee for Geography, *Atlas of Ireland*, Dublin, 1979.

O'Tuama, Sean and Thomas Kinsella, *An Duanaire, An Irish Anthology: 1600–1900. Poems of the Dispossessed*, Philadelphia, 1981.

Vaughan, W. E. and A. J. Fitzpatrick (eds.), *Irish Historical Statistics: Population 1821–1971*, Dublin, 1978.

Walker, Brian M. (ed.), *Parliamentary Election Results in Ireland, 1801–1922*, Dublin, 1978.

Index

land meeting (June 1879), 221–9, 235,
   267
linen market, 60
linen and manufacturing industry, 62–4
Poor Law Union, 110, 123, 138, 180–1,
   201
Wexford, Co., 82, 281
Whiteboys, 74

Wilde, William, 71
women, in the land and national
   movements, *also see*: Ladies'
   National Land League, 294–303;
   women in post-Famine society,
   297–9

Young, Arthur, 52, 54, 58–9, 61

Past and Present Publications

General Editor: PAUL SLACK, *Exeter College, Oxford*

Family and Inheritance: Rural Society in Western Europe 1200–1800, edited by Jack Goody, Joan Thirsk and E. P. Thompson*

French Society and the Revolution, edited by Douglas Johnson

Peasants, Knights and Heretics: Studies in Medieval English Social History, edited by R. H. Hilton*

Town in Societies: Essays in Economic History and Historical Sociology, edited by Philip Abrams and E. A. Wrigley*

Desolation of a City: Coventry and the Urban Crisis of the Late Middle Ages, Charles Phythian-Adams

Puritanism and Theatre: Thomas Middleton and Opposition Drama under the Early Stuarts, Margot Heinemann*

Lords and Peasants in a Changing Society: The Estates of the Bishopric of Worcester 680–1540, Christopher Dyer

Life, Marriage and Death in a Medieval Parish: Economy, Society and Demography in Halesowen 1270–1400, Zvi Razi

Biology, Medicine and Society 1840–1940, edited by Charles Webster

The Invention of Tradition, edited by Eric Hobsbawm and Terence Ranger*

Industrialization before Industrialization: Rural Industry and the Genesis of Capitalism, Peter Kriedte, Hans Medick and Jürgen Schlumbohm*

The Republic in the Village: The People of the Var from the French Revolution to the Second Republic, Maurice Agulhon†

Social Relations and Ideas: Essays in Honour of R. H. Hilton, edited by T. H. Aston, P. R. Coss, Christopher Dyer and Joan Thirsk

A Medieval Society: The West Midlands at the End of the Thirteenth Century, R. H. Hilton

Winstanley: 'The Law of Freedom' and Other Writings, edited by Christopher Hill

Crime in Seventeenth-Century England: A County Study, J. A. Sharpe†

The Crisis of Feudalism: Economy and Society in Eastern Normandy c. 1300–1500, Guy Bois†

The Development of the Family and Marriage in Europe, Jack Goody*

Disputes and Settlements: Law and Human Relations in the West, edited by John Bossy

Rebellion, Popular Protest and the Social Order in Early Modern England, edited by Paul Slack

Studies on Byzantine Literature of the Eleventh and Twelfth Centuries, Alexander Kazhdan in collaboration with Simon Franklin†

The English Rising of 1381, edited by R. H. Hilton and T. H. Aston*

Praise and Paradox: Merchants and Craftsmen in Elizabethan Popular Literature, Laura Caroline Stevenson

The Brenner Debate: Agrarian Class Structure and Economic Development in Pre-Industrial Europe, edited by T. H. Aston and C. H. E. Philpin*

Eternal Victory: Triumphal Rulership in Late Antiquity, Byzantium, and the Early Medieval West, Michael McCormick†*

East-Central Europe in Transition: From the Fourteenth to the Seventeenth Century, edited by Antoni Mączak, Henryk Samsonowicz and Peter Burke†

Small Books and Pleasant Histories: Popular Fiction and its Readership in Seventeenth-Century England, Margaret Spufford*

Society, Politics and Culture: Studies in Early Modern England, Mervyn James*

Horses, Oxen and Technological Innovation: The Use of Draught Animals in English Farming 1066–1500, John Langdon

Nationalism and Popular Protest in Ireland, edited by C. H. E. Philpin

Rituals of Royalty: Power and Ceremonial in Traditional Societies, edited by David Cannadine and Simon Price*

The Margins of Society in Late Medieval Paris, Bronisław Geremek†

Landlords, Peasants and Politics in Medieval England, edited by T. H. Aston

Geography, Technology, and War: Studies in the Maritime History of the Mediterranean, 649–1571, John H. Pryor*

Church Courts, Sex and Marriage in England, 1570–1640, Martin Ingram*

Searches for an Imaginary Kingdom: The Legend of the Kingdom of Prester John, L. N. Gumilev

Crowds and History: Mass Phenomena in English Towns, 1780–1835, Mark Harrison

Concepts of Cleanliness: Changing Attitudes in France since the Middle Ages, Georges Vigarello†

The First Modern Society: Essays in English History in Honour of Lawrence Stone, edited by A. L. Beier, David Cannadine and James M. Rosenheim

The Europe of the Devout: The Catholic Reformation and the Formation of a New Society, Louis Châtellier†

English Rural Society, 1500–1800: Essays in Honour of Joan Thirsk, edited by John Chartres and David Hey

From Slavery to Feudalism in South-Western Europe, Pierre Bonnassie†

Lordship, Knighthood and Locality: A Study in English Society c. 1180–c. 1280, P. R. Coss

English and French Towns in Feudal Society: A Comparative Study, R. H. Hilton

An Island for Itself: Economic Development and Social Change in Late Medieval Sicily, Stephan R. Epstein

Epidemics and Ideas: Essays on the Historical Perception of Pestilence, edited by Terence Ranger and Paul Slack

The Political Economy of Shopkeeping in Milan, 1886–1922, Jonathan Morris

After Chartism: Class and Nation in English Radical Politics, 1848–1874, Margot C. Finn

Commoners: Common Right, Enclosure and Social Change in England, 1700–1820, J. M. Neeson

Land and Popular Politics in Ireland: County Mayo from the Plantation to the Land War, Donald E. Jordan Jr.*

The Castilian Crisis of the Seventeenth Century: New Perspectives on the Economic and Social History of Seventeenth-Century Spain, edited by I. A. A. Thompson and Bartolomé Yun Casalilla

* Published also as a paperback
† Co-published with the Maison des Sciences de l'Homme, Paris